The Force of Technology

Understanding Innovation, Risk, Cybersecurity

Second Edition

D. Schippers, Sc.D., M. Simko, Sc.D.

The Force of Technology (Second Edition)

The Force of Technology (Second Edition)

Understanding Innovation, Risk Management, Cybersecurity

Dave Schippers, Sc.D.
Michael Simko, Sc.D.

Iron Dog LLC
Grand Rapids

Cover art created with Dall-E, ChatGPT.

Published in the United States by Iron Dog LLC

Dave Schippers, Michael Simko.
The force of technology: understanding innovation, risk management, cybersecurity

Includes bibliographical references and index.
ISBN 9-798992-2934-2-5
1. Innovation. 2. Risk management. 3. Cybersecurity.

Contents

The Editor's Foreword

In the rapidly evolving world of technology, the need for thoughtful, forward-thinking literature has never been greater. **The Force of Technology: Understanding Innovation, Risk Management, and Cybersecurity** provides readers with a comprehensive and insightful exploration of these interconnected areas, offering both practical guidance and theoretical understanding. However, as with innovation itself, the journey to bringing this book to life has been anything but linear.

At times, life introduces unexpected changes, requiring a shift. The development of this book encountered such moments. In the process of its creation, changes in authors and editors became necessary. While transitions of this nature can often bring uncertainty, they ultimately allowed us to forge a stronger, more cohesive work—one aligning with the present and future landscape of technology innovation, risk management, and cybersecurity.

The challenges we faced brought fresh perspectives, and with them, the opportunity to refine and elevate the content, ensuring it is both relevant and adaptable to the dynamic technological world we inhabit. Technology was embraced to experiment and improve the process. Generative artificial intelligence was used in collaboration with outlines and author knowledge to create initial drafts. Authors completed the writing process, ensuring content and expertise were maintained. Every chapter now reflects a collaborative effort infused with innovative technological approaches and diverse expertise, which has made for a better and more refined product. These contributions from different minds mirror the very themes of this book: innovation thrives in change, and adaptability is essential in managing risks and securing the future.

As readers delve into the topics of innovation, risk, and security, it is important to remember technology, like life, is constantly changing. **The Force of Technology** not only reflects the technical challenges and solutions of today but also looks toward the future, guiding readers on how to navigate the evolving technological landscape.

I invite you to engage with this book as both a resource and a roadmap, prepared not only for the world as it is but also for the world as it may become.

-Nastrodavus

Introduction – Understanding the Connected Landscape

Overview

While COVID-19 spread across the globe in 2020, the United States (U.S.) Health and Human Services (HHS) was hit with a cyber-attack [1]. John Ullyot, from the National Security Council, indicated the attack attempted to impact HHS responses to the COVID-19 crises. During COVID-19 in Asia, another group, dubbed Advanced Persistent Threat (APT) 36 and believed to be associated with Pakistan, launched a spear phishing campaign with a fake health advisory masquerading as an official communication from the government of India [2]. Other groups, including Vicious Panda, Mustang Panda, Kimsuky, Hades, Emotet and Lokibot, employed COVID-19 lures to compromise targets [2].

Figure I.1. Cyber.[1]

Massive global issues and problems are often leveraged to create compromises and scams by state-sponsored threat actors and cyber criminals. The threat to HHS from APT36 is a prime example of threat actors' tenacity to leverage fear, misinformation and hysteria for gain. These unscrupulous actions should be viewed as warning signs for organizations and institutions in our digital world.

We live in a connected age and these interconnections pose serious threats to our organizations, institutions, data and way of life.

Despite ongoing breaches, failures, and scams, some organizations and leaders still question the value of technology and security measures to mitigate cybersecurity risks. Government, private and public sectors have been and still ask the following questions:

- How do I justify the cost of cybersecurity expenditures?
- What is the return on investment on cybersecurity?

Terms To Know

Advanced Persistent Threat (APT) – Highly motivated and capable attackers, often associated with nation states or very capable cybercriminal gangs who use continuous, clandestine and sophisticated attack techniques to gain access to targets.

Cyber Criminal – Technically savvy attacker who leverages compromise of remote systems for gain.

Spear Phishing – Attacks targeting a specific individual, often an executive or high-ranking official at an organization.

Threat Actors – Any group or individual employing cyber-attacks for gain.

- Why do we need to implement cybersecurity early when we can add it after things are working?

Introduction Learning Objectives

1. Investigate attack sources
2. Evaluate industry attack frequency
3. Examine historical attacks to comprehend the risks associated with digital technology
4. Articulate the complexity of security factors associated with Internet connectivity

This book will provide context on why business leaders need to understand technology operations and protections. Reliable strategies and leadership in modern organizations requires a proper perspective regarding technology and cybersecurity. To understand this perspective, a technology background may be helpful but is not required on a deep level. This book will provide the following:

- **Unit 1** - Overview of enterprise environments and approaches to designing, leading and managing those enterprise environments.
- **Unit 2** - Overview of risk, threats, and risk management strategies to build critical strategies for organizational effectiveness and longevity.
- **Unit 3** - Overview of cybersecurity and how to effectively lead efforts to protect the organization and its people.

In this Introduction, historical events will be reviewed. These events serve as cautionary sign posts on the Internet timeline. They were chosen to help illustrate the complexity, intensity, and problematic nature of building, leading, and defending organizations in the volatile environment of a connected landscape.

Understanding Technology & Cybersecurity Impacts

Views about cybersecurity and technology vary greatly. A primary misperception is that big organizations are the primary targets of cyber-attacks. Sixty-six percent of small business decision makers believe they are not targets of cybercrime [3]. Depending on the year, however, small businesses -- including manufacturing businesses -- account for about half of all breaches [3].

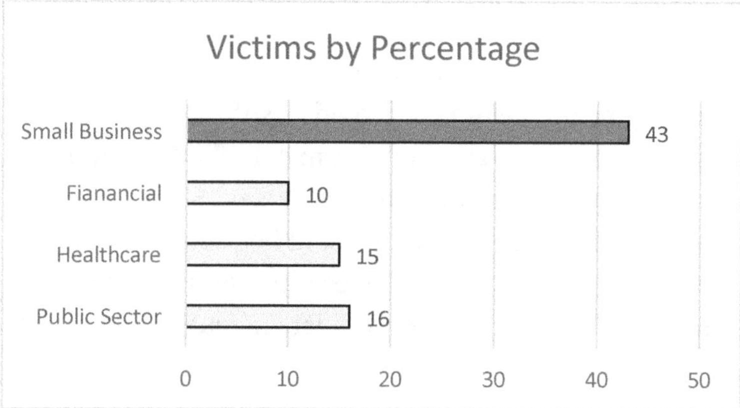

Figure 1.2. Small Business Breaches. Adapted [3]

In 2019, small business victims accounted for 43% of breaches. Sixty percent of small businesses who are attacked close within six months [4]. In addition to knowing they are a target nearly half of the time, small businesses need to understand that threat actors can fund their own criminal organizations or nation state operations by extorting smaller sums of money from a larger group of targets. Economics and economy of scale also applies to cybercrime. Individuals and organizations are more likely to be a victim of cybercrime than physical crime [5]. Anybody from anywhere in the world can attack through the Internet. A physical crime, on the other hand, requires direct confrontation and access to the target.

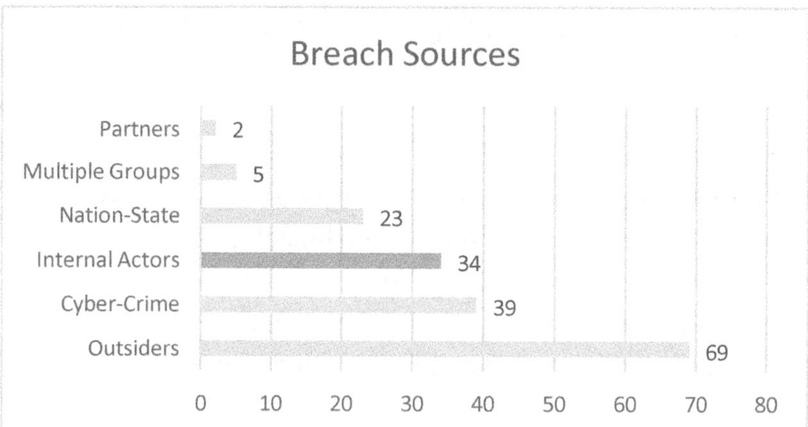

Figure 1.3. Breach Sources. Adapted [3]

Unfortunately, there are other threat actors in addition to foreign countries/nation states and cyber criminals. Internal threats account for one third of attacks. Internal actors are contractors, partners, or employees working in or for the organization.

Several historical breaches will now be presented. The root cause of, broader impacts of, and lessons learned from each breach will be discussed. These breaches were chosen based on their significance to organizations. The first example is the infamous Office of Personnel Management (OPM) hack.

2015 – Anthem Healthcare

The **Anthem data breach**, discovered in early 2015, was one of the largest cyberattacks targeting the healthcare sector. Anthem, a leading health insurance provider, suffered a significant breach that compromised the sensitive information of approximately **78.8 million individuals**. The stolen data included highly personal information such as names, Social Security numbers, birth dates, addresses, and employment details, all of which could be used for identity theft and other malicious activities. This breach underscored the vulnerabilities in healthcare-related data and had wide-ranging implications for how healthcare providers manage and protect personal information.

Scope of Breach

The **Anthem breach** affected a massive number of individuals, primarily current and former members of Anthem's health insurance plans. The **78.8 million affected individuals** included both patients and employees, with exposed data encompassing **names, birthdates, medical identification numbers, Social Security numbers, addresses, phone numbers, employment details**, and in some cases, **income data**. Anthem clarified that **medical records and financial information** such as credit card numbers were not exposed in the breach, but the theft of other personal data still posed a substantial risk for identity theft and fraud.

As one of the largest healthcare data breaches, the incident highlighted the particular **vulnerabilities in healthcare organizations**, which manage large amounts of sensitive data that cybercriminals can easily monetize on black markets.

Attack Mechanism

The attack on Anthem was a **targeted and sophisticated phishing campaign**, initiated by external attackers who gained access to Anthem's internal systems. The breach began in **December 2014** when attackers used phishing emails to trick employees into providing login credentials for Anthem's network. Once inside the system, the attackers were able to move laterally across the network and gain access to sensitive personal information over the course of several weeks before being detected.

Investigators later determined that the attackers were able to **exfiltrate data** by querying Anthem's databases directly, leading to the massive data theft. **No encryption** was applied to the stolen personal information, making it easier for attackers to extract and use the data. The breach, attributed to a **nation-state actor**, demonstrated the growing threat of highly organized cybercriminal groups with the capability to bypass corporate security measures and target sensitive industries such as healthcare.

Response and Investigation

Anthem responded to the breach by notifying affected individuals and regulatory authorities in **early 2015**. The company also engaged cybersecurity experts to assess the scope of the breach and determine the vulnerabilities that led to the attack. As part of its response, Anthem offered affected individuals **credit monitoring and identity protection services** to mitigate the risk of identity theft and fraud.

The investigation into the breach involved the **Federal Bureau of Investigation (FBI)** and cybersecurity firms that traced the attack back to external attackers linked to nation-state entities. The breach was believed to be part of a larger espionage campaign aimed at gathering information on U.S. citizens. The sophistication of the attack and its ties to foreign actors made it clear that Anthem was targeted for the valuable personal information it held.

In 2017, Anthem agreed to pay a **$115 million settlement** to resolve consumer class-action lawsuits related to the breach, marking one of the largest data breach settlements in history. This settlement covered expenses such as credit monitoring services, compensation for victims, and cybersecurity improvements. Regulatory fines followed, as government bodies determined that Anthem had failed to adequately protect personal information.

Lessons Learned

Several important lessons emerged from the Anthem breach, especially for the healthcare sector and industries handling sensitive personal data:

1. **Data Encryption**: One of the most critical shortcomings in Anthem's defenses was the **lack of encryption** for sensitive data. Had the stolen data been encrypted, it would have been much harder for attackers to use it maliciously. This breach reinforced the importance of encrypting personal and healthcare-related data, even when stored internally.

2. **Phishing Vulnerabilities**: The attack demonstrated the effectiveness of **phishing campaigns** in infiltrating even large and well-established organizations. Anthem's employees were tricked into providing their credentials, which gave attackers direct access to the network. This emphasized the need for better **employee training** and **awareness programs** to prevent such attacks.

3. **Improved Cybersecurity Infrastructure**: Anthem's existing cybersecurity measures were insufficient to detect and prevent this sophisticated attack. As a result, the healthcare industry took note of the need for more **advanced security monitoring**, **multi-factor authentication**, and **real-time threat detection** systems to combat evolving cyber threats.
4. **Incident Response Preparedness**: Anthem's response was swift, but the breach revealed the importance of having a well-prepared **incident response plan**. In such cases, rapid action to contain the breach, notify affected individuals, and provide remedies such as credit monitoring services is essential to minimize damage.

Broader Implications

The Anthem breach had far-reaching implications for both the healthcare sector and data protection regulations. In the aftermath of the breach, the healthcare industry began taking steps to strengthen its cybersecurity posture, recognizing the valuable nature of personal and medical data.

On a regulatory level, the breach added momentum to efforts for **stricter data protection regulations**. In the U.S., it highlighted the need for more comprehensive security standards in the healthcare sector under the **Health Insurance Portability and Accountability Act (HIPAA)**. Globally, it contributed to the push for stricter data protection laws, with regions such as the **European Union (EU)** later adopting the **General Data Protection Regulation (GDPR)** to address similar risks.

Additionally, the breach prompted companies in industries beyond healthcare to review their **third-party risk management** practices. Since healthcare providers often rely on multiple third-party vendors for data storage and processing, organizations began reassessing the cybersecurity practices of their vendors to ensure robust data protection across their supply chains.

Conclusion

The **Anthem breach** was a landmark event in the history of cybersecurity breaches, affecting millions of individuals and exposing critical vulnerabilities in the healthcare sector's ability to safeguard personal data. The attack demonstrated the growing sophistication of cybercriminals and the increasing value of personal information in the digital age. Anthem's experience highlighted key lessons around the need for **encryption**, **phishing prevention**, and **stronger cybersecurity infrastructure**. Ultimately, the breach underscored the necessity for organizations—particularly in sensitive sectors like healthcare—to adopt a **proactive approach to cybersecurity**, ensuring that sensitive information is protected against a rising tide of cyber threats.

2015 – United States Office of Personnel Management

The **United States Office of Personnel Management (OPM) Breach**, discovered in 2015, was a devastating cyberattack that compromised the personal data of approximately **22.1 million individuals** [6]. OPM is the federal agency responsible for managing the U.S. government's civilian workforce, which includes conducting background checks on federal employees and security clearance applicants. The breach was significant not only because of the sheer volume of personal information stolen, but also because of the **sensitive nature of the data** involved, including detailed background investigation files [7]. This breach was a wake-up call for the U.S. government regarding the cybersecurity vulnerabilities within its agencies and the consequences of inadequate security practices.

Scope of Breach

The OPM breach had a far-reaching impact, affecting **current and former federal employees**, as well as contractors and applicants for security clearances. The attack exposed a variety of personal data, including **names, Social Security numbers, dates of birth, addresses, fingerprints**, and highly sensitive information contained in **Standard Form 86 (SF-86) questionnaires**, which are used in the vetting process for security clearances. SF-86 forms include personal history, foreign contacts, financial records, mental health details, and past legal troubles, making the breach especially harmful to national security.

The breach affected **two separate OPM databases**: one containing personnel records of about **4.2 million current and former federal employees**, and another containing **detailed background investigation information** of over **21.5 million individuals** [9]. This included not only employees but also their families and associates, further expanding the breach's impact.

Attack Mechanism

The OPM breach was carried out through a sophisticated **advanced persistent threat (APT)**, believed to have originated from a foreign nation-state actor. Attackers first gained access to OPM's systems in **late 2013** and remained undetected for months, conducting extensive reconnaissance before exfiltrating large volumes of sensitive data.

The attack likely began with **phishing campaigns**, which allowed attackers to gain credentials from an external contractor. Once inside the network, the attackers used **privilege escalation techniques** to gain administrative access, giving them the ability to move laterally through OPM's systems. During this time, the attackers installed **custom malware** to extract and transmit data, all while evading detection.

The breach was not discovered until **April 2015**, well after the attackers had gained significant control over OPM's systems. By then, millions of records had already been stolen. It was later revealed that OPM's cybersecurity infrastructure was weak, with **outdated systems**, **insufficient encryption**, and poor **identity management practices** contributing to the severity of the breach.

Response and Investigation

OPM's response to the breach was criticized for being slow and inadequate. When the breach was discovered, the agency initially disclosed that **4.2 million personnel records** had been compromised. However, it was later revealed the breach also included **detailed background investigation files** for millions more individuals, bringing the total number affected to **22.1 million**. The delayed and incomplete disclosure raised concerns about the agency's transparency and ability to manage such a significant breach.

In response to the breach, OPM launched an internal investigation, working with cybersecurity firms and the **Department of Homeland Security (DHS)** to understand the scope of the attack. The **Federal Bureau of Investigation (FBI)** was also involved, as the breach was considered a serious national security threat. Congressional hearings were held to investigate the breach, leading to the resignation of OPM's director and chief information officer [9].

The U.S. government also implemented several measures to assist affected individuals, including offering **credit monitoring** and **identity theft protection services**. However, the response was seen as insufficient given the sensitive nature of the stolen data, especially the compromise of fingerprints and SF-86 forms [9].

Lessons Learned

The OPM breach highlighted several critical cybersecurity shortcomings, particularly within the federal government. The lessons learned from this breach are relevant not only to government agencies but to any organization handling large amounts of sensitive personal data:

1. **Importance of Identity and Access Management (IAM)**: Attackers were able to escalate their privileges and gain administrative access, highlighting the need for **stronger access controls**, such as **multi-factor authentication** (MFA) and **least privilege** principles. At the time of the breach, OPM's identity management practices were outdated, allowing attackers to easily navigate through the system.

2. **Need for Encryption of Sensitive Data**: One of the most glaring issues was the lack of **encryption** for highly sensitive data, including Social Security numbers and fingerprints. Encrypting such data could have made it significantly harder for attackers to make use of the stolen information.

3. **Regular Security Audits and Modernization**: OPM was operating with **outdated legacy systems** that had numerous known vulnerabilities. This breach demonstrated the

critical need for **regular cybersecurity audits** and the modernization of systems to protect against emerging threats.

4. **Early Detection and Monitoring**: The attackers remained undetected in OPM's systems for over a year, highlighting the need for better **intrusion detection systems (IDS)** and **continuous monitoring** to detect suspicious activity earlier and prevent data exfiltration.
5. **Transparency and Incident Communication**: OPM's initial response and communication regarding the breach were viewed as insufficient and delayed, underscoring the importance of **clear and transparent communication** during cybersecurity incidents. Timely notification can help affected individuals take protective actions sooner.

Broader Implications

The OPM breach had significant implications for national security and cybersecurity policy in the U.S. The **compromise of sensitive background check data**, including personal details of individuals with security clearances, raised concerns about potential espionage and the targeting of individuals by foreign adversaries. The breach also underscored the vulnerabilities present in **government IT infrastructure**, prompting federal agencies to reassess their cybersecurity practices [6].

In response to the breach, the U.S. government launched several initiatives to strengthen cybersecurity within federal agencies, including the **Federal Information Security Modernization Act (FISMA)**, which mandated stricter security protocols and oversight. The breach also accelerated the adoption of the **Continuous Diagnostics and Mitigation (CDM) Program**, aimed at improving real-time threat detection and response across government networks.

On a broader scale, the OPM breach served as a wake-up call for governments around the world, emphasizing the need for robust cybersecurity measures to protect critical national data. It also highlighted the growing threat posed by **nation-state actors** in cyberspace, pushing forward discussions on cyber defense and international cybersecurity standards [7].

Conclusion

The **OPM breach** was a watershed moment in the history of cybersecurity, revealing the critical vulnerabilities in federal government agencies' cybersecurity infrastructures. The attack compromised sensitive personal data of over 22 million individuals, putting national security at risk and leading to widespread reforms in how the U.S. government handles and protects personal information. The lessons learned from this breach—especially around identity management, encryption, and cybersecurity modernization—are valuable for both public and private sectors. As cyber threats continue to evolve, the OPM breach remains a stark reminder of the importance of maintaining strong, up-to-date cybersecurity defenses to protect sensitive information from increasingly sophisticated attackers.

2016 – Uber Drives into a Data Breach

The Uber breach of 2016 is a significant case in cybersecurity history, revealing how poor security practices and mishandled incident responses can lead to severe legal and reputational consequences. The breach compromised the personal information of 57 million customers and drivers, and Uber concealed the breach for over a year before it was publicly disclosed in 2017. This incident involved paying attackers to delete the stolen data and maintain silence, which raised ethical concerns and legal ramifications.[11].

Figure 1.2. Vehicle View [26].

Scope of the Breach

The 2016 breach exposed the personal data of 57 million Uber users, including names, email addresses, and phone numbers, along with the driver's license information of 600,000 Uber drivers. Although no payment data or Social Security numbers were reportedly stolen, the volume and sensitivity of the exposed information significantly impacted Uber's users and drivers. The breach remained concealed for more than a year before Uber's new management disclosed it in 2017 [10].

Terms To Know

Github – This service provides an Internet repository for software development code. Programmers often leverage Github for version control, archives and cross collaboration.

Bug Bounty Program – This program offers rewards to security researchers who identify security vulnerabilities in software and report them to the company offering the bounty. This program is intended to inspire people to report vulnerabilities instead of selling them to threat actors for malicious use.

The Attack Mechanism

The breach occurred due to human error and a failure to adhere to proper security protocols. Uber's developers accidentally left credentials for its Amazon Web Services (AWS) account embedded in a private GitHub repository. Attackers gained unauthorized access to Uber's GitHub account, located the credentials, and used them to infiltrate Uber's AWS cloud environment [10].

Once inside, the attackers found large quantities of unencrypted personal data stored in Uber's AWS servers. They downloaded the data, which included millions of user records. Uber chose to pay the attackers $100,000 under the guise of a bug bounty reward to ensure that the stolen data was deleted, further complicating the ethical and legal aspects of the breach [10].

Response and Investigation

Uber's response to the breach has been widely criticized. Instead of reporting the incident to affected individuals and regulators, Uber attempted to cover up the breach. The company paid the attackers through its bug bounty program, intending to ensure the stolen data was destroyed. However, this delay in reporting triggered investigations and legal actions [11].

Regulatory bodies, including the Federal Trade Commission (FTC), launched investigations into Uber's failure to disclose the breach in a timely manner. In 2018, Uber agreed to a settlement of $148 million with various U.S. states for violating data breach notification laws. The company's decision to conceal the breach exacerbated the legal and reputational damage [11].

> **Looking Further**
>
> **Breach Disclosure Laws** – Many states have passed breach disclosure laws. Breach disclosure laws require public notification of data breaches where personally identifiable information (PII) is stolen.

Lessons Learned

Several important cybersecurity lessons emerged from the Uber breach:

1. **Credential Management**: Uber's failure to securely manage credentials, leaving AWS access keys exposed in a GitHub repository, illustrates the importance of proper secret management. Credentials should never be hardcoded in code repositories, and secure vaulting solutions should be used to manage sensitive keys.
2. **Data Encryption**: Storing unencrypted personal data in the cloud increased the breach's severity. Encrypting sensitive data both at rest and in transit could have significantly mitigated the breach's impact.
3. **Incident Response and Transparency**: Uber's failure to promptly report the breach compounded its legal issues. The incident demonstrates the importance of transparency and prompt reporting of breaches to mitigate damage to both individuals and organizations.
4. **Ethical Use of Bug Bounties**: Uber's decision to misuse its bug bounty program to pay off attackers raised ethical concerns. Bug bounties are designed to reward ethical hackers, not to cover up ransom payments, which compromises the integrity of such programs.

Broader Implications

The Uber breach had far-reaching implications for the tech industry and cybersecurity practices. It emphasized the need for robust security protocols, especially regarding credential management and incident response. The incident also drew attention to the ethical complexities of bug bounty programs and the risks posed by attempting to conceal data breaches.

For organizations, this breach highlighted the necessity of encryption, secure storage practices, and the importance of timely reporting in managing cybersecurity incidents. The regulatory penalties faced by Uber demonstrated the growing global demand for accountability in handling user data, which has become a critical factor in maintaining public trust.

Conclusion

The Uber breach of 2016 serves as a cautionary tale about the risks of poor security management and the consequences of attempting to conceal a breach. With 57 million user records exposed and a delayed response leading to a $148 million settlement, Uber's actions highlight the critical importance of secure credential management, encryption, transparent incident response, and the ethical administration of bug bounty programs. This breach underscores the necessity of proactive cybersecurity measures and the need for organizations to remain vigilant against evolving threats to protect their users and data.

2017 – We All Cry with WannaCry

Infections of the WannaCry ransomware appeared first in Europe on May 12, 2017, and then spread quickly across the globe, impacting over 200,000 organizations [13]. WannaCry is a great example of the true wild and dangerous nature of the Internet. WannaCry also illustrates the severe challenges faced by organizations that fail to embrace and employ security effectively.

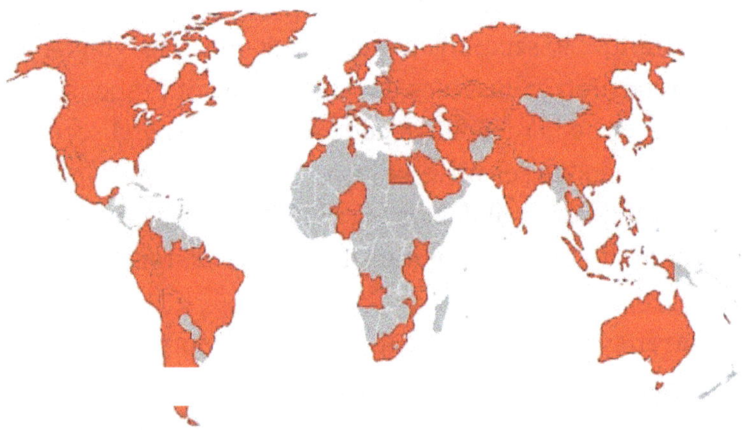

Figure 1.5. WannaCry Impact. [25]

The WannaCry story does not begin in May of 2017, but in August of 2016 with The Shadow Brokers and Equation Group.

Equation Group, nicknamed by the cybersecurity research group from Kaspersky Lab [14], has been assumed to be associated with the National Security Agency's (NSA) Tailored Access Operations (TAO). TAO is an elite group of US hackers, credited with participating in the hunt for Osama Bin Laden by collecting intelligence from smart phones of al-Qaeda operatives [13]. TAO's cyber toolkit was assumed to contain zero-day exploits to breach TAO's hacking targets. In August 2016, The Shadow Brokers, another hacking group, audaciously claimed they had stolen TAO's toolkit. The Shadow Brokers gained the attention of security experts by releasing exploits claimed to be from the TAO/Equation Group toolkit [15]. These exploits affected Cisco ASA, Cisco PIX, and Cisco Firewall Services. Three specific exploits, EXTRABACON, EPICBANANA and JETPLOW, enabled remote code execution and persistence options for

attacker [15]. Organizations raced to install security patches for the exploits, providing credibility to the Shadow Brokers' claims.
The Shadow Brokers tweeted "We find cyber weapons made by creators of Stuxnet, Duqu, Flame" to gain even more attention [16]. The Shadow Brokers first attempted to sell the TAO toolkit for one million bitcoins, valued at $500 million. The group then tried to auction the kit, but by October 2016 had called off the auction and were instead demanding 10,000 bitcoins for the release of files from the kit. When those strategies also failed, the Shadow Brokers did something highly unusual for a cybercriminal or nation state hacking group: they simply released the toolkit to the public, for anyone to weaponize.

Looking Further

APT Group Names –
In the world of cybersecurity, malware derives from the names of APT groups. After malware infects targets, malware artifacts (residual data markers left behind after attacks) are reviewed. Over time, repetitive code sequences help indicate malware attacks associated with a specific group, sometimes leading to nicknames associated with the code sequences for the APT group credited with the malware creation.

In the larger discussion of malware, nation states sponsor and operate hacking groups. Nation states can leverage hacking groups to: combat terrorism, conduct espionage, steal data and sow discord in collaboration with military campaigns.

Security experts wondered how The Shadow Brokers obtained the toolkit. Doubting that The Shadow Brokers directly hacked the NSA and TAO, security experts assumed The Shadow Brokers compromised a TAO command-and-control (CNC) server to obtain the tools [16]. In Fall 2016, however, former government contractor Harold Martin was reported to be the prime suspect of the TAO's toolkit theft [16]. As events unfolded, the NSA alleged Martin stole over 50 terabytes of data, including the TAO toolkit with exploits impacting Microsoft operating systems [16]. Martin's defense attorneys claimed Martin took the tools to enhance his contract work capabilities [16]. It is still unclear whether Martin sold the toolkit, or The Shadow Brokers compromised Martin to obtain the tools, or if something else happened entirely.

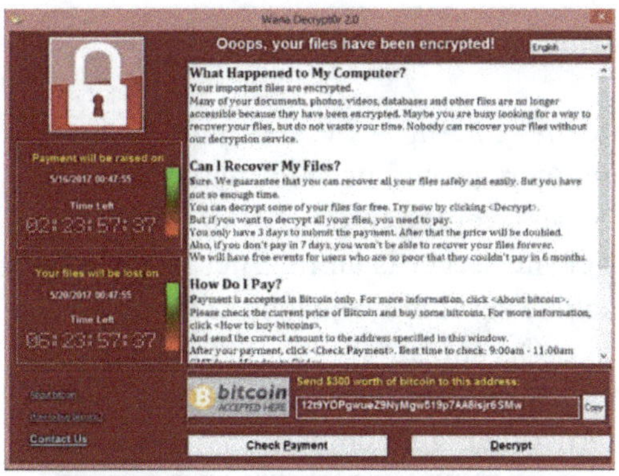

Figure 1.6. WannaCry Screenshot. [22]

What is clear, on the other hand, is that the exploits in the TAO toolkit were poised to have a profound impact on businesses everywhere. Microsoft, in another unusual security, was apparently covertly forewarned with a request for anonymity about the Windows XP exploits in the toolkit. Recognizing the devastating global impact these exploits would have, Microsoft released a patch for the vulnerabilities, despite the fact that it was no longer supporting Windows XP [16].

Analysis of WannaCry suggests the Lazarus Group, an APT cybercrime group made up of an unknown number of individuals, weaponized the critical vulnerabilities exposed by the TAO toolkit by merging them with ransomware, forcing victims to pay to get their files back. Lazarus Group has been identified as a North Korean sponsored hacking group associated with the Sony Pictures breach, South Korean media hacks, bank hacks across the globe, and the $81 million Bangladesh Bank cyber heist [14].

WannaCry is an excellent example of how businesses can fall victim to cybercrime through no fault of their own. Those who ended up paying WannaCry ransoms were ultimately caught in the crossfire of three powerful hacking groups, two of which had national ties. It would have been difficult, if not impossible, for businesses to anticipate the series of events that led to the WannaCry ransomware attacks. This situation underscores the need for businesses to be vigilant about employing security best practices.

Looking Forward

In Unit 1, innovation and digital strategy will be reviewed. In Unit 2, risk management will cover how to assess and address risk. It is important to realize – conducting business on the Internet is not just about organizational goals and costs. Unit 3 will present cybersecurity considerations for business leaders.

Lessons Learned –

1. **Maintain effective patch management with licensed software:** Microsoft provided the Windows XP security update a month before WannaCry hit. Organizations with effective patch management were protected from the attack. Many organizations, however, run unlicensed versions of Windows and other software, which means they do not have access to regular updates or security patches. When an organization invests in technologies for innovation, licensed software and security updates are an integral portion of the equation.

2. **Turn off unnecessary services:** WannaCry's cocktail of exploits attacked Windows' Server Message Block (SMB) service, which enables file sharing across systems [18]. WannaCry leveraged weaknesses in SMB version 1, an older version of SMB. Network traffic analysis of WannaCry indicated it was scanning Internet facing machines for exploitability [18]. Organizations who did not utilize and had thus turned off SMBv1 were immune to the attacks. Their immunity serves as an important reminder to run only necessary services, especially on Internet facing machines.

Terms To Know

Internet Facing – Servers and computers providing information and services over the Internet. For example, a website server is an Internet facing machine serving webpages to Internet users. Organizations should have all unnecessary services turned off on Internet facing machines.

3. **Educate users on phishing attacks:** Security companies informed the media that WannaCry was spreading via malicious emails campaigns [18]. Ransomware is often spread via phishing attacks. Organizations should continually educate users on how to identify email scams and address phishing attacks [18].

4. Maintain usable backups:_WannaCry allowed attackers to encrypt files on vulnerable machines and demand ransom payments to release the files. A simple countermeasure to ransomware is usable backups. Creating backups is a relatively simple task. Organizations, however, often fail to test their backups, which leaves the organization exposed. During a ransomware attack is not the time to test backups to determine if they work. Organizations should conduct ongoing tests to ensure backups are available and usable in times of need. (Unit 1 will cover technology strategies and approaches, specifically business continuity planning.)

2016 – Yahoo

The **Yahoo data breach**, one of the largest and most severe cybersecurity breaches in history, unfolded over several years and was first disclosed in **2016**. This breach, however, impacted Yahoo between **2013 and 2014** and wasn't fully understood until much later. It compromised the personal data of **3 billion user accounts**, making it the largest known data breach to date. The breach had far-reaching consequences, not only for the company and its users but also for Yahoo's reputation, especially as it was in the process of selling its core business to Verizon at the time. Although first discovered in **2016**, litigation, regulatory actions, and fallout from the breach continued through **2017-2019**, highlighting significant issues with how Yahoo managed its data security and incident response.

Scope of Breach

The **Yahoo breach** was massive in scope, affecting **every single user account** that existed on the platform at the time, totaling **3 billion accounts**. The stolen data included **names, email addresses, dates of birth, telephone numbers, hashed passwords**, and **security questions and answers**, both encrypted and unencrypted. The breach exposed both personal and account-related information, raising serious concerns about the potential misuse of this data for **identity theft**, **credential stuffing**, and other forms of cybercrime.

Although Yahoo initially reported in **2016** that **500 million accounts** were affected, further investigations revealed that the breach had compromised **3 billion user accounts**—the entire user base of Yahoo at the time. This scale of compromise made it one of the most extensive breaches in history, affecting users globally.

Attack Mechanism

The Yahoo breach was attributed to **state-sponsored actors** who infiltrated Yahoo's systems in **2013 and 2014**. Attackers were able to exploit vulnerabilities in Yahoo's security infrastructure to gain unauthorized access to its networks. The exact details of how the attackers initially breached the system have not been fully disclosed, but they used a variety of tactics, including **phishing attacks** to gain employee credentials, which allowed them to navigate Yahoo's internal systems.

Once inside, the attackers installed **backdoors** and **malware** that enabled them to maintain persistent access over an extended period. Yahoo's systems were poorly monitored, allowing attackers to remain undetected for a long time. The attackers stole valuable account data, including **security questions and answers**, which, when unencrypted, could be used to reset passwords and access other user accounts. The fact that Yahoo was using outdated encryption mechanisms, including **MD5 hashing**, made it easier for attackers to crack password hashes.

Response and Investigation

Yahoo's response to the breach was heavily criticized, primarily for its delayed disclosure of the full scope of the breach. Although the breaches occurred in **2013 and 2014**, they were not made public until **2016**, long after the damage had been done. Even then, Yahoo initially downplayed the number of affected accounts, reporting **500 million accounts** in the first announcement, only to later admit the breach had affected **3 billion accounts** in **2017** after further investigation. Once Yahoo disclosed the breach, it offered **identity theft protection services** and encouraged users to **change their passwords**. However, many users were already vulnerable to attacks by that point. Verizon, which was in the process of acquiring Yahoo, renegotiated the deal after the full extent of the breach was disclosed, eventually acquiring Yahoo for **$350 million less** than the originally agreed price.

Investigations into the breach revealed that Yahoo had several security weaknesses, including outdated encryption methods and inadequate **incident response processes**. The **U.S. Department of Justice** eventually indicted **four individuals**, including two Russian intelligence officers, for their roles in the attack. Yahoo also faced significant scrutiny from regulatory bodies and settled numerous **class-action lawsuits**, agreeing to a **$117.5 million settlement** to compensate affected users.

Lessons Learned

The Yahoo breach exposed several critical lessons about the importance of cybersecurity, particularly for large organizations managing vast amounts of user data:

1. **Strong Encryption**: Yahoo's use of outdated **MD5 hashing** to secure passwords and **unencrypted security questions** was a major vulnerability. This breach emphasized the need for organizations to use strong encryption algorithms like **bcrypt** or **SHA-256** to protect user credentials and sensitive data.
2. **Timely Breach Disclosure**: Yahoo waited several years to disclose the full extent of the breach, which prevented users from taking swift action to protect their accounts. The breach underscored the importance of timely and transparent communication when a cybersecurity incident occurs.
3. **Proactive Monitoring and Threat Detection**: The attackers maintained access to Yahoo's systems for a long period without being detected. This highlighted the need for organizations

to implement **continuous monitoring**, **intrusion detection systems (IDS)**, and **threat intelligence tools** to identify and respond to attacks in real-time.

4. **Incident Response Preparedness**: Yahoo's inadequate response to the breach demonstrated the importance of having a well-defined **incident response plan** in place. Organizations need to be prepared to quickly contain and mitigate a breach, notify affected parties, and provide clear guidance on next steps.

Broader Implications

The Yahoo breach had far-reaching implications beyond the company itself. As one of the most significant breaches in history, it highlighted the **global nature of cybersecurity threats** and the importance of safeguarding user data across different regions and platforms. The breach affected not only Yahoo users but also had ripple effects across other online services, as many individuals reused the same passwords for multiple accounts.

The breach also prompted a global conversation about **data privacy**, **user protection**, and the **regulation of technology companies**. Governments worldwide began to take a closer look at how companies were securing user data, eventually leading to stricter regulations like the **General Data Protection Regulation (GDPR)** in the European Union. The Yahoo breach, along with other major cyber incidents, demonstrated the need for better regulatory oversight to ensure companies were adequately protecting sensitive data.

From a business perspective, the breach significantly affected **Yahoo's valuation** and its acquisition by Verizon, illustrating how a cybersecurity incident can impact not only a company's reputation but also its financial standing. The incident also led to more intense scrutiny of cybersecurity practices during mergers and acquisitions, with cybersecurity now becoming a critical part of due diligence in corporate transactions.

Conclusion

The **Yahoo breach** remains one of the most consequential cybersecurity incidents to date, not only because of the sheer number of affected users but also due to the delayed disclosure, weak security practices, and the lasting impact on Yahoo's business and reputation. The breach demonstrated the importance of **modern encryption techniques**, **proactive threat monitoring**, and **timely breach notifications**. Its fallout over the years, including the renegotiation of Yahoo's sale to Verizon and numerous legal settlements, further emphasized the long-term consequences of failing to secure user data. As cyber threats continue to evolve, the lessons from the Yahoo breach serve as a reminder that organizations must remain vigilant in their cybersecurity efforts to protect against similar large-scale breaches in the future

2017 – Equifax Goes Full Dumpster Fire

Figure 1.7. Dumpster Fire. [27]

The **Equifax Data Breach of 2017** stands as one of the most significant cybersecurity incidents in recent history, impacting the sensitive personal information of approximately **147 million people**. As one of the largest credit reporting agencies in the U.S., Equifax collects vast amounts of data, including **Social Security numbers**, credit card details, and personal identification information. The breach exposed critical vulnerabilities within the company's security practices and underscored the potential risks associated with large-scale data storage. While the breach itself occurred in 2017, its repercussions—legal battles, regulatory fines, and public scrutiny—continued well into 2021 [17].

Scope of Breach

The **scale of the Equifax breach** was unprecedented, affecting nearly **half of the U.S. population**. Sensitive information that was compromised included **Social Security numbers, names, birth dates, addresses**, and in some cases, **driver's license numbers and credit card information**. Given the nature of Equifax's business, the data breached was particularly harmful, as it could easily be used for identity theft and financial fraud. This made the attack one of the most consequential breaches in terms of the potential harm to consumers [18].

In addition to personal data, **credit report data**—a key product of Equifax's services—was also exposed. This data is critical in determining an individual's financial standing, and its exposure created risks not only for individuals but also for the financial institutions that rely on such reports for lending decisions.

Attack Mechanism

The breach was enabled by a vulnerability in **Apache Struts**, an open-source web application software used by Equifax. This particular vulnerability, **CVE-2017-5638**, was publicly disclosed in March 2017, with security patches made available shortly thereafter. Despite the known risk, Equifax failed to patch the vulnerability in its systems, leaving them exposed to attackers. The hackers exploited this weakness and gained access to the company's internal systems over several months, from **mid-May to July 2017** [17].

Once inside the system, the attackers were able to **exfiltrate massive amounts of sensitive data** undetected. The breach wasn't discovered until late July, and Equifax did not publicly disclose it until **September 7, 2017**, nearly two months after discovering the attack [18].

Terms To Know

Apache Software Foundation – A non-profit American corporation created to support Apache software projects. The most notable project – Apache Web Server – is the most popular web server.

Apache Struts – A web development framework enabling the creation of portals with Java software.

Open Source – Freely available and distributable software.

Web Application Framework – Software designed for web portal creation and mainenanc.e

Response and Investigation

Equifax's response to the breach was widely criticized for being both slow and insufficient. The company did not inform the public for several weeks after discovering the breach, delaying the ability of affected individuals to take protective measures, such as freezing their credit or monitoring for fraud. This delay in communication added to the company's reputational damage [17].

Upon disclosing the breach, Equifax offered free credit monitoring services to the affected individuals, but these efforts were seen as reactive rather than preventive. Regulatory bodies, including the **Federal Trade Commission (FTC)**, as well as state and federal prosecutors, launched investigations into Equifax's security practices and handling of the breach. The investigations uncovered systemic flaws in Equifax's security infrastructure, such as the failure to patch known vulnerabilities, poor internal controls, and inadequate data protection measures [17].

In July 2019, Equifax reached a settlement with the FTC, the **Consumer Financial Protection Bureau (CFPB)**, and 50 U.S. states. The company agreed to pay up to **$700 million** in fines, compensation, and credit monitoring services. However, the long-term impacts of the breach continued, with litigation and consumer lawsuits persisting through 2021 [18].

Lessons Learned

The Equifax breach underscored several important lessons for organizations handling sensitive data, particularly regarding **cybersecurity hygiene** and **incident response**:

1. **Timely Patching of Vulnerabilities**: The breach occurred due to Equifax's failure to apply a critical security patch to Apache Struts. This highlights the importance of staying current with patches and updates, particularly when vulnerabilities are widely known and have been actively exploited in the wild.
2. **Internal Security Controls**: The lack of proper monitoring and internal controls allowed attackers to remain within Equifax's systems for several months, undetected. The importance of **robust monitoring, intrusion detection systems**, and regular security audits cannot be overstated.
3. **Incident Response and Communication**: Equifax's delayed notification to the public damaged its reputation. Organizations need clear and effective incident response plans that prioritize transparency and provide timely communication to affected parties.
4. **Data Encryption**: Equifax's failure to adequately encrypt sensitive information allowed hackers to exfiltrate data more easily. The breach underscored the critical need for **encrypting personal data**, especially in large-scale databases that hold sensitive information.
5. **Nation States May be in Play -** On February 10, 2020, U.S. Attorney General Bill Barr announced charges against the Chinese Military for the Equifax breach. According to the Department of Justice allegations, the Chinese Military stole personal and financial data and Equifax's trade secrets. When cyber criminals steal data, the stolen data is often monetized. When a nation state steals the data, it is often unclear as to when and how the stolen data will be leveraged or monetized. The table below shows records of what the Chinese APT groups have harvested across the Anthem, OPM and Equifax hacks.

Table I.1. Compromise Comparisons

Hack	Records Compromised
Anthem	80,000,000 Americans
OPM	4,200,000 Federal Applicants/Workers
Equifax	145,500,500 Americans
	693,665 UK Citizens
	8,000 Canadians

Broader Implications

The Equifax breach had wide-reaching implications for both the private and public sectors. The attack highlighted vulnerabilities in **critical financial infrastructure**, raising concerns about the broader security of consumer financial data. It also sparked a national conversation about the role of **credit reporting agencies** in protecting sensitive data and whether such entities should be subject to stricter oversight and regulation.

The breach triggered a wave of regulatory and legislative actions aimed at increasing **consumer protection**. Several states passed laws requiring companies to provide **free credit freezes** and increased transparency about breaches. Furthermore, the breach acted as a wake-up call for other large organizations handling sensitive data to reevaluate their own **security practices** and their readiness to respond to cybersecurity incidents.

On an industry level, the breach had a significant impact on **third-party risk management**, as financial institutions and businesses that relied on Equifax had to assess their own exposure due to the breach.

Conclusion

The Equifax breach is a cautionary tale of the potential consequences when a large organization fails to maintain adequate cybersecurity defenses. The exposure of sensitive data for 147 million individuals, along with the long-lasting financial and reputational damage to Equifax, illustrates the importance of timely patching, strong internal security measures, and transparent communication in the aftermath of a breach. As the fallout from the breach continued into 2021, it served as a stark reminder that large organizations must prioritize cybersecurity at every level to protect against both current and emerging threats.

2018 – Marriot Checks In For an Extended Stay

In November 2018, **Marriott International**, one of the world's largest hotel chains, disclosed a significant data breach affecting the **Starwood Hotels** guest reservation database. The breach, which began in **2014** and went undetected for four years, resulted in the exposure of the personal information of **approximately 383 million guests**. This incident was one of the most substantial breaches in the hospitality industry, bringing attention to the vulnerabilities in corporate data management systems [28].

The compromised data included a wide array of sensitive information, such as **names, phone numbers, email addresses, passport numbers, and travel itineraries**. While Marriott later revealed that **payment card information** and **encrypted passport numbers** were also part of the breach, there was no evidence that encryption keys were compromised. The breach raised serious concerns about customer privacy, security, and the potential for future exploitation of the stolen data [28].

Scope of the Breach

The scope of the Marriott data breach was vast, impacting millions of individuals globally, including both **personal and travel-related information**:

- **Personally Identifiable Information (PII)**: The breach exposed sensitive personal details, such as **names, contact information, birthdates, and passport numbers**. Passport data exposure, in particular, was alarming due to the risk of identity theft.
- **Financial Information**: Although Marriott confirmed that payment card data was encrypted, the fact that it had been compromised raised concerns about the **security of financial transactions** conducted through the Starwood reservation system.
- **Global Impact**: With guests from all over the world, the breach affected individuals across multiple countries, leading to regulatory scrutiny from authorities, including the **European Union (EU)** under its **General Data Protection Regulation (GDPR)** laws, which require strict data protection practices.

The breach was initially linked to Starwood Hotels, a company that Marriott acquired in **2016**. This meant the vulnerability existed long before Marriott took control of Starwood's systems, highlighting potential **due diligence and integration issues** during the acquisition process. The prolonged access to this data allowed attackers to gather a significant amount of information over an extended period [28].

The Attack Mechanism

The Marriott breach was the result of a highly **sophisticated and persistent attack** that remained undetected for years. Here's how the attack unfolded:

- **Initial Intrusion**: The breach was believed to have started in **2014**, when attackers gained unauthorized access to the Starwood guest reservation system. The attackers used **advanced persistent threat (APT)** tactics to infiltrate the network and **exfiltrate data slowly** over several years.
- **Undetected Presence**: For four years, the attackers had access to the system, quietly collecting data while evading detection. This prolonged presence allowed them to gather **millions of records** before the breach was identified.
- **Discovery**: Marriott only became aware of the breach in **September 2018**, when a security tool detected an attempt to access the guest reservation database. Upon investigation, the company realized that unauthorized access had been occurring since 2014, affecting hundreds of millions of guest records.
- **Types of Data Stolen**: The attackers gained access to **guest profiles** that included names, email addresses, phone numbers, passport numbers, and travel itineraries. Although some of the stolen data was encrypted (such as credit card information), Marriott was unable to confirm whether encryption keys were compromised, raising concerns about the security of payment information.

Response and Investigation

Once the breach was uncovered, **Marriott** initiated a widespread investigation and took immediate steps to secure its systems. The company collaborated with cybersecurity experts and government authorities to understand the scope of the attack and the full extent of the data that had been compromised [28].

- **Disclosure and Public Notification**: On **November 30, 2018**, Marriott publicly disclosed the breach, notifying affected guests and regulators. The announcement triggered widespread concern, given the scale of the data involved and the sensitivity of the stolen information.

- **Regulatory Investigations**: Given the global impact of the breach, **regulators** from multiple jurisdictions, including the **U.S. Federal Trade Commission (FTC)** and **European GDPR authorities**, launched investigations into Marriott's data protection practices. The GDPR's strict data privacy laws put Marriott under intense scrutiny, and the company faced potential fines for failing to protect guest data adequately.

- **Internal Investigation**: Marriott conducted a thorough investigation into the breach, working with external security experts to determine how the attackers gained access and why the intrusion went undetected for so long. This investigation revealed weaknesses in **Starwood's legacy IT systems**, which Marriott had inherited during the acquisition but had not fully integrated into its own infrastructure.

Lessons Learned

The Marriott breach provided several key lessons for the hospitality industry and other sectors handling vast amounts of **customer data**:

1. Due Diligence During Acquisitions: The Marriott breach underscored the importance of conducting thorough **cybersecurity audits** during mergers and acquisitions. Starwood's systems were already compromised when Marriott acquired the company, indicating a potential lapse in security due diligence. Organizations must ensure that they assess the **cybersecurity posture** of the companies they are acquiring to prevent inheriting vulnerabilities.

2. Long-term Presence of Threat Actors: The breach highlighted the dangers of **advanced persistent threats (APTs)**, where attackers remain undetected within systems for extended periods. Organizations need to enhance **threat detection** capabilities to identify and respond to suspicious activity before attackers can exfiltrate large amounts of data.

3. Regulatory Compliance and Data Protection: The regulatory fallout from the breach, particularly under **GDPR**, emphasized the need for companies to comply with **stringent data protection standards**. Organizations must have strong **encryption policies** in place and ensure they have processes for detecting and reporting breaches within the legally mandated timeframes.

4. Incident Response and Crisis Management: Marriott's handling of the breach demonstrated the importance of having a well-prepared **incident response plan**. Although the breach had been ongoing for years, Marriott's quick action after the discovery—public disclosure, engagement with regulators, and launching an investigation—helped mitigate some of the reputational damage. Companies need robust **crisis management** strategies that include transparent communication and rapid response to data breaches.

Broader Implications

The **Marriott breach** had significant implications for both the company and the broader hospitality industry. With **383 million guest records** compromised, it reinforced the importance of **data privacy** and security, especially for companies handling large amounts of **personal and financial information**. The breach also spurred **regulatory changes**, leading to stricter enforcement of data protection laws and higher fines for companies that fail to safeguard customer data.

In the wake of the breach, Marriott committed to improving its **cybersecurity practices**, investing in **advanced threat detection tools**, and enhancing the **encryption of sensitive data**. The company also pledged to work closely with regulators to prevent similar incidents in the future.

Conclusion

In conclusion, the Marriott breach was a stark reminder of the risks associated with **legacy systems** and the long-term damage that data breaches can cause. It highlighted the need for **proactive cybersecurity measures** and greater **transparency** in the handling of personal data.

2019 – Facebook Goes For a Meta Breach

In April 2019, **Facebook** faced yet another major data breach that exposed personal information belonging to approximately **530 million users**. The breach was not a direct hack into Facebook's systems, but rather a result of data scraping due to vulnerabilities in Facebook's platform. These vulnerabilities allowed third-party actors to collect user information over time, impacting users across **106 countries** [29].

This breach included sensitive information such as **phone numbers, email addresses, full names, locations, and other personal details**, all of which were obtained without users' consent. While Facebook claimed that the vulnerability had been fixed by 2019, the scraped data surfaced online in April 2021, when a massive dataset containing the compromised information was made publicly available on hacking forums [29].

Scope of the Breach

The Facebook data breach affected a **vast range of users**, including both private individuals and public figures. The exposure of **530 million users' data** was significant due to the types of information compromised, such as:

- **Phone numbers** and **email addresses**, which could be used in subsequent phishing or social engineering attacks.
- **Names** and **locations**, potentially compromising individuals' privacy and safety.
- Additional personal details that could be used for **identity theft** or sold on the dark web for malicious purposes.

While no sensitive financial or password information was compromised, the scope of the data breach raised concerns about **personal privacy**, especially considering that Facebook's platform had already been scrutinized for its data handling practices in previous incidents, like the **Cambridge Analytica scandal** [29].

The Attack Mechanism

A vulnerability in Facebook's **contact importer feature** was present, which enabled attackers to scrape vast amounts of personal information over a period of time. The mechanism of the breach can be explained in the following steps:

- **Data Scraping**: Using the platform's contact importer, attackers were able to automate the process of gathering data from Facebook users' profiles. Although this tool was designed to help users find their friends, it was exploited to collect massive amounts of personal data.
- **Mass Data Exposure**: Attackers built databases of information on millions of users over several years. Even though Facebook claimed the vulnerability was fixed in 2019, the data that had already been scraped continued to circulate online.
- **Public Disclosure**: In April 2021, the entire dataset was leaked to public hacking forums, making the information easily accessible to anyone with malicious intent. This resulted in a renewed focus on the data privacy practices of social media giants like Facebook.

Response and Investigation

Once the breach was widely reported, **Facebook** responded by asserting that the vulnerability responsible for the data scraping had been resolved back in 2019. However, the release of the scraped data in 2021 triggered a series of investigations and heightened scrutiny regarding how Facebook manages user data [29].

- **Facebook's Official Response**: Facebook emphasized that this breach did not involve direct hacking of their systems, but rather the exploitation of a **vulnerability** that allowed for data scraping. They reiterated that the vulnerability had been fixed and that no passwords or financial data were exposed. However, they faced criticism for the delayed detection and response to the ongoing misuse of the platform.
- **Regulatory Scrutiny**: Various regulatory bodies, particularly in the European Union, where strict data privacy laws like the **General Data Protection Regulation (GDPR)** apply, initiated investigations into whether Facebook had sufficiently protected users'

data. GDPR regulators sought to determine if Facebook's handling of personal information met the standards required by law, potentially leading to further fines and restrictions.

- **Public Backlash**: The breach contributed to growing public concern over the privacy practices of **social media platforms**. Given Facebook's repeated privacy scandals, including the high-profile Cambridge Analytica affair, users began questioning whether their data was safe on the platform. The timing of the breach, so close to other data privacy incidents, fueled calls for stronger **data protection measures**.

Lessons Learned

The **Facebook Data Breach (2019)** highlighted several key lessons, particularly in the areas of **data privacy** and **corporate responsibility** for securing user information.

1. The Importance of Data Privacy: This breach emphasized the need for platforms like Facebook to prioritize **data privacy** and enforce stricter security controls, especially when handling **personal data**. The company's contact importer feature was vulnerable to exploitation for years, raising questions about Facebook's oversight of user data and its **vulnerability management processes**.

2. Transparency and Timely Reporting: Facebook's delayed response and lack of timely notification to users further eroded public trust. The breach revealed the importance of **transparent communication** with users when their data is exposed, as well as the need for **early detection systems** that can mitigate the impact of such breaches before data is widely disseminated.

3. Global Data Protection Laws: With GDPR in full effect, this breach underscored the importance of **compliance with international data protection laws**. Regulatory bodies increased their scrutiny of how companies like Facebook manage personal data, pushing for better safeguards and more severe penalties for non-compliance.

4. The Long-term Impact of Data Breaches: Even though the breach occurred due to vulnerabilities patched in 2019, the long-term implications of the breach became apparent in 2021 when the dataset was released publicly. This highlighted that breaches can have **lasting consequences**, particularly when stolen data continues to be traded or shared long after the vulnerability is fixed.

Broader Implications

The **Facebook Data Breach (2019)** had significant implications for the way social media platforms and large tech companies manage **user data**. As one of the largest breaches in terms of the sheer number of affected users, it pushed regulators, governments, and tech firms to take a more proactive approach toward **data security**.

In the wake of the breach, Facebook (now Meta) has invested more heavily in **improving security** across its platforms and **strengthening privacy settings** for users. However, this incident continues to serve as a stark reminder of the potential risks associated with personal data on social media platforms.

The breach also played a role in accelerating global conversations around **data privacy regulations** and the **responsibility of tech companies** to protect user information. As a result, calls for stronger **data governance** and **consumer protection measures** have gained momentum, influencing both corporate policy and government legislation in the tech sector.

Conclusion
In conclusion, the **Facebook Data Breach (2019)** exemplified the challenges of securing personal data on large social media platforms and underscored the growing demand for accountability and transparency in the digital age.

2020 – The SolarWinds of Change
In December 2020, a supply chain attack on SolarWinds, a major IT management software provider, became one of the most significant cybersecurity breaches in recent history, impacting both the private and public sectors. The breach, attributed to an Advanced Persistent Threat (APT) group likely backed by the Russian government, resulted in widespread compromise across thousands of organizations globally, including critical U.S. government agencies like the Treasury Department, Department of Homeland Security, and large corporations such as Microsoft [30].

The attack originated when malicious code was injected into SolarWinds' Orion software during a software update. Orion is widely used for IT infrastructure management, making it an ideal target. The attackers exploited the SolarWinds update process, embedding their malware into an update, which was distributed to around 18,000 customers between March and June 2020.
The SolarWinds breach began between March and June of 2020, when attackers successfully infiltrated the company's software build environment. During this time, they inserted a sophisticated backdoor, later known as **Sunburst**, into SolarWinds' widely used Orion software. In June 2020, the compromised software update was distributed to SolarWinds' customers, which included major corporations and government agencies. Upon installation, this update allowed the attackers to gain unauthorized access to the affected systems, providing them with a secret gateway to spy on networks and gather sensitive data [30].

The breach remained undetected for months until December 2020, when the cybersecurity firm **FireEye** uncovered that its own systems had been compromised by the same malicious actors. FireEye's discovery led to the revelation of the broader SolarWinds attack. On **December 13,**

2020, SolarWinds publicly acknowledged the breach, sparking widespread alarm as organizations across the globe realized their networks might have been compromised [30].

The **SolarWinds breach** was vast in its scope, impacting a wide range of organizations across both the public and private sectors. Among the hardest hit were **U.S. federal agencies**, including critical departments such as **Commerce, Energy, and Justice**. The infiltration of these government entities raised serious concerns about potential threats to national security, as sensitive information within these agencies was exposed [30].

In addition to government agencies, the **private sector** also suffered significant impacts. Major technology companies like **Microsoft** and **Cisco** were among the targets. While some of these private organizations chose to closely monitor the situation, many refrained from taking immediate action, likely due to the complexity of the attack and the desire to assess the full extent of the breach before responding [30].

The attackers took advantage of SolarWinds' Orion software by deploying a **layered strategy**. This approach allowed them to embed themselves deeply within the systems of affected organizations. Through this layered access, they were able to maintain long-term control over their targets, moving laterally within compromised networks. This method enabled them to remain undetected for extended periods, exfiltrating data and performing espionage activities without raising immediate alarms. The breach not only compromised sensitive systems but also highlighted the attackers' ability to operate stealthily for months, extracting valuable information at will [30].

Response and Investigation

Once the SolarWinds breach was uncovered in December 2020, it triggered an immediate and large-scale response from both the **U.S. government** and cybersecurity experts around the globe. Recognizing the severity of the attack and the breadth of its impact, the first priority was to assess the full extent of the compromise. Affected organizations were swiftly instructed to **disconnect compromised systems** to prevent further damage and to **patch vulnerabilities** in their networks. This included both government agencies and private sector companies, as the breach's scale was unprecedented [30].

Federal agencies, led by entities such as the **Cybersecurity and Infrastructure Security Agency (CISA)** and the **Federal Bureau of Investigation (FBI)**, coordinated efforts to identify how deeply the attackers had penetrated critical infrastructure. Immediate actions were taken to secure sensitive government data, and intelligence-sharing initiatives were expanded to ensure other organizations could defend themselves against the ongoing threat. CISA issued **Emergency Directive 21-01**, which required all federal agencies using SolarWinds software to disconnect or power down their Orion products to limit further exploitation [30].

As the investigation unfolded, it became clear that the **attackers had been lurking within systems for months**, dating back to as early as **March 2020**. During this time, they had quietly infiltrated networks and **exfiltrated sensitive data**, gathering intelligence from high-profile targets. Their ability to move laterally within compromised networks without detection for such an extended period raised serious concerns about the security of both **government systems** and **critical private sector infrastructure** [30].

In response, **Congress** held several **oversight hearings** to scrutinize the handling of the breach and SolarWinds' security practices. These hearings involved testimony from key stakeholders, including the **CEO of SolarWinds**, representatives from cybersecurity firms like **FireEye**, and leaders from affected government agencies. Congress explored how the attackers had managed to infiltrate such a widely-used software platform undetected for so long, and what security failures had contributed to the breach. In these hearings, it was revealed that **SolarWinds' own internal security measures** were alarmingly lax, with reports surfacing about weak password policies and outdated security protocols during the software build process [30].

The breach also prompted broader discussions about the state of **cybersecurity in critical infrastructure**. Lawmakers and cybersecurity experts debated the need for stronger regulations governing **supply chain security** and called for greater **transparency** from software vendors about their security practices. Some proposed that software companies should undergo more rigorous **third-party security audits** to detect vulnerabilities before they can be exploited by sophisticated attackers [30].

As SolarWinds faced intense scrutiny, the company vowed to improve its security posture. It announced plans to strengthen its **software development practices**, including more robust security reviews and **advanced threat detection** mechanisms. Additionally, cybersecurity recommendations such as implementing **Zero Trust Architecture** and expanding **endpoint monitoring** became focal points of the industry's response to prevent future incidents.

The long-term investigation also sparked an increased focus on **attribution**—identifying the actors behind the attack. By early 2021, U.S. intelligence agencies officially attributed the attack to **Russia's Foreign Intelligence Service (SVR)**, a state-sponsored group known for conducting espionage campaigns against Western targets. This attribution further fueled geopolitical tensions, as the U.S. considered retaliation in the form of **sanctions** and **cyber countermeasures** [30].

Ultimately, the SolarWinds breach underscored the vulnerability of global IT supply chains and demonstrated the need for more rigorous **cybersecurity governance** across industries. The breach served as a wake-up call for governments and businesses alike, pushing them to reconsider how they manage **cyber risks** and defend against **state-sponsored threats** in an increasingly interconnected world.

Lessons Learned

The SolarWinds breach provided the following key lessons learned:

1. Supply Chain Security: The SolarWinds attack underscored the need for stronger security within the software supply chain. Organizations need to vet their vendors more rigorously and establish protocols for monitoring software integrity throughout the development lifecycle. SolarWinds' lack of robust security protocols for its build process facilitated the attack.

2. Implementing Zero Trust Architecture (ZTA): A more comprehensive implementation of Zero Trust principles could have helped limit the lateral movement of attackers. In traditional security models, trust is granted within a perimeter, but Zero Trust emphasizes never assuming trust and consistently validating identities and behaviors.

3. Network Segmentation and Anomaly Detection: Proper segmentation of critical infrastructure and better anomaly detection mechanisms might have helped detect malicious activity earlier. In this case, the attackers successfully disguised their communication as legitimate traffic, which went undetected for months.

4. Incident Response Readiness: The need for an agile and well-prepared incident response team is essential in mitigating damage. In this case, once the breach was identified, FireEye's quick response helped uncover the attack's full scope.

Conclusion

The SolarWinds breach serves as a stark reminder of the evolving complexity of cybersecurity threats in a hyperconnected world. This attack not only revealed the vulnerabilities within supply chain security but also highlighted the devastating impact such breaches can have on both private and public sectors. From government agencies to multinational corporations, the attackers' ability to operate undetected for months showcases the need for stronger, more resilient cybersecurity strategies.

As technology advances, so too must our defenses. The breach underscored the importance of adopting robust security frameworks like Zero Trust Architecture, enhancing network segmentation, and deploying advanced threat detection systems. Organizations must rethink their approach to software supply chain security, ensuring that vendors and third-party providers are rigorously vetted and monitored. Additionally, the incident demonstrated the critical need for agile incident response teams that can quickly adapt to and mitigate emerging threats.

Ultimately, the SolarWinds breach was a wake-up call for the global cybersecurity community, urging businesses and governments to reassess their risk management strategies and embrace a more proactive, security-first mindset. As we look to the future, it is essential to prioritize the development of secure technologies and foster international collaboration to defend against state-sponsored cyber espionage and other sophisticated cyber threats. The lessons from this breach should guide the path forward, ensuring a more secure and resilient digital ecosystem for all.

2020 Twitter

In **July 2020**, **Twitter** experienced a highly publicized and disruptive security breach that affected some of the platform's most influential accounts, including those of prominent figures such as **Bill Gates**, **Elon Musk**, **Barack Obama**, and major corporations like **Apple**. The attackers used these compromised accounts to promote a **cryptocurrency scam**, deceiving users into sending Bitcoin with the false promise of receiving double the amount in return. This hack was not just an embarrassing incident for Twitter but also a concerning example of how social engineering attacks can target **high-profile users** and platforms [31].

The hack involved **social engineering techniques** to compromise internal Twitter systems. The attackers used these methods to gain access to Twitter's administrative tools, which allowed them to take control of **45 accounts**, alter account details, and bypass two-factor authentication. The scam managed to collect **more than $100,000** worth of Bitcoin in a short period before it was stopped, exposing vulnerabilities in Twitter's internal security practices and raising concerns about the security of **verified accounts** and the platform's wider user base [31].

Scope of the Breach

The Twitter hack was significant due to the **high-profile nature of the accounts** targeted and the potential for large-scale **disinformation**:

- **Compromised Accounts**: Affected accounts included celebrities, political figures, and major corporations. The attackers sent out coordinated tweets from these accounts, urging followers to participate in a Bitcoin giveaway scam [31].
- **Public Trust and Influence**: The hack not only led to financial losses for users but also eroded trust in the platform's ability to secure sensitive, high-value accounts. With control over such influential voices, the attackers had the potential to cause substantial disruption or disinformation [31].
- **Global Attention**: Due to the stature of the accounts affected, the hack attracted **global attention**, forcing Twitter to take drastic measures, such as **temporarily disabling verified accounts** from posting and limiting functionalities on the platform to mitigate further damage [31].

The Attack Mechanism

The attackers employed a **social engineering attack** targeting Twitter employees with administrative access to internal systems [31]. Here's how the attack unfolded:

- **Social Engineering**: The hackers reportedly used **phishing attacks** to trick Twitter employees into providing access to internal tools. They successfully obtained credentials that allowed them to log into Twitter's systems.
- **Internal Control Exploitation**: Once inside, the attackers used these administrative tools to take over prominent accounts. They bypassed security measures such as two-factor authentication, altered recovery email addresses, and posted messages from the compromised accounts.
- **Coordinated Bitcoin Scam**: The hackers used the compromised accounts to tweet messages encouraging followers to send Bitcoin to a specific wallet address with the promise of doubling their investment. This scam targeted the massive followings of these influential accounts, and the attackers managed to collect over **$100,000** in Bitcoin before Twitter could intervene.

Response and Investigation

The response to the Twitter hack was swift but raised questions about **platform security** and **internal protocols**:

- **Immediate Response**: Twitter took drastic action by temporarily **disabling all verified accounts** from posting new tweets to prevent further misuse. The company also locked down compromised accounts and restored control to their rightful owners [31].
- **Public Communication**: Twitter quickly communicated with the public, confirming the breach and assuring users that they were investigating the situation. The platform worked closely with law enforcement and external security experts to identify the attackers and secure internal systems [31].
- **Federal Investigation**: Given the scale and high-profile nature of the hack, the **FBI** and other federal agencies launched an investigation into the incident. Authorities later arrested **three individuals**, including a 17-year-old who was considered the mastermind behind the attack. These individuals were charged with orchestrating the breach using social engineering tactics to access internal systems [31].
- **Twitter's Internal Review**: Twitter conducted an internal review of its security practices, particularly around how its employees could access sensitive tools. The company acknowledged that the attackers had exploited weaknesses in employee training and security protocols [31].

Lessons Learned

The Twitter hack provided several key lessons for organizations managing **high-profile accounts** and handling **internal security**:

1. The Importance of Social Engineering Defense: The hack highlighted the effectiveness of **social engineering** techniques in breaching large organizations. Despite Twitter's sophisticated systems, the attackers successfully manipulated employees to gain access. This underscores the need for **comprehensive security training** for all employees, especially those with access to critical systems.

2. Securing Administrative Tools: The breach exposed vulnerabilities in how Twitter handled access to its **administrative tools**. With these tools, attackers could bypass security measures and compromise accounts directly. The incident emphasized the need for **better internal access controls**, such as **limiting access privileges** to only essential personnel and **implementing stronger multi-factor authentication** for employees managing critical systems.

3. Rapid Incident Response: Twitter's decision to temporarily suspend verified accounts from tweeting was a critical step in preventing further damage. The incident demonstrated the importance of having a **well-coordinated incident response plan** that allows for rapid action to mitigate the impact of ongoing cyberattacks. However, the public fallout also highlighted the need for **transparent communication** with users during a security breach.

4. Protecting High-Value Accounts: Given the influential nature of the accounts compromised, the hack reinforced the need for **additional security layers** for high-profile accounts, such as **enhanced monitoring** and **manual review** for any suspicious account changes or activity. Twitter subsequently implemented new security measures for accounts tied to significant individuals or organizations to prevent similar incidents in the future.

Broader Implications

The **Twitter Hack (2020)** had broader implications for **social media security** and the potential dangers of **platform manipulation**. With control over such influential accounts, attackers could have easily spread misinformation, created geopolitical unrest, or disrupted financial markets. The breach prompted widespread concern about the ability of social media platforms to safeguard against attacks that target both **internal systems** and **human weaknesses**.
In response to the hack, Twitter committed to enhancing the security of its **internal tools**, improving employee training, and strengthening **authentication processes** for high-profile accounts. The incident also sparked discussions across the tech industry about the need for **better protection against social engineering attacks** and the importance of **internal security protocols** for companies that hold vast amounts of user data and influence.

Conclusion

In conclusion, the Twitter Hack (2020) exposed the vulnerabilities of even the largest platforms to **social engineering** and highlighted the importance of **securing internal systems** and tools. It served as a wake-up call for both Twitter and other social media platforms to reassess their security practices, especially in the face of increasingly sophisticated cyber threats.

2021 - Accellion Breach

In early 2021, **Accellion**, a provider of secure file-sharing and transfer solutions, suffered a major breach involving its legacy **File Transfer Appliance (FTA)**. The breach resulted in the **compromise of sensitive data** from multiple high-profile organizations, including **Stanford University**, **Kroger**, and **Shell**. The incident occurred due to vulnerabilities in the **20-year-old FTA software**, which had not been designed to meet modern security standards. Attackers exploited these vulnerabilities to infiltrate the systems of Accellion's customers, accessing highly sensitive personal, financial, and corporate data [32].

This breach highlighted the risks associated with the continued use of **outdated software** and **legacy systems** in critical operations. Despite being informed that the FTA would be decommissioned and replaced by more secure alternatives, many organizations were still reliant on the tool, which made them vulnerable to this attack [32].

Scope of the Breach

The **Accellion breach** affected a broad range of organizations across various industries, including healthcare, education, retail, and government institutions:

- **Healthcare and Education**: Universities, including **Stanford University**, were severely impacted by the breach. Sensitive **student and staff information**, including academic records and personal identification data, was exposed. Similarly, healthcare providers were affected, with confidential patient information potentially compromised.
- **Corporate and Financial**: Large corporations like **Kroger** and **Shell** had customer data exposed, including **financial details** and **corporate secrets**. The breach also impacted **financial services**, leading to the exposure of sensitive transactional and internal financial records.
- **Widespread Data Exposure**: The attackers gained access to personal information such as **names, Social Security numbers, health data, and payment card information**, exposing individuals and organizations to significant risks, including **identity theft** and **fraud**.

The breach was notable for the range of industries affected, demonstrating the **cross-sector vulnerabilities** that can arise from using outdated technology. As the attack unfolded, it became clear that more than **100 organizations** worldwide were affected by this breach [32].

The Attack Mechanism

The Accellion breach occurred due to **multiple zero-day vulnerabilities** in its legacy **FTA** software. Attackers used a combination of **SQL injection vulnerabilities** and **remote code execution (RCE)** to gain unauthorized access to the file-sharing systems of Accellion's clients.

- **Zero-Day Exploits**: The attackers exploited previously unknown vulnerabilities in Accellion's FTA software to **inject malicious code**. These zero-day vulnerabilities allowed them to bypass security controls and execute commands within compromised environments.

- **Data Exfiltration**: Once inside, the attackers used **web shells** and **backdoors** to extract sensitive data stored within the file transfer system. This method allowed them to exfiltrate large amounts of confidential data over time without detection.

- **Ransom and Extortion**: After exfiltrating data, the attackers shifted to **ransom and extortion tactics**. Victims were contacted and threatened with the public release of their data unless they paid substantial ransoms. The **Clop ransomware group**, which was linked to the attack, published some of the stolen data on the dark web to pressure organizations into paying.

Response and Investigation

The response to the Accellion breach involved both the company and its affected customers, with efforts focused on **mitigating the ongoing threat** and preventing further data loss:

- **Accellion's Response**: Accellion quickly released patches for the identified vulnerabilities in the FTA software. The company urged its customers to **immediately apply the updates** and transition to its newer, more secure platform, **Kiteworks**, which was designed to replace the FTA. However, for many organizations, the patches came too late, as their data had already been exfiltrated [32].

- **Incident Reporting and Notifications**: Accellion notified affected organizations and worked with cybersecurity firms to investigate the breach. However, the timing of the notifications was a point of criticism, as some organizations felt they had not been informed promptly enough to prevent significant data loss [32].

- **Law Enforcement Involvement**: Given the scope and impact of the breach, the **FBI** and other international law enforcement agencies launched investigations to track down the attackers. The **Clop ransomware group**, believed to be behind the attack, was identified as a primary culprit. Authorities coordinated efforts to pursue the individuals responsible and mitigate the effects of the breach [32].

Despite the patching efforts, many organizations faced long-term consequences, including data recovery challenges, reputational damage, and legal repercussions related to the exposed data.

Lessons Learned

The Accellion breach emphasized several critical lessons for organizations and the tech industry, particularly concerning **legacy systems** and **cybersecurity readiness**:

1. Risks of Legacy Systems: The Accellion breach demonstrated the dangers of relying on **outdated software** in critical operations. Organizations that failed to migrate from Accellion's legacy FTA to more modern solutions were left vulnerable to this sophisticated attack. This breach reinforced the need for organizations to **regularly audit** and **upgrade legacy systems** to ensure they are meeting contemporary security standards.

2. The Importance of Timely Patching and System Decommissioning: Accellion had communicated plans to retire its FTA solution, yet many organizations continued to use the outdated system, either due to inertia or integration complexities. This breach highlighted the importance of **timely decommissioning** and upgrading legacy infrastructure. Applying **patches quickly** when vulnerabilities are discovered is essential to mitigating the risk of compromise.

3. Stronger Incident Response and Communication: Accellion's response, while swift, faced criticism for the perceived delay in notifying customers. The breach emphasized the need for **transparent and immediate communication** during cybersecurity incidents to allow affected organizations to take protective action as soon as possible. An effective **incident response plan** must include clear **communication protocols** for both internal teams and external stakeholders.

4. Defending Against Ransomware and Extortion: The attack's progression from data theft to ransom demands underscored the need for organizations to be prepared for **extortion tactics** used by cybercriminals. Companies should invest in **proactive defense measures** like **ransomware prevention** tools and **data encryption** to limit the impact of a breach. Having a robust **backup strategy** is also essential to recovering data without yielding to ransom demands.

Broader Implications

The **Accellion breach** had significant implications for the **file-sharing industry** and for organizations dependent on third-party vendors for secure data transmission. The attack shed light on the risks of **supply chain vulnerabilities**, particularly when legacy systems are involved. It also reignited conversations about **third-party risk management** and the **responsibility of vendors** to provide secure, up-to-date solutions.

In the wake of the breach, many organizations reevaluated their **cybersecurity practices** around third-party software, particularly legacy solutions. Accellion, while continuing to push its newer **Kiteworks** platform, faced reputational challenges as customers sought more secure alternatives. The incident also highlighted the need for **regulatory oversight** and **industry standards** to ensure that legacy systems with known vulnerabilities are either replaced or adequately secured.

Conclusion

In conclusion, the **Accellion (2021) breach** served as a stark reminder of the risks posed by **legacy technology** and emphasized the importance of proactive **cybersecurity measures** and **vendor management**. It underscored the need for organizations to stay ahead of **emerging threats** by continually modernizing their systems and implementing **strong incident response plans**

2021 T-Mobile Phones in a Breach

The **T-Mobile Data Breach of 2021** was one of the most significant cyber incidents to affect the telecommunications industry, exposing the personal data of over **40 million current and former customers**. T-Mobile, a major provider of wireless services in the United States, found itself the target of a sophisticated cyberattack that compromised sensitive customer information, including Social Security numbers and driver's license details. The breach raised serious concerns about data privacy and security within telecommunications, an industry that manages vast amounts of personal and financial data. This breach had wide-reaching implications for both T-Mobile and its customers, highlighting vulnerabilities in the company's cybersecurity practices [33].

Scope of Breach

The **scope of the T-Mobile breach** was extensive, affecting **approximately 47.8 million customers**, including current, former, and prospective customers who had applied for T-Mobile services. The stolen data included highly sensitive personal information, such as **Social Security numbers, driver's license numbers, names, dates of birth**, and **phone numbers**. While no financial data, such as credit card numbers, was exposed, the personal information compromised could still be exploited for **identity theft**, **fraud**, and **phishing schemes** [33].

The breach impacted both **postpaid** and **prepaid customers**, with millions of Social Security numbers and driver's licenses stolen, along with the **International Mobile Equipment Identity (IMEI)** and **International Mobile Subscriber Identity (IMSI)** numbers linked to customers' phones. The exposure of this data posed significant security risks, as it provided cybercriminals with the necessary details to impersonate individuals, conduct account takeovers, and target customers with further attacks [33].

Attack Mechanism

The attackers responsible for the breach gained access to T-Mobile's systems by exploiting a **vulnerability in the company's infrastructure**. A **teenage hacker** claimed responsibility for the attack, stating that they were able to penetrate T-Mobile's **test environment**. From there, the attacker used weak security controls and **misconfigurations** within the system to escalate privileges and gain access to sensitive customer data [33].

Once inside T-Mobile's systems, the attackers **exfiltrated data** over an extended period without being detected. The breach went unnoticed until the stolen data was offered for sale on **underground forums**, prompting T-Mobile to investigate the situation. The attacker exploited a lack of robust security measures, particularly in **endpoint security** and **network segmentation**, which allowed them to move laterally across the network and access critical customer databases [33].

Response and Investigation

T-Mobile publicly disclosed the breach in **August 2021**, shortly after becoming aware that customer data had been compromised. The company launched an investigation and collaborated with **cybersecurity firms** and **law enforcement agencies** to assess the scope of the breach and mitigate further damage. The Federal Bureau of Investigation (FBI) also became involved, given the scale of the breach and the potential for widespread identity theft [33].

T-Mobile immediately implemented **containment measures**, such as securing the compromised systems and enhancing its security infrastructure. The company offered affected customers **two years of free identity protection services**, including **credit monitoring**, through **McAfee's ID Theft Protection Service**. T-Mobile also encouraged customers to change their **PINs** and passwords to reduce the risk of account takeovers [33].

Despite these efforts, T-Mobile faced significant criticism for its handling of the breach. Many customers expressed dissatisfaction with the company's response, particularly the delay in notifying affected individuals and the perceived lack of transparency around the full extent of the breach. T-Mobile's CEO issued a public apology, acknowledging the breach and promising to invest in stronger cybersecurity defenses to prevent future incidents [33].

Lessons Learned

Several important lessons emerged from the T-Mobile breach, not only for the company but for the entire telecommunications industry:

1. **Stronger Security Controls**: The breach revealed weaknesses in T-Mobile's **network security**, particularly around how data was stored and accessed. The attackers were able to infiltrate the system through the test environment, highlighting the need for stronger **segmentation of networks** and **restricted access controls**. T-Mobile has since committed to bolstering its security infrastructure.

2. **Improved Monitoring and Detection**: T-Mobile was unaware of the breach until the stolen data was offered for sale on dark web forums. This breach emphasized the need for enhanced **real-time monitoring**, **intrusion detection systems (IDS)**, and **automated threat detection tools** to identify and stop suspicious activity before significant data can be exfiltrated.

3. **Data Minimization and Encryption**: While T-Mobile stored large amounts of sensitive data, it failed to **adequately encrypt** key elements like Social Security numbers. Encrypting customer data, even within internal systems, could have reduced the risk of the data being exploited once it was stolen. The breach also highlighted the importance of **data minimization**, ensuring that only necessary data is stored and retained.

4. **Timely Disclosure**: T-Mobile faced criticism for the delay in disclosing the breach to customers. The incident highlighted the importance of **quickly notifying affected parties** to enable them to take proactive steps, such as changing passwords and monitoring their accounts for fraudulent activity.

Broader Implications

The T-Mobile breach had far-reaching implications for the telecommunications industry, as it demonstrated how attackers can target critical infrastructure to access large volumes of sensitive personal data. The breach raised concerns about how **telecom companies** secure customer data and their vulnerability to cyberattacks, especially as the industry manages sensitive information that can be easily monetized by cybercriminals.

This breach also reignited discussions about **data privacy** and **regulatory oversight**. Many lawmakers and regulators questioned whether telecom companies should face stricter requirements for securing customer data. The incident prompted calls for stronger data protection regulations, similar to the **General Data Protection Regulation (GDPR)** in Europe, to ensure that companies are held accountable for the way they handle personal information.

From a business standpoint, the breach affected T-Mobile's reputation and customer trust. With several large breaches already in its history, this incident further strained the company's relationship with its customers. The breach also underscored the importance of cybersecurity in **mergers and acquisitions**, as T-Mobile had recently completed a high-profile merger with Sprint. The integration of two massive networks may have created additional vulnerabilities that attackers exploited.

Conclusion

The **T-Mobile data breach of 2021** was a sobering reminder of the growing threat of cyberattacks in critical sectors like telecommunications. The breach exposed sensitive personal data of millions of customers, highlighting weaknesses in T-Mobile's security practices and underscoring the need for stronger protections around customer data. The breach's lessons—ranging from better encryption and network segmentation to faster breach disclosure—are applicable across industries that handle sensitive data. As cyberattacks continue to evolve in scale and complexity, the T-Mobile breach emphasizes the importance of **robust cybersecurity defenses**, **proactive threat monitoring**, and **prompt incident response** to safeguard against future breaches.

2021 Microsoft Exchange Server

In early 2021, a series of vulnerabilities in **Microsoft Exchange Server** were discovered and exploited by a **state-sponsored group** known as **Hafnium**, allegedly backed by the Chinese government. These vulnerabilities, referred to as **zero-day vulnerabilities**, allowed attackers to gain unauthorized access to on-premises Exchange Servers. The breach quickly evolved into a global cybersecurity crisis, as hundreds of thousands of organizations were affected, including government agencies, businesses, and institutions worldwide [34].

The attack targeted **Microsoft Exchange email servers**, which are used by a significant number of organizations to manage email communications. By exploiting these vulnerabilities, Hafnium was able to bypass authentication mechanisms and execute arbitrary code within the affected systems. This allowed the attackers to gain control over the servers, steal sensitive information, and plant backdoors for future access [34].

Scope of the Breach

The scope of the **Microsoft Exchange Server breach** was vast, affecting both **private and public sector organizations** globally:

- **Government Agencies**: Multiple government agencies across the U.S. and other nations were impacted by the breach. Sensitive information, such as internal communications and classified data, was potentially compromised, raising concerns about national security.
- **Private Sector Organizations**: Businesses of all sizes, including law firms, healthcare providers, and financial institutions, found their Exchange email servers compromised. This attack left them vulnerable to data theft and future exploitation, as backdoors were left in many affected systems.

The attack unfolded in two stages. Initially, Hafnium used the vulnerabilities to steal data from compromised organizations, but as the breach was publicly disclosed, **opportunistic cybercriminals** and other malicious groups began to exploit the vulnerabilities for widespread attacks. This led to a secondary wave of attacks, which involved the deployment of ransomware and the establishment of persistent backdoors within networks [34].

The Attack Mechanism

The Microsoft Exchange Server breach exploited four **zero-day vulnerabilities** in the software. These vulnerabilities, collectively known as **ProxyLogon**, allowed attackers to gain full control of the server through a **remote code execution** exploit [34]. Here's a breakdown of the attack mechanism:

- **Initial Exploit**: The attackers used the vulnerabilities to gain unauthorized access to the affected Exchange Servers without needing valid login credentials. This gave them administrative control over the servers.
- **Web Shell Installation**: Once inside, the attackers installed **web shells**—malicious scripts that provided them with persistent access to the compromised systems. These web shells allowed the attackers to execute commands remotely and maintain control over the servers even after patches were applied.
- **Data Exfiltration and Lateral Movement**: Hafnium primarily focused on **data exfiltration**, targeting sensitive communications, intellectual property, and internal organizational data. Additionally, the attackers used their foothold in the compromised servers to move laterally across networks, increasing the scope of the breach.

Response and Investigation

The **Microsoft Exchange breach** prompted an immediate response from the global cybersecurity community, as well as government agencies and Microsoft itself. The **U.S. Cybersecurity and Infrastructure Security Agency (CISA)** issued emergency directives, urging organizations to apply the necessary patches immediately.

- **Microsoft's Response**: Upon discovering the vulnerabilities, **Microsoft** released patches in March 2021. However, many organizations were slow to apply the patches, leaving thousands of servers vulnerable even after the patch was made available. Microsoft also collaborated with law enforcement agencies and cybersecurity firms to identify affected systems and mitigate the damage [34].

- **U.S. Government's Response**: Recognizing the severity of the breach, the U.S. government launched a full-scale investigation. The **FBI** played a critical role in identifying victims of the attack and aiding with remediation efforts. The **Department of Justice** (DOJ) also obtained court orders to **remove malicious web shells** from compromised servers, a proactive measure aimed at reducing the attack's impact [34].

- **International Response**: Similar actions were taken by government agencies worldwide, as the breach affected a large number of organizations across Europe, Asia, and other regions. International cybersecurity organizations collaborated with affected entities to contain the breach and prevent further exploitation [34].

Despite these efforts, the attack resulted in significant data loss for many organizations. The failure to apply patches quickly also allowed cybercriminals to take advantage of the vulnerabilities, leading to subsequent ransomware attacks and further exploitation [34].

Lessons Learned

The Microsoft Exchange Server breach highlighted several critical lessons for organizations and the broader cybersecurity community:

Lesson 1 – Patch Management and Vulnerability Disclosure

The breach underscored the importance of prompt **patch management**. Although Microsoft released patches to fix the vulnerabilities, many organizations delayed their implementation, leaving themselves exposed. This demonstrated the urgent need for better **vulnerability management** and faster patching processes.

Lesson 2 – Advanced Persistent Threat (APT) Preparedness

The breach, orchestrated by a **state-sponsored group**, reinforced the need for organizations to be prepared for **Advanced Persistent Threat (APT)** actors. These well-resourced groups often exploit zero-day vulnerabilities and operate with long-term goals, such as espionage and intellectual property theft. Organizations must adopt **proactive defense measures**, including **threat hunting** and **continuous monitoring**.

Lesson 3 – Endpoint Detection and Response (EDR) and Network Segmentation
Effective **Endpoint Detection and Response (EDR)** systems could have helped organizations detect suspicious activity earlier, potentially reducing the impact of the breach. Additionally, **network segmentation**—isolating critical systems from other parts of the network—could have limited the attackers' ability to move laterally and access sensitive data.

Lesson 4 – Zero Trust Security Model
The breach emphasized the need for adopting a **Zero Trust Security** model, which assumes that every request, whether internal or external, must be verified before granting access. Had a Zero Trust approach been in place, organizations could have reduced the likelihood of attackers gaining full administrative control over their systems.

Broader Implications
The **Microsoft Exchange Server breach** had significant implications for global cybersecurity, particularly in the context of **state-sponsored cyberattacks**. The incident demonstrated the sheer scale and speed at which vulnerabilities can be exploited and the potential for cascading consequences across industries and countries.

In the aftermath of the breach, governments and cybersecurity firms increased their focus on **coordinated threat intelligence sharing** and **collaborative defense efforts**. **Microsoft** itself pledged to further strengthen the security of its software products and improve its patch release processes to better protect its customers.

The breach also raised awareness about the critical importance of **cloud migration** and **cloud security**. As organizations move away from on-premises systems like Exchange Server and adopt cloud-based solutions, they must invest in securing these environments and ensuring that they are resilient against future threats.

Summary

Every organization faces considerable challenges while conducting business over the Internet. From China's APTs to COVID-19 scams, challenges will continually arise, often at inopportune times. There are three core competencies necessary to adequately create, plan, lead and secure an organization's digital capabilities. Designing and maintaining information technology infrastructure is critical to organizational health and stability. Risk planning, assessment, and mitigation plays an important role in design and ongoing operations. Lastly, cyber resiliency and cybersecurity ensure ongoing operations in an uncertain and volatile Internet business environment. Let's begin to investigate technology and innovation for business success.

Discussion Questions

Answer the questions as they relate to the organization.

1) In 2013, Target was breached, impacting millions of people.
    a) What organization was the source of Target's breach?
    b) What was the initial attack leveraged at the source organization?
    c) What lessons learned would you recommend?
2) In 2015, Anthem was breached.
    a) What organization was the source of Anthem's breach?
    b) What was the initial attack leveraged at the source organization?
    c) What lessons learned would you recommend?
3) In 2013, Yahoo was breached.
    a) What organization was the source of Yahoo's breach?
    b) What was the initial attack leveraged at the source organization?
    c) What lessons learned would you recommend?
4) In 2014, eBay was breached.
    a) What organization was the source of eBay's breach?
    b) What was the initial attack leveraged at the source organization?
    c) What lessons learned would you recommend?

References

[1] S. Stein and J. Jacobs, "Cyber-Attack Hits U.S. Health Agency Amid Covid-19 Outbreak," 16 March 2020. [Online]. Available: https://www.bloomberg.com/news/articles/2020-03-16/u-s-health-agency-suffers-cyber-attack-during-covid-19-response.. [Accessed 19 March 2020].

[2] Threat Intelligence Team, "APT36 jumps on the coronavirus bandwagon, delivers Crimson RAT," Malware Bytes Lab, 16 March 2020. [Online]. Available: https://blog.malwarebytes.com/threat-analysis/2020/03/apt36-jumps-on-the-coronavirus-bandwagon-delivers-crimson-rat/. [Accessed 19 March 2020].

[3] Verizon, Verizon, 2019. [Online]. Available: https://enterprise.verizon.com/resources/reports/2019-data-breach-investigations-report.pdf. [Accessed 2019].

[4] S. Steinberg, "CNBC.com," 13 October 2019. [Online]. Available: https://www.cnbc.com/2019/10/13/cyberattacks-cost-small-companies-200k-putting-many-out-of-business.html. [Accessed 20 March 2020].

[5] NIST, "What is the Internet of Things (IoT) and how can we secure it?," NIST, [Online]. Available: https://www.nist.gov/video/what-internet-things-iot-and-how-can-we-secure-it. [Accessed 31 August 2020].

[6] E. Nakashima, "Hacks of OPM databases compromised 22.1 million people, federal authorities say," The Washington Post, 9 July 2015. [Online]. Available: https://www.washingtonpost.com/news/federal-eye/wp/2015/07/09/hack-of-security-clearance-system-affected-21-5-million-people-federal-authorities-say/. [Accessed 1 Apri 2020].

[7] J. Fruhlinger, "The OPM hack explained: Bad security practices meet China's Captain America," CSOonline.com, 12 February 2020. [Online]. Available: https://www.csoonline.com/article/3318238/the-opm-hack-explained-bad-security-practices-meet-chinas-captain-america.html. [Accessed 2 April 2020].

[8] B. Gertz, "FBI Alert Reveals 'Groups' Behind OPM Hack," The Washington Free Beacon, 10 June 2015. [Online]. Available: https://freebeacon.com/national-security/fbi-alert-reveals-groups-behind-opm-hack/. [Accessed 10 April 2020].

[9] B. Koerner, "Inside the Cyberattack That Shocked the US Government," Wired.com, 23 October 2016. [Online]. Available: https://www.wired.com/2016/10/inside-cyberattack-shocked-us-government/. [Accessed April 2020].

[10] M. d. Cava, "Uber to pay $148 million over undisclosed data breach that ex-CEO paid hackers to keep quiet," 26 September 2018. [Online]. Available: https://www.usatoday.com/story/tech/news/2018/09/26/uber-pay-148-million-over-undisclosed-data-breach-ex-ceo-paid-hackers-keep-quiet/1432335002/. [Accessed 19 June 2020].

[11] A. Greenberg, "Wired.com," 21 November 2017. [Online]. Available: https://www.wired.com/story/uber-paid-off-hackers-to-hide-a-57-million-user-data-breach/. [Accessed 20 March 2020].

[12] J. Dunn, "Uber data breach aided by lack of multi-factor authentication," 8 February 2018. [Online]. Available: https://nakedsecurity.sophos.com/2018/02/08/uber-data-breach-aided-by-multi-factor-authentication-weakness/. [Accessed 20 March 2020].

[13] M. Hayden, "A timeline of the WannaCry cyberattack," ABC News, 12 May 2017. [Online]. Available: https://abcnews.go.com/US/timeline-wannacry-cyberattack/story?id=47416785. [Accessed 26 March 2020].

[14] C. Cimpanu, "How US authorities tracked down the North Korean hacker behind WannaCry," ZDNet, 6 September 2018. [Online]. Available: https://www.zdnet.com/article/how-us-authorities-tracked-down-the-north-korean-hacker-behind-wannacry/. [Accessed 30 March 2020].

[15] O. Santos, "The Shadow Brokers EPICBANANA and EXTRABACON Exploits," Cisco Blogs, 20 April 2017. [Online]. Available: https://blogs.cisco.com/security/shadow-brokers. [Accessed 26 March 2020].

[16] D. Goodin, "NSA-leaking Shadow Brokers just dumped its most damaging release yet," Arstechnica.com, 14 April 2017. [Online]. Available: https://arstechnica.com/information-technology/2017/04/nsa-leaking-shadow-brokers-just-dumped-its-most-damaging-release-yet/. [Accessed 30 March 2020].

[17] G. Dan, "Arstechnica.com," 14 March 2017. [Online]. Available: https://arstechnica.com/information-technology/2017/03/in-the-wild-exploits-ramp-up-against-high-impact-sites-using-apache-struts/. [Accessed 31 August 2020].

[18] J. Fruhlinger, "CSO Online," 12 February 2020. [Online]. Available: https://www.csoonline.com/article/3444488/equifax-data-breach-faq-what-happened-who-was-affected-what-was-the-impact.html. [Accessed 31 August 2020].

[19] R. J. II, "60 Percent Of Small Companies Close Within 6 Months Of Being Hacked," Cybercrime Magazine, 2 January 2019. [Online]. Available: https://cybersecurityventures.com/60-percent-of-small-companies-close-within-6-months-of-being-hacked/. [Accessed 16 April 2020].

[22] OpenAI. (2024). Raging dumpster fire in an alleyway, New York City [AI-generated image]. DALL·E. https://chat.openai.com

[24] Wikipedia, "Screenshot of a WannaCry ransomware attack on Windows 8," Wikipedia, May 2017. [Online]. Available: https://en.wikipedia.org/wiki/WannaCry_ransomware_attack#/media/File:Wana_Decrypt0r_screenshot.png. [Accessed 30 March 2020].

[25] Dall-E, ChatGPT, [Online]. Available: https://chatgpt.com/g/g-2fkFE8rbu-dall-e. [Accessed 3 November 2024].

[26] Wikimedia Commons, "File:Countries initially affected in WannaCry ransomware attack.png," Wikimedia Commons, [Online]. Available: https://commons.wikimedia.org/wiki/File:Countries_initially_affected_in_WannaCry_ransomware_attack.png. [Accessed 30 March 2020].

[27] Dall-E, ChatGPT, [Online]. Available: https://chatgpt.com/g/g-2fkFE8rbu-dall-e. [Accessed 3 November 2024]..

[28] CSO Online, "Marriott data breach FAQ: How did it happen and what was the impact?", [Online]. Available: https://www.csoonline.com/article/567795/marriott-data-breach-faq-how-did-it-happen-and-what-was-the-impact.html [Accessed 16 October 2024]

[29] NordVPN, "Facebook data breaches: A detailed look at the most prominent data leaks." [Online]. Available: https://nordvpn.com/blog/facebook-data-breach/. [Accessed 16 October 2024]

[30] Government Accountability Office, "SolarWinds Cyberattack demands significant federal and private sector response. [Online]. Available: https://www.gao.gov/blog/solarwinds-cyberattack-demands-significant-federal-and-private-sector-response-infographic. [Accessed 16 October 2024]

[31] New York State Department of Financial Services, "Twitter investigation report", [Online]. Available: https://www.dfs.ny.gov/Twitter_Report. [Accessed 12 October 2024]

[32] Purplesec. "Accellion Data Breach: What happened & who was impacted?", [Online]. Available: https://purplesec.us/breach-report/accellion-data-breach/. [Accessed 10 October 2024].

[33] Forbes, "T-Mobile data breach: Hackers stole 37 million customers' info, company says". [Online]. Available https://www.forbes.com/sites/nicholasreimann/2023/01/19/t-mobile-data-breach-hackers-stole-37-million-customers-info-company-says/. [Accessed 12 October 2024].

[34] CSO Online. "The Microsoft Exchange Server hack: A timeline", [Online]. Available: https://www.csoonline.com/article/570653/the-microsoft-exchange-server-hack-a-timeline.html. [Accessed 1 October 2024]

UNIT 1: INFORMATION TECHNOLOGY AND THE ORGANIZATION

Chapter 1 - Technological Innovation and the Organization

Overview

In today's rapidly evolving business landscape, technology acts as a powerful force multiplier, enhancing the resilience, capabilities and impact of organizations across all sectors. From streamlining operations to enhancing decision-making and driving innovation, technology has become the cornerstone of modern business success. Savvy business leaders recognize effectively leveraging information technology (IT) requires more than just adopting new tools—it demands strategic planning and visionary leadership. By understanding how to align IT investments with organizational goals and fostering a culture of technological integration, these leaders are able to unlock new opportunities for growth, efficiency, and competitive advantage. In an era where agility and digital transformation are critical, successful leaders view IT not as a support function but as a central component of their long-term business strategy.

Chapter 1 Learning Objectives

1. **Analyze** the influence of today's consumer on the growth of digital organizations.
2. **Defend** the organization's need to adapt to changing technological trends.
3. **Distinguish** between information systems and information technology within an organization.
4. **Evaluate** the integration of hardware, software, and human resources in supporting the organization's infrastructure.
5. **Differentiate** among the various types of software systems.
6. **Explain** the responsibilities of individuals at all levels within the IT department.
7. **Compare** and **contrast** different IT sourcing models.

Transformative Times

Transformative times encapsulates an era where change is not just constant but accelerating. Transformative periods are rife with swift technological advancements, rapidly evolving consumer behaviors, and the blurring of boundaries between physical and digital realms. Businesses thriving in such times are those who adapt quickly, leveraging technology not just to survive but to redefine their industries [1].

The Essence of Transformative Times

Transformative times represent an era where traditional business models are continuously challenged and redefined [2]. The emergence of the internet, mobile technology, artificial intelligence (AI), blockchain, and the Internet of Things (IoT) has not only changed how businesses operate but also how they deliver value to their customers. This period is characterized by:

- **Speed of Change**: The pace at which technological advancements occur today is unprecedented. Innovations that took decades to mature and adopt are now reaching mainstream acceptance within a few years, if not months.
- **Customer Empowerment**: Customers today have access to more information and choices than ever before. They demand personalized experiences, seamless service, and ethical practices from businesses.
- **Global Connectivity**: The digital age has made the world smaller. Businesses can reach global markets with ease, but this also means increased competition from every corner of the globe.

Digital Darwinism and Business Evolution

Digital Darwinism refers to the phenomenon where technology in combination with its impact on society evolve faster than businesses can adapt. It is a wakeup call for organizations to recognize adaptation is not optional; it is a survival imperative. Charles Darwin's "survival of the fittest" principle enacts a new context here — it is not the strongest businesses who survive but the most adaptable [1].

In this era, businesses must evolve through:

- **Digital Transformation**: Incorporating new technologies into all areas of business, fundamentally transforming the operation and delivery of value to an organization's customers. It's not just about adopting new technology but about changing the culture to embrace digital innovation.
- **Customer-centricity**: Placing the customer at the heart of the business strategy. Understanding and anticipating customer needs and behaviors is crucial. This requires leveraging data analytics, AI, and other technologies to gain insights and foster a personalized experience.
- **Agility and Innovation**: The ability to move quickly and efficiently, adapting to market changes and embracing innovation. This involves iterative development, continuous learning, and fostering an environment where experimentation is encouraged.
- **Sustainable Practices**: The recognition of the evolving importance of sustainability combined with ethical practices in the perception of consumers. Businesses need to integrate resiliency and sustainability into their key organizational strategies, leveraging technology to reduce their environmental impact and improve social outcomes.

Navigating the Transformative Landscape

To navigate these transformative times, businesses must:

1. **Embrace a Digital-First Mindset**: Recognize digital is not a part of the business but the foundation upon which the future business will stand.
2. **Invest in Talent and Culture**: Cultivate a culture that embraces change, fosters innovation, and values continuous learning. Attracting and retaining talent that can drive digital initiatives is crucial.

3. **Leverage Data for Decision Making**: Use AI, machine learning and data science/data analytics to understand market trends, customer behavior, and operational efficiency. Data-driven decision-making is key to staying ahead.
4. **Focus on Experience and Value**: Differentiate not just on products or services but on the experiences and value provided to customers. This effort involves synthesizing and comprehending the entire customer experience and journey, ensuring every touchpoint adds value for the customer.
5. **Build Resilience and Flexibility**: Develop strategies that allow for quick pivots and adaptation to unforeseen challenges. This includes diversifying supply chains, investing in cybersecurity, and maintaining financial flexibility.

In conclusion, the transformative times we are experiencing today, fueled by rapid technological advancements and changing consumer expectations, demand that businesses adapt or face obsolescence. Digital Darwinism underscores the urgency of this adaptation, highlighting that in the race for relevance, it's not the biggest who survive but the most adaptable. As businesses navigate this landscape, they must embrace change, invest in digital capabilities, and always put the customer at the center of their strategy. This is not just a path to survival but an opportunity to thrive and lead in the new digital era [2].

In a transformative business world, Information Technology (IT) plays a central role, acting not just as a support function but as a strategic driver of change and innovation. The evolution of IT from a back-office function to a front-line strategic asset reflects the critical role it plays in enabling businesses to adapt, compete, and prosper in a rapidly changing environment. Below are key aspects of how IT is shaping the transformative business world.

Strategic Enabler of Business Transformation

IT has become a strategic enabler of business transformation, empowering organizations to reimagine their operations, customer engagement models, and product offerings. Through digital transformation initiatives, IT helps businesses leverage digital technologies for the creation of new — or modification existing — business processes, culture, and customer experiences to meet changing business and market requirements. This transformation goes beyond mere automation to fundamentally alter business operations and value delivery for customers [3].

Acceleration of Innovation

The role of IT in accelerating innovation cannot be overstated. With the integration of multiple technologies, such as big data analytics, AI, cloud computing, and the Internet of Things (IoT), businesses can leverage IT to innovate rapidly. These technologies enable companies to develop new products and services, enhance customer experiences, and enter new markets. Moreover, IT facilitates a culture of experimentation, where businesses can test new ideas at a low cost and with reduced risk, fostering a more agile and innovative organization.

Enhancing Customer Experience

In today's customer-centric business environment, IT plays a crucial role in enhancing the customer experience. Through the use of CRM systems, mobile applications, social media, and data analytics, businesses can understand and anticipate customer needs, preferences, and behaviors. This enables personalized engagement and service delivery, improving customer satisfaction and loyalty. IT ensures that businesses can provide seamless, omnichannel experiences, meeting customers where they are and when they need service.

Operational Efficiency and Agility

IT is fundamental in driving operational efficiency and agility. Through the automation of business processes and the implementation of enterprise resource planning (ERP) systems, businesses enable agile and efficient operations, reducing costs, and improving productivity. Cloud computing, moreover, provides scalable resources for enhancing business agility, allowing organizations to rapidly adjust to market demands, expectations and opportunities without the need for significant upfront investment in infrastructure [4].

Data-Driven Decision Making

The transformative business world is increasingly data-driven, with IT at the core of this shift. Businesses leverage IT to collect, store, and analyze vast amounts of data, gaining insights that inform strategic decisions. From understanding market trends to optimizing operations and personalizing customer interactions, data analytics and AI enable organizations to make informed decisions from data to enable and drive growth and competitiveness.

Cybersecurity in a Digital Age

As businesses become more digital, the importance of IT in ensuring cybersecurity has grown exponentially. Protecting sensitive information, maintaining customer trust, and complying with regulatory requirements are paramount. IT provides the tools, policies, and practices necessary to secure digital assets, manage risk, and ensure business resiliency and continuity in the face of rapidly evolving cyber threats.

Enabling Remote Work and Collaboration

The transformative business world has seen a significant shift towards remote work and digital collaboration. IT enables this transition through cloud-based collaboration tools, virtual meeting platforms, and secure remote access solutions. This not only supports business continuity in challenging times but also opens up new possibilities for talent acquisition and work-life balance.

In conclusion, IT is at the heart of the transformative business world, driving strategic change, innovation, and competitive advantage. Its role extends beyond traditional support functions to being a critical enabler of business transformation. As businesses navigate the ongoing and evolutionary complexities of the digital age, leveraging IT strategically is key to achieving operational excellence, enhancing customer experiences, and ensuring long-term growth and sustainability.

Digital transformation and digital Darwinism are two concepts that frequently come up in discussions about the impact of technology on businesses and society. While they are interconnected, they address different aspects of the digital evolution landscape. Understanding the distinction between them is crucial for organizations determined to embrace and overcome the complexities of the digital age successfully.

Digital Transformation

Digital transformation is the process organizations use to integrate digital technology into all operational areas, fundamentally transforming operations and value delivery for their customers. It is an intentional, strategic overhaul that touches every part of the organization, from its internal processes to customer interactions and product or service delivery. Key characteristics of digital transformation include:

- **Strategic Integration**: It involves a top-down approach where technology initiatives are aligned with strategic business goals and initiatives. It's not just about adopting new technologies but about rethinking existing business models, processes, and culture to leverage these technologies effectively.
- **Customer-Centricity**: Digital transformation is often forced from evolving and changing customer expectations. Businesses use technology to enhance customer experiences, offering personalized and seamless interactions across digital and physical channels.
- **Innovation and Agility**: It encourages innovation and supports a culture of agility within organizations. Businesses become more responsive to market changes, able to iterate on products and services quickly based on data-driven insights.
- **Comprehensive Scope**: Digital transformation encompasses all areas of the business, including operations, customer service, marketing, and HR. It involves rethinking how teams collaborate, how data is used, and how value is delivered.

Digital Darwinism

Digital Darwinism describes the phenomenon wherein technological and societal evolution outpaces the ability of businesses to adapt. This concept is a wake-up call for organizations failing to acknowledge the importance of digital transformation. Digital Darwinism highlights the survival-of-the-fittest aspect within the digital age, emphasizing:

- **Rapid Pace of Change**: Technology and customer expectations evolve at an unprecedented speed, and businesses who cannot keep up risk becoming obsolete [5].
- **Involuntary Evolution**: Unlike digital transformation, which is a strategic choice, digital Darwinism represents an involuntary pressure to evolve. Businesses are forced to adapt due to external pressures rather than internal strategic decisions [6].
- **Survival and Extinction**: Digital Darwinism posits that businesses must adapt or die. It underscores the harsh reality that being slow to adapt to digital changes can lead to business failure.
- **Market and Environmental Forces**: It stresses the influence of market and environmental forces in driving change, highlighting how these external factors can dictate the need for adaptation and transformation.

Comparison and Interplay

The relationship between digital transformation and digital Darwinism is one of proactive versus reactive adaptation to digital change. Digital transformation is about actively pursuing change to capitalize on digital opportunities and meet evolving customer needs. In contrast, digital Darwinism represents the consequences of failing to engage with digital transformation, where businesses are passively shaped by external forces, risking obsolescence if they cannot adapt quickly enough.

In essence, digital transformation is the strategic response to the challenges, demands and opportunities presented by digital Darwinism. While digital Darwinism outlines the inevitability of change and the survival challenges businesses face, digital transformation provides a pathway for businesses to navigate and thrive in the digital era.

To remain competitive and viable in the face of digital Darwinism, businesses must embrace digital transformation as a continuous, strategic initiative. It's about foreseeing changes, adapting proactively, and ensuring that digital technology is at the core of business innovation and customer engagement strategies. By doing so, businesses can not only survive but lead in an era defined by rapid digital evolution.

The terms Information Technology (IT) and Information System (IS) are often used interchangeably, but they refer to distinct concepts within the realm of digital infrastructure and operations in organizations. Understanding the differences between IT and IS are crucial for effectively leveraging them to achieve business objectives.

Information Technology (IT)

Information Technology encompasses the hardware, networks, and software used to create, process, store, secure, and exchange all forms of electronic data. IT is focused on technology itself and its operational aspects . Key elements include:

- **Hardware**: This includes computers, servers, data centers, switches, hubs, routers, printers, and other devices that are used to perform IT functions.
- **Software**: Applications, programs and operating systems running on the hardware, including productivity tools, databases, and more specialized programs designed for specific tasks.
- **Networks**: The infrastructure that allows for the transmission of data. This includes the internet, intranet, LANs (Local Area Networks), and WANs (Wide Area Networks).

IT's primary concern is the efficient and effective deployment, maintenance, and management of these technologies to facilitate the processing and flow of information within an organization. It is a function within organizations tasked with ensuring that all technology tools and infrastructure are available, operational, and secure [7].

Information System (IS)

An Information System, on the other hand, is a coordinated network of components, which collect, obtain, process, store, and distribute information to support control, coordination decision making, analysis, and visualization in an organization [7]. An IS focuses not just on the technology but on the interaction between people, processes, data, and technology. Key components include:

- **People**: Users who interact with the information system, including IT specialists and end-users.
- **Processes**: Procedures and operations that define how data is collected, processed, and disseminated.
- **Data**: The raw facts and figures processed into useful information.
- **Technology**: The IT component of IS, including hardware, software, and networks.
- **Information**: Data that has been organized and processed to provide meaning and improve decision-making.

An IS is concerned with how IT is used to solve business problems and support the strategic goals of an organization. It emphasizes the value of harnessing IT to collect, store, and disseminate knowledge in a way that enhances business processes, improves decision-making, and provides a competitive advantage [8].

Comparison and Interplay

While IT focuses on the technical aspects of managing and operating technology infrastructure, IS encompasses a broader spectrum including not only the technology but also the way in which people interact with the technology to support business processes. In essence, IT provides the tools that make up an information system, and IS is the bridge connecting these technological capabilities to the business needs.

The interplay between IT and IS is fundamental to achieving organizational goals. IT infrastructure and capabilities are the backbone of modern information systems, enabling the collection, processing, and distribution of information. IS, however, determines how this technology is used strategically to fulfill organizational objectives, enhance productivity, and drive innovation.

In summary, while Information Technology and Information Systems are closely related, recognizing their distinct roles and how they complement each other is essential for leveraging technology to meet business needs effectively. IT provides the technological foundation, and IS ensures that technology serves the broader strategic aims of the organization through the integration of people, processes, data, and technology [9].

Components of Information Technology

Information Technology (IT) is an umbrella term encompassing all technology used to handle telecommunications, information dissemination, and data management. IT is instrumental in businesses and organizations to facilitate operations, improve efficiency, and enhance communications. The components of IT can be broadly classified into hardware, software, networking, and data management. Let's explore each of these components with examples to illustrate their roles and significance.

1. Hardware

Hardware is defined as the physical components of technology, storing and running software. These are the tangible parts of a computer system, network, or IT environment, including:

- **Computers**: Desktop PCs, laptops, tablets, and smartphones.
- **Servers**: Powerful machines that store, send, and process data 24/7. Examples include web servers, mail servers, file servers, print servers and database servers.
- **Storage Devices**: Includes hard drives, SSDs (Solid State Drives), USB flash drives, and memory cards, used for storing data.
- **Networking Hardware**: Such as routers, switches, modems, and hubs, which are used to create and manage networks.
- **Input/Output Devices**: Keyboards, mice, printers, scanners, and monitors, which are used to interact with computers.

2. Software

Software is instructional programming code telling the hardware what to do and how to operate. The following categories will be used to define software:

- **Firmware:** Firmware is low-level software that is embedded directly into the hardware to control its specific functions. This base-level coding provides the key/core instructions for the hardware to operate, acting as the intermediary between the hardware and higher-level software. Firmware is often stored in non-volatile memory and is rarely changed, although updates can occasionally improve performance or add features [31]. Examples include the software embedded in printers, routers, and computer BIOS/UEFI.
- **System Software**: This includes operating systems (like Windows, MacOS, & Linux) that manage the hardware and create an environment for running application software.
- **Application Software**: Programs performing unique or specialized tasks for users. Examples include office productivity suites (Microsoft Office, & Google Workspace), web browsers (Edge, Chrome, & Firefox), customer relationship management (CRM) software, and specialized tools like Adobe Photoshop or AutoCAD.

3. Networking

Networking involves connecting multiple computing devices together to share data, resources, and communications [33]. Networking components include:

- **LAN (Local Area Network)**: A network connecting digital devices, such computers, servers and specialized digital equipment, in a defined area limited in size, such as a manufacturing area, home, home office, school, or office building.
- **WAN (Wide Area Network)**: Covers broader areas, such as cities, regions, or countries. The internet is the largest WAN.

- **Internet**: A global network connecting millions of private, public, academic, business, and government networks.
- **Wi-Fi & Ethernet**: Technologies for connecting devices to a network. Wi-Fi is used for wireless connections, while Ethernet involves cables.
- **Protocols**: Rules and standards that enable networked devices to communicate, such as TCP/IP (Transmission Control Protocol/Internet Protocol).

4. Data Management

Data management involves the organization, storage, preservation, and retrieval of data. Components include:

- **Databases**: Organized collections of data. Examples include relational databases like MySQL, PostgreSQL, and Oracle, which store data in tables, and NoSQL databases like MongoDB, which store data in formats like JavaScript Object Notation (JSON) documents.
- **Data Warehouses**: Specialized systems for analyzing and storing large amounts of data. They are used for business intelligence and data analysis.
- **Cloud Storage**: Services like Amazon S3, Google Cloud Storage, and Microsoft Azure Storage offer scalable and accessible data storage options over the internet.

Examples in Practice

A company may use a combination of IT components to operate efficiently:

- **E-commerce Business**: Utilizes web servers (hardware) running e-commerce software (application software) accessible via the internet (networking) to sell products. It stores customer and product information in databases (data management).
- **Remote Work**: Employees use laptops or tablets (hardware) with VPN software (application software) to securely connect to their company's network (networking) and access work files stored on company servers (data management).

Understanding the components of IT is crucial for leveraging technology effectively in any organizational or business context. Each component fulfills a unique role in ensuring information is processed, stored, and communicated efficiently, enabling modern enterprises to achieve objectives and innovate continuously.

Computing models have evolved significantly over the years to meet the growing demands for processing power, data storage, and connectivity. This evolution has introduced various architectures and concepts, each designed to optimize efficiency, scalability, and performance in data processing and networking. Here's an overview of some pivotal computing models, including mainframe, client-server, and the Internet of Things (IoT), along with definitions of key terms.

Mainframes

Mainframes are large computers with specialized equipment used primarily by large organizations for critical applications, bulk data processing (such as census, industry, and consumer statistics), and transaction processing [22]. They are known for their high level of reliability, scalability, and security. Mainframe computers can handle processing millions of transactions per day and are used in sectors where massive data processing is required, such as banking and healthcare.

Distributed Computing

Distributed computing refers to models where components of designed systems are shared among multiple devices, improving performance, and efficiency. This approach contrasts with traditional centralized models by distributing tasks, work, or databases across several machines, which work together to achieve a common goal. It enhances the processing power and storage capacity beyond what a single machine could provide.

Client-Server Model

The **client-server model** is a distributed computing structure which divides tasks or workloads between providers of a resource or service, known as servers, and requesters of a service, known as clients [24]. Clients start communications with servers, which await incoming requests. Examples include web browsers (clients) requesting pages from web servers.

- **Client**: A client is a computer accessing shared network services provided by another computer (the server).
- **Server**: A server is hardware providing many types of resources to other computers, known as clients, over a network [25].
- **Server Farms**: Server farms (or server clusters) are groups of computer servers used to provide redundancy and high availability of server resources [25]. They are commonly used in data centers for load balancing, offering improved performance and reliability for web hosting, database management, and cloud storage.

Cloud Computing

Cloud computing is providing computing services—including databases, servers, networking, software, analytics, and intelligence—over the Internet to enable flexible resources, new opportunities and economies of scale [26]. It allows users and organizations to use software applications without local installation and access their personal files on any system with internet access. This technology provides significant efficiencies for scaling resources, reducing the need for physical infrastructure. Cloud computing can be categorized into the following categories:

1. **Infrastructure as a Service (IaaS)**: IaaS is a cloud computing model where providers offer essential infrastructure resources such as virtualized servers, storage, and networking over the Internet. This model enables organizations to avoid the expenses and complexities of directly owning and managing physical servers, letting them scale their computing needs up or down as required. IaaS is ideal for users who need control over infrastructure resources but want the flexibility and cost-efficiency of cloud delivery.

2. **Platform as a Service (PaaS)**: This platform type provides a cloud environment for developing, testing, and deploying applications. In this model, users get access to a complete development and deployment ecosystem, including databases, middleware, development tools, and operating systems, all managed by the provider. PaaS simplifies the application development process, allowing developers to focus on software creation and functionality without distractions from underlying infrastructure management, making it suitable for agile development and efficient collaboration.
3. **Software as a Service (SaaS)**: SaaS is a model delivering software applications over the Internet. Users access these software applications from web browsers without requiring them to install or maintain the software on local devices. SaaS enables businesses and individuals to use software on a subscription basis, offering accessibility, scalability, and cost savings. Common examples of SaaS include web-based email services, customer relationship management (CRM) systems, and productivity applications.

Internet of Things (IoT)

The **Internet of Things** is a grouping of physical objects embedded with software, physical sensors and other technologies designed specifically to connect and exchange data about the physical world with other devices and systems over networks and the Internet [27]. These devices range from ordinary household objects to sophisticated industrial tools.

Industrial Internet of Things (IIoT)

The **Industrial Internet of Things** is a subset of IoT focusing on the application of connected and smart devices in industrial sectors and applications [28]. The IIoT encompasses industrial applications, including manufacturing, logistics, oil and gas, and agriculture, which benefit from the integration of smart devices, automation technologies, and other software to improve efficiency, safety, and productivity.

Smart Devices

Smart devices are electronic gadgets connected via wireless protocols such as Bluetooth, NFC, Wi-Fi, LiFi, 3G, etc., to operate interactively and autonomously. Typical examples include smartphones, smart TVs, smart home devices (like smart thermostats and smart lights), and wearable technology such as smart watches.

In summary, the evolution of computing models from mainframes to the IoT reflects the technological advancements and growing needs for data processing, storage, and connectivity. Each model offers unique advantages and serves different requirements, from massive data processing in mainframes to distributed computing models like client-server systems, and the interconnectedness of everyday objects through the IoT and IIoT. These models and concepts have fundamentally transformed how data is processed, stored, and accessed, enabling new levels of efficiency and innovation across industries.

The realm of information systems encompasses various types of systems, each designed to facilitate the collection, processing, storage, and dissemination of information. The following differentiates between various types of information systems:

Application Systems

Application systems are computer programs designed to perform specific tasks or functions for the user. They can range from simple standalone applications like word processors to complex, integrated systems managing enterprise-wide functions. The primary purpose is to fulfill particular user requirements, such as accounting, inventory management, or customer data management [29].

Software Systems

Software systems refer to a collection of software components or programs that work together to provide a specific functionality. This term is broader than application systems, encompassing not just applications designed for end-users but also the underlying infrastructure software (like databases and operating systems) enabling these applications to function.

Applications

In the context of information systems, applications are software programs designed to help users perform tasks. These can include business applications (like CRM and ERP systems), educational software, gaming applications, and utility software. Applications are a subset of software systems focused on end-user tasks.

Enterprise Resource Systems (ERS)

Enterprise Resource Systems are comprehensive software platforms that provide the technological backbone for managing the resources and processes of an entire organization. They integrate various organizational functions like into a single system to improve efficiency and data accuracy.

Enterprise Resource Planning (ERP)

ERP systems are a type of ERS designed to plan and manage all the major functions of an organization. They help in integrating processes across different departments, facilitating the flow of information, and ensure decisions are based on accurate and up-to-date information. ERP systems are critical for large organizations to coordinate their efforts and optimize resources.

Supply Chain Management Systems (SCMS)

SCMS are designed to manage the flow of information, goods and finances as a product or service moves from supplier to manufacturer to wholesaler to retailer to consumer. These systems help organizations in optimizing their supply chain operations, improving efficiency, reducing costs, and ensuring that products are delivered on time.

Customer Relationship Management Systems (CRMS)

CRMS are designed to manage company interactions with current and potential future customers. These use data analysis about customers' history with a company to improve customer retention, customer-business relationships, and ultimately driving sales growth.

Managed Information Systems (MIS)

MIS, often simply called Information Systems, are organized systems for storing, collecting and processing data and for delivering information, knowledge, and digital products. Businesses and other organizations use MIS to manage business operations, interact with customers and partner organizations, and enable success in their industry. MIS supports decision-making, coordination, control, analysis, and visualization in an organization.

Decision Support Systems (DSS)

DSS are computer-based information systems that support business or organizational decision-making activities. DSS enables agile decision making in the face of rapidly changing conditions. Each of these systems plays a crucial role in modern organizations, enabling them to manage their operations more efficiently, make better decisions, and maintain competitiveness in their respective industries.

Information Technology Roles

In the rapidly evolving field of Information Technology (IT), roles and responsibilities are diverse, catering to different facets of technology management and implementation. These roles can generally be categorized into executive and mid-level positions, each with its own set of responsibilities that contribute to the organization's overall IT strategy and operational efficiency [21].

Executive Roles in IT

Chief Information Officer (CIO)

- **Responsibilities**: The CIO is responsible for the overall IT strategy and technology vision of the organization. This role involves overseeing the IT department, aligning IT strategy with business goals, managing IT investments, and ensuring the compliance, resilience and security of IT systems.

- **Key Activities**: Developing IT policies, liaising with executive management, managing IT budgets, and leading digital transformation initiatives.

Chief Technology Officer (CTO)

- **Responsibilities**: The CTO focuses on the organization's technological needs and research and development (R&D) of new technologies. This role often involves identifying opportunities for technological advancements, overseeing the development of new IT products or services, and ensuring the technology stack supports the company's goals.
- **Key Activities**: Researching new technologies, guiding product development, overseeing technical teams, and strategic planning of technology adoption.

Chief Security Officer (CSO) or Chief Information Security Officer (CISO)

- **Responsibilities**: Responsible for ensuring the security of IT systems and data. This role involves developing security policies, managing risks, overseeing compliance with regulations, and responding to security incidents.
- **Key Activities**: Conducting risk assessments, developing disaster recovery plans, managing security operations, and ensuring data privacy and compliance.

Mid-Level Roles in IT

IT Manager

- **Responsibilities**: IT Managers oversee the day-to-day operations of IT departments. This role includes managing IT staff, overseeing IT projects, ensuring system uptime, and liaising between the IT department and other business units.
- **Key Activities**: Project management, staff supervision, budget management, and reporting on IT performance.

Network Architect

- **Responsibilities**: Network Architects design and implement computer networks, such as intranets, extranets, and local area networks (LANs). They ensure the network meets the organization's needs for reliability, performance, and scalability.
- **Key Activities**: Designing network infrastructure, selecting hardware and software, planning network installation, and monitoring network performance.

Systems Analyst

- **Responsibilities**: Systems Analysts act as a bridge between business problems and technology solutions. They analyze business processes and design or recommend technology solutions to improve efficiency.
- **Key Activities**: Requirements gathering, process analysis, system design, and implementing technology solutions.

Database Administrator (DBA)

- **Responsibilities**: DBA duties include the performance, integrity, and security of databases. They also ensure that data remains consistent across the database, is clearly defined, and can be accessed by users as needed.
- **Key Activities**: Database design, maintenance, backup, and recovery, security, and performance tuning.

System Administrator (SysAdmins)

- **Responsibilities**: System administrators (SysAdmins) are responsible for maintaining the overall health, performance, and security of an organization's IT infrastructure. This includes managing servers, ensuring uptime, monitoring system performance, applying security patches, and addressing vulnerabilities in a timely manner.
- **Key Activities**: server installation, server management, patching and vulnerability management

Information Security Analyst

- **Responsibilities**: This role involves protecting an organization's computer systems and networks from infiltration and cyber-attacks. They implement security measures and monitor networks for security breaches.
- **Key Activities**: Installing security software, conducting regular security audits, monitoring for security breaches, and investigating security incidents.

These roles, among others, form the backbone of IT operations within organizations. The exact titles and responsibilities can vary depending on the company's size, industry, and specific needs. However, each role is crucial in ensuring that IT resources are used effectively, securely, and in alignment with the organization's strategic goals.

Technology Investments

Technology serves as a powerful force multiplier for businesses, amplifying the efficiency, innovation, and effectiveness of various functions across an organization. Given its pivotal role in driving innovation, optimizing decision-making, and safeguarding information, information technology (IT) must be treated as a core strategic asset. Rather than being seen merely as a cost center, IT should be valued as an investment that can significantly boost overall business performance. To ensure this potential is fully realized, the executive team—including the Chief Information Officer (CIO), Chief Security Officer (CSO), and Chief Technology Officer (CTO)—must carefully evaluate and allocate IT budgets. Strategic budgeting decisions are essential not only to meet the current technological needs of the organization but also to position it for future growth, security, and adaptability in an increasingly digital and competitive landscape.

Many organizations encounter significant challenges when it comes to IT budgeting, largely due to a disconnect between the IT and finance departments. IT teams may lack a deep understanding of financial planning processes, while finance professionals may not fully grasp the complexities and evolving nature of IT infrastructure and services. This misalignment can create tension during budget discussions, making it difficult to allocate resources effectively. However, it is crucial for organizations to shift their perspective and recognize IT as something more than an operational expense. It is a strategic investment directly contributing to the company's mission and long-term goals. By fostering better collaboration between IT and finance, organizations can ensure that budgeting decisions are made with a comprehensive view of how technology can drive innovation, improve efficiency, and secure the company's digital assets. Aligning IT investments with the organization's broader vision helps unlock its full potential, ensuring that technology solutions support growth, competitiveness, and resilience in a fast-paced business environment.

A well-crafted IT sourcing strategy is essential for ensuring technology effectively supports and drives business success. Whether a company chooses to manage its IT needs internally through insourcing or leverage external expertise via outsourcing, the decision should be strategically aligned with the organization's overall goals. **Insourcing** allows businesses to maintain control over IT operations, offering greater responsiveness and the ability to tailor solutions specifically to internal needs. However, it can also come with higher costs and the challenge of maintaining cutting-edge skills within the team. On the other hand, **outsourcing** IT functions can reduce costs and convert technology expenditures into predictable budget items, but it requires entrusting critical data and operations to external providers, which may introduce concerns around security and quality control. The optimal sourcing model will depend on factors such as the company's core competencies, the need for flexibility, and the importance of proprietary technology. Ultimately, a strategic IT sourcing plan should be designed to meet immediate operational needs and enable future growth and innovation.

Service Level Agreements (SLAs) are formalized agreements between a service provider and a client defining the expected levels of service, performance, and accountability. They play a crucial role in managing performance, key expectations and ensuring both parties understand their responsibilities. SLAs clearly outline what specific services will be delivered, the measurable performance metrics (such as system uptime or response times), and remedies if the agreed standards are not met, such as financial penalties or service credits. These agreements are important because they mitigate risks by formalizing the terms of service, helping build trust between the client and provider, and providing a clear mechanism for resolving conflicts when issues arise. SLAs are especially critical in industries like IT services, telecommunications, and cloud computing, where consistent service delivery is essential to business operations.

A **Memorandum of Understanding (MOU)** is a non-binding document that outlines the basic terms of cooperation between two or more parties. MOUs are often used at the early stages of negotiations, allowing the parties to ensure that they are aligned in terms of their goals, roles, and expectations before formalizing a more detailed agreement. Unlike formal contracts, MOUs do not create enforceable legal obligations but serve as a reference point for future formal agreements. They are important because they provide flexibility and clarity, helping to establish the groundwork for further collaboration without committing the parties to specific legal responsibilities.

In contrast, a **Memorandum of Agreement (MOA)** is generally more formal and often legally binding. An MOA provides a detailed description of the terms and conditions agreed upon by the parties, including specific roles, responsibilities, and timelines for deliverables. MOAs differ from MOUs in that they typically create enforceable obligations. This makes MOAs essential when parties want to ensure a formal commitment, as they clearly define each party's responsibilities and the consequences for non-compliance. MOAs are often used in government, research collaborations, and complex projects involving multiple organizations.

A **Non-Disclosure Agreement (NDA)** is a legal contract created to protect confidential information shared between parties. NDAs are used to prevent unauthorized disclosures of trade secrets, intellectual property, or business strategies during negotiations, employment, or business collaborations. An NDA will specify what information is considered confidential, the requirements of each party receiving the confidential information, the duration of confidentiality, and the consequences of breaching the agreement. NDAs are critical because they protect intellectual property, establish trust in business relationships, and provide legal recourse in case of a breach. NDAs are widely used across industries like technology and manufacturing, where safeguarding proprietary information is essential to maintaining a competitive edge.

Together, SLAs, MOUs, MOAs, and NDAs provide the foundation for successful business relationships by establishing clear expectations, protecting sensitive information, and ensuring legal and operational accountability. They help ensure that partnerships are built on trust and transparency, with clear mechanisms in place to manage risks and resolve disputes.

Sourcing models for IT management range from fully in-house operations to outsourcing and off-shoring, each presenting its own set of advantages and drawbacks. In-house management allows a company to maintain full control over its technology infrastructure, providing immediate responsiveness to internal demands and enabling closer alignment with business objectives. However, this model can be costly to maintain, requiring ongoing investments in infrastructure, talent, and skills development. Outsourcing, on the other hand, offers cost savings and access to specialized expertise by shifting certain IT functions to third-party providers, which can transform technology spending into a more predictable, fixed expense. Yet, this approach comes with trade-offs, as it involves relinquishing some control over critical operations and trusting external partners to uphold security, confidentiality, and service quality. Off-shoring extends outsourcing by leveraging global talent, often reducing costs even further while enabling continuous operations across different time zones. However, challenges such as communication barriers, cultural differences, and potential loss of agility can arise. Ultimately, choosing the right sourcing model depends on a company’s specific needs, priorities, and risk tolerance, and balancing cost efficiencies with the need for control and responsiveness.

Choosing the right IT sourcing model is a critical decision requiring a thorough assessment of several key factors, including security, cost, and the specific needs of the organization. Security is paramount, especially for businesses handling sensitive or proprietary data, where outsourcing certain IT functions could introduce vulnerabilities or risk breaches of confidentiality. Cost considerations also play a major role, as some models, like in-house management, can be expensive to maintain but offer greater control, while others, like outsourcing or off-shoring, can reduce expenses but may come with hidden costs related to quality control or loss of operational agility. Additionally, the unique needs of the organization must be taken into account—whether the business requires rapid innovation, specialized skills, or round-the-clock IT support will influence which model is the most suitable. Failing to properly evaluate these factors can lead to costly mistakes, such as inefficiencies, increased downtime, slow incident response times, loss of profitability due to service outages, or a lack of alignment with business objectives. Given the long-term implications of IT sourcing decisions, companies must approach this choice with strategic foresight, ensuring the selected model not only meets immediate operational needs but also supports sustainable growth and competitiveness.

Modern IT budgets have become more intricate as organizations increasingly adopt advanced technologies such as cloud computing, artificial intelligence (AI), cybersecurity solutions, and automation tools. These technologies drive innovation and efficiency but also introduce ongoing costs for infrastructure, security updates, and continuous training, skill building and learning to keep up with emerging technologies and the rapid pace of change. Traditional budgeting methods, which involve setting financial plans once a year, can quickly become outdated in this dynamic environment. To address this complexity, many organizations are shifting toward a rolling forecast model, where budgets are reviewed and adjusted several times throughout the year. This approach offers greater flexibility, allowing companies to respond swiftly to market changes, emerging threats, or new opportunities. By revisiting budget allocations regularly, decision-makers can make more informed choices, ensuring investments in technology remain aligned with both current demands and future strategic goals. A rolling forecast model helps organizations stay agile in a fast-evolving digital landscape, improving both financial management and operational efficiency.

Collaboration between IT and other departments is crucial for creating a more accurate and efficient budgeting process, particularly when planning for new development projects. When IT works closely with departments such as finance, operations, and marketing, it ensures that technology investments align with the broader organizational goals and operational needs. This cross-functional collaboration helps identify the specific technological requirements of each department, allowing for better resource allocation and more strategic financial planning. Furthermore, the use of specialized budgeting and forecasting applications streamline the budgeting process, enabling real-time data, advanced analytics, and greater visibility into how resources are being utilized. Such tools not only simplify the complex task of managing IT budgets but also offer valuable insights that support more informed decision-making. By fostering open communication and leveraging technology to support financial planning, organizations can ensure IT budgets are both accurate and adaptable, particularly when it comes to planning for new development initiatives, as will be discussed in the next chapter.

Chapter Summary

Today's connected consumer, with constant access to information and evolving expectations, is compelling organizations to quickly adapt to shifting market demands. In this fast-paced environment, companies who embrace digital transformation are far better positioned to stay competitive by leveraging cutting-edge technologies. Digital transformation not only requires the adoption of innovative tools but also necessitates a robust IT infrastructure capable of supporting these advancements. This infrastructure must be backed by skilled IT professionals who understand how to integrate and optimize technology within the organization, ensuring processes are efficient and aligned with business objectives. By fostering this synergy between technology, talent, and streamlined workflows, companies can respond more effectively to consumer needs, drive innovation, and enhance overall operational performance. Organizations who prioritize these elements are better equipped to thrive in a modern, digitally-driven marketplace

Discussion Questions

1. In 2003, writer Nicholas G. Carr stirred up controversy with his article "IT Doesn't Matter." Carr posited that since information technology has gone mainstream and worldwide, it is no longer a differentiator and is more of a business commodity. Read his article at https://hbr.org/2003/05/it-doesnt-matter and explain why this is still thought provoking today. Do you agree with his assessment of IT? Why or why not?

2. Defend the use of cryptocurrency over traditional, central banking systems. What companies or retailers accept them presently? What are the pros and cons of cryptocurrency?

3. We discussed companies such as YouTube or Hulu that only have a digital presence. Identify 2 - 3 other digital companies, where no storefront exists, the product is digital, and even payment is completed electronically. Consider the management challenges these companies face. Might a fully digital company run into issues that a brick-and-mortar company would not?

4. Consider the difference between the terms logistics, transportation, supply chain, and purchasing. How are they similar? How are they different? How does technology enable each of them?

5. Read an article on monthly budget forecasting at https://www.truesky.com/monthly-rolling-forecast-financial-forecasting/ and debate the merits of using a monthly versus annual forecast for the IT department for a healthcare industry. How might the need for a monthly forecast differ for a financial institution? Focus on the information technology needs for each industry.

Exercises

1. Visit http://claytonchristensen.com/ and click on the link to Christensen's "key concepts." Read through several concepts and identify one that resonates with you. Prepare a 60-second elevator speech on your selected concept and be prepared to defend your pitch by explaining why you chose it and why it is important.

2. Research the rise of blockchain technology. What new challenges does it present to today's business retailer? Deconstruct a blockchain, identify its components, and describe what each component contributes to the process.

3. Visit https://www.bls.gov/ooh/computer-and-information-technology/home.htm and, based on the statistics presented, explain which areas in IT are growing and why. Identify

which industries or sectors may become increasingly reliant on tech workers to support their strategic goals.

4. Amazon has disrupted many brick-and-mortar retailers. Read https://www.cnn.com/2018/10/03/tech/amazon-go/index.html and research how Amazon handles logistics. Explain why you think they can do this. What and why is the reason for their innovative approach? What are they doing differently and how do they use technology to do so?

5. Persuade your organization's leadership to move to cloud computing. Prepare a presentation that will persuade the executives in your organization that this is what they should use and why. Make sure you list the pros and the cons. Remember, this is an executive-level presentation.

References

[1] E. Schwarz, Digital Darwinism., New York, NY: Random House Publishing, 1999.

[2] C. Christensen and J. Bower, Disruptive Technologies: Catching the Wave., Cambridge MA: Harvard Business Review Press., 1995.

[3] C. Christensen, "Disruptive Innovation.," n.d.. [Online]. Available: http://claytonchristensen.com/key-concepts/. [Accessed 1 February 2020].

[4] L. Karjewski, J. Malhotra and L. Ritzman , Operations Management: Processes and Supply Chains, Boston, MA: Pearson Education, Inc., 2019.

[5] S. Hyder, "Forget the Millennials, The Connected Consumer is Who You Should Be Chasing," 2018. [Online]. Available: https://www.forbes.com/sites/shamahyder/2018/01/18/forget-the-millennials-the-connected-consumer-is-who-you-should-be-chasing/#78eb7b014172. [Accessed 20 June 2020].

[6] S. O'Dea, "Number of Smartphone Users WorldWide from 2016 to 2021.," [Online]. Available: https://www.statista.com/statistics/330695/number-of-smartphone-users-worldwide/. [Accessed 10 July 2020].

[7] S. Tilley, in *Systems Analysis and Design, Twelfth Edition*, Boston MA, Cengage, 2020.

[8] A. Dennis, B. H. Wixom and R. R. Roth, in *Systems Analysis & Design (7E)*, New York, NY, John Wiley & Sons, 2018.

[9] M. B. D. a. M. A. Westerman, Leading Digital: Turning Technology into Business Transformation, Cambridge, MA: Harvard Business Review Press, 2014.

[10] PMI, "10th Global Project Management Survey: Expanding the Value Delivery Landscape to Address the High Cost of Low Performance," 2018. [Online]. Available: https://www.pmi.org/-/media/pmi/documents/public/pdf/learning/thought-leadership/pulse/pulse-of-the-profession-2018.pdf. [Accessed 5 March 2020].

[11] PMI, "Success in Disruptive Times.2018," [Online]. Available: https://www.pmi.org/-/media/pmi/documents/public/pdf/learning/thought-leadership/pulse/pulse-of-the-profession-2018.pdf. [Accessed 10 May 2020].

[12] B. Solis, "The State of Digital Transformation 2019.," 2019. [Online]. Available: https://www.prophet.com/. [Accessed 2 March 2020].

[13] Y. Noguchi, "Why Borders Failed While Barnes & Noble Survived," 2011. [Online]. Available: https://www.npr.org/2011/07/19/138514209/why-borders-failed-while-barnes-and-noble-survived. [Accessed 1 February 2020].

[14] Sandeep, "Top 8 Information Technology Trends in 2019.," 2017. [Online]. Available: https://techieword.com/top-8-information-technology-trends-in-2017/. [Accessed March 2020].

[15] Sandeep, "Top 8 Information Technology Trends in 2019.," 2017. [Online]. Available: https://techieword.com/top-8-information-technology-trends-in-2017/. [Accessed 1 March 2020].

[16] HP , "HP Inc. and Partners Mobilize 3D Printing Solutions to Battle COVID-19. [Press Release]," [Online]. Available: https://press.ext.hp.com/us/en/press-releases/2020/hp-inc--and-partners-mobilize-3d-printing-solutions--to-battle-c.html. [Accessed 2020 March 2020].

[17] N. Bashir, " Designed a New Ventilator in 10 days. He's Making 15,000 for the Pandemic Fight.," 27 March 2020. [Online]. Available: https://www.cnn.com/2020/03/26/tech/dyson-ventilators-coronavirus/index.html. [Accessed 2 April 2020].

[18] A. Hasnie, "Couple Uses 3D Printers to Help Protect Health Care Workers for Free.," 26 March 2020. [Online]. Available: https://www.foxnews.com/tech/couple-uses-3d-printers-to-help-protect-health-care-workers-for-free. [Accessed 2 April 2020].

[19] B. Dictionary., "Information Technology (IT).," [Online]. Available: http://www.businessdictionary.com/definition/information-technology-IT.html. [Accessed April 2020].

[20] T. Laurence, "What Is Cryptocurrency?," [Online]. Available: https://www.dummies.com/personal-finance/what-is-cryptocurrency/. [Accessed April 2020].

[21] U. B. o. L. Statistics., "Computer and Information Technology Occupations," 10 April 2020. [Online]. Available: https://www.bls.gov/ooh/computer-and-information-technology/home.htm. [Accessed April 2020].

[22] P. Christensson, "Mainframe Definition.," TechTerms, 2006. [Online]. Available: https://techterms.com/definition/mainframe. [Accessed April 2020].

[23] IBM, "IBM mainframes.," [Online]. Available: https://www.ibm.com/it-infrastructure/servers/mainframes.

[24] W. C. contributors., " File:Client-server-model," 28 November 2019. [Online]. Available: https://commons.wikimedia.org/w/index.php?title=File:Client-server-model.svg&oldid=378309837. [Accessed April 2020].

[25] Techopedia, "Server Farm," 11 December 2016. [Online]. Available: https://www.techopedia.com/definition/4202/server-farm. [Accessed April 2020].

[26] Techopedia, "Cloud," 12 May 2017. [Online]. Available: https://www.techopedia.com/definition/26514/cloud. [Accessed April 2020].

[27] W. Kenton, "The Internet of Things," Investopedia, 9 February 2020. [Online]. Available: https://www.investopedia.com/terms/i/internet-things.asp. [Accessed April 2020].

[28] J. Gould, "What is the Industrial internet of things? Essentials of IIoT," Network World, 9 February 2018. [Online]. Available: https://www.networkworld.com/article/3243928/what-is-the-industrial-internet-of-things-essentials-of-iiot.html. [Accessed April 2020].

[29] R. K. Rainer and B. Prince, Introduction to Information Systems 7th Edition, Hoboken NJ: John Wiley and Sons, 2018.

[30] B. J. Copeland, "Artificial Intelligence," Britannica, 11 August 2020. [Online]. Available: https://www.britannica.com/technology/artificial-intelligence. [Accessed August 2020].

[31] T. Terms, "Firmware," [Online]. Available: https://techterms.com/definition/firmware. [Accessed April 2020].

[32] T. Terms, "Utility," [Online]. Available: https://techterms.com/definition/utility. [Accessed August 2020].

[33] R. Cockerham, "What Is Networking Software?," Techwalla, 23 September 2018. [Online]. Available: https://www.techwalla.com/articles/what-is-networking-software. [Accessed April 2020].

[34] P. Wallace, Introduction to Information Systems 3rd Edition, Upper Saddle River, New Jersey: Pearson Education, 2018.

[35] K. Schwalbe, An Introduction To Project Management 6th Edition, Minneapolis MN: Schwalbe Publishing, 2017.

Chapter 2 - Strategic Alignment through Project Management

Overview

In today's fast-paced, technology-driven world, organizations must navigate complex environments while ensuring their projects and initiatives remain tightly aligned with their strategic goals. This chapter, *Strategic Alignment through Project Management*, explores how organizations can bridge the gap between their long-term vision [1] and the tactical execution of projects, enabling them to maintain a competitive edge [2], achieve operational efficiency, and maximize the value of their investments.

Chapter Learning Objectives

1. Compare and contrast between a mission and vision statement.
2. Articulate the need for a strategic plan that will support a long-term vision.
3. Explain the reason behind integrating technology into the strategic plan.
4. Differentiate among strategic planning tools.
5. Explain the relationship between portfolios, programs, and projects.
6. Describe key deliverables of the project life cycle, such as a project charter and work breakdown structure.
7. Identify the ways in which project, program and portfolio oversight can contribute to organizational initiatives.
8. Explain how the systems development life cycle integrates within a project.
9. Identify modeling and design tools used in the systems analysis and design process.

Strategic alignment begins with a clear understanding of the organization's **Mission and Vision Statements**, which define its purpose and long-term aspirations [3]. From these guiding principles, **Strategy, Objectives, and Strategic Plans** are developed to outline how the organization will achieve its goals. The chapter delves into the role of **Operational Planning**, **Information Technology (IT) Governance**, and **Enterprise Content Management** (ECM) in ensuring technology initiatives support broader business objectives.

Chapter 2 also introduces a range of **Strategic Planning Tools** that are essential for navigating internal and external forces. These tools, including **SWOT Analysis**, **Porter's Five Forces**, and **PEST Analysis**, provide a framework for understanding competitive dynamics, market pressures, and environmental factors that influence strategic decision-making. Additionally, the **Balanced Scorecard** approach allows organizations to monitor performance from multiple perspectives, ensuring that projects are not only aligned with financial goals but also with customer satisfaction, internal processes, and innovation.

A critical aspect of strategic alignment is the effective management of **Portfolios, Programs, and Projects**. The chapter breaks down the characteristics of projects, including key factors such as **Duration**, **Scope**, **Time**, **Cost**, and the **Triple Constraints** that every project manager must balance. It also highlights the importance of programs, with their **Program Managers** and **Program Roadmaps**, and explains how project portfolios help organizations prioritize initiatives that deliver the most value. Through tools like the **Business Case**, **Cost-Benefit Analysis**, and **Return on Investment (ROI)**, the chapter guides readers through the **Project Selection Process**, ensuring that the right projects are chosen to support strategic goals.

The **Project Management Life Cycle** is a core focus of the chapter, detailing each phase of project management—**Initiating**, **Planning**, **Executing**, **Monitoring/Controlling**, and **Closing**. Additionally, the chapter contrasts different project management methodologies, such as the **Waterfall** and **Agile** approaches, helping readers understand when each methodology is most effective. Key phases like **Initiation**, with the **Business Case, Feasibility Study**, and **Planning**, in conjunction with the **Scope Statement** and **Risk Management Plan**, are explored in depth to provide a comprehensive understanding of project management best practices.

Finally, the chapter covers the **Systems Development Life Cycle (SDLC)**, detailing the five primary phases: **Requirements Gathering and Analysis**, **Design**, **Development**, **Testing**, and **Deployment or Implementation**. This process ensures technology systems are developed in a structured, efficient manner meeting both business and user requirements. The role of the **Systems Analyst** is emphasized as critical in translating business needs into functional specifications. The chapter also explores advanced topics such as **Unified Modeling Language (UML)** and **Data Modeling**, guiding readers through the complexities of system design, testing, and final deployment.

By integrating strategic planning with robust project management practices and technical methodologies, this chapter provides a roadmap for aligning projects with organizational goals, ensuring that every initiative delivers measurable value and contributes to long-term success.

Organizational Strategy & Governance

Effective governance in an organization involves more than simply managing day-to-day operations—it is about aligning all activities, including project management, with the overarching strategy of the organization [4]. This alignment helps ensure resources, decisions, and processes work toward common goals, enhancing efficiency and accountability across all levels [5].

Mission Statement

The mission statement articulates the core purpose of the organization, describing what it does and why it exists. In terms of project management, every project must serve the mission by contributing to the organization's overall purpose. Whether a project aims to improve customer service, innovate new products, or streamline operations, it must be rooted in the organization's mission to ensure relevance and focus.

Vision Statement

The vision statement describes the long-term aspirations of the organization—or where it aims to be in the future. Projects should not only align with immediate objectives but also contribute toward this vision. For project managers, understanding organizational vision helps in prioritizing projects to propel the organization toward its desired future state, ensuring all efforts build a bridge between present and future goals.

Strategy, Objectives, and Strategic Plan

The organizational strategy outlines the key actions the organization will take to achieve its mission and move toward its vision. This strategy is often broken down into specific objectives and a strategic plan, which guides operational decision-making. Project management is the tactical mechanism for implementing these strategic objectives. A project manager's role is to ensure every project is scoped, planned, and executed to support the strategic plan, translating high-level objectives into concrete outcomes.

Operational Planning

Operational planning bridges the gap between strategy and execution, detailing the specific activities required to implement the strategy at the tactical level [6]. For project managers, operational plans provide a roadmap for managing resources, timelines, and deliverables to achieve strategic objectives. Effective operational planning ensures each project contributes to the overall operational efficiency of the organization while aligning with strategic priorities [7].

Information Technology Governance

Information technology (IT) governance is crucial in today's digitally driven organizations. It ensures IT resources and systems are managed effectively to support an organization's strategy. Project management in this context involves ensuring technology projects are aligned with IT governance policies, optimizing the use of IT resources to deliver business value. IT governance frameworks provide guidelines for decision-making and

Figure 2.1. IT Governance Framework.

accountability in technology investments, ensuring projects align with both operational and strategic needs.

Information Management and Enterprise Content Management (ECM)
Information management is about ensuring that data, knowledge, and content are efficiently captured, stored, and used across the organization. Enterprise Content Management (ECM) systems play a key role in this by managing the lifecycle of information—from creation to storage, retrieval, and eventual disposal. In project management, having well-governed information systems is essential for managing project data, ensuring seamless communication, and enhancing decision-making. Project managers must ensure systems and processes used in a project adhere to the organization's ECM practices, helping the organization leverage information as a strategic asset.

Strategic Planning Tools
Strategic planning tools help organizations align their resources, operations, and initiatives with long-term visions. In project management, these tools guide the prioritization of projects, ensuring they contribute to high-level objectives and fit within the strategic framework. See below for a detailed explanation of the key strategic planning components:

Internal Drivers
Internal drivers are the forces within an organization that influence its strategic direction. These may include the organization's resources, culture, capabilities, and operational processes. For project managers, understanding these drivers is essential for selecting and executing projects that align with internal strengths, address weaknesses, and capitalize on available resources.

External Drivers
External drivers are factors outside the organization, impacting its strategy, such as market trends, economic conditions, regulatory changes, and technological advancements. Project managers must be adept at responding to these external influences, ensuring projects are not only reactive to changes in the business environment but also proactive in leveraging external opportunities.

Vision Statement
The vision statement defines where the organization wants to go in the future, serving as a guiding star for strategic planning. When using strategic planning tools, project managers should ensure all projects align with the long-term vision, contributing to the realization of the organization's aspirations.

High-Level Objectives

High-level objectives translate the vision into actionable goals. These objectives provide clear targets for the organization, and, in turn, help prioritize projects. Each project undertaken should align with one or more of these high-level objectives, ensuring the organization's resources are focused on what matters most.

Implementation Plan

The implementation plan is the roadmap for turning strategy into action. It outlines specific steps, timelines, and responsibilities for achieving high-level objectives. In project management, the implementation plan provides structure for delivering projects on time, within scope, and with desired outcomes. Successful implementation requires alignment between the strategic plan and day-to-day operations managed through projects.

Analytical Frameworks

Several analytical frameworks are used to support strategic planning. These frameworks help organizations analyze their environment, evaluate their competitive position, and make informed decisions about which projects will best support their strategy.

SWOT Analysis

SWOT Analysis (Strengths, Weaknesses, Opportunities, and Threats) is a widely used tool for evaluating internal and external factors affecting the organization. Project managers use this tool to assess the strategic environment in which their projects will operate. By understanding the organization's strengths and weaknesses, as well as external opportunities and threats, project teams can design projects to maximize strengths, address weaknesses, and mitigate risks.

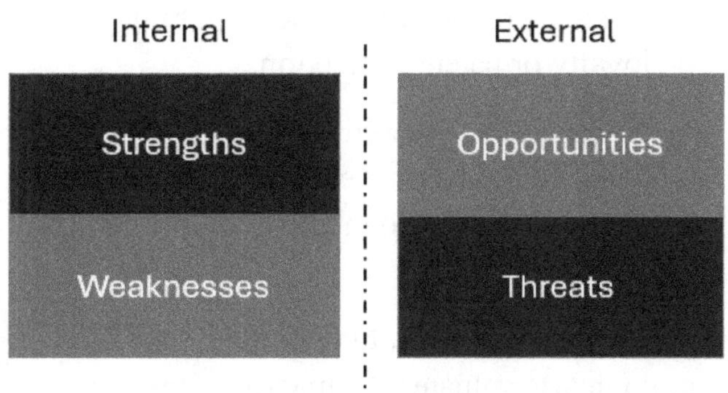

Figure 2.1. IT Governance Framework.

Porter's Five Forces Model

Porter's Five Forces Model delivers a structured approach/framework to analyze the competitive forces in an industry [8]. This model is critical for understanding the dynamics of competition and how projects might position the organization to succeed in its market. The model includes:

- **Buyer Power**: The influence customers have on pricing and demand. Projects focused on innovation or customer experience may be prioritized to reduce buyer power.
- **Supplier Power**: The influence suppliers have on the cost and availability of goods. Projects that develop alternative supply chains or improve supplier relationships can mitigate risks.

Figure 2.3. Porter's Five Forces [62].

- **Threat of Substitute Products**: The risk posed by alternative products or services. Projects should consider how to innovate or differentiate offerings to reduce the impact of substitutes.
- **Threat of New Entrants**: The likelihood of new competitors entering the market. Strategic projects may focus on building barriers to entry, such as strengthening brand loyalty or patent protection.
- **Competitive Rivalry**: The intensity of competition within the industry. Projects that enhance operational efficiency or market positioning help organizations thrive in highly competitive environments.

PEST Analysis

PEST Analysis (Political, Economic, Social, and Technological) evaluates the macro-environmental factors that can impact an organization [9]. Project managers use this tool to assess how these external forces may affect project outcomes and adapt strategies accordingly. For example, changes in government regulations or technological advancements could influence the direction or scope of a project [10].

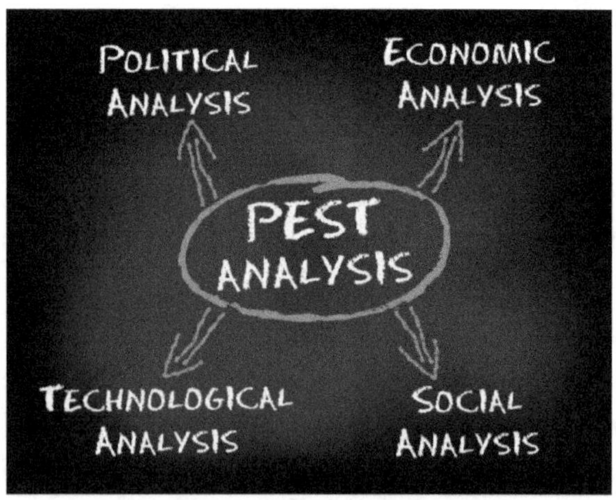

Figure 2.4 PEST Analysis [10].

Balanced Scorecard

The Balanced Scorecard is a performance management framework, enabling organizations to convert their vision and strategy into actionable and measurable goals. [11]. It looks at performance from four perspectives: financial, customer, internal processes, and learning and growth. In project management, the balanced scorecard ensures that projects are not just measured by financial success but also by their ability to improve internal processes, enhance customer satisfaction, and foster innovation.

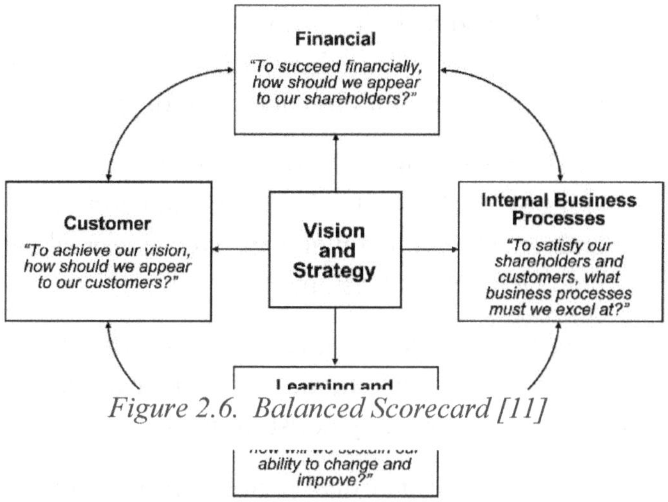

Figure 2.6. Balanced Scorecard [11]

Companies – Business Environment and Technology Quotient

Finally, understanding the broader business environment and an organization's "technology quotient" (TQ) is vital [12]. The business environment includes market dynamics, regulatory constraints, and industry trends, all of which shape strategic priorities. The TQ refers to the organization's ability to adopt and leverage new technologies effectively. High TQ organizations are better positioned to take advantage of technological innovations, making technology-focused projects a strategic priority. By considering these elements, project managers ensure projects not only respond to current conditions but also position the organization to thrive in an evolving technological landscape.

In conclusion, strategic planning tools play a crucial role in aligning project management with organizational objectives. By considering both internal and external drivers, employing analytical frameworks such as SWOT, Porter's Five Forces, PEST Analysis, and the Balanced Scorecard, and taking into account the business environment and technology quotient, project managers can ensure their initiatives are aligned with the broader strategic goals of the organization [13].

Portfolios, Programs, and Projects

At the heart of project management are portfolios, programs, and projects, each playing a distinct yet interconnected role in delivering value to an organization. Managing them effectively ensures the right projects are selected, aligned with strategic objectives, and executed to deliver intended benefits [16].

Project

A **project** is a temporary initiative aimed at delivering a distinct product, service, or outcome. Projects are defined by a clear scope, specific goals, and a limited timeframe.

- **Duration**: Projects have a start and end date, which sets them apart from ongoing operational work. The duration of a project is determined by its objectives and complexity, and it is critical for project managers to plan and manage a timeline carefully.

- **Key Characteristics**: Projects are unique, one-off undertakings designed to achieve specific goals within the constraints of scope, time, and cost. They require cross-functional collaboration and clear objectives to guide decision-making and execution.
- **Project Manager**: The project manager is responsible for leading the project, ensuring it stays on track, meets objectives, and adheres to the constraints of scope, time, and budget. The project manager plays a crucial role in communication, stakeholder management, and risk mitigation.
- **Scope**: Scope defines the boundaries of what the project will deliver. A well-defined scope ensures stakeholders and the team have a clear understanding of the project's deliverables and any constraints or limitations.
- **Time**: Time is a critical factor in project management, representing the timeline within which the project must be completed. Managing time effectively requires careful scheduling, monitoring progress, and adjusting plans to keep the project on track.
- **Cost**: Every project has a budget, representing financial resources required to complete the project. The project manager must ensure the project is delivered within the allocated budget, while balancing costs with resources and time.
- **Triple Constraints**: The triple constraints refer to the delicate balance between scope, time, and cost. Any change to one of these elements affects the others, and successful project management requires maintaining an equilibrium that ensures quality and meets project objectives.

Program

A program is a coordinated grouping of related projects managed together to achieve benefits and control that would not be attainable if managed separately. Programs emphasize the strategic alignment of projects and their combined impact.

- **Program Manager**: A program manager oversees the program, ensuring projects within it are aligned, well-coordinated, and collectively achieve desired benefits. The program manager is responsible for managing interdependencies, risks, and resources across multiple projects.
- **Program Roadmap**: A program roadmap outlines the timeline, major milestones, and key deliverables of the projects within the program. It serves as a strategic guide for program execution, ensuring all projects contribute toward the program's goals.

Portfolio

A **portfolio** is a collection of programs and projects which are managed and prioritized to meet the strategic objectives of the organization. Portfolios ensure the organization is investing in the right initiatives and that resources are being allocated to projects that align with strategic goals.

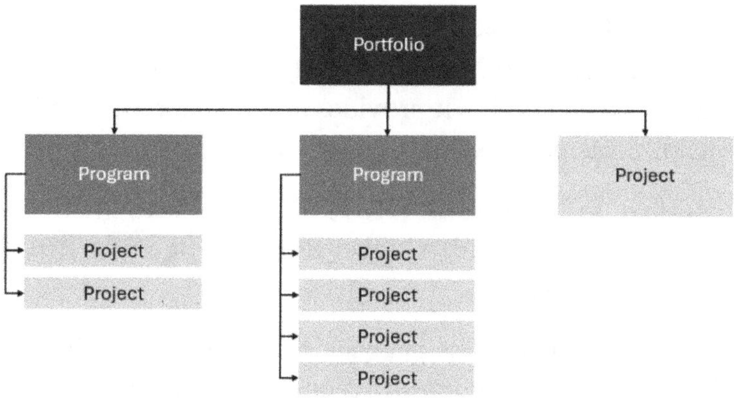

Figure 2.8. Portfolio Hierarchy.

- **Portfolio Management**: Portfolio management involves selecting and managing the right mix of projects and programs to deliver maximum value to the organization. It focuses on aligning investments with the organization's strategy, managing risks, and ensuring an optimal allocation of resources.

Project Selection Process

Selecting the right projects to include in a portfolio is crucial for maximizing the value delivered to the organization. The project selection process ensures projects align with business objectives and offer a favorable return on investment (ROI).

- **Business Case**: A business case justifies the initiation of a project by outlining its benefits, costs, and alignment with strategic goals. It helps decision-makers understand the value the project will deliver and supports the selection process.
- **Sponsor**: The sponsor is a senior stakeholder who advocates for the project and provides necessary support and resources. The sponsor ensures the project aligns with organizational priorities and helps remove obstacles that may arise during its execution.
- **Operational Projects**: These are projects focused on improving the efficiency and effectiveness of the organization's operations. They may include process improvements, cost-saving initiatives, or projects aimed at enhancing service delivery.
- **Project Selection Process and Underlying Purpose**: The project selection process involves reviewing and evaluating potential projects based on their alignment with strategic goals, resource availability, and expected benefits. The underlying purpose is to ensure that only projects with high potential for success and alignment with the organizational strategy are chosen for execution.

Evaluation and Analysis Tools
Several tools and methodologies are used to assess the viability and value of potential projects during the selection process. Some of those tools include:

- **Cost Benefit Analysis**: This analysis compares the expected costs of a project with the anticipated benefits. It provides a financial rationale for proceeding with a project and helps decision-makers assess whether the benefits justify the investment.
- **Return on Investment (ROI)**: ROI measures the financial return of a project relative to its cost. Projects with a higher ROI are often prioritized, as they provide greater value to the organization.
- **Payback Period**: The payback period is the amount of time it takes for a project to generate enough benefits to recover its costs. Projects with shorter payback periods are typically favored, as they provide quicker returns on investment.
- **Weighted Matrix or Weighted Scoring Model**: This model assigns weights to different criteria (such as cost, benefit, risk, and strategic alignment) and scores each project accordingly. The weighted matrix helps organizations prioritize projects by quantifying their relative value based on key decision criteria.

In summary, the framework of portfolios, programs, and projects, supported by a structured project selection process and analytical tools, ensures organizations focus their resources on initiatives offering the highest value. By strategically managing these elements, project managers can contribute to the broader alignment of projects with organizational goals, driving both efficiency and long-term success.

Project Management Life Cycle
The **Project Management Life Cycle** is a structured approach that helps guide projects from inception to completion. Understanding the phases of the project life cycle is essential for successful project management, as each phase involves distinct tasks and objectives ensuring projects are delivered effectively, on time, and within budget. Below is a detailed explanation of the project life cycle and its phases.

The project management life cycle is a framework that divides a project into manageable phases, each serving a specific purpose. These phases—**Initiating**, **Planning**, **Executing**, **Monitoring/Controlling**, and **Closing**—form the backbone of project management, ensuring that projects are systematically planned, executed, and evaluated.

Project Life Cycle Phases Overview and Brief Listing
1. Initiating
The **Initiating** phase is the starting point of any project, where the groundwork is laid for project success. This phase involves defining the project's purpose, identifying key stakeholders, and

developing the project charter, which formally authorizes the project. The key activities in this phase include:

- Defining the project's objectives and scope.
- Identifying stakeholders and understanding their needs and expectations.
- Developing the project charter, which outlines the purpose, goals, and authorization to proceed with the project.

The initiating phase is critical for setting the direction and ensuring aall stakeholders are aligned on the project's goals before moving forward.

2. Planning

The **Planning** phase is where the project's roadmap is developed. This phase involves creating detailed plans for how the project will be executed, monitored, and controlled. It includes defining the scope in more detail, estimating time and cost, identifying risks, and establishing the project's baseline. Key activities in this phase include:

- Developing the project management plan, which serves as the comprehensive guide for the project.
- Defining tasks, activities, and resources required to achieve the project objectives.
- Creating a detailed schedule, estimating costs, and identifying required resources.
- Risk identification and developing risk management strategies to mitigate potential challenges.

Effective planning is crucial for guiding projects to successful execution, ensuring resources are allocated efficiently, and timelines are realistic.

3. Executing

The **Executing** phase is where the project work begins. In this phase, the project plan is put into action, and deliverables are created according to the planned scope, timeline, and budget. It involves coordinating people and resources, managing stakeholder expectations, and ensuring tasks are being completed as scheduled. Key activities include:

- Directing and managing project execution.
- Allocating resources and ensuring team members understand their roles and responsibilities.
- Ensuring project deliverables are being produced to meet the defined quality standards.
- Managing communication between stakeholders and keeping everyone informed of progress.

Successful execution depends on careful coordination, clear communication, and effective management of resources to achieve the project's objectives.

4. Monitoring/Controlling

The **Monitoring and Controlling** phase runs concurrently with project execution and involves tracking progress to ensure the project stays on course. This phase focuses on comparing actual performance with the project plan and making adjustments as needed to meet the project's goals. Key activities include:

- Measuring project performance and progress against the baseline schedule, budget, and scope.
- Identifying any deviations or risks that could impact project success.
- Implementing corrective actions to bring the project back on track if necessary.
- Managing changes to the project scope, cost, and schedule through an established change control process.

This phase ensures the project remains aligned with the plan, with adjustments made as necessary to ensure the final outcomes meet stakeholder expectations.

5. Closing

The **Closing** phase marks the formal conclusion of the project. It involves completing all project activities, delivering the final product or service to stakeholders, and documenting the lessons learned. This phase ensures that the project is wrapped up methodically and that any remaining obligations are fulfilled. Key activities include:

- Completing and handing over project deliverables.
- Conducting final project reviews and gaining stakeholder approval.
- Documenting lessons learned and best practices for future projects.
- Closing contracts and releasing project resources.

The closing phase is essential for ensuring that all objectives have been met and that there is a clear end to the project, allowing the organization to reflect on what went well and what could be improved for future endeavors.

Project Methodologies

Project methodologies play a crucial role in determining how projects are executed and delivered. Two of the most prominent methodologies in project management are the **Waterfall Methodology** and the **Agile Methodology**. Each offers distinct approaches and is suited to different types of projects based on factors like flexibility, complexity, and the need for iterative development. Understanding these methodologies allows organizations to choose the right approach for their projects, ensuring alignment with both project objectives and organizational strategy.

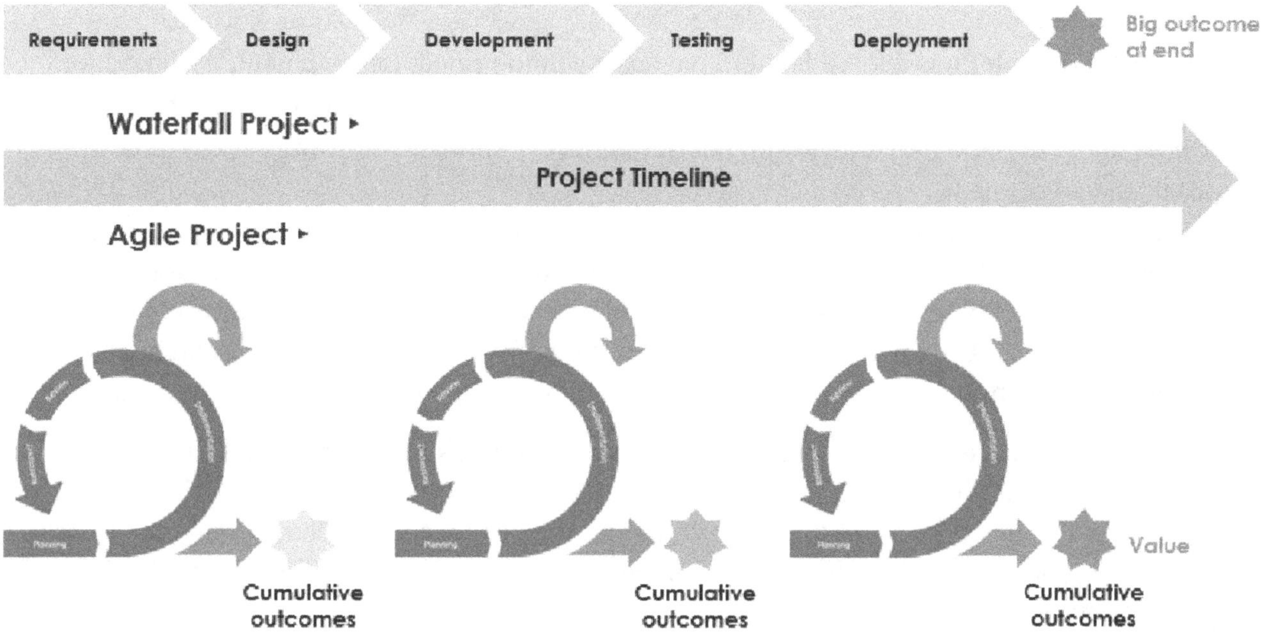

Figure 2.11. Waterfall methodology versus Agile methodology [14]

Waterfall Methodology

The **Waterfall Methodology** is a linear, sequential approach to project management emphasizing the completion of one phase before the next can begin. It follows a structured path, making it suitable for projects with well-defined requirements and where changes are minimal during the execution phase.

- **Phases**: The Waterfall Methodology breaks the project down into distinct phases: initiation, planning, execution, monitoring/controlling, and closure. Each phase must be completed in full before the project moves on to the next phase.
- **Predictability**: Waterfall's linear nature makes it highly predictable. The project manager and team have a clear view of what needs to be done at each phase, making it easier to track progress and manage resources. This predictability is ideal for projects where the scope, requirements, and deliverables are clearly defined from the start.
- **Documentation**: One of the key features of Waterfall is its emphasis on documentation. Detailed planning documents, scope statements, and schedules are prepared upfront, providing a comprehensive roadmap for the project. This documentation helps ensure all stakeholders have a shared understanding of the project's objectives and deliverables.
- **Limitations**: While the Waterfall approach offers clear structure and control, it can be inflexible. Changes in requirements late in the project can be costly and difficult to manage. Waterfall is best suited for projects with minimal scope changes, such as construction or hardware development.

Agile Methodology

The **Agile Methodology** is a flexible, iterative approach to project management, designed for projects where requirements may evolve over time or where rapid delivery of small increments is critical. Agile breaks the project into smaller iterations or "sprints," allowing for continuous feedback and adjustment.

- **Iterative Development**: Agile focuses on delivering small, functional increments of the project throughout its life cycle. Each sprint results in a working product, enabling teams to adapt quickly to changes or new requirements as the project progresses. This iterative nature makes Agile particularly well-suited for software development, research, and innovative projects where the final outcome may not be fully known at the outset.
- **Customer Involvement**: Agile places a strong emphasis on customer and stakeholder collaboration. Frequent feedback is gathered at the end of each sprint, ensuring the product is meeting customer expectations and that any necessary changes are made early in the process. This ongoing interaction helps to keep the project aligned with business objectives.
- **Flexibility**: One of the biggest advantages of Agile is its ability to adapt to changing requirements. Unlike Waterfall, Agile projects are not rigidly bound to the initial plan. Instead, they embrace change, with teams adjusting scope, features, and priorities based on real-time feedback and emerging needs.
- **Minimal Upfront Planning**: Agile does not require exhaustive upfront planning. Instead, it focuses on incremental planning, where the team plans for each sprint based on the outcomes of the previous one. This allows for more dynamic and responsive project management.
- **Challenges**: Agile's flexibility can also present challenges, particularly in environments where there is a need for a high level of predictability or where scope and budget constraints are tightly controlled. Additionally, Agile requires highly collaborative teams and can be difficult to implement in organizations who are not accustomed to continuous feedback loops.

Choosing the Right Methodology

The choice between Waterfall and Agile depends on the nature of the project and the organization's priorities:

- **Waterfall** is ideal for projects where scope and requirements are fixed, and there is a need for predictability and detailed documentation. Again, this methodology works well in industries like construction, manufacturing, or any field where there are clear, unchanging goals.
- **Agile** is best for projects that require flexibility and adaptability, particularly where requirements may change or evolve. It is particularly effective in software development, research, and innovation-focused industries where speed and stakeholder input are critical to success.

By understanding the strengths and limitations of both methodologies, organizations can align their project management approach with their strategic goals, ensuring they select the methodology that best meets the needs of each project.

In conclusion, both the **Waterfall Methodology** and the **Agile Methodology** offer valuable frameworks for managing projects, each with its own set of benefits. Waterfall provides structure and predictability, while Agile offers flexibility and continuous improvement. The choice of methodology plays a pivotal role in ensuring projects are executed efficiently and effectively, contributing to the overall strategic alignment of the organization.

Initiation Phase

The **Initiation Phase** is the foundational stage of any project, where the project's purpose is defined, and key elements are established to ensure alignment with strategic objectives. This phase is critical for setting the project on the right path, ensuring all stakeholders are aligned with the goals, and that the project has a strong justification for proceeding. Below is a detailed explanation of the core elements involved in the Initiation Phase.

The **Initiation Phase** marks the formal beginning of a project. It involves identifying the project's purpose, stakeholders, and key constraints. By the end of this phase, the project should have clear objectives, defined parameters, and the necessary approval to proceed. The four primary elements of the Initiation Phase include the **Business Case**, **Project Charter**, **Stakeholder Register**, and **Feasibility Study**.

Business Case

The **Business Case** is the document that provides the justification for the project. It outlines why the project is being proposed, what benefits it will bring, and how it aligns with the organization's strategic goals. The business case typically includes the following components:

- **Purpose**: Describes why the project is necessary, including the problem it aims to solve or the opportunity it seeks to capitalize on.
- **Benefits**: Lists the tangible and intangible benefits that the project will provide, such as increased revenue, cost savings, or enhanced customer satisfaction.
- **Costs**: Estimates the financial and resource costs required to complete the project, ensuring decision-makers understand the investment needed.
- **Risks**: Identifies any potential risks or challenges that could affect the success of the project and proposes mitigation strategies.
- **Alignment with Strategic Goals**: Demonstrates how the project supports the organization's broader objectives, ensuring that the project contributes to long-term success.

The business case is essential for securing approval from senior management or project sponsors, as it provides a clear rationale for why the project should move forward.

Project Charter

The **Project Charter** is a formal document authorizing the project and outlines its objectives, scope, and stakeholders. It serves as a reference for the project manager and team, providing clear guidance on what the project will achieve and how it will be structured. Key components of the project charter include:

- **Project Objectives**: Defines the specific goals the project will accomplish, providing a clear target for the project team.
- **Scope**: Details the boundaries of the project, including what is within and outside the project's scope. This ensures all stakeholders have a shared understanding of what the project will deliver.
- **Stakeholders**: Identifies the key stakeholders involved in the project, including sponsors, customers, and team members, along with their roles and responsibilities.
- **Deliverables**: Specifies the tangible outcomes or products the project will produce.
- **Authorization**: Grants the project manager the authority to begin planning and executing the project, ensuring they have the necessary resources and support.

The project charter is critical for establishing the project's legitimacy and providing the project manager with the authority to proceed.

Stakeholder Register

The **Stakeholder Register** is a document identifying all individuals, groups, and organizations who have an interest in the project. It ensures the project team understands who the stakeholders are, what their interests and expectations are, and how they should be engaged throughout the project lifecycle. Key elements of the stakeholder register include:

- **Stakeholder Identification**: Lists all stakeholders who have a vested interest in the project, such as customers, project sponsors, team members, regulatory bodies, and external partners.
- **Roles and Interests**: Describes the role of each stakeholder in the project and their specific interests or concerns. This helps the project team anticipate potential challenges or support from stakeholders.
- **Communication Requirements**: Defines how each stakeholder will be kept informed about the project's progress, including the frequency and methods of communication.

By maintaining an accurate and up-to-date stakeholder register, the project team can ensure effective communication and manage stakeholder expectations, reducing the risk of misunderstandings or conflicts.

Feasibility Study

A **Feasibility Study** assesses whether the project is viable and likely to succeed. It evaluates technical, financial, and operational factors to determine if the project can realistically achieve its goals given the available resources and constraints. The feasibility study typically includes:

- **Technical Feasibility**: Evaluates whether the necessary technology, expertise, and infrastructure are available to complete the project.
- **Financial Feasibility**: Assesses whether the project is financially viable, considering the estimated costs and potential returns on investment. It helps decision-makers determine if the project's benefits justify its costs.
- **Operational Feasibility**: Examines whether the organization has the necessary processes, personnel, and resources to support the project's execution and long-term success.

The feasibility study provides a comprehensive analysis of the project's potential success, helping stakeholders make informed decisions about whether to proceed with the project.

Importance of the Initiation Phase

The **Initiation Phase** is essential for laying the groundwork for the project's success. By developing a robust business case, project charter, stakeholder register, and feasibility study, the project team ensures the project is strategically aligned, well-supported, and grounded in a realistic assessment of its potential. Without a strong initiation phase, projects risk moving forward without clear objectives, inadequate resources, or misaligned stakeholder expectations, all of which can lead to failure.

In conclusion, the **Initiation Phase** of the **Project Management Life Cycle** is where the project takes shape. Through careful development of the business case, project charter, stakeholder register, and feasibility study, a foundation is laid for a project aligned with organizational goals, supported by stakeholders, and viable in terms of resources and technical requirements. These elements are critical to ensure a project can proceed to the next phase with confidence and clarity.

Planning Phase

The **Planning Phase** is a critical stage in the **Project Management Life Cycle**, where detailed plans are developed to guide the project toward successful execution. This phase involves defining the project's scope, setting objectives, identifying deliverables, and planning how to manage risks, stakeholders, and changes. The Planning Phase sets the foundation for all subsequent project activities and ensures the project remains aligned with organizational goals.

The **Planning Phase** translates the high-level vision and objectives outlined during the Initiation Phase into actionable steps. The main goal of this phase is to create a comprehensive roadmap detailing how the project will be executed, monitored, and controlled. The following elements are key to a successful Planning Phase.

Scope Statement

The **Scope Statement** clearly defines the boundaries of the project by outlining what is included and what is not. It establishes the deliverables and major objectives of the project, ensuring all stakeholders have a shared understanding of what the project will achieve. The scope statement includes:

- **Deliverables**: The products, services, or results the project will produce.
- **Project Boundaries**: What is and isn't included in the project.
- **Acceptance Criteria**: The conditions and standards the deliverables must meet to be acceptable by stakeholders.

The scope statement is essential for preventing scope creep, where uncontrolled changes can lead to project delays, cost overruns, or missed objectives.

Project Plan

The **Project Plan** is the master document that outlines how the project will be managed and executed. It integrates all aspects of the project, including scope, time, cost, quality, communication, risk, and resources. The project plan provides a comprehensive roadmap for the team, ensuring everyone is aligned with the project's objectives and strategy.

Project Schedule

The **Project Schedule** outlines the timeline for completing all tasks and milestones within the project. It breaks down the work into manageable tasks, assigns resources, and sets deadlines. The project schedule is typically presented using tools such as Gantt charts to provide a visual timeline of the project's progress.

- **Milestones**: Key points in the project where progress is evaluated.
- **Deadlines**: Specific dates for the completion of tasks and deliverables.

A well-defined project schedule ensures the project stays on track and that resources are managed efficiently.

Objectives

Project **Objectives** provide specific, measurable goals a project must achieve. These objectives are aligned with the organization's strategic goals and should be clearly defined to guide the project team. Well-crafted objectives are essential for ensuring the project delivers value to the organization.

Requirements

Requirements specify the features, functions, or characteristics the project's deliverables must meet. Gathering and documenting requirements ensures the project outputs align with stakeholder expectations. This process includes:

- **Functional Requirements**: The technical or operational needs the project deliverables must fulfill.
- **Non-Functional Requirements**: Other criteria, such as security, performance, or usability, that must be met.

Deliverables

Deliverables are the tangible or intangible outputs produced by the project. These could be products, services, reports, or other results. Clearly defining deliverables ensures all stakeholders understand what the project will produce and how success will be measured.

Baseline

The **Baseline** is the approved version of the project plan, including scope, schedule, and cost. It serves as a reference point for measuring project performance. Any deviations from the baseline are carefully tracked, and corrective actions are taken to keep the project aligned with its objectives. The baseline helps project managers control the project and maintain focus on the agreed-upon goals.

Gantt Chart

A **Gantt Chart** is a visual tool used to represent the project schedule. It shows the start and end dates of each task, their dependencies, and the overall project timeline. The Gantt chart is a valuable tool for tracking progress and ensuring the project remains on schedule. It allows project managers to quickly identify any delays or resource constraints.

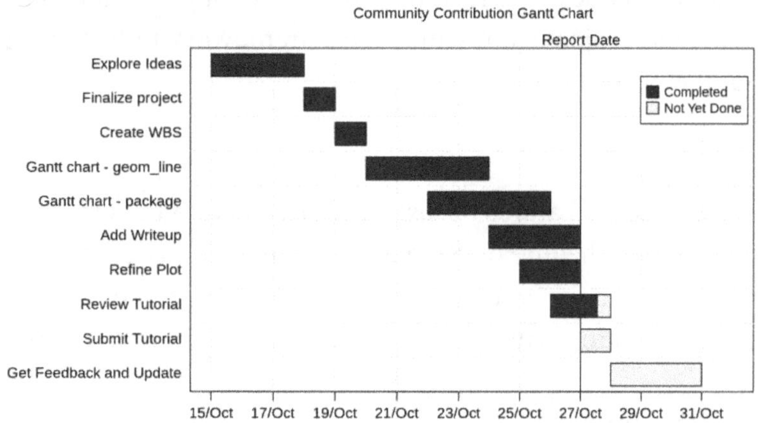

Figure 2.12 Project Schedule with Gantt Chart [20].

Stakeholder Engagement Plan

The **Stakeholder Engagement Plan** outlines how the project will communicate with and manage stakeholders. It ensures stakeholders are informed, involved, and supportive throughout the project. The plan includes strategies for engaging different stakeholder groups, considering their needs, expectations, and influence on the project's success.

- **Communication Methods**: How information will be shared (meetings, reports, emails, etc.).
- **Frequency of Communication**: How often stakeholders will receive updates.
- **Key Stakeholders**: Those who have a significant impact or interest in the project.

A well-executed stakeholder engagement plan helps prevent misunderstandings and builds support for the project.

Risk Management Plan and Issues Log

The **Risk Management Plan** identifies risks potentially impacting the project and outlines strategies to mitigate them. It includes a risk register that tracks each identified risk, its potential impact, and the actions needed to reduce or eliminate it.

- **Risk Assessment**: Evaluating the likelihood and impact of each risk.
- **Mitigation Strategies**: Actions to reduce the likelihood or impact of risks.

The **Issues Log** is used to document problems which may arise during the project. It tracks the issue, the steps taken to resolve it, and its impact on the project. By maintaining an issues log, the project team ensures all problems are addressed in a timely and organized manner.

Project Plan Documents

Project Plan Documents refer to all the formal documents created during the planning phase, including the project charter, scope statement, risk management plan, and communication plan. These documents provide the project team with a clear framework to follow and ensure consistency throughout the project.

Scope Creep

Scope Creep occurs when added features or tasks are amended to the project without proper approval or adjustments to the schedule or budget. This can lead to delays, cost overruns, and resource depletion. Preventing scope creep requires careful management of changes to the project scope, clear communication with stakeholders, and adherence to the project's objectives.

Importance of the Planning Phase

The **Planning Phase** is vital for ensuring the project has a clear direction and that all stakeholders are aligned with its goals. By creating a detailed scope statement, project plan, schedule, and risk management plan, the project team can anticipate challenges and proactively address them. Without proper planning, projects often encounter delays, budget overruns, and misaligned stakeholder expectations.

In conclusion, the **Planning Phase** of the **Project Management Life Cycle** is where the groundwork is laid for successful project execution. With detailed planning around scope, objectives, deliverables, risks, and stakeholder engagement, the project team ensures the project is well-organized and prepared for any challenges. Proper planning is the key to delivering projects on time, within budget, and to the satisfaction of all stakeholders.

Execution Phase

The **Execution Phase** is where the project plan is put into action, and the work required to deliver the project's objectives is performed. This phase is the most resource-intensive and involves managing people, processes, and changes to ensure the project stays on track. It requires continuous monitoring and adaptation to handle any deviations from the original plan. Below is a detailed explanation of the key elements involved in the Execution Phase.

The **Execution Phase** is the core of the project lifecycle, where the project team works to produce the deliverables outlined in the project plan. Success in this phase depends on effective communication, team collaboration, and the ability to manage changes dynamically. Several key components play critical roles in ensuring the project is executed efficiently and aligned with its strategic objectives.

Project Change Requests

As the project progresses, it's common for changes to arise, whether due to evolving requirements, unforeseen issues, or new opportunities. **Project Change Requests** are formal proposals for modifications to the project's scope, timeline, or budget. These changes need to be documented, evaluated, and approved before being implemented to avoid disrupting the project. Key steps include:

- **Identification**: Recognizing the need for change, whether it's scope-related, time-line-driven, or resource-based.
- **Evaluation**: Assessing the impact of the requested change on the overall project, including how it affects the triple constraints (scope, time, & cost).
- **Approval**: Ensuring change requests are authorized through a formal process before implementation.

Change Form

A **Change Form** is the document used to capture all necessary details about a project change request. This form ensures the request is thoroughly documented and that all stakeholders are informed of the proposed change. The change form typically includes:

- **Description of the change**: What the proposed modification involves.

- **Reason for the change**: Why the change is necessary and how it benefits the project.
- **Impact analysis**: An assessment of how the change affects the project's scope, timeline, budget, and resources.
- **Approval section**: Signatures from key stakeholders or the project sponsor, indicating their agreement with the change.

The change form formalizes the process, ensuring transparency and traceability.

Change Review Board

The **Change Review Board (CRB)** is responsible for reviewing and approving or rejecting project change requests. This board typically consists of senior project stakeholders, including the project sponsor, project manager, and relevant functional managers. The CRB's role is to:

- **Evaluate the change**: Consider the benefits, risks, and costs associated with the requested change.
- **Prioritize changes**: Determine whether the requested change is critical to the project's success or if it can be deferred or rejected.
- **Authorize implementation**: Approve changes that align with the project's goals and strategic objectives, ensuring the project remains viable and on track.

Capability Maturity Model

The **Capability Maturity Model (CMM)** is a framework used for assessing and improving an organization's project management processes. In the execution phase, it helps evaluate the maturity of the project management practices in use. This model defines levels of process maturity, from ad-hoc processes (lower levels) to optimized processes (higher levels). It encourages continuous improvement and helps project teams identify areas for process optimization.

Using CMM, project managers can ensure that their team's processes are scalable, repeatable, and adaptable to the project's needs, reducing risks and improving project performance.

Project Team

The **Project Team** is responsible for carrying out the tasks outlined in the project plan. The project manager must effectively lead and coordinate the team to ensure that each member understands their role and responsibilities. Team dynamics, clear communication, and collaboration are essential to delivering project objectives. Key management tasks include:

- **Resource allocation**: Ensuring each team member has the resources needed to perform their tasks.
- **Task management**: Monitoring individual and team progress to ensure timely completion of deliverables.
- **Team cohesion**: Fostering a collaborative and motivated team environment.

Responsibility Assignment Matrix

The **Responsibility Assignment Matrix (RAM)** is a tool that defines the roles and responsibilities of each team member in relation to specific tasks. It ensures clarity in who is responsible for each aspect of the project, preventing confusion and overlap. The RAM provides a structured way to assign ownership for different tasks, making sure everyone knows their specific duties.

RACI (Responsible, Accountable, Consulted, Informed)

The **RACI Matrix** is a type of Responsibility Assignment Matrix that clarifies who is:

- **Responsible**: The person who does the work to complete the task.
- **Accountable**: The individual who is ultimately answerable for the task's success and who must ensure it gets done.
- **Consulted**: Individuals who provide input or advice for the task.
- **Informed**: Stakeholders who need to be kept up to date on the progress of the task.

Using the RACI model ensures each task has clear ownership, with no ambiguity about roles or responsibilities. This clarity helps streamline communication and accountability throughout the project execution phase.

Histograms and Stacked Histograms

Histograms and **Stacked Histograms** are graphical tools used to visually represent data related to resource allocation and task distribution during the execution phase.

- **Histograms**: These show the distribution of work across different team members or resources, helping to identify if anyone is over- or under-allocated. This allows project managers to adjust workloads and ensure that resources are optimally utilized.
- **Stacked Histograms**: These build on regular histograms by displaying multiple data sets in a single graph, often used to track different resource categories or time periods simultaneously. This visual tool helps project managers get a clearer picture of how different aspects of the project are progressing, enabling them to manage resources and time more effectively.

Importance of the Execution Phase

The **Execution Phase** is where the project moves from planning to action. By managing changes effectively through tools like change requests, change forms, and the Change Review Board, the project team can stay adaptable while maintaining alignment with project goals. The use of frameworks like the Capability Maturity Model and tools like the RACI matrix ensures responsibilities are clear and resources are allocated efficiently. Visual tools like histograms further support effective management of the project's resources and timeline.

Without effective execution, even the most well-planned project is unlikely to succeed. Therefore, clear communication, strong team management, and a structured process for managing changes and responsibilities are crucial to delivering the project successfully.
In conclusion, the **Execution Phase** of the **Project Management Life Cycle** is where the actual work happens. By following structured processes for managing changes, clearly defining team roles with tools like the RACI matrix and using data visualization tools like histograms to manage resources, project managers can ensure their teams stay on track and the project remains aligned with its strategic goals. Effective execution is key to turning a project plan into tangible results.

Monitoring and Controlling Phase
The **Monitoring and Controlling Phase** is crucial for ensuring the project remains aligned with its objectives throughout its execution. This phase involves tracking the project's progress, managing changes, and making adjustments as needed to ensure the project stays on track in terms of scope, time, cost, and quality. Below is a detailed explanation of the key elements involved in the Monitoring and Controlling Phase.

The **Monitoring and Controlling Phase** runs concurrently with the execution phase of the project and plays a pivotal role in ensuring the project delivers its intended outcomes. This phase allows the project manager and team to observe project performance, compare it against the planned baseline, and make necessary adjustments to keep the project on course. The two main activities in this phase are **Monitoring Project Performance** and fulfilling the **Project Manager's Duties** related to controlling deviations and ensuring changes are managed appropriately.

Monitoring Project Performance
Monitoring project performance involves continuously tracking and measuring the project's progress against the baseline established in the planning phase. This ongoing process helps identify any variances or deviations from the project plan and ensures that corrective actions can be taken promptly to minimize disruptions. Monitoring activities include:

- **Performance Metrics**: Key performance indicators (KPIs) are used to assess the progress of the project. These metrics may include milestones achieved, percentage of tasks completed, budget expenditure, and time utilization. Performance metrics provide real-time insights into whether the project is on track or falling behind.

- **Comparing Actual vs. Planned Performance**: By comparing actual progress with the planned schedule, cost, and scope, the project manager can quickly detect any discrepancies. For example, if the project is behind schedule or over budget, the project team can take corrective actions to address the issues.

- **Tracking Deliverables**: Monitoring whether the project is producing the required deliverables as planned is essential for ensuring that project outcomes meet defined quality standards. Quality assurance checks may be conducted to confirm each deliverable meets its acceptance criteria.

- **Risk Management**: Risks identified during the planning phase are actively monitored, and new risks that arise during execution are logged and evaluated. Continuous risk monitoring helps the project team respond proactively to potential threats to the project's success.

- **Change Monitoring**: Any changes to the project—whether scope, timeline, or budget—are tracked to ensure they are authorized, documented, and implemented in a controlled manner. Monitoring the impact of these changes is crucial for maintaining project alignment with the original goals.

Effective monitoring provides early warnings of potential issues, allowing the project team to adjust their approach and implement mitigation strategies.

Project Manager Duties During the Monitoring and Controlling Phase

The project manager plays a central role during the Monitoring and Controlling phase. Their primary responsibility is to ensure the project remains aligned with the baseline plan while managing changes and deviations effectively. Key duties of the project manager during this phase include:

- **Tracking and Reporting**: The project manager is responsible for tracking progress and reporting it to stakeholders. This involves regular status updates, highlighting performance metrics, and informing stakeholders about any risks or changes that may affect the project. Clear and timely communication is essential for keeping all stakeholders informed and aligned.

- **Managing Changes**: One of the most important duties in this phase is managing change requests. The project manager must ensure any proposed changes to the project are thoroughly evaluated through a formal change control process. This process involves assessing the impact of changes on scope, schedule, and cost, and seeking approval from the Change Review Board before making any adjustments.

- **Implementing Corrective Actions**: When monitoring identifies variances from the project plan, the project manager must take corrective actions to bring the project back on track. These actions may include reallocating resources, adjusting timelines, or renegotiating scope. The goal is to minimize deviations and ensure the project achieves its objectives.

- **Ensuring Compliance with Baseline**: The project manager must ensure the project adheres to the established baseline for scope, cost, and schedule. Any deviations must be tracked, and the necessary approvals must be obtained for any adjustments.

- **Managing Stakeholder Expectations**: The project manager must continually engage with stakeholders to manage their expectations and ensure their needs are being met. This involves addressing any concerns they may have about progress or changes and ensuring they remain informed and satisfied with the project's trajectory.
- **Quality Assurance**: The project manager ensures quality assurance processes are implemented throughout the execution phase. This includes reviewing deliverables to ensure they meet the agreed-upon quality standards and conducting regular inspections or tests to verify their compliance with the project requirements.
- **Risk Mitigation**: The project manager actively monitors risks and ensures mitigation strategies are in place. When new risks are identified, the project manager must assess their impact and adjust the project plan accordingly to minimize any negative effects.

By fulfilling these duties, the project manager ensures the project remains on course and that all changes are managed in a controlled, transparent manner. The goal is to deliver the project's outcomes within the agreed-upon constraints of scope, time, and cost, while maintaining high-quality standards.

Importance of the Monitoring and Controlling Phase
The **Monitoring and Controlling Phase** is essential for ensuring the project remains aligned with its strategic goals and delivers value to the organization. Without effective monitoring, projects can quickly veer off track, leading to delays, cost overruns, and failure to meet stakeholder expectations. By continuously measuring performance, managing changes, and taking corrective actions, project managers can keep the project on target and ensure it achieves its desired outcomes.

In conclusion, the **Monitoring and Controlling Phase** of the **Project Management Life Cycle** is where the project manager ensures the project stays on track by monitoring performance, managing changes, and keeping stakeholders informed. Through effective monitoring and proactive management of risks and changes, the project manager plays a crucial role in ensuring the project delivers its intended results within the defined scope, time, and cost constraints.

Systems Development Life Cycle (SDLC)
The **Systems Development Life Cycle (SDLC)** is a framework outlining the stages involved in developing and delivering an information system. The SDLC provides a structured approach to system development, ensuring all necessary steps are followed to create a high-quality system to meet user needs. Below is a high-level overview of the five primary phases of the SDLC and the role of the **Systems Analyst**.

The **SDLC** consists of a sequence of phases guiding the development and implementation of systems. Each phase has its own objectives and deliverables, ensuring the system is developed in a logical, organized manner. By following this structured approach, organizations can minimize risks, optimize resources, and ensure the successful delivery of the system.

The Project Management Life Cycle and the SDLC

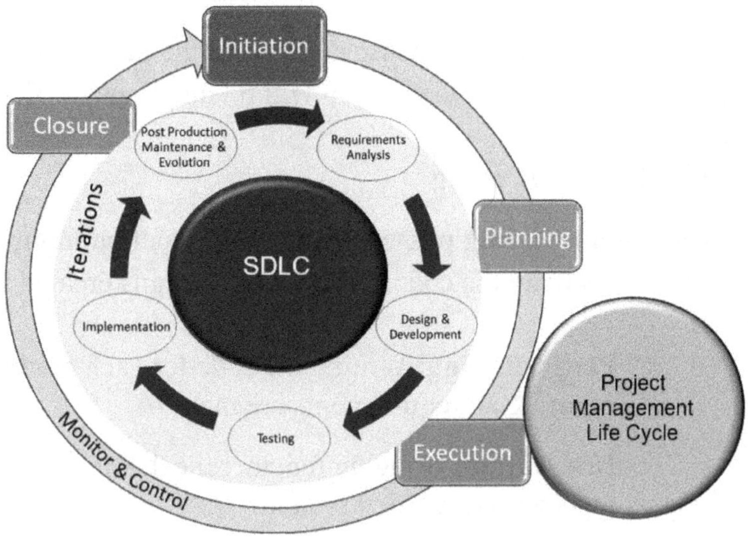

Figure 2.13. SDLC and Project Management Life Cycle [16]

Five Primary Phases – High-Level Overview

1. **Requirements Gathering and Analysis**

The **Requirements Gathering and Analysis** phase is the foundation of the entire SDLC. During this phase, the project team works closely with stakeholders to identify and document the specific needs and requirements of the system. The goal is to understand what the users need from the system and to capture all functional and non-functional requirements in detail.

- **Functional Requirements**: These define what the system should do—specific tasks or functions it needs to perform.
- **Non-Functional Requirements**: These cover other system attributes such as performance, security, usability, and scalability.

Once gathered, the requirements are analyzed to determine their feasibility, and any potential constraints or challenges are identified. This phase is critical because it ensures that the system being developed aligns with the needs of the organization and its users.

2. **Design**

In the **Design** phase, the system's architecture and structure are developed based on the requirements gathered in the previous phase. This involves creating detailed designs outlining how the system will function and how different components will interact. The design phase typically includes:

- **System Architecture Design**: A high-level view of the system, including hardware and software components and how they will work together.
- **Database Design**: The structure of the data that will be stored and how it will be accessed and managed.

- **User Interface (UI) Design**: The layout and structure of the user interface, focusing on how users will interact with the system.

The design phase is critical because it serves as the blueprint for the development phase. A well-thought-out design ensures the system will be functional, efficient, and aligned with user expectations.

3. **Development/Coding**

The **Development/Coding** phase is where the actual building of the system takes place. In this phase, developers write the code based on the designs created in the previous phase. This phase involves:

- **Programming**: Writing the code for each module or component of the system, ensuring all requirements are met.
- **Integration**: Bringing together the different components and ensuring they work together as a unified system.
- **Version Control**: Managing changes to the code through version control systems to ensure the development process is organized and trackable.

The success of the development phase depends heavily on the quality of the design and the accuracy of the requirements. A collaborative approach between developers, analysts, and testers ensures the system is built efficiently and correctly.

4. **Testing**

In the **Testing** phase, the system undergoes rigorous testing to identify and fix any issues or bugs before deployment. The goal of this phase is to ensure the system works as intended and meets the quality standards set during the planning phase. Different types of testing are conducted:

- **Unit Testing**: Tests individual components or modules for functionality.
- **Integration Testing**: Ensures different modules work together as expected.
- **System Testing**: Tests the system as a whole to verify it meets the functional and non-functional requirements.
- **User Acceptance Testing (UAT)**:

  Involves end users testing the system to ensure it meets their needs and expectations.

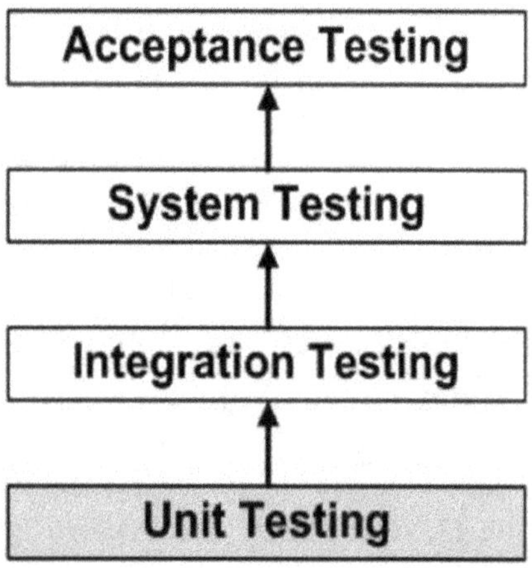

Figure 2.15. Progression of Testing [18]

Testing is crucial because it helps identify any issues before the system goes live, minimizing the risk of failure during deployment. A thorough testing phase ensures a smooth and successful system implementation.

5. **Deployment or Implementation**

The **Deployment or Implementation** phase is the final phase of the SDLC, where the system is installed, configured, and made available to users. This phase involves:

- **System Deployment**: Moving the system from the testing environment to the production environment.
- **Training and Support**: Providing users with training and resources to help them understand how to use the system effectively.
- **Post-Deployment Monitoring**: Ensuring the system operates as expected and addressing any issues that arise after deployment.

A successful deployment ensures the system is fully operational, meets user needs, and integrates seamlessly with the organization's existing processes and systems.

Role of the Systems Analyst

A **Systems Analyst** plays a critical role throughout the SDLC, acting as the liaison between the business stakeholders and the technical team. Their primary responsibility is to ensure the system being developed aligns with the organization's business objectives and user requirements. Key responsibilities of the systems analyst include:

- **Requirements Gathering**: Working closely with stakeholders to define and document system requirements, ensuring both business and technical needs are addressed.
- **Feasibility Analysis**: Analyzing the feasibility of the system, including technical, operational, and financial considerations, to ensure the project is viable.
- **Design Coordination**: Collaborating with designers and developers to ensure the system's architecture and design align with the requirements.
- **Testing Oversight**: Working with testers and end users to ensure the system meets quality standards and user expectations during the testing phase.
- **Continuous Improvement**: Identifying opportunities for system improvements and enhancements based on feedback from users and stakeholders.

The systems analyst is a key bridge between the business and technical aspects of the project, ensuring the system delivers real value to the organization.

Importance of the Systems Development Life Cycle

The **Systems Development Life Cycle (SDLC)** provides a clear, structured approach to system development which helps ensure success. By following the five primary phases—**Requirements Gathering and Analysis**, **Design**, **Development/Coding**, **Testing**, and **Deployment**—organizations can ensure their systems are developed efficiently, meet user needs, and align with strategic goals. The role of the **Systems Analyst** is critical throughout this process, as they ensure the system is both technically feasible and aligned with the organization's business objectives.

In conclusion, the **Systems Development Life Cycle** and the role of the **Systems Analyst** are integral to the successful development and implementation of systems. By following the SDLC's structured phases and leveraging the expertise of systems analysts, organizations can deliver high-quality systems supporting their strategic objectives while providing value to users.

Requirements Gathering and Analysis Phase

The **Requirements Gathering and Analysis Phase** is a critical first step in the **Systems Development Life Cycle (SDLC)**. This phase ensures the system's purpose is clearly defined, and the project team fully understands the business needs, user requirements, and technical constraints before development begins. Gathering accurate and comprehensive requirements is key to delivering a system that meets stakeholder expectations and aligns with the organization's strategic goals. Below is a detailed explanation of the key components involved in the Requirements Gathering and Analysis Phase.

The **Requirements Gathering and Analysis Phase** involves working closely with stakeholders, end users, and technical teams to understand the needs of the business and to define what the system should achieve. This phase sets the foundation for all subsequent SDLC phases, ensuring the project is properly scoped and all requirements are documented and agreed upon.

Business Requirements

Business Requirements refer to the high-level needs and objectives the system must fulfill to support the organization's goals. These requirements focus on what the business aims to achieve with the system and how it will improve or transform existing processes. Examples of business requirements include increasing efficiency, enhancing customer experience, or automating specific workflows.

- **High-Level Project Goals**: The overarching goals the project seeks to accomplish, usually tied to the organization's strategic objectives.
- **Objectives**: Specific, measurable outcomes the system must deliver, such as reducing transaction times by a certain percentage or improving data accuracy.

Specifications

Specifications are detailed descriptions of the system's functionality, performance, and technical requirements. These specifications outline how the system will fulfill the business requirements and ensure the design and development phases have clear, actionable guidance.

- **Functional Specifications**: Define what the system should do, including specific tasks, features, and workflows.

- **Non-Functional Specifications**: Define how the system should perform, including speed, security, scalability, and usability.

Project Specifications

Project Specifications are the detailed technical requirements that guide the system's development. These specifications ensure the system will meet the performance, security, and operational standards required by the organization.

- **Technical Requirements**: Outline the necessary hardware, software, network infrastructure, and other technical aspects the system must integrate with.
- **User Interface (UI) Requirements**: Define how users will interact with the system, focusing on usability, accessibility, and ease of navigation.

Process Modeling and Data Modeling

Process Modeling and **Data Modeling** are used to visualize and document how the system will function. These models help the project team understand the flow of information, interactions between different system components, and how data will be stored and retrieved.

- **Process Modeling**: Maps out the business processes the system will support, showing the sequence of activities, decision points, and information flows.
- **Data Modeling**: Defines the structure of the data, including relationships between different data elements, how data will be stored, and how it will be accessed. Data modeling ensures the system's database architecture supports the requirements for data storage, retrieval, and management.

Unified Modeling Language (UML)

Unified Modeling Language (UML) is a standardized visual language used to model system designs and processes. UML helps stakeholders and developers communicate complex system interactions through diagrams and models that represent the system's structure and behavior.

- **UML Tools**: Software tools that help create UML diagrams, which provide a clear visual representation of the system's architecture and processes.
- **Use Case Diagram**: A key UML diagram that illustrates the interactions between users (actors) and the system. It shows the various ways users engage with the system and the system's responses to those interactions.
    - **Actors**: Represent the users or other systems that interact with the system being developed. An actor can be a person, another system, or an external device that communicates with the system.
    - **Use Cases**: Specific functions or activities the system performs in response to an actor's input. Each use case represents a different way the system is used, ensuring all functional requirements are covered.

  - **Use Case List**: A comprehensive list of all the use cases identified during the requirements gathering process. This list serves as a reference to ensure system development covers all necessary interactions.

The use of UML and related tools ensures the design phase will have clear, structured documentation of how the system will function from both the user and system perspectives.

Requirements Specifications Document

The **Requirements Specifications Document** is the formal record of all business, functional, and technical requirements gathered during this phase. This document serves as a blueprint for the design and development phases and provides a shared understanding between stakeholders, developers, and the project team.

- **Purpose**: To serve as a reference throughout the SDLC, ensuring that the system is built according to the agreed-upon requirements.
- **Content**: Includes business goals, detailed requirements, UML diagrams, process models, and data models, offering a comprehensive view of the system's intended functionality and structure.

The **Requirements Specifications Document** is crucial because it prevents misunderstandings and ensures all parties are aligned on what the system should deliver. Any changes to requirements after this document is finalized will require formal change requests to ensure scope creep is controlled.

Importance of the Requirements Gathering and Analysis Phase

The **Requirements Gathering and Analysis Phase** is critical to the success of the project. It ensures the project is based on a clear understanding of business needs, provides detailed guidance for the design and development phases, and establishes a solid foundation for building a system that aligns with both business objectives and user needs. Any gaps or misunderstandings in this phase can lead to costly changes later in the project, so thorough documentation and communication are essential.

In conclusion, the **Requirements Gathering and Analysis Phase** sets the stage for the entire Systems Development Life Cycle. Through detailed requirements collection, process and data modeling, and the use of UML diagrams, the project team ensures that the system will meet business needs and user expectations. The **Requirements Specifications Document** formalizes these findings, providing a clear roadmap for the system's design and development, helping to minimize risk and maximize the chances of project success.

Design Phase

The **Design Phase** of the **Systems Development Life Cycle (SDLC)** focuses on translating the requirements gathered into a detailed blueprint for how the system will function and how the data will be structured. One of the critical aspects of this phase is the design of the database, which will house the data and ensure that it can be stored, accessed, and manipulated efficiently. Below is a detailed explanation of the design phase, focusing on database design and the data modeling process.

The **Design Phase** is where the system's architecture is created, ensuring it meets both functional and non-functional requirements. This phase focuses on how the system will be structured, including the design of databases, data flow, and how data will be modeled and stored. A well-thought-out design ensures the system is efficient, scalable, and capable of handling the necessary data and operations.

Database Design

Database Design is a crucial part of the system design, as it ensures the system can store and manage data effectively. The goal of database design is to create a structure that organizes data in a way that optimizes performance, maintains data integrity, and supports the system's functional requirements.

- **Data Modelers / Database Analysts**: Data modelers or database analysts are responsible for designing the database structure. They work closely with the systems analysts and developers to ensure the database supports the system's functionality and meets the requirements outlined during the analysis phase. These professionals focus on defining how data will be organized, accessed, and maintained, ensuring the design aligns with both user needs and technical constraints.

Data Flow Diagrams

Data Flow Diagrams (DFDs) are visual representations of how data moves through the system. These diagrams map out the flow of information between different parts of the system, including inputs, processes, and outputs. DFDs help the project team visualize the flow of data and identify how information is transferred between system components.

- **Purpose of DFDs**: To illustrate how data is processed, stored, and retrieved in the system, ensuring all processes are accounted for, and that data moves efficiently between different system modules.

DFDs are essential for ensuring the system's design supports the intended data flows and there are no bottlenecks or inefficiencies in data processing.

Data Modeling – Relationships Between Data Objects, Where and How Data Will Be Stored

Data Modeling is the process of defining the relationships between data objects and determining where and how data will be stored in the system. Data modeling ensures the database structure supports the system's operations and can handle the required data volume and complexity. Key elements of data modeling include:

- **Relationships Between Data Objects**: Defining how different data elements relate to one another is critical for ensuring the database structure reflects real-world relationships. For example, in a customer management system, a customer entity might be related to an order entity, which in turn relates to a product entity.
- **Where and How Data Will Be Stored**: Data modeling helps determine the physical storage structure, ensuring the system's database can handle the necessary data types and volumes, as well as the specific access and retrieval requirements.

Data modeling creates a foundation for building an efficient database supporting the system's needs for both performance and data integrity.

Logical Data Model

The **Logical Data Model** is an abstract representation of how the data will be structured in the system, independent of how it will be physically stored. This model focuses on the business perspective, defining the data elements, their relationships, and how they interact within the system.

- **Entity**: An entity represents a real-world object or concept in the system, such as a customer, product, or order. Entities are the core building blocks of the logical data model.
- **Attributes**: Attributes are the properties or characteristics of an entity. For example, a customer entity might have attributes such as name, address, and phone number. Attributes define the specific data that will be stored for each entity.
- **Entity Relationship Diagram (ERD)**: An **Entity Relationship Diagram** is a visual representation of the entities and their relationships. It shows how different entities are connected and how data flows between them. ERDs are critical for visualizing the structure of the database and ensuring the relationships between entities accurately reflect business requirements.

The logical data model provides a high-level view of the system's data architecture, ensuring all necessary data elements and their interactions are well-defined before moving into physical implementation.

Physical Data Model – Schema

The **Physical Data Model** translates the logical data model into the actual database schema that will be used to implement the system. The schema defines how data will be stored in the database, including the specific tables, columns, data types, and relationships between tables.

- **Schema**: The schema is the blueprint for how data will be organized at the physical level. It includes detailed definitions of database tables, columns, data types, indexes, and constraints. The schema ensures the database is optimized for performance, security, and data integrity.

- **Example**: In a customer management system, the physical schema might define a **Customer** table with columns for CustomerID, Name, Email, and PhoneNumber, along with relationships to other tables such as **Orders** and **Products**.

The physical data model ensures the database can efficiently store and retrieve data while maintaining the relationships and integrity defined in the logical data model.

Role of Data Modelers and Database Analysts

Data Modelers and **Database Analysts** are responsible for designing and optimizing the database structure. They ensure the data models support the system's functional and performance requirements, and that the database design is scalable, secure, and efficient [17]. Their role includes:

- **Collaboration with Development Teams**: Working closely with developers to ensure the database design supports the system's architecture.
- **Data Integrity and Security**: Implementing mechanisms to ensure data is accurate, consistent, and secure.
- **Optimization**: Ensuring the database is optimized for fast access and efficient data storage.

Importance of the Design Phase in SDLC

The **Design Phase** is critical for translating business requirements into a detailed blueprint for system development. By carefully designing the database, creating data models, and using tools like data flow diagrams and entity relationship diagrams, the project team ensures the system's data architecture is well-structured, efficient, and scalable. This phase sets the stage for a successful development process and helps avoid costly rework during later phases of the SDLC.

In conclusion, the **Design Phase** of the **Systems Development Life Cycle** focuses on creating a detailed data architecture that meets the system's functional requirements. Through careful **Database Design**, **Data Modeling**, and the creation of **Logical** and **Physical Data Models**, the project team ensures the system can handle its data efficiently and securely. Tools like **Entity Relationship Diagrams** and **Data Flow Diagrams** help visualize the system's structure, making it easier for stakeholders to understand how the system will operate. This phase is essential for ensuring the system is built on a solid foundation, capable of supporting both current and future needs.

Testing Phase

The **Testing Phase** of the **Systems Development Life Cycle (SDLC)** is critical for ensuring the quality and reliability of the system before it is deployed for use [18]. During this phase, the system is rigorously tested to identify and resolve any defects, confirm that all components work together as expected, and ensure the system meets both technical and business requirements. The

Testing Phase involves various levels of testing, each serving a specific purpose in validating different aspects of the system. Below is a detailed explanation of the key components of the Testing Phase.

The **Testing Phase** is designed to validate the system operates correctly, meets user requirements, and is free from critical defects. This phase helps ensure the system performs as expected in real-world scenarios and that any issues are addressed before deployment. Testing is performed in multiple stages, each targeting different levels of system functionality, integration, and user expectations.

Unit Testing

Unit Testing is the first level of testing, focusing on individual components or modules of the system. During unit testing, each piece of code is tested independently to ensure that it functions correctly on its own, without interference from other parts of the system. The primary goals of unit testing are to:

- **Verify Functionality**: Ensure each component performs its intended function correctly.
- **Identify Early Defects**: Catch bugs and issues at the earliest stage, making it easier and less costly to fix them before they affect other parts of the system.
- **Isolated Testing**: Test each unit in isolation, without dependency on other system components, to ensure that the logic and algorithms within that unit are sound.

Unit testing is typically performed by developers as they write code and is often automated to allow for continuous validation during the development process.

Integration Testing and Systems Testing

Once individual components have been tested and verified through unit testing, the next step is **Integration Testing** and **Systems Testing**.

- **Integration Testing**: Integration testing focuses on testing the interactions between different components or modules. The goal is to verify that when combined, the components work together as expected. This type of testing helps identify issues related to data flow, communication between modules, and interaction between components that were developed separately. Key objectives include:
    - **Compatibility**: Ensure modules interface correctly with one another and data is passed between them accurately.
    - **Detecting Integration Issues**: Identify any problems that arise when independent modules are combined, such as mismatches in data formats or timing issues.
- **Systems Testing**: Once integration testing is complete, **Systems Testing** evaluates the entire system as a whole. This phase ensures all system components, including hardware, software and network infrastructure, work together as intended. Systems

testing is typically conducted in an environment that closely mirrors the production environment to validate real-world performance. The goals include:

- **End-to-End Functionality**: Ensure the complete system meets all functional and non-functional requirements.
- **Performance Testing**: Assess how the system performs under various conditions, such as high load, stress, or potential failure scenarios.
- **Security Testing**: Identify any vulnerabilities or weaknesses in the system's security controls.

Systems testing is essential for ensuring the system can handle the operational requirements and perform well under expected conditions.

User Acceptance Testing (UAT)

The final stage of the testing phase is **User Acceptance Testing (UAT)**, where end users test the system to ensure that it meets their needs and expectations. UAT focuses on validating the system aligns with the business requirements and that users can perform their tasks effectively using the system. Key aspects of UAT include:

- **Real-World Scenarios**: Users test the system using real-world scenarios to ensure it behaves as expected in their day-to-day operations.
- **Feedback from Users**: UAT provides an opportunity for users to give feedback on the system's functionality, usability, and performance. Any issues or improvements suggested by users are addressed before the system goes live.
- **Final Approval**: UAT serves as the final checkpoint before the system is deployed. Once users confirm the system meets their requirements, the project team can proceed with deployment.

User Acceptance Testing (UAT) is essential to ensure the system satisfies technical requirements while also meeting user needs and expectations.

Importance of the Testing Phase

The **Testing Phase** is one of the most critical stages in the SDLC because it ensures the system functions correctly, is free of major defects, and meets both business and technical requirements. By conducting thorough testing—starting from unit testing and moving through integration, systems, and user acceptance testing—organizations can minimize the risk of system failures, security vulnerabilities, and performance issues post-deployment. Proper testing ensures the system will deliver value to the organization and its users while operating reliably and securely in production.

In conclusion, the **Testing Phase** of the **Systems Development Life Cycle** provides a structured approach to validating the system's functionality, performance, and usability. By conducting

Unit Testing, **Integration and Systems Testing**, and **User Acceptance Testing**, the project team ensures the system is ready for deployment and capable of meeting both technical requirements and user expectations. A comprehensive testing process is essential for delivering a high-quality system supporting organizational goals and provides a positive user experience.

Deployment or Implementation Phase

The **Deployment or Implementation Phase** and **Closing Phase** are the final steps in the **Systems Development Life Cycle (SDLC)**. These phases focus on transitioning the system from development to real-world use and ensuring all project objectives have been met before closing out the project. Below is a detailed explanation of these two phases.

The **Deployment or Implementation Phase** marks the point where the system is made operational and available for use by the end users. This phase is critical because it involves installing the system in a production environment, configuring it to meet operational requirements, and ensuring a smooth transition from development to actual use.

- **System Deployment**: This involves moving the system from the testing environment into the production environment. It may include installing software on servers, configuring network components, and integrating the system with existing technologies. Deployment can be done in phases (staged rollouts) or all at once (big bang approach), depending on the complexity of the system and the organization's risk tolerance.
- **User Training and Support**: During this phase, users are trained to operate the new system. The training program ensures end users understand how to use the system's features and can perform their tasks efficiently. Support teams are also put in place to help users navigate any issues or questions which may arise during the initial use of the system.
- **Data Migration**: In many cases, existing data must be transferred to the new system. This data migration process ensures all relevant information is securely and accurately moved to the new environment, maintaining data integrity and continuity of operations.
- **Post-Deployment Monitoring**: Once the system is deployed, it is monitored to ensure it operates as expected. This monitoring phase helps identify any performance issues, bugs, or user difficulties that might not have been evident during testing. The project team remains engaged during this period to provide fixes or updates as needed.

Deployment is a critical phase because it is the moment when the system goes live. Any issues at this stage could disrupt business operations, so careful planning, coordination, and support are essential to ensuring a successful deployment.

Closing Phase

The **Closing Phase** is the final step of the SDLC, where the project is formally concluded, and the system is transitioned to ongoing support or operational teams. This phase ensures all project objectives have been met, documentation is completed, and lessons learned are captured for future projects.

- **Formal Acceptance**: The project team seeks formal acceptance from the project stakeholders, confirming that the system meets all agreed-upon requirements and deliverables. Once the stakeholders are satisfied, they provide sign-off, officially completing the project.
- **Transfer of Ownership**: In the closing phase, ownership of the system is transferred to the relevant operational or IT teams. This transfer includes the responsibility for ongoing maintenance, support, and any future updates or enhancements. The project team ensures the operational team has all the necessary documentation, including user manuals, system architecture, and troubleshooting guides.
- **Administrative Closure**: This involves completing all remaining administrative tasks, such as finalizing contracts, making any outstanding payments, and ensuring all project-related resources are released or reassigned.
- **Final Project Report**: The project manager compiles a final project report summarizing the overall project performance, highlighting successes, challenges, and any deviations from the original plan. This report is used for future reference and helps improve the organization's project management processes.
- **Lessons Learned**: The project team conducts a post-project review to identify lessons learned. This review focuses on what went well, what could be improved, and any challenges that arose during the project. Documenting these lessons helps the organization refine its processes for future projects and avoid repeating mistakes.
- **Archiving Project Documentation**: All project documentation, including the project plan, requirements, design documents, testing records, and final reports, are archived for future reference. These documents provide a historical record of the project and can be useful for audits, future system upgrades, or similar projects.
- **Disbanding the Project Team**: The final step in the Closing Phase is releasing the project team. Team members are reassigned to new projects or roles, and the project manager ensures all loose ends are tied up before formally closing the project.

The Closing Phase ensures that the project is completed in a structured and formal manner, with no outstanding issues left unresolved. It also helps the organization capture valuable insights and maintain a comprehensive record of the project's lifecycle.

Importance of the Deployment and Closing Phases

The **Deployment or Implementation Phase** and **Closing Phase** are crucial because they ensure the system is fully operational and the project is wrapped up effectively. Successful deployment minimizes operational disruptions, while a thorough closing phase ensures all project goals have been met, and future projects benefit from the lessons learned. These phases complete the SDLC, transitioning the project from development to ongoing operations and support.

In conclusion, the **Deployment or Implementation Phase** and **Closing Phase** are vital to the success of any project within the **Systems Development Life Cycle**. Deployment facilitates the successful introduction of the system to its users, while the Closing Phase marks the formal conclusion of the project, capturing lessons learned and ensuring a seamless transition to operational teams. Together, these phases ensure the system not only meets technical and business requirements but also delivers long-term value to the organization.

Chapter Summary

This chapter on *Strategic Alignment through Project Management* equips business students with an understanding of how organizations ensure their projects and initiatives align with broader strategic goals. It emphasizes the importance of connecting long-term vision with tactical execution, particularly in technology-driven environments. By exploring strategic planning tools, project management frameworks, and the Systems Development Life Cycle (SDLC), the chapter provides a comprehensive guide to managing projects that deliver real value to the organization.

Key Takeaways for Business Students:

1. **Organizational Strategy & Governance**:
   - A clear **Mission Statement** and **Vision Statement** are foundational to an organization's strategic direction.
   - Effective **Operational Planning** and **Information Technology (IT) Governance** ensures that projects are aligned with the organization's overall objectives and regulatory requirements.
   - **Enterprise Content Management (ECM)** supports the organized management and utilization of business information.
2. **Strategic Planning Tools**:
   - Internal and external factors drive organizational decisions. Tools like **SWOT Analysis**, **Porter's Five Forces**, and **PEST Analysis** help identify strengths, weaknesses, market forces, and external risks.
   - The **Balanced Scorecard** provides a multi-perspective approach to performance measurement, ensuring alignment with both financial and operational goals.
   - **High-Level Objectives** and **Implementation Plans** guide organizations toward executing their strategic plans efficiently.
3. **Portfolios, Programs, and Projects**:
   - **Project Management** balances the triple constraints of **Scope**, **Time**, and **Cost** (often referred to as the triple constraints) to deliver successful outcomes.

- **Program Management** ensures that related projects are aligned and managed for maximum benefit, while **Portfolio Management** focuses on selecting and prioritizing the right projects to support organizational goals.
- Tools like the **Business Case**, **Cost-Benefit Analysis**, and **Return on Investment (ROI)** are essential in the **Project Selection Process** for evaluating and choosing the most valuable initiatives.

4. **Project Management Life Cycle**:
   - The project life cycle includes five core phases: **Initiating**, **Planning**, **Executing**, **Monitoring/Controlling**, and **Closing**.
   - **Waterfall** and **Agile** methodologies offer different approaches to project management, with Waterfall providing a linear process and Agile promoting flexibility through iterative releases.
   - Key elements in the **Initiation Phase** include the **Business Case** and **Feasibility Study**, which justify and authorize the project, while the **Planning Phase** covers detailed project documentation such as the **Scope Statement** and **Risk Management Plan.**
5. **Systems Development Life Cycle (SDLC)**:
   - The SDLC ensures that technology systems are developed through a structured process, starting from **Requirements Gathering and Analysis** and moving through **Design**, **Development**, **Testing**, and **Deployment/Implementation**.
   - Tools like **Unified Modeling Language (UML)** and **Entity Relationship Diagrams (ERD)** aid in defining system structures, while **User Acceptance Testing (UAT)** confirms that systems meet user needs before full deployment.
6. **Finalizing Projects**:
   - The **Closing Phase** is crucial for ensuring that project deliverables are transferred to stakeholders, that administrative tasks are completed, and that lessons learned are documented for future reference.
   - **Post-Project Evaluation**, such as gathering feedback and documenting best practices, ensures continuous improvement in project management processes.

By understanding how strategic alignment through project management operates, business students will gain insights into how successful organizations manage their projects to not only deliver on time and within budget but also support long-term organizational goals. These skills are critical for any future business leader, project manager, or strategist.

Discussion Questions

1. Discuss the importance of aligning projects with an organization's mission and vision statements. Identify an organization of your choice and evaluate how well its recent projects reflect its mission and vision.

2. Choose one strategic planning tool discussed in the chapter (e.g., SWOT Analysis, PEST Analysis, or Porter's Five Forces). How does this tool help organizations prioritize projects? Provide an example of a company or industry where this tool is particularly effective.

3. Analyze how the triple constraints of scope, time, and cost impact project outcomes. Reflect on a project you've been involved with and explain how managing these constraints contributed to or detracted from its success.

4. Debate the suitability of the Waterfall methodology versus Agile for different types of projects. What factors should a project manager consider when deciding between the two?

5. How does integrating the Systems Development Life Cycle (SDLC) within a project management framework contribute to project success? Provide an example of a project that required the SDLC and discuss the role of the systems analyst.

Exercises

1. Select a hypothetical project and create a detailed project charter. Include objectives, scope, stakeholders, deliverables, and project authorization.

2. Conduct a SWOT Analysis for a startup in the technology industry. Based on the results, recommend strategic projects the company should prioritize to align with its long-term goals.

3. Using a software tool or a manual template, create a Gantt chart for a project of your choice. Include at least five tasks, dependencies, and milestones. Explain how the chart aids in visualizing the project timeline and managing resources.

4. Develop a Balanced Scorecard for an organization focusing on four perspectives: financial, customer, internal processes, and learning/growth. Identify key performance indicators for each perspective and suggest a project aligned with improving one of these areas.

5. Perform a Porter's Five Forces analysis for an e-commerce company. Identify strategies the company can use to strengthen its market position and discuss how project management can facilitate these strategies.

References

[1] Kickstarter, "About Us: Vision Statement," 2020. [Online]. Available: https://www.kickstarter.com/about.

[2] Microsoft, "Mission and Vision Statement," 2020. [Online]. Available: https://mission-statement.com/google/. [Accessed July 2020].

[3] Tesla, "Tesla Mission and Vision Statement Analysis," 2013. [Online]. Available: https://mission-statement.com/tesla/. [Accessed 2020].

[4] L. Krajewski, J. Malhotra and L. Ritzman, Operations Management: Processes and Supply Chains, Boston, MA: Pearson Education, Inc., 2019.

[5] KathySchwalbe, Information Technology Project Management 9th Edition, Boston, MA: Cengage, 2019.

[6] Aiim, "What is Enterprise Content Management (ECM)?," 2020. [Online]. Available: https://www.aiim.org/What-is-ECM#. [Accessed July 2020].

[7] P. Wallace, Introduction to Information Systems 3rd Edition, Upper Saddle River, New Jersey: Pearson Education, 2018.

[8] W. Commons, Artist, *Porter's Five Forces Model.* [Art]. https://upload.wikimedia.org/wikipedia/commons/6/66/Porters_five_forces.PNG, 2020.

[9] O. Jurevicius., "PEST & PESTEL Analysis.," 13 February 2013. [Online]. Available: https://strategicmanagementinsight.com/tools/pest-pestel-analysis.html. [Accessed July 2020].

[10] J. Post, "What Is a PEST Analysis?," 21 September 2018. [Online]. Available: https://www.businessnewsdaily.com/5512-pest-analysis-definition-examples-templates.html. [Accessed July 2020].

[11] S. Strategies, "Implementing Law Firm Strategy Using a Balanced Scorecard," 30 January 2013. [Online]. Available: http://sterlingstrat.com/implementing-law-firm-strategy-using-a-balanced-scorecard.html. [Accessed July 2020].

[12] PMI, "The Future of Work: Leading the Way with PMTQ.," 2019. [Online]. Available: https://www.pmi.org/-/media/pmi/documents/public/pdf/learning/thought-leadership/pulse/pulse-of-the-profession-2019.pdf. [Accessed July 2020].

[13] K. Tavrizyan, "16 Project Management Stats You Can't Ignore," 2019. [Online]. Available: https://medium.com/crowdbotics/hips-dont-lie-15-project-management-stats-you-can-t-ignore-6f655060ef30. [Accessed July 2020].

[14] V. Paradigm, "Scrum vs Waterfall vs Agile vs Lean vs Kanban," [Online]. Available: https://www.visual-paradigm.com/scrum/scrum-vs-waterfall-vs-agile-vs-lean-vs-kanban/. [Accessed July 2020].

[15] S. White, "What is CMMI? A model for optimizing development processes.," 2018. [Online]. Available: https://www.cio.com/article/2437864/process-improvement-capability-maturity-model-integration-cmmi-definition-and-solutions.html. [Accessed July 2020].

[16] U. o. Waterloo., "Project Management.," n.d.. [Online]. Available: https://uwaterloo.ca/ist-project-management-office/methodologies/project-management. [Accessed July 2020].

[17] V. Paradigm, "Data Flow Diagram with Examples - Vehicle Maintenance Depot," 2015. [Online]. Available: https://www.visual-paradigm.com/tutorials/data-flow-diagram-example-vehicle-maintenance-depot.jsp. [Accessed July 2020].

[18] K. Munot, "Unit Testing- Important role in Software Development," November 2015. [Online]. Available: https://medium.com/nonstopio/unit-testing-important-role-in-software-development-1f52f7c810f8. [Accessed July 2020].

[19] S. Pogue, "18 Best Gantt Chart Software for Project Management in 2020.," 11 January 2020. [Online]. Available: https://www.workzone.com/blog/gantt-chart-software/ . [Accessed July 2020].

[20] W. Wang & J Jiang, "Chapter 13 Plotrix for complex visualizations.," 31 October 2024. [Online]. Available: https://jtr13.github.io/cc19/gantt-charts.html . [Accessed October 2024].

Chapter 3 - Data and Knowledge Management

Overview
In today's rapidly evolving business environment, technology is not merely a tool; it is a strategic organizational asset. This chapter explores how modern organizations leverage cutting-edge technological innovations to optimize operations, improve decision-making, and enhance overall performance. It delves into key concepts such as **big data**, **data lakes**, and the **4Vs of Big Data**—volume, variety, velocity, and veracity—that underscore the vast potential of data in shaping business strategies.

Chapter Learning Objectives

1. Compare and contrast different data sources.
2. Articulate foundational reasons for the growth of "big data" and the challenges associated with it.
3. Differentiate between the Internet of Things and the Industrial Internet of Things.
4. Explain the importance of artificial intelligence and additive manufacturing in today's organizations.
5. Identify the options available for data storage and retrieval.
6. Compare and contrast network types.
7. List the data warehouse process steps.
8. Differentiate between business intelligence and data analytics.

As organizations increasingly rely on connected devices, the rise of the **Internet of Things (IoT)** and its subdomains—**wearables**, the **Industrial Internet of Things (IIoT)**, and **Military Internet of Things (MIoT)**—create digital ecosystems offering unprecedented insights into operational performance. **Artificial intelligence (AI)** further transforms how organizations function by introducing **progressive learning algorithms**, **neural networks**, and various AI forms, such as **reactive machines** and **self-aware AI**. With the integration of **robotics**, **drones**, and **constrained AI**, businesses can redefine their processes and automate complex tasks.

A core component of managing technology lies in the efficient handling of organizational data. This chapter provides a comprehensive look at how **computer networks**, such as **local area networks (LANs)** and **wide area networks (WANs)**, interconnect businesses globally, fostering communication through **URLs**, **HTTP**, and the **World Wide Web (WWW)**. The roles of **network equipment**, from core to edge devices, as well as the debate between **centralized** and **decentralized networks**, are also highlighted.

At the heart of any organization is its ability to manage data effectively. Concepts like **databases**, **SQL**, **transactional data**, and **data warehouses** provide the foundation for understanding how businesses extract actionable insights from raw data through processes like **extract, transform, and load (ETL)**. The chapter also touches on **data mining** and the importance of **scrubbing data** to maintain integrity.
Organizations today rely heavily on **data analytics** and **business intelligence (BI)** to make informed decisions. The chapter examines how **predictive analytics**, **trend analysis**, and tools like **online analytical processing (OLAP)** support **data-driven decision-making**. Through **systems thinking**, **design thinking**, and **critical thinking**, leaders can approach problems from multiple perspectives and drive innovation.

Moreover, the chapter discusses **root cause analysis**, **feedback loops**, and the importance of **troubleshooting** in refining business processes. These problem-solving methodologies guide professionals in pinpointing issues and developing effective solutions.
Finally, the ethical dimension of technology is considered, with a focus on **ethics**, **professional codes of conduct**, and ethical decision-making frameworks. Understanding the ethical implications of technology is crucial for maintaining trust and transparency in both business practices and technological advancements.

By the end of this chapter, readers will grasp how technology serves as a transformative force within organizations, driving efficiency, innovation, and ethical responsibility across every level of operation.

Technology as a Strategic Asset
In the modern business landscape, technology plays a central role in shaping how organizations operate, compete, and innovate. As a strategic asset, technology empowers organizations to harness data, streamline processes, and create more responsive and efficient operations. Key technological advancements such as **big data**, the **Internet of Things (IoT)**, **artificial intelligence (AI)**, and **robotics** provide organizations with tools to analyze vast amounts of information, automate complex tasks, and enhance decision-making. This section delves into the essential technologies that are transforming businesses and enabling them to become more agile and data driven.

Big Data and Data Lakes
Big data refers to the massive volumes of structured and unstructured data generated by organizations, customers, and devices. The ability to collect and analyze big data is critical for organizations looking to gain insights into market trends, customer preferences, and operational efficiencies. The characteristics of big data are commonly summarized as the **4Vs**:

- **Volume**: Refers to the sheer amount of data being collected, which can reach petabytes or even exabytes.

- **Variety**: This includes data from different sources and formats, such as text, images, video, and sensor data.
- **Velocity**: The rate at which data is generated and requires real-time processing to enable timely decision-making.
- **Veracity**: The trustworthiness and accuracy of the data, ensuring that insights drawn from it are reliable.

To manage these large datasets, organizations are increasingly adopting **data lakes**, which store raw data in its native format until it is needed for processing [1]. This approach provides flexibility in how data is accessed and used, allowing for more dynamic and comprehensive analytics [2].

The Internet of Things and Smart Devices

The **Internet of Things (IoT)** is another transformative technology which has expanded the boundaries of data collection and connectivity. IoT refers to the interconnected network of devices—ranging from **smart devices** like smartphones and wearables to industrial equipment—that collect and transmit data over the internet. These devices leave behind **digital trails**, providing organizations with valuable information on usage patterns, performance, and environmental conditions [3] [4].

In particular, the **Industrial Internet of Things (IIoT)** has revolutionized sectors such as manufacturing, logistics, and energy by enabling real-time monitoring of machines and systems, improving operational efficiency, and reducing downtime. Similarly, the **Military Internet of Things (MIoT)** integrates IoT into defense operations, enhancing situational awareness and decision-making capabilities.

Another emerging field is **operational technology (OT)**, which refers to hardware and software identifying or generating changes through the direct systematic monitoring, updating and control of physical devices, processes, and infrastructure. OT is especially relevant in industries like energy, transportation, and manufacturing, where real-time data collection and automation can drive significant improvements in performance and safety.

Artificial Intelligence

Artificial intelligence (AI) is a critical element of organizational resilience and strategy, enabling businesses to leverage machine intelligence to identify and solve complex problems, automate repetitive tasks, and predict future outcomes. AI encompasses a wide range of evolving technologies, from **progressive learning algorithms** to **neural networks**, which mimic the way the human brain processes information [2].

AI can be categorized based on its capabilities:

- **Reactive Machines**: AI systems that can respond to specific inputs but do not retain past experiences. They are typically used for tasks like playing chess or diagnosing diseases. Chess grandmaster Gary Kasparov lost to the supercomputer Deep Blue in 1997, illustrating a significant milestone in machine capabilities.
- **Limited Memory AI**: These systems can use past experiences to inform future actions, such as self-driving cars that learn from previous trips.

Figure 3.1 Chess Match 1997 Kasparov versus Deep Blue [8]

- **Theory of Mind AI**: Still in the experimental phase, this type of AI would understand emotions, thoughts, and beliefs, allowing it to interact more naturally with humans.
- **Self-aware AI**: This represents the future of AI, where machines would have a form of consciousness, enabling them to be truly autonomous.

Machine perception, which allows AI systems to interpret and understand the world through sensors, combined with **predictive analytics**, enables organizations to forecast trends, customer behavior, and potential risks. These AI-driven insights help companies make more informed, data-driven decisions, positioning them for success in competitive markets.

Robotics, Drones, and Constrained AI

Robotics is another area where technology acts as a powerful asset for organizations. Robots are increasingly utilized to carry out repetitive tasks, manage hazardous materials, and operate in environments too risky or inefficient for human presence. In industries like manufacturing, robotics has significantly improved productivity by automating tasks that require precision and consistency.

Drones are another example of technology enabling businesses to operate in new and innovative ways. Drones are used for aerial surveillance, delivery services, and even infrastructure inspections, offering companies an efficient way to gather data and perform tasks in hard-to-reach areas.

Finally, **constrained AI** refers to AI systems designed for a specialized tasks or sets of tasks, rather than the more general intelligence found in advanced AI models. These constrained systems are highly effective in their areas of specialization, offering solutions that are often more practical and cost-effective for businesses looking to automate or optimize specific processes [9].

In conclusion, technology as an organizational asset is no longer just a support function—it is central to driving innovation, efficiency, and competitive advantage. Whether through big data, IoT, AI, or robotics, organizations today have an array of powerful tools at their disposal to transform the way they operate and achieve their strategic goals [10]. Understanding how to harness these technologies effectively is key to remaining agile and forward-thinking in the face of rapid technological advancement.

Organizational Data Management

Effective data management is at the core of modern organizations, enabling them to store, process, and analyze the vast amounts of data they collect. In a digital economy, managing organizational data involves a range of technologies and systems that ensure seamless data flow, accessibility, and security across networks, databases, and business processes. This section explores the foundational concepts and infrastructure supporting data management, while covering topics such as computer networks, databases, and advanced data analytics techniques.

Computer Networks and Types

Computer networks form the backbone of data management by connecting devices and systems, allowing information to be shared and accessed efficiently. Networks are broadly classified into three primary types:

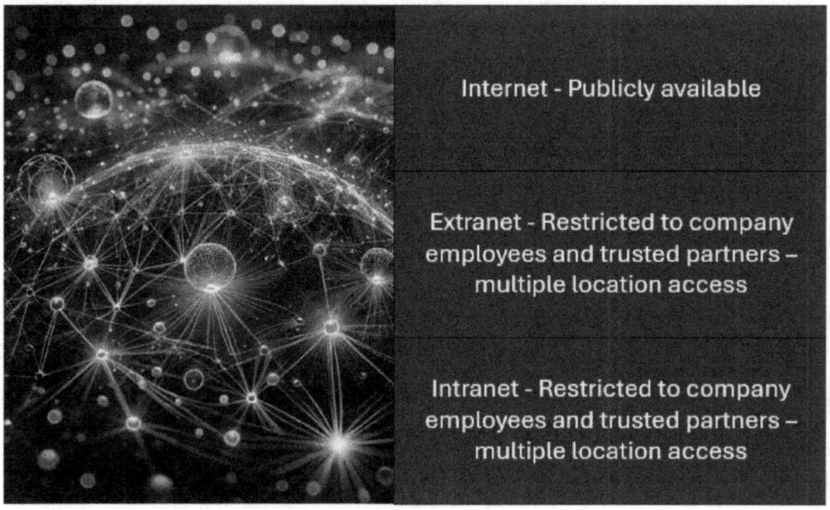

Figure 3.2 Network Types

- **Internet**: The global network that connects billions of devices worldwide, enabling access to vast resources such as websites, cloud services, and online databases.
- **Intranets**: Private networks within an organization that allow employees to securely share information, collaborate on projects, and access internal resources.
- **Extranets**: Secure networks that extend the intranet to external partners, vendors, or customers, allowing for controlled access to specific organizational data or services [12].

Two commonly used network structures are the **local area network (LAN)**, which connects devices within a specific, limited area (like a building), and the **wide area network (WAN)**, which connects devices over larger geographical areas, such as cities or countries. **Campus Area Networks (CANs)** interconnect multiple local area networks (LANs) within a defined campus area, such as a university, corporate campus, or industrial complex, facilitating efficient data exchange and resource sharing across multiple buildings within the campus. Organizations often use a mix of these network types to ensure efficient communication and data exchange, both internally and externally [11].

Key Internet Technologies

Several essential technologies enable data to move seamlessly across networks. **URLs (Uniform Resource Locators)** serve as the addresses that identify web resources, while **HTTP (Hypertext Transfer Protocol)** is the protocol used to transmit data over the internet. The **World Wide Web (WWW)** is the system of interlinked hypertext documents users can access through web browsers. **Portals**, which are user interfaces that aggregate and present information from different sources, are often used by organizations to provide employees, customers, or partners with a unified view of data and applications.

Network Equipment and Segmentation

To support these networks, organizations rely on various **network equipment types**, including routers, switches, firewalls, and gateways, each serving specific roles in directing traffic, securing the network, and managing data flow [13].

Networks are often segmented into different layers, from **core devices**, which are central to the network infrastructure, to **edge devices**, which include the devices users directly interact with, such as computers, smartphones, or IoT devices. Segmenting a network into Virtual Local Area Networks (VLANs) help enhance security, improve performance, and simplify management [14].

Centralized versus Decentralized Networks

Organizations must decide whether to adopt a **centralized** or **decentralized** network architecture. In a centralized network, all data and services are managed from a single location, offering greater control but potentially creating bottlenecks. In contrast, a decentralized network spreads data and services across multiple locations, increasing redundancy and resilience but requiring more complex management. The choice between these architectures depends on factors such as the size of the organization, its geographic distribution, and its security requirements.

Databases and Data Management Systems

Databases are critical for storing and managing organizational data in structured formats. They consist of **tables** made up of rows and columns, where **attributes** (or fields) define the types of data that can be stored, and **records** represent individual entries [15][16]. The structure of databases is maintained using **relational databases**, which use relationships between tables to efficiently manage and retrieve data [2]. Key elements in relational databases include:

- **Primary keys**: Unique identifiers for each record in a table.
- **Joins**: Methods for combining data from multiple tables based on a related column.

Organizations often use **Database Management Systems (DBMS)** to handle their databases. A **DBMS** ensures data is structured, searchable, and accessible [16]. It provides tools for data storage, retrieval, and management, allowing organizations to maintain data integrity and security. **Database administrators (DBAs)** are responsible for overseeing the performance, security, and availability of databases.

SQL and Data Queries

Structured Query Language (SQL) is the standard language used to interact with relational databases [16]. SQL allows users to create, retrieve, update, and delete data stored in databases. Some common SQL queries include:

- **SELECT**: Retrieves specific data from a table.
- **INSERT**: Adds new data into a table.
- **UPDATE**: Modifies existing data within a table.
- **DELETE**: Removes data from a table.

SQL's simplicity and power make it an essential tool for data analysis, enabling organizations to generate insights by querying their data in highly customizable ways.

Advanced Data Management Concepts

In addition to traditional databases, organizations often deal with complex, large-scale data systems. **Data mining** is a process used to discover patterns, correlations, and trends in large datasets, while **transactional data** refers to data generated from everyday transactions such as sales, payments, or inventory movements.

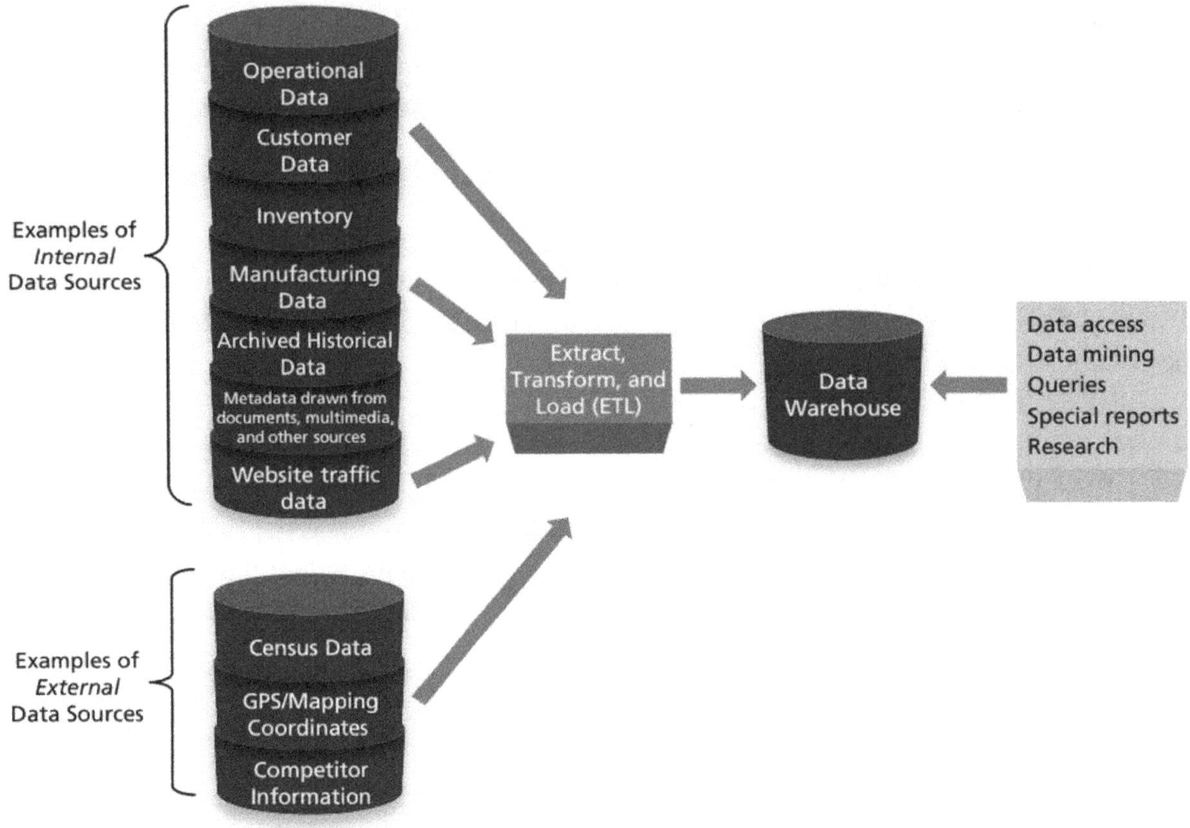

Figure 3.3 Data Warehouse [2]

To manage massive datasets, organizations use **data warehouses**, which store large amounts of historical data for analysis and reporting. **Transaction processing systems** capture transactional data in real-time, supporting day-to-day operations. A fundamental process in data management is ETL (**Extract, Transform, and Load**), which entails extracting data from multiple sources, converting it into a usable format, and loading it into a data warehouse.

Scrubbing Data and Data Marts

Scrubbing data (or data cleansing) ensures that data is accurate, complete, and free from errors. This process is vital for maintaining the quality and reliability of data used for analysis. **Data marts** are subsets of data warehouses which focus on specific business areas or departments, providing a streamlined view of the most relevant data for certain users [16].

Supercomputers and High-Performance Data Processing

For organizations requiring the processing of exceptionally large datasets or complex algorithms, **supercomputers** provide the computing power needed to handle these tasks. Supercomputers are often used for advanced data analytics, simulations, and other high-performance applications, particularly in industries such as finance, healthcare, and scientific research [17].

In summary, organizational data management is a multifaceted discipline that integrates a wide range of technologies to ensure data is effectively captured, stored, and used. By leveraging the right combination of networks, databases, and analytics tools, organizations can unlock valuable insights, drive new innovations, and maintain a competitive edge in an increasingly data-driven world. Understanding how to manage data efficiently is crucial for any organization looking to thrive in today's digital economy [18].

Business Intelligence and Data Analytics

In today's technology-driven world, organizations rely heavily on **business intelligence (BI)** and **data analytics** to gain insights, make informed decisions, and stay competitive. These tools and methodologies allow businesses to transform raw data into meaningful and actionable insights, helping them to anticipate trends, optimize operations, and solve complex problems. This section explores the critical components of business intelligence and data analytics, including their definitions, challenges, and techniques for leveraging data to drive decision-making.

Business Intelligence – Definition and Challenges

Business intelligence (BI) refers to the technologies, tools, and strategies organizations use to collect, analyze, and present business information. BI systems provide a comprehensive view of a company's data, enabling decision-makers to understand past performance, monitor current operations, and make more informed strategic choices [19]. The goal of BI is to improve the quality of decision-making by providing accurate, timely, and actionable insights.

However, implementing and maintaining BI systems comes with several challenges:

- **Data Integration**: Organizations often struggle to combine data from multiple sources, including legacy systems, third-party applications, and cloud-based platforms.
- **Data Quality**: Poor data quality—such as incomplete, inconsistent, or inaccurate data—can undermine the value of BI.
- **User Adoption**: Ensuring employees across all levels of the organization understand how to use BI tools and interpret the insights is crucial for success.

Data-Driven Decision Making

One of the core benefits of business intelligence is facilitating **data-driven decision-making (DDD)**, where decisions are based on data analysis rather than intuition or guesswork [21]. By relying on data, organizations can reduce uncertainty, minimize risks, and ensure strategies are backed by factual evidence. Data-driven decision-making empowers businesses to:

- Identify trends and patterns in customer behavior, market shifts, or operational performance.
- Forecast future outcomes with greater accuracy.
- Allocate resources more efficiently.

Data Analytics – Goals

Data analytics goes beyond BI by applying statistical and computational techniques to identify hidden patterns, relationships, and insights within data. The main goals of data analytics include:

- **Understanding historical trends**: Analyzing past data to identify trends and factors influencing business outcomes.
- **Improving decision-making**: Providing insights to enable more effective decision-making at strategic, tactical, and operational levels.
- **Optimizing processes**: Identifying inefficiencies in business operations and developing data-driven solutions for improvement.
- **Predicting future outcomes**: Using predictive models to anticipate future trends and behaviors.

Trend Analysis

Trend analysis is a key component of data analytics that involves examining data over time to identify patterns or shifts. Organizations use trend analysis to understand changes in customer preferences, market dynamics, or operational performance. This approach enables businesses to adapt and evolve their strategies proactively rather than reactively, gaining a competitive edge.

Correlation and Causation Analysis

Correlation analysis examines the relationships between variables, helping organizations understand how different factors might be linked. However, correlation does not imply causation—just because two variables move together does not mean one causes the other. To make sound decisions, organizations must differentiate between correlation and **causation**, ensuring they don't draw incorrect conclusions from their data. For example, a correlation between high sales and increased social media engagement may indicate a relationship, but deeper analysis is needed to confirm if one drives the other.

Predictive Analytics

Predictive analytics leverages historical data, statistical models, and machine learning techniques to anticipate future outcomes. By identifying patterns in past behavior, predictive models can help organizations anticipate customer demand, detect potential risks, and optimize their operations. Common applications of predictive analytics include:

- Sales forecasting
- Risk management
- Customer retention strategies

Predictive analytics enables businesses to make forward-looking decisions and stay ahead of potential challenges.

Online Analytical Processing (OLAP)

Online Analytical Processing (OLAP) is a technology allowing users to interactively analyze multidimensional data from various perspectives. OLAP systems enable quick querying and reporting of large datasets, helping decision-makers understand complex data through detailed views and summaries. With OLAP, organizations can:

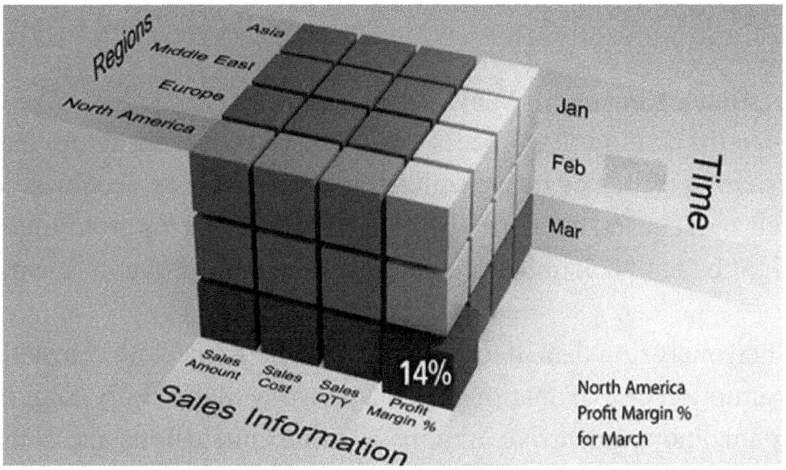

Figure 3.4. Graphical Representation of OLAP [20]

- Drill down into data for granular insights.
- Slice and dice data to view it from different dimensions (e.g., time, region, product line).
- Aggregate data for summary reporting.

OLAP is especially valuable for organizations needing to analyze large datasets in real time, supporting quick and flexible decision-making.

Decision-Making with Data

At the heart of both business intelligence and data analytics is the ability to make **data-informed decisions**. Effective decision-making requires more than just data; it also involves **critical thinking**, **systems thinking**, and **design thinking** approaches:

- **Critical thinking**: Involves questioning assumptions, evaluating evidence, and reasoning through complex problems. In the context of data, it requires analyzing the accuracy, relevance, and implications of the data being used [21].
- **Systems thinking**: Looks at the organization as an ecosystem where changes create other impacts within the connected system. Systems thinking helps decision-makers understand the broader context and consider the ripple effects of their choices [16].
- **Design thinking**: A problem-solving approach focusing on comprehension of user's needs to create innovative and impactful solutions. By combining creativity with data analysis, organizations can develop strategies that are both data-driven and customer-centric.

Root Cause Analysis and Workarounds

In problem-solving, identifying the **root cause** of an issue is essential for implementing lasting solutions. **Root cause analysis (RCA)** helps organizations trace problems back to their origin, preventing recurrence. When an immediate solution is not possible, organizations often rely on

workarounds—temporary measures to address the symptoms of a problem until the root cause can be fully resolved.

Feedback Loops and Working Hypotheses

A **feedback loop** is a process where the results of an action or decision are fed back into the system to influence future actions. In data analytics, feedback loops help organizations refine their models and strategies by continuously learning from outcomes. For instance, sales data might be fed back into a predictive model to improve its accuracy over time.

When analyzing data, decision-makers often start with a **working hypothesis**—an initial assumption or explanation tested against the data. By testing and refining hypotheses, organizations can arrive at more accurate conclusions and solutions.

Troubleshooting

Troubleshooting is a problem-solving process that involves diagnosing and resolving issues systematically. In the context of business intelligence and data analytics, troubleshooting might involve investigating data anomalies, resolving system errors, or addressing performance bottlenecks in data processing. The ability to quickly identify and address issues is crucial for maintaining the reliability and accuracy of BI and analytics systems [16].

In summary, business intelligence and data analytics are vital tools for organizations seeking to leverage data for better decision-making. By understanding how to collect, analyze, and interpret data, businesses can uncover valuable insights, optimize operations, and anticipate future trends. The integration of critical thinking, systems thinking, and design thinking ensures data-driven strategies are not only effective but also aligned with the broader organizational context. Ultimately, the ability to make informed, data-driven decisions is what enables businesses to thrive in a dynamic and competitive environment.

Ethics in Technology

As technology becomes increasingly integrated into every aspect of business and society, the importance of ethical considerations in its development, implementation, and use has grown significantly. Organizations must navigate complex ethical landscapes to ensure technology is used responsibly, with attention to its potential impact on individuals, communities, and the environment [22]. This section explores the concept of ethics in technology, key ethical models, and professional codes of conduct that guide responsible behavior in the technological sphere.

Definition of Ethics

Ethics refers to the principles and standards that govern an individual's or organization's behavior, determining what is right and wrong in a given context. In the realm of technology,

ethics focuses on the responsible use of technology, taking into account the rights, privacy, and well-being of all stakeholders affected by technological advancements.
In essence, ethics in technology asks critical questions such as:

- **Is this technology being used in a way that benefits society?**
- **Does it respect the rights and privacy of individuals?**
- **What are the potential unintended consequences of this technology, and how can they be mitigated?**

Ethical considerations ensure technology serves humanity rather than exploiting or harming it. The broader the impact of a technology—such as artificial intelligence, surveillance systems, or genetic engineering—the more critical it is to carefully evaluate its ethical implications.

Ethical Model Examples
Several **ethical models** can be applied to technology, each offering different perspectives on what constitutes ethical behavior. Here are a few prominent models:

1. **Utilitarianism**: This ethical framework focuses on maximizing overall happiness or benefit while minimizing harm. In technology, utilitarianism would advocate for the development and use of systems that provide the greatest good for the largest number of people. For instance, when designing an AI algorithm for healthcare, a utilitarian approach would seek to optimize patient outcomes while minimizing potential risks or biases.
2. **Deontology**: Deontological ethics emphasize duty and adherence to rules or principles, regardless of the outcomes. In technology, this might involve adhering to strict data privacy regulations, even if it means limiting the efficiency or profitability of a system. A deontological approach prioritizes actions which are inherently right or wrong, such as ensuring that algorithms do not discriminate against certain groups of people, even if it leads to more complex system designs.
3. **Virtue Ethics**: This model focuses on the moral character of the individuals or organizations involved, rather than the outcomes of their actions. In the context of technology, virtue ethics would encourage developers, engineers, and decision-makers to embody virtues such as honesty, fairness, and accountability in their work. For instance, a tech company valuing transparency might disclose how user data is being used and seek informed consent before collecting it.
4. **Rights-Based Ethics**: This model is centered on respecting and protecting the inherent rights of individuals, such as the right to privacy, autonomy, and freedom from harm. In technology, this approach requires systems and applications to be designed with a focus on safeguarding user rights, such as ensuring robust security measures to prevent data breaches or allowing users to control how their data is collected and used.
5. **Social Contract Theory**: This model suggests that ethical behavior arises from the implicit agreements individuals and organizations make with society to promote social welfare. In the technological world, this might mean adhering to societal expectations of

fairness, safety, and accountability. For example, tech companies that develop autonomous vehicles must ensure their safety protocols and implementations meet societal standards and that they responsibly address any accidents or malfunctions.

Ethics and Professional Codes of Conduct Examples

To ensure ethical behavior is consistently applied in the tech industry, many organizations and professional bodies have established **codes of conduct** that set out guidelines and standards for ethical practice. These codes provide a clear framework for professionals working in technology fields, ensuring that their actions align with the broader ethical principles and values of their industry. Some examples of professional codes of conduct in technology include:

1. **The ACM Code of Ethics and Professional Conduct**: Developed by the Association for Computing Machinery (ACM), this code provides guidelines for computing professionals to follow ethical practices in areas like data privacy, intellectual property, and system reliability. It emphasizes the importance of contributing to society, avoiding harm, and respecting the rights of individuals affected by computing technologies.
2. **IEEE Code of Ethics**: The Institute of Electrical and Electronics Engineers (IEEE) provides a code of ethics governing the behavior of its members, particularly those involved in engineering and technology development. The IEEE Code stresses the importance of honesty, fairness, and public welfare, urging professionals to disclose risks, avoid conflicts of interest, and prioritize the safety and well-being of society.
3. **The Data Protection Code of Conduct (GDPR)**: In response to growing concerns about data privacy, the European Union's General Data Protection Regulation (GDPR) establishes a legal and ethical framework for how organizations should handle personal data. This code ensures individuals' rights to privacy are respected and protected by requiring transparency in data collection and storage practices and enforces strict penalties for non-compliance.
4. **Code of Ethics for AI Researchers**: As artificial intelligence grows in influence, there are increasing calls for AI researchers and developers to adhere to ethical guidelines promoting fairness, transparency, and accountability in AI systems. For instance, ethical codes for AI may require algorithms to be explainable and free from bias, ensuring they do not perpetuate discrimination or harm vulnerable groups.

These codes of conduct help shape ethical standards in the technology sector, providing a foundation for responsible innovation and reinforcing the notion technology should advance human well-being.

Conclusion

As technology continues to evolve, organizations and individuals must remain vigilant about its ethical implications. Understanding and applying ethical principles in technology helps to ensure that innovation serves the greater good while respecting individual rights and societal values. Through the application of ethical models and adherence to professional codes of conduct, businesses and technologists can navigate the complexities of modern technology with integrity, ensuring that their actions contribute positively to both their organizations and society at large. Ethics in technology is not a static concept but an ongoing conversation, continually evolving in response to the challenges and opportunities that new technologies present.

Chapter Summary

This chapter explored how organizations can strategically leverage technological advancements to drive operational efficiency, improve decision-making, and maintain a competitive edge in the digital era. The chapter highlights the pivotal role technology plays in transforming businesses and shaping their strategic initiatives through cutting-edge innovations such as big data, the Internet of Things (IoT), artificial intelligence (AI), and robotics.

Key Takeaways:

1. **Big Data and Data Lakes**: Organizations today deal with massive volumes of data, both structured and unstructured. The **4Vs of Big Data—volume**, **variety**, **velocity**, and **veracity**—represent the challenges and opportunities of processing and analyzing this data. **Data lakes** allow organizations to store large datasets in their raw format, providing flexibility and scalability for real-time analytics.
2. **Internet of Things (IoT)**: IoT connects smart devices, wearables, industrial equipment, and military technologies, creating digital ecosystems that offer unparalleled insights into operational performance and decision-making. The rise of **Industrial Internet of Things (IIoT)** and **Military Internet of Things (MIoT)** has revolutionized sectors like manufacturing and defense, enhancing efficiency, safety, and intelligence gathering.
3. **Artificial Intelligence (AI)**: AI empowers organizations to solve complex problems and automate tasks through **machine learning**, **neural networks**, and **predictive analytics**. Different AI models—**Reactive Machines**, **Limited Memory AI**, **Theory of Mind**, and **Self-aware AI**—enable businesses to tailor AI capabilities to their needs. AI helps predict customer behavior, optimize processes, and improve decision-making through real-time data analysis.
4. **Robotics, Drones, and Constrained AI**: **Robotics** and **drones** are used across industries for tasks ranging from manufacturing automation to infrastructure inspections, while **Constrained AI** is designed for specific tasks, making it a cost-effective solution for many businesses. These technologies allow organizations to operate efficiently in hazardous or hard-to-reach environments and improve productivity by automating repetitive tasks.
5. **Organizational Data Management**: Effective management of organizational data is critical for maintaining seamless operations. **Computer networks**, such as LANs and WANs, connect devices and enable data sharing, while **databases** store and organize this data. Tools like **SQL** help in querying and retrieving valuable information from relational

databases, and processes like **data mining, ETL (Extract, Transform, and Load)**, and **scrubbing data** ensures data quality and integrity.

6. **Business Intelligence (BI) and Data Analytics**: BI and data analytics provide the foundation for **data-driven decision-making**, allowing organizations to turn raw data into actionable insights. By leveraging **predictive analytics**, **trend analysis**, and **online analytical processing (OLAP)**, businesses can forecast trends, optimize performance, and remain agile in a competitive market. Critical thinking, systems thinking, and design thinking help leaders address problems from multiple angles and develop innovative solutions.
7. **Ethics in Technology**: As technology becomes more pervasive, ethical considerations grow in importance. Organizations must apply ethical frameworks—such as **utilitarianism**, **deontology**, and **virtue ethics**—to ensure that technology is used responsibly and in a way that benefits society. Adhering to professional **codes of conduct**, such as the **ACM Code of Ethics** and **GDPR regulations**, helps ensure transparency, fairness, and accountability in technological practices.

Technology is no longer a mere operational tool—it is a vital organizational asset enabling businesses to innovate, adapt, evolve, compete, and grow in a rapidly evolving digital world. From leveraging big data and IoT to employing AI and robotics, businesses can enhance decision-making, automate complex processes, and stay ahead of industry trends. However, organizations must also prioritize ethical considerations, ensuring that their technological innovations align with societal values and professional standards. By understanding how to effectively manage and harness these technologies, businesses can position themselves for sustained success in a data-driven economy.

Discussion Questions

1. The chapter introduces the 4Vs of big data: volume, variety, velocity, and veracity. Which of these characteristics do you think organizations struggle with the most when leveraging data for strategic decision-making, and why? Can you suggest solutions to overcome these challenges?

2. The Internet of Things (IoT) has expanded into various industries through devices like wearables, industrial equipment, and military technologies. Identify two specific use cases of IoT in industries and discuss how these applications improve operational efficiency and decision-making.

3. AI models such as reactive machines and limited memory AI serve distinct purposes. Which type of AI would you prioritize for a startup looking to automate customer service? Justify your choice based on the startup's potential needs and resources.

4. Ethical considerations in data management are critical for ensuring transparency and trust. Discuss how the principles of utilitarianism or rights-based ethics might guide decision-making in an organization deploying AI-driven customer profiling tools.

5. Compare the benefits and drawbacks of centralized and decentralized network architectures for a multinational corporation. Which architecture would you recommend, and why?

Exercises

1. Research a company that uses AI to drive its operations. Prepare a short analysis highlighting how the company uses AI to solve problems or create value. Include at least one ethical consideration related to the use of AI.

2. Imagine you are tasked with introducing IoT into a logistics company to optimize fleet operations. Create a proposal outlining the steps for integrating IoT devices, the anticipated benefits, and potential risks.

3. Using a free data visualization tool or software (e.g., Tableau Public or Excel), create a chart to display data trends for a hypothetical retail company. Your chart should highlight how volume, variety, and velocity impact business operations. Include a brief explanation of your findings.

4. Design a hands-on exercise where participants identify the root cause of a declining customer retention rate in a case study company. Use a feedback loop model to propose actionable solutions.

5. Draft a code of conduct for developers working on an AI project. Your framework should address fairness, transparency, accountability, and privacy. Provide examples of how each principle could be implemented.

References

[1] Bryner, J. (2020, March 13). 1st Known case of coronavirus traced back to November in China. Retrieved from: https://www.livescience.com/first-case-coronavirus-found.html

[2] NIST. (2011, March). Special Publication 800-39: Managing Information Security Risk. [PDF].

[3] Jaeger, J. (2019, December 30). Top 10 Risk to Keep Executives on their Toes in 2020. *Compliance Week.* Retrieved from https://www.complianceweek.com/risk-management/top-10-risks-to-keep-executives-on-their-toes-in-2020/28239.article

[4] Usmani, F. (2020, February). Risk Appetite, Risk Tolerance, and Risk Threshold. PM Study Circle. Retrieved from https://pmstudycircle.com/2014/05/risk-appetite-risk-tolerance-and-risk-threshold/

[5] Fazlida, M. R., & Said, J. (2015, April). Information Security: Risk, Governance and Implementation Setback. Paper presented at the proceedings of the Financial Criminology, 2015 7th International Conference, Oxford, UK. doi: 10.1016/S2212-5671(15)01106-5

[6] Pearson, T. (n.d.). OODA. How to Turn Uncertainty into Opportunity. Retrieved from https://taylorpearson.me/ooda-loop/#Why_is_the_OODA_loop_so_important

[7] Fulford, M. (2018, April). How a RACI Matrix can Enhance Your Risk Management Program. *Ballast.* Retrieved from https://ballastsecure.com/resource/how-a-raci-matrix-can-enhance-your-risk-management-program/

[8] Jameel, S. (2017, September 22). Privilege Creep: Prevention & Correction. Retrieved from https://cgscomputer.com/privilege-creep-prevention-correction/

[9] Purcell, J. E. (n.d.). Secure coding. Practical Steps to Defend Your Web Apps. SANS. Retrieved from https://software-security.sans.org/resources/paper/cissp/employee-management-security-controls

[10] Mikkelson, D. (2001, February 22). The Salami Embezzlement Technique. Snopes. Retrieved from https://www.snopes.com/fact-check/the-salami-technique/

[11] Johnson, A. & Ludema, J. (2018, June 5). Three Reasons Your Company Should Make Vacation Mandatory. Forbes. Retrieved from https://www.forbes.com/sites/amberjohnson-jimludema/2018/06/05/three-reasons-your-company-should-make-vacation-mandatory/#39ea7b5238ec

[12] PCI Certificate. (2015, April 23). Dual Control or Segregation of Duties? PCI DSS. Retrieved from https://www.pcicertificate.com/dual-control-or-segregation-of-duties/

[13] Behr, A. & Coleman, K. (2017, August 3). Separation of Duties and IT Security. CSO Online. Retrieved from https://www.csoonline.com/article/2123120/separation-of-duties-and-it-security.html

[14] Struck, M. (2018, April 16). HR Risk Management – Top 8 Sources of Human Resource Risk. [Web log post]. Retrieved from http://blog.treadstonerisk.com/hr-risk-management-top-8-sources-of-human-resource-risk

[15] Donaldson, C. (2009, November 3). Human Factors: How to Manage People Risk in your Business. Finance. Retrieved from https://finance.nine.com.au/small-business/human-factors-how-to-manage-people-risk-in-your-business/65eaed43-07b4-41af-8429-374eac6d3115
[16] NIST. (n.d.). Computer Security Resource Center. Retrieved from https://csrc.nist.gov/glossary/term/vulnerability
[17] Tech Plan Inc. Environmental Threats to Your Data Center. [Web log post]. Retrieved from https://techplaninc.com/environmental-threats-to-your-data-center/
[18] Tripp Lite. (n.d.). The Five Main Power Problems. Retrieved from https://www.tripplite.com/support/common-power-problems
[19] Fire Line. (2014, December 30). 4 Types of Sprinkler Systems. [Web log post]. Retrieved from https://www.fireline.com/blog/4-types-fire-sprinkler-systems/
[20] NIST. (2013, April). Special Publication 800-53: Security and Privacy Controls for Federal Information Systems and Organizations (Rev. 4). [PDF].
[21] Christiansen, B. (2018, August 10). MTTR, MTBF, or MTTF? – A Simple Guide to Failure Metrics. Limble. Retrieved from https://limblecmms.com/blog/mttr-mtbf-mttf-guide-to-failure-metrics/
[22] Mizoguchi, T. (2012). Information Technology Risks in Today's Environment. Retrieved from https://chapters.theiia.org/san-diego/Documents/Seminars/SD_IIA___ISACA_Event_041112_Deloitte_IA_Top_Ten_Risks.pdf

Unit 1 Key Terms

Actor

- **Definition:** A component of a **use case diagram** that represents the roles users play as they interact with a system. These users can be individuals, other systems, or external devices.
- **Purpose:** Helps visualize who or what interacts with the system and defines the functionality required to meet their needs.

Agile Project Management Methodology

- **Definition:** A flexible project management approach that delivers work in **iterative releases** rather than a single final deliverable.
- **Purpose:** Promotes adaptability and continuous improvement, often used in software development to ensure frequent delivery of value.

Application Systems

- **Definition:** Software solutions that support **core business processes** like payroll, human resources, and marketing.
- **Purpose:** Enables organizations to streamline operations and maintain efficiency in their primary functions.

Artificial Intelligence (AI)

- **Definition:** A branch of computer science dedicated to creating systems that can perform tasks requiring **human intelligence**, such as problem-solving and decision-making.
- **Purpose:** Enhances automation, analytics, and user interactions across industries.

Attributes

- **Definition:** Characteristics that define an **entity**, such as name, size, or location.
- **Purpose:** Provides detailed descriptions and distinctions for entities within a system.

Balanced Scorecard

- **Definition:** A performance management tool that evaluates an organization's operations and functions from a balanced perspective, including financial, customer, internal processes, and growth dimensions.
- **Purpose:** Helps organizations align activities to strategic goals and measure progress effectively.

Baseline

- **Definition:** A fixed reference point in a **project plan**, defining the original scope, budget, and schedule.
- **Purpose:** Serves as a benchmark to measure project progress and manage changes.

Big Data

- **Definition:** Vast volumes of unstructured data in various formats collected from diverse sources like social media and sensors.
- **Purpose:** Provides valuable insights when processed and analyzed using advanced data analytics techniques.

Blockchain

- **Definition:** A decentralized and digitized ledger used to record transactions, commonly associated with **cryptocurrency**.
- **Purpose:** Ensures transparency, security, and immutability in digital transactions.

Business Analyst

- **Definition:** A professional who identifies business needs, gathers requirements, and acts as a bridge between technical teams and user departments.
- **Purpose:** Ensures that technology solutions align with business objectives.

Business Case

- **Definition:** A formal document presenting the justification, scope, and expected benefits of a project.
- **Purpose:** Provides stakeholders with a clear rationale for investment.

Business Intelligence (BI)

- **Definition:** The use of accurate, actionable information by decision-makers to support **effective decision-making**.
- **Purpose:** Enables organizations to identify trends, make informed decisions, and achieve competitive advantages.

Centralized

- **Definition:** An IT structure where all computing resources are managed from a central location.
- **Purpose:** Simplifies management and enhances resource efficiency but may reduce flexibility for individual departments.

Charter

- **Definition:** A formal document that authorizes the start of a project.
- **Purpose:** Defines project scope, objectives, and stakeholder responsibilities.

Chief Information Officer (CIO)

- **Definition:** The executive responsible for aligning IT strategies with organizational goals.
- **Purpose:** Ensures IT operations contribute to the organization's success.

Chief Information Security Officer (CISO)

- **Definition:** The executive in charge of securing information assets and technologies.

- **Purpose:** Protects the organization from cybersecurity threats and ensures compliance with regulations.

Chief Knowledge Officer (CKO)

- **Definition:** An executive responsible for maximizing the value of organizational knowledge.
- **Purpose:** Drives innovation and efficiency through effective knowledge management.

Chief Security Officer (CSO)

- **Definition:** The executive responsible for protecting an organization's physical and digital assets.
- **Purpose:** Oversees data security, risk management, and regulatory compliance.

Chief Technology Officer (CTO)

- **Definition:** The executive responsible for monitoring and adopting emerging technologies.
- **Purpose:** Ensures the organization remains competitive through technological innovation.

Client

- **Definition:** A device that requests services or resources from a more powerful **server** in a **client-server model**.
- **Purpose:** Separates user interfaces from centralized computing power.

Client-Server Model

- **Definition:** A computing architecture that divides tasks between a **client** (interface) and a **server** (processing).
- **Purpose:** Balances workloads and improves efficiency in distributed systems.

Closing Phase

- **Definition:** The final phase of the project lifecycle, focusing on documentation, obtaining signoff, and disbanding the project team.
- **Purpose:** Ensures the project is formally completed and lessons learned are documented.

Cloud

- **Definition:** A global network of servers providing scalable resources like storage, computing, and networking.
- **Purpose:** Enables on-demand access to IT resources without the need for local infrastructure.

Code of Conduct

- **Definition:** A formal policy outlining expected behaviors for managing and handling data.
- **Purpose:** Promotes ethical and secure data management practices.

Connected Consumers

- **Definition:** Digitally engaged customers who research, interact with, and provide feedback on products or services.
- **Purpose:** Highlights the importance of delivering consistent and engaging digital experiences.

Cost-Benefit Analysis

- **Definition:** A financial assessment comparing the costs and benefits of a project.
- **Purpose:** Determines whether a project is economically viable.

Critical Thinking

- **Definition:** The objective evaluation of factual evidence to guide decisions.
- **Purpose:** Improves problem-solving and decision-making.

Cryptocurrency

- **Definition:** A digital asset used for financial transactions, often secured by **blockchain** technology.
- **Purpose:** Enables decentralized and secure digital payments.

Customer Relationship Management (CRM)

- **Definition:** Systems designed to manage and enhance interactions with customers.
- **Purpose:** Improves sales, marketing, and customer service effectiveness.

Data

- **Definition:** Raw characters and numbers collected for processing.
- **Purpose:** Forms the basis for information and decision-making.

Data Analytics

- **Definition:** The process of examining data to uncover patterns and insights.
- **Purpose:** Supports faster, more informed decision-making.

Data-Driven Decision Making (DDDM)

- **Definition:** The practice of basing decisions on factual data rather than intuition.
- **Purpose:** Enhances accuracy and reduces biases in decision-making.

Data Flow Diagram (DFD)

- **Definition:** A diagram showing how data moves through a system.
- **Purpose:** Visualizes system processes and their interactions.

Data Lake

- **Definition:** A repository for storing large volumes of unstructured data in its raw format.
- **Purpose:** Provides a foundation for advanced analytics and machine learning.

Data Mart

- **Definition:** A subset of a data warehouse focusing on a specific business area.
- **Purpose:** Facilitates faster and more targeted data access for specific functions.

Data Mining

- **Definition:** A process used to analyze large datasets to uncover patterns, relationships, and insights that can be useful for decision-making or strategic planning.
- **Purpose:** Helps organizations turn raw data into actionable information, such as identifying customer trends or optimizing business operations.

Data Modeling

- **Definition:** An analytical process that determines the optimal way to structure and store data for efficient storage and retrieval.
- **Purpose:** Ensures that databases are designed for scalability, accuracy, and ease of access, enabling effective data management.

Data Repository

- **Definition:** A centralized infrastructure used to collect, manage, and store datasets for analysis, sharing, and reporting.
- **Purpose:** Provides a secure and accessible environment for managing large volumes of data, often used in big data analytics.

Data Warehouse

- **Definition:** A specialized system designed for storing key organizational data, optimized for reporting and analysis across different business units.
- **Purpose:** Enables businesses to analyze historical data and make informed decisions by aggregating data from multiple sources.

Database

- **Definition:** A structured collection of data files that are systematically organized for easy access and retrieval.
- **Purpose:** Serves as the backbone of data-driven operations, allowing businesses to store and manage information efficiently.

Database Administrators

- **Definition:** Professionals responsible for designing, implementing, and maintaining databases to ensure data integrity and performance.
- **Purpose:** Ensures that organizational databases operate smoothly, securely, and efficiently.

Database Management System (DBMS)

- **Definition:** Software that allows users to create, manage, and access databases.

- **Purpose:** Provides tools to handle data structure, retrieval, and updates, ensuring consistent data management across an organization.

Decentralized Files

- **Definition:** A system where each department maintains its own proprietary data files, often leading to duplicated and inconsistent data across the organization.
- **Purpose:** While sometimes necessary for specific departments, it often creates inefficiencies and inconsistencies.

Decision Support Systems (DSS)

- **Definition:** Systems designed to assist with critical decision-making activities, such as predictions and trend analyses.
- **Purpose:** Helps organizations analyze data to make strategic decisions, often incorporating real-time insights.

Deliverable

- **Definition:** A tangible, measurable outcome or item produced as part of a project.
- **Purpose:** Serves as a milestone or final product that reflects project progress or completion.

Developers

- **Definition:** Professionals who write, test, and maintain software code.
- **Purpose:** Create the programs and systems that power an organization's digital operations.

Differentiation

- **Definition:** The process of offering products or services that are distinct and superior to competitors' offerings.
- **Purpose:** Helps businesses gain a competitive edge by standing out in the market.

Digital

- **Definition:** The use of technology to automate processes, reduce human intervention, and improve efficiency.
- **Purpose:** Enables innovation and optimization in business operations.

Digital Darwinism

- **Definition:** A phenomenon where companies fail to adapt to technological advancements and become obsolete.
- **Purpose:** Highlights the importance of embracing innovation to remain competitive.

Digital Organization

- **Definition:** A company that leverages digital technologies to manage operations, interact with customers, and respond to market demands.

- **Purpose:** Enhances agility, efficiency, and customer engagement.

Digital Trail

- **Definition:** The data generated through interactions with technology, such as online activities or system usage.
- **Purpose:** Provides valuable insights into user behavior and system performance.

Digital Transformation

- **Definition:** The adoption of digital tools and processes to achieve strategic business goals.
- **Purpose:** Drives efficiency, innovation, and competitive advantage.

Disruptive Technology

- **Definition:** Innovative technology that displaces existing methods, creating new industries or revolutionizing markets.
- **Purpose:** Drives significant change and innovation but may also disrupt traditional businesses.

Endpoint

- **Definition:** Any device connected to a network, such as computers, printers, or smartphones.
- **Purpose:** Represents potential entry points for data access and security vulnerabilities.

Enterprise Content Management (ECM)

- **Definition:** A system for organizing and managing information for a designated audience, such as executives or employees.
- **Purpose:** Streamlines content management and ensures accessibility for decision-making.

Enterprise Resource Planning (ERP)

- **Definition:** Integrated systems that manage and streamline organizational data across departments.
- **Purpose:** Enhances collaboration, data accuracy, and operational efficiency.

Entities

- **Definition:** Objects or "actors" in a data flow diagram with which data interacts, defined by specific attributes.
- **Purpose:** Helps identify and describe the key elements in a database.

Entity Relationship Diagram (ERD)

- **Definition:** A diagram that models the relationships between data elements and their attributes in a system.
- **Purpose:** Visualizes database structures, aiding in the design of efficient systems.

Ethics

- **Definition:** Principles that guide behavior and decision-making regarding what is right or wrong.
- **Purpose:** Promotes integrity and accountability in business practices.

Execution Phase

- **Definition:** The phase of project management where the planned work is executed to meet project objectives.
- **Purpose:** Delivers on project requirements, ensuring customer satisfaction.

Executive Support Systems (ESS)

- **Definition:** Systems that generate high-level reports for executives, often summarizing enterprise data in an easy-to-understand format.
- **Purpose:** Supports strategic decision-making by providing a big-picture view.

External Drivers

- **Definition:** Events or situations outside a company that influence its operations, such as market trends or regulatory changes.
- **Purpose:** Helps organizations anticipate and adapt to external pressures.

External Factors

- **Definition:** Opportunities or threats from outside the organization that affect its performance.
- **Purpose:** Forms part of **SWOT analysis**, helping organizations strategize effectively.

Extranet

- **Definition:** A network that combines internal systems with controlled external access for partners or customers.
- **Purpose:** Facilitates secure collaboration with external stakeholders.

Feasibility Study

- **Definition:** An evaluation of a project's viability, including its goals, timeline, technology, and costs.
- **Purpose:** Determines whether a project is practical and worth pursuing.

File

- **Definition:** A collection of related records or data fields that share an association.
- **Purpose:** Organizes data for retrieval and use in systems.

Firewall

- **Definition:** A security system that protects networks from unauthorized access.
- **Purpose:** Acts as a barrier to secure sensitive information and prevent cyberattacks.

Firmware

- **Definition:** Software embedded in hardware to control its functions.
- **Purpose:** Ensures devices operate efficiently and securely.

Follow-the-Sun

- **Definition:** A business model where work is distributed globally to extend productivity across time zones.
- **Purpose:** Enhances efficiency and speeds up project completion.

Force Multiplier

- **Definition:** A factor that significantly increases the effectiveness of a resource or process.
- **Purpose:** Amplifies outcomes without requiring proportional increases in effort.

Group Decision Support Systems (GDSS)

- **Definition:** Systems that enable interactive, computer-based communication and decision-making processes, often used in collaborative environments.
- **Examples:** Tools like Zoom and Google Meet facilitate real-time discussions, brainstorming, and decision-making.
- **Purpose:** Helps teams make informed decisions by fostering collaboration and enhancing communication efficiency.

Headless Systems

- **Definition:** Computers designed to operate without peripherals like monitors, keyboards, or mice.
- **Purpose:** Commonly used in servers or embedded systems where user interaction is minimal or unnecessary.

Histogram

- **Definition:** A type of bar chart used to visualize the distribution of data, tasks, or resource allocations.
- **Purpose:** Aids in identifying patterns, such as workload distribution or project timelines.

Hypertext Transfer Protocol (HTTP)

- **Definition:** The protocol used for transmitting data over the World Wide Web.
- **Purpose:** Facilitates the communication between web browsers and servers, enabling the display of web pages.

Industrial Internet of Things (IIoT)

- **Definition:** The use of connected devices and systems in industrial settings to automate processes and monitor infrastructure.
- **Examples:** Smart sensors on factory floors or systems that monitor energy usage in real time.
- **Purpose:** Enhances efficiency, reduces costs, and improves safety in industrial environments.

Information

- **Definition:** Data that has been processed, contextualized, or transformed into a format that provides value.
- **Purpose:** Supports decision-making and communication by providing meaningful insights.

Information Management

- **Definition:** The structured approach organizations use to collect, store, access, and dispose of information.
- **Purpose:** Ensures data security, accessibility, and compliance with regulations.

Information Systems

- **Definition:** A combination of hardware, software, processes, and people designed to manage and disseminate information within an organization.
- **Purpose:** Enables efficient operations, communication, and decision-making.

Information Technology (IT)

- **Definition:** The tools and resources used in computing, including hardware, software, and networks.
- **Purpose:** Supports organizational operations and innovation by enabling data processing and communication.

Information Technology Governance

- **Definition:** The policies and processes implemented to ensure IT strategies align with business objectives and deliver value.
- **Purpose:** Ensures accountability and strategic alignment in IT projects.

In-House

- **Definition:** A business model where IT functions are managed internally within the organization.
- **Purpose:** Provides greater control over IT operations but may require higher resource investment.

Initiation Phase

- **Definition:** The first phase of the project lifecycle where the project's value and feasibility are assessed.
- **Purpose:** Determines whether the project is viable and worth pursuing.

Innovation

- **Definition:** The process of applying novel ideas or technologies to solve problems or create new opportunities.
- **Purpose:** Drives competitive advantage and growth.

Internal Drivers

- **Definition:** Factors within a company's control that influence operations, such as leadership decisions or organizational culture.
- **Purpose:** Helps organizations identify and leverage internal strengths for growth.

Internal Factors

- **Definition:** Elements within an organization that can either support its success (**strengths**) or hinder its progress (**weaknesses**).
- **Purpose:** Forms the foundation for **SWOT analysis**, guiding strategy development.

Internet

- **Definition:** A global network of interconnected computer systems.
- **Purpose:** Facilitates communication, data sharing, and access to information.

Internet of Things (IoT)

- **Definition:** A network of interconnected smart devices that collect, transmit, and process data over the internet.
- **Purpose:** Enables automation, real-time monitoring, and enhanced user experiences.

Intranet

- **Definition:** A private network used within an organization for internal communication and data sharing.
- **Purpose:** Provides a secure environment for collaboration and access to resources.

Issues Log

- **Definition:** A document used to track problems encountered during a project and their resolutions.
- **Purpose:** Ensures that all project-related issues are addressed systematically.

Join

- **Definition:** The process of linking records from two tables using a common field.
- **Purpose:** Facilitates data integration and query efficiency in relational databases.

Key Field

- **Definition:** A unique identifier for records within a database table.
- **Purpose:** Ensures data accuracy and supports efficient retrieval.

Knowledge

- **Definition:** Information that has been contextualized and is actionable by the right individuals.
- **Purpose:** Drives decision-making and innovation.

Local Area Network (LAN)

- **Definition:** A network that connects devices within a limited geographical area, such as a building.
- **Purpose:** Enables resource sharing and communication within an organization.

Logical Data Model

- **Definition:** A detailed diagram of proposed data structures without implementation details.
- **Purpose:** Guides database design by describing relationships and data flow.

Mainframe

- **Definition:** A powerful computer designed for high-volume, processor-intensive tasks.
- **Purpose:** Supports large-scale operations like transaction processing and enterprise resource planning.

Management Information Systems (MIS)

- **Definition:** Systems focused on collecting, storing, and reporting data for management decision-making.
- **Purpose:** Enhances operational efficiency and strategic planning.

Metadata

- **Definition:** Data that provides context or information about other data, such as file size or creation date.
- **Purpose:** Facilitates data organization, retrieval, and analysis.

Mission Statement

- **Definition:** A concise declaration of an organization's purpose and objectives.
- **Purpose:** Guides strategic decision-making and aligns stakeholders.

Modems

- **Definition:** Devices that convert digital signals into formats suitable for transmission and vice versa.
- **Purpose:** Enables communication over telephone lines or cable networks.

Monitoring and Controlling Phase

- **Definition:** The phase in project management focused on tracking progress and ensuring alignment with plans.
- **Purpose:** Identifies deviations and implements corrective actions.

Near-Shoring

- **Definition:** Outsourcing work to nearby countries, often with shared time zones or borders.
- **Purpose:** Balances cost savings with improved communication and collaboration.

Network

- **Definition:** A system of interconnected devices that share resources and communicate with each other.
- **Purpose:** Enables data exchange, resource sharing, and collaboration.

Network Cards

- **Definition:** Hardware devices that enable computers to connect to a network.
- **Purpose:** Facilitates network communication for devices.

Network Software

- **Definition:** Operating systems and applications that manage network operations, such as routing and security.
- **Purpose:** Ensures efficient and secure communication across networks.

Neural Networks

- **Definition:** AI systems modeled after the human brain, using interconnected nodes to process and analyze data.
- **Purpose:** Supports tasks like pattern recognition, machine learning, and predictive analytics.

Off-Shoring

- **Definition:** Outsourcing work to countries on different continents, often to reduce costs.
- **Purpose:** Provides access to global talent and cost advantages.

Online Analytical Processing (OLAP)

- **Definition:** Technology designed for multidimensional data analysis, enabling tasks like reporting, complex calculations, and "what-if" scenarios.
- **Purpose:** Enhances decision-making through advanced data exploration and visualization.

Operating Systems (OS)

- **Definition:** Software managing a computer's hardware and software resources, delivering essential services for other programs.
- **Purpose:** Acts as the backbone of a computer platform, ensuring smooth operation and user interaction.

Operational Planning

- **Definition:** The process of creating actionable plans to address routine organizational activities, primarily handled by middle management.
- **Purpose:** Ensures that day-to-day operations align with strategic objectives and function efficiently.

Operational Project

- **Definition:** Mandatory initiatives, such as government-mandated upgrades, infrastructure maintenance, or essential system improvements.
- **Purpose:** Ensures the organization meets regulatory standards and maintains operational continuity.

Operational Technology

- **Definition:** The use of information technology to control physical processes, manage production, and support business infrastructure.
- **Purpose:** Enhances efficiency, safety, and reliability in industrial environments.

Outsource

- **Definition:** A strategy where a third party manages parts or all of an organization's technology infrastructure.
- **Purpose:** Reduces costs and allows businesses to focus on core activities by leveraging external expertise.

Payback Period Analysis

- **Definition:** A method to calculate how long it will take for a project to generate enough cash inflows to cover its initial investment.
- **Purpose:** Helps evaluate the financial viability of projects.

Peripheral Devices

- **Definition:** External devices connected to a computer, such as keyboards, mice, printers, and headphones.
- **Purpose:** Expands a computer's functionality for various tasks.

Physical Data Model

- **Definition:** A detailed representation of database tables, attributes, relationships, primary and foreign keys, and constraints.
- **Purpose:** Guides the physical implementation of a database system.

Planning Phase

- **Definition:** The second phase of the project lifecycle, involving the creation of a project plan, scope statement, and schedule.
- **Purpose:** Establishes the foundation for project execution and monitoring.

Political, Economic, Social, and Technological (PEST) Analysis

- **Definition:** A strategic tool for analyzing external factors that could impact an organization.
- **Purpose:** Helps organizations anticipate challenges and opportunities in their environment.

Porter's Five Forces Model

- **Definition:** An analytical framework examining five forces: buyer power, supplier power, new entrants, substitute goods/services, and competitive rivalry.
- **Purpose:** Assesses industry competitiveness and informs strategic decisions.

Portfolio

- **Definition:** A collection of projects, programs, and sub-portfolios managed to achieve strategic goals.
- **Purpose:** Aligns initiatives with organizational objectives for maximum impact.

Predictive Analytics

- **Definition:** The use of data mining, machine learning, and statistical modeling to predict future events.
- **Purpose:** Provides insights that help businesses make proactive, informed decisions.

Primary Key

- **Definition:** A unique identifier for each record in a database table.
- **Purpose:** Ensures data integrity and facilitates efficient data retrieval.

Process Modeling

- **Definition:** Analyzing how a system interacts with its users and other systems to improve workflows.
- **Purpose:** Optimizes system design and user experience.

Program

- **Definition:** A coordinated set of related projects managed together to achieve shared benefits.
- **Purpose:** Enables more efficient resource allocation and goal alignment.

Program Roadmap

- **Definition:** A high-level overview of project progress and interdependencies within a program at a specific point in time.
- **Purpose:** Provides strategic insights for program planning and management.

Progressive Learning Algorithm

- **Definition:** A computational method that mimics brain neurons to solve problems or perform tasks through incremental learning.
- **Purpose:** Powers machine learning and artificial intelligence systems.

Project

- **Definition:** A unique, time-bound initiative defined by its scope, cost, and objectives.
- **Purpose:** Delivers specific outcomes or solutions within a set timeframe.

Project Management Life Cycle

- **Definition:** A five-phase framework guiding projects from initiation to closure.
- **Purpose:** Ensures structured and successful project delivery.

Project Manager

- **Definition:** The individual responsible for ensuring a project stays on time, within scope, and within budget.
- **Purpose:** Oversees all aspects of project execution and delivery.

Project Plan

- **Definition:** A document outlining project assumptions, decisions, communication plans, and scope, cost, and schedule baselines.
- **Purpose:** Serves as a roadmap for project execution and monitoring.

Project Schedule

- **Definition:** A detailed document identifying tasks, start and end dates, and assigned resources.
- **Purpose:** Ensures tasks are completed on time and responsibilities are clear.

Project Selection Process

- **Definition:** Evaluating and deciding whether to approve, deny, or defer project requests.
- **Purpose:** Prioritizes initiatives that align with organizational goals and resources.

Query

- **Definition:** A coded request for data retrieval from a database.
- **Purpose:** Facilitates data access for analysis or reporting.

RACI

- **Definition:** A framework identifying who is **Responsible**, **Accountable**, **Consulted**, and **Informed** for project tasks.
- **Purpose:** Clarifies roles and responsibilities, ensuring accountability and efficient communication.

Reactive Machines

- **Definition:** Intelligent systems designed to react to specific scenarios without learning from past experiences.
- **Purpose:** Executes predefined tasks reliably, often used in basic AI systems.

Release

- **Definition:** A formal distribution of software or system updates.
- **Purpose:** Provides users with new features, enhancements, or bug fixes.

Reshoring

- **Definition:** Bringing previously outsourced or offshored IT functions back to the home country.
- **Purpose:** Improves control, quality, and alignment with organizational standards.

Responsibility Assignment Matrix (RAM)

- **Definition:** A document identifying project roles and responsibilities, often using a RACI framework.
- **Purpose:** Ensures clarity in task assignments and accountability.

Return on Investment (ROI)

- **Definition:** A financial metric evaluating the profitability of an investment relative to its cost.
- **Purpose:** Assists in project selection and financial decision-making.

Rolling Forecast

- **Definition:** A budgeting model that updates projections periodically throughout the year.
- **Purpose:** Provides flexibility and accuracy in financial planning.

Router

- **Definition:** A device that directs network traffic and connects different networks.
- **Purpose:** Ensures efficient and secure data transmission across networks.

Schema

- **Definition:** A diagram representing a **physical data model**, providing detailed information about database tables, fields, and their relationships.
- **Purpose:** Helps visualize and organize how data will be stored, accessed, and managed in a database.

Scope

- **Definition:** Defines the boundaries of a project, detailing what will be delivered and what is excluded.
- **Purpose:** Ensures alignment between stakeholders and the project team on deliverables and objectives.

Scope Statement

- **Definition:** A formal document specifying what a project will deliver, often referred to as the **statement of work**.
- **Purpose:** Serves as a reference to manage expectations and guide project execution.

Scrubbed

- **Definition:** The process of cleaning and standardizing **transactional data** during its preparation for a data warehouse.
- **Purpose:** Ensures data quality by removing errors, duplicates, and inconsistencies.

Server

- **Definition:** A powerful computer that provides resources or services to **clients** in a **client-server model**.
- **Purpose:** Centralizes processing and data management, supporting multiple users or devices.

Server Farms

- **Definition:** Collections of interconnected servers used to perform large-scale computing tasks.
- **Purpose:** Provides scalability, reliability, and redundancy for handling high-demand applications and services.

Smart Devices

- **Definition:** Electronics capable of connecting, sharing, and interacting with users and other devices over a network.
- **Examples:** Smartphones, IoT-enabled appliances, and wearable devices.
- **Purpose:** Enhances automation and user convenience.

Software System

- **Definition:** A collection of interconnected programs that enable and manage the operation of a computer.
- **Purpose:** Provides a cohesive platform for performing various tasks and functions.

Sourcing Strategy

- **Definition:** An organizational decision about how IT solutions and services are delivered, whether internally or externally.
- **Purpose:** Aligns IT capabilities with business objectives, balancing cost, quality, and efficiency.

Sponsor

- **Definition:** An individual or group responsible for approving and championing a project.
- **Purpose:** Provides resources, support, and oversight to ensure project success.

Stacked Resource Histogram

- **Definition:** A bar chart that displays resources over time, stacking bars to show cumulative allocation.
- **Purpose:** Aids in resource leveling and identifying overcommitments.

Stakeholder

- **Definition:** An individual or group with a vested interest in a project, such as employees, customers, or project team members.
- **Purpose:** Ensures all perspectives and needs are considered in project planning and execution.

Stakeholder Register

- **Definition:** A document listing all project stakeholders, including their roles, responsibilities, and contact information.
- **Purpose:** Facilitates communication and stakeholder engagement throughout the project.

Strategic Plan

- **Definition:** A formal document outlining the steps needed to achieve an organization's vision and long-term goals.
- **Purpose:** Provides direction and sets priorities for the organization.

Strategy

- **Definition:** A coordinated set of actions aimed at achieving measurable goals over a specified period.
- **Purpose:** Guides decision-making and resource allocation to achieve objectives.

Supply Chain Management (SCM)

- **Definition:** Systems designed to oversee the movement of goods and services, from sourcing raw materials to delivering final products.
- **Purpose:** Enhances efficiency, reduces costs, and improves customer satisfaction.

Sustaining Technology

- **Definition:** Technologies that offer incremental improvements to existing products or processes.
- **Purpose:** Helps businesses maintain competitiveness and enhance current offerings.

Switches

- **Definition:** Devices that connect endpoints (e.g., computers, printers) within a network.
- **Purpose:** Facilitates efficient data transmission between connected devices.

SWOT Analysis

- **Definition:** A framework for identifying an organization's **Strengths**, **Weaknesses**, **Opportunities**, and **Threats**.
- **Purpose:** Guides strategic planning by evaluating internal and external factors.

Systems Analyst

- **Definition:** A tech-savvy professional who gathers requirements and designs solutions, working closely with IT teams.
- **Purpose:** Ensures technology aligns with business needs.

Systems Development Life Cycle (SDLC)

- **Definition:** A process for determining IT needs, designing, building, and maintaining solutions to meet those needs.
- **Purpose:** Provides a structured approach to developing and deploying systems.

Systems Thinking

- **Definition:** A holistic approach to problem-solving that considers the entire organization and its interdependencies.
- **Purpose:** Improves decision-making and long-term outcomes by understanding systemic impacts.

Table

- **Definition:** A structured arrangement of related data in rows and columns within a database.
- **Purpose:** Stores and organizes data for easy retrieval and analysis.

Technology Quotient (TQ)

- **Definition:** A person's ability to adapt to and integrate new technology to meet organizational needs.
- **Purpose:** Measures technological adaptability and proficiency.

Theory of Mind AI

- **Definition:** Artificial intelligence capable of observing behavior and building models to predict actions, also known as **machine perception**.
- **Purpose:** Enhances interaction by understanding human behavior patterns.

Transaction Processing Systems (TPS)

- **Definition:** Systems that manage and report on day-to-day business transactions.
- **Purpose:** Ensures accurate and efficient processing of operational data.

Transactional Data

- **Definition:** Information generated and used during daily business transactions.
- **Purpose:** Supports operational decision-making and reporting.

Trend Analysis

- **Definition:** A long-term examination of data to identify consistent patterns or trends.
- **Purpose:** Guides strategic planning and forecasting.

Unified Modeling Language (UML)

- **Definition:** A standardized visual tool for designing and documenting system architectures.
- **Purpose:** Simplifies system development by providing clear design representations.

Uniform Resource Locator (URL)

- **Definition:** A human-readable web address that maps to an IP address, making it easier to access websites.
- **Purpose:** Simplifies navigation and access to web resources.

Unit Testing

- **Definition:** A software testing method focusing on individual components or programs.
- **Purpose:** Ensures that each unit functions as intended before integration.

Use Case

- **Definition:** A scenario describing a series of actions between a system and its users to achieve a goal.
- **Purpose:** Captures functional requirements and guides system design.

Use Case Diagram

- **Definition:** A visual representation of interactions between people and machines in a system.
- **Purpose:** Documents and models system processes.

User Experience (UX)

- **Definition:** The overall experience and satisfaction of a user when interacting with a system or application.
- **Purpose:** Enhances usability, accessibility, and engagement.

User Interface (UI)

- **Definition:** The physical or virtual space where users interact with a system (e.g., screens, buttons).
- **Purpose:** Facilitates user interactions and provides feedback.

Utility Software

- **Definition:** Software designed to maintain, optimize, and manage a computer system.
- **Examples:** Disk cleanup tools and antivirus programs.
- **Purpose:** Ensures system performance and reliability.

Vision Statement

- **Definition:** A formal declaration of what an organization aims to become or achieve in the future.
- **Purpose:** Inspires and aligns stakeholders toward long-term goals.

Waterfall Project Methodology

- **Definition:** A sequential project management approach where tasks are completed in distinct stages.
- **Purpose:** Provides a clear structure and timeline for project completion.

Wearables

- **Definition:** Smart devices worn on the body, such as fitness trackers or smartwatches.
- **Purpose:** Enhances user convenience and health monitoring.

Weighted Matrix or Weighted Scoring Model

- **Definition:** A project selection tool that assigns weight to criteria based on organizational priorities.
- **Purpose:** Helps choose projects that align best with strategic goals.

Wide Area Network (WAN)

- **Definition:** A network that spans large geographical areas, connecting multiple LANs.
- **Purpose:** Enables communication across cities, countries, or continents.

World Wide Web (WWW)

- **Definition:** The multimedia content accessible on the Internet, including websites, images, and videos.
- **Purpose:** Provides an interconnected platform for information sharing and communication.

UNIT 2: RISK MANAGEMENT

Chapter 4 – Identifying and Categorizing Risk

Overview

Risk is often associated with how people make decisions. Risk is not limited to decisions, however: the level of risk is a product of the probability and impact of decisions, scenarios, disasters, or even outcomes. Risk can further expand into technology and data and can contribute to how organizations conduct operations and implement information technology governance. This unit dives into the realm of risk. This chapter will discuss risk identification, risk mediums, and risk environments.

Chapter 4 Learning Objectives

1. Evaluate the fundamentals of organizational risk management.
2. Elaborate on the importance of a risk-aware culture within an organization.
3. Determine the risk appetite and risk threshold of an organization.
4. Choose the best method for making risk-aware business decisions.
5. Differentiate between technology- and data-related risk scenarios.
6. Compare and contrast the risk of disgruntled employees and insider threats.
7. Determine overall risk associated with loss or compromise of assets.

In November 2019, the first known case of COVID-19 was identified in China. In early March of 2020, this epidemic was documented with over one-hundred and forty-eight thousand known cases around the world [1]. Governments, large corporations, and even small businesses had some type of contingency plan established for countering environmental risks; no one, however, had ever imagined the impact such a large-scale risk would pose both nationally and globally. Had the probability of a mass virus outbreak ever truly been a possibility? American families had not planned to counter the risk of local stores having no home essentials, such as toilet paper, cleaning products, and bottled water. Businesses had not prepared for a nationwide mandated quarantine that resulted in no choice but to impose telework-oriented operations. Risk scenarios or tabletop exercises had not been conducted to counter the overwhelming amount of stress that organizational virtual private networks would face from the magnitude of remote workers. All these issues directly correlate to the likeliness of a risk-based scenario, risk assessment and management, and the severity various risks can pose.

Introduction to Risk

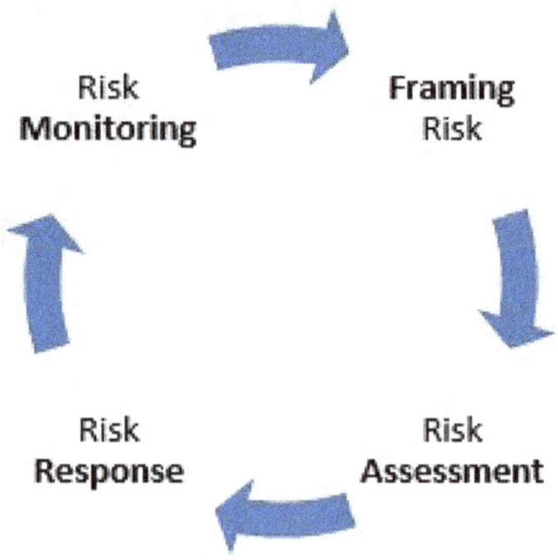

Figure 4.1. Risk Management

Prior to risk being explored in detail, it is imperative to understand the meaning of risk as it pertains to Information Technology. **Risk** is defined as any potential threat or vulnerability that may result in damage, loss, or disruption to company people, assets, technology, data, operations, or productivity. **Risk management** is a process consisting of several components. As shown in Figure 4.1, the risk management process begins with how an organization perceives risk or frames it as relevant to their environment/ecosystem. The second component identifies or assesses the various risks and threats to the organization that pertain to people, technology, data, or assets. Responding to various identified risks is the third component. Lastly, once risk is mitigated, reduced to a tolerable level, or responded to within the organization, established controls and residual risk are monitored to continually verify the actions being taken are effective [2]. **Residual risk** describes the amount of risk that remains after implementing a control. Security controls are put in place as preventative measures to assist in lowering identified risks. Although security controls will be referenced on a few occasions here in Chapter 4, Chapter 6 will explore various types of controls, their purpose, and where to utilize each. There are typically three primary types of controls: administrative, technical (also known as logical), and physical. The risk management cycle process is iterative, repeating each phase or component continually to ensure due diligence in organizational risk management [2]. **Due diligence** is just another term for actions the organization has taken to reduce risk.

An example of a real-life risk scenario will help illustrate key concepts. A business evaluates their risk environment and given the historical environmental data, discovers that a flood is likely. The organization anticipates the flood would impact personnel, infrastructure, and buildings in the area, and perceives the risk as high and probable. "High" and "probable" are examples of risk designation used for this example; additional levels of designation will be discussed in Chapter 5. The organization responds to the risk by establishing a hot site approximately seventy miles inland. A **hot site** is the term for a fully prepared backup location that offers the same information technology capabilities as the primary location. Alternatively, a **warm site** is only partially equipped with infrastructure and IT capabilities, and a **cold site** is simply a backup location without much of any infrastructure available. The company can then continually monitor the flood risk by studying historical data, staying current on flood trends, and running through emergency response plans. Assessing risk must be done early in planning processes and frequently throughout the life cycles of projects or equipment. Identifying risk early on can assist with stakeholder decisions, funding for countermeasures, and potential mitigation techniques. Risk mitigation will be discussed in further detail in Chapter 6.

Creating a Risk-Aware Culture

Risk culture summarizes the demeanor, ethics, and core values pertaining to risk within a company. In a fully established risk culture, every employee from the top to the bottom of the organizational hierarchy understands risk. Upper management should ensure all workers are educated on how to identify risk, how to manage risk, where to document risk, and what the benefits of risk management are. Risk culture is all about how employees react to risk. The most effective method for validating organizational risk culture is to study how risk is identified and to evaluate whether employees adhere to policies and procedures of risk scenarios.
At minimum, a central location must be identified to record risks pertaining to the organization. A **risk register** contains necessary information for categorizing risk. This information includes the likeliness of each risk occurring, the impact each risk could have, strategies for mitigating each risk, and a method of scoring a risk's severity. The risk register will be discussed in greater detail in Chapter 6.

A report conducted by Protiviti summarized executive perspectives on the top risks for 2020, highlighting three specific risk dimensions: macroeconomic risk, strategic risk, and operational risk [3]. **Macroeconomic risk** pertains to markets and outside factors, primarily dealing with finance and currency. **Strategic risk** correlates to business strategy, innovation, and opportunity-related risk. **Operational risk** relates to the employees, business processes, and technologies within the organization. One of the top risks identified by the report is that organizational culture may not advocate the identification and escalation of risk-related concerns quickly enough [3]. In other words, a risk-aware culture is critical to identifying, categorizing and mitigating risk. Risk culture and climate are linked to mature processes. Mature processes in the organization drive success. Making risk-aware decisions at all levels assists organizations in achieving the next level of organizational maturity. Promoting **risk awareness** and continually improving upon the current organizational posture to risk leads to a risk-aware culture.

Risk appetite is the amount of total risk an organization can withstand without suffering any financial or operational loss. Risk appetite must align with the objectives of the organization. If the cost to mitigate a risk outweighs the cost of the risk being exploited, that risk may be accepted; critical or high risks, on the other hand, must be mitigated, as they would pose severe financial or operational hardships to the company. **Risk tolerance** is the agreed-upon level of risk the organization is willing to withstand. Both risk appetite and risk tolerance are measurable and specific to each individual company.

An example of risk tolerance can occur when an employee arrives to work late. Arriving 8 minutes late for a 7 AM to 3:30 PM shift will change the employee's work time to 7:08 AM to 3:38 PM. If the employee's manager is willing to allow this deviation from the schedule, the manager is exhibiting risk tolerance. **Risk threshold** is yet another term that addresses the amount of risk a company will deem acceptable [4]. If the employee above had instead arrived 45 minutes late and the manager refused to let the employee work until 4:15 PM, the manager's decision indicates that employees arriving 45 minutes late is beyond the company's risk threshold.

As IT governance aligns technology with business processes, **risk governance** seeks to align risk management with both business and decision-making processes. Risk governance also branches off IT governance by expanding objectives, such as creating and preserving a perspective of risk that is common and recognizable by all. Risk management must be integrated into the enterprise as a whole and utilized for making risk-conscientious decisions. Furthermore, controls implemented in support of risk management must be frequently evaluated and monitored to ensure effectiveness, leveraging an iterative loop from lessons learned [5]. When IT and risk governance are adequately integrated, corporate governance will advance the organization with successful processes and operations.

Once the organization's risk appetite, tolerance, and threshold have been determined, all risks must be assessed. Identifying or evaluating risk is described as the process of **risk assessment**. Specific methods for assessing risk will be discussed in Chapter 6. Categorizing risks by type, severity, and probability helps the organization prioritize which risks it must address. Once risks are prioritized, a company can create controls and allocate funding to mitigate those risks based on criticality and severity of risk impact. Risks are generally categorized as critical, high, medium, and low. Critical or high risks must be mitigated first, as they pose the highest threat of damage to the organization. Each risk is mitigated in order to drop the overall risk to the organization's level of risk tolerance, in accordance with its risk appetite. This process of mitigating individual risks to meet the organization's risk appetite and tolerance is known as **risk reduction**.

Disaster recovery and business continuity closely correlate to risk management. A **disaster recovery plan** will help identify potential disasters, ranging from environmental to personnel related. Part of assessing risk relies upon the success rate of previous disaster recovery operations and lessons learned. If an established disaster recovery plan has proven successful with previous environmental disasters, such as a tornado, the risk of a tornado threatening the organization has been addressed and reduced to an acceptable level by established preventative measures. **Business continuity planning (BCP)** is a predetermined plan to enact during a disaster. BCP establishes planning and preventative controls to ensure continuous operations. Conducting routine risk audits and assessments help maintain the validity of identified risks and associated controls. Disaster recovery and business continuity will be further discussed in Unit 3.

Making Risk-Conscientious Decisions

One of the main objectives of identifying and categorizing risk is to use the results to make sound risk-based decisions. Each scenario possesses some form of risk and repercussion which must be analyzed thoroughly prior to action. Several methodologies exist for making risk-aware decisions; however, the decision-making process must first be understood sufficiently to incorporate risk-based decision-making techniques. The **OODA Loop** is a decision-making process originated by military strategist, Colonel John Boyd. Risks must be considered in each phase of the OODA loop: observe, orient, decide and action.

In the observation phase, the goal is to take in surroundings, information, and any other relevant data that may contribute to the end goal or decision [6]. In the context of risk, imagine an individual attempting to pry open a door to a facility that houses critical information technology infrastructure. A sign indicates authorized IT personnel only. The person being observed looks suspicious and is not recognized as an individual who has authorized access to the facility. The facility, infrastructure, assets, and data of the company are at risk due the attempted breach of physical security.

The orientation phase of the OODA loop involves calling upon past experiences and decisions in similar situations: the well-known phrase "learn from past mistakes" will serve as a driver moving forward [6]. From a risk perspective, this is where risk analysis comes into play. For example, the intruder above may or may not break into the facility -- but the risk is there. If the intruder will probably not be able to pry the door open, the risk of breaching the facility is low. If the intruder probably will break the door open, a high risk of breach or exposure exists. Technology-related equipment or data could be stolen, trade secrets exposed, or malicious hardware installed to provide a backdoor to the enterprise network. Key considerations during the initial observation stage include whether personnel know how to handle an intruder attempting to break in, as well as how the situation must be handled based on organizational policy and procedure. Key considerations during the orientation stage, on the other hand, include options, such as whether the intruder will choose to run away or engage in physical force after being discovered. Brainstorming possibilities within each stage of the OODA process will support producing a well thought out risk-based decision.

The OODA's decision phase requires careful discussion or strategizing to determine the best course of action. When an individual person is contemplating a decision, it may be instinctive [6]. Realistically, there may not always be time to discuss the next best option, and acting on rationality, experience, and the severity of the risk may be the best action to take. In the specific scenario provided, however, engaging the threat actor may not be a smart move. Contacting authorities or facility security immediately is usually the best course of action to avoid conflict. Contacting authorities will keep the individual from facing the risk of confronting the perpetrator and will also address the risk faced by the facility from the perpetrator. It is important to always base decisions on organizational policy and procedure to ensure incidents are handled appropriately.

Decisions are carried out in the act phase [6]. Stopping the intruder on the spot may have been an option, but that action was determined to have a high risk with potential consequences. A better action in terms of risk was to contact security or the police. Upon making a decision, the OODA loop begins again -- this time, for example, to consider what should be done if security or the police fail to show up. The process begins at the observation stage and transitions to the orient, decide, and act phases yet again.

A well-developed risk strategy still needs to be practiced and executed based on the objectives of the organization's risk management strategy. Getting employees and management to execute risk-based decision making can be challenging: successfully executing risk-based decisions is an indication of organizational process maturity. Common hurdles to implementing risk management include obtaining both buy-in and participation. Often, a risk assessment is performed but no action is implemented afterward [7]. As discussed in Chapter 3, a RACI matrix is an appropriate and formal way of ensuring responsibility is clearly assigned. A **RACI Matrix** will help ensure accountability and participation with overall decision making and enterprise risk strategies. Let's revisit the purpose of a RACI matrix in the context of risk management.

A RACI Matrix will help ensure accountability and participation with overall decision making and enterprise risk strategies. RACI stands for responsibility, accountability, consulted, and informed.

Responsibility indicates who is responsible for a given task [7]. In the realm of risk, tasks can include assuming risk, performing risk assessments, and updating the risk register. A specific task pertaining to information technology is applying patches to mitigate enterprise vulnerabilities, thereby reducing organizational risk to an acceptable level. Identifying the individuals or positions who are responsible for specific tasks negates any possibility of confusion and holds each individual liable for making risk-based decisions.

Liability is further associated with accountability, the second element of RACI. Being accountable means ensuring that individuals complete the tasks for which they are responsible [7]. If employee A is responsible for performing a risk assessment, whomever is accountable for

Role ➡ Task ⬇	Michael	Terri	Dave	Chris
Perform risk assessment	R	R	R	R
Identify Risk	R	A	A	R
Categorize Risk	I	R	R	I
Mitigate Risk	R	I	C	R

Figure 4.2. The RACI Matrix

the risk assessment must ensure that employee A has completed all phases of the risk assessment thoroughly and accurately.

The consulted phase involves individuals who provide data, advice, or general discussion pertaining to a given task [7]. Although these individuals could be from any department, management often fills this role. For example, after a risk assessment has been performed by the responsible team and a first level supervisor has ensured accountability, it may be the director of the IT department who is consulted to review the risk assessment results. The director offers feedback derived from years of experience to provide more detail and insight regarding specific risks, and the risk assessment will be updated accordingly.

The informed stage ensures that all necessary individuals are notified of a task's completion [7]. In the case of the risk assessment example, the organization's board of directors or upper management would be informed that the assessment has been completed. The final product of the risk assessment will be delivered to assist the board or upper management in making risk-aware decisions, such as prioritizing mitigation and allocating financial resources to the risks identified as the most critical.

In summary, the RACI matrix identifies who is responsible for each identified task or risk action, and how an organization can ensure accountability of risk-based decisions for ensuring a risk-aware culture. An example of a simple RACI Matrix is Figure 4.2 above. Note that letters assigned to each box on the matrix are one of the four letters in the word RACI. Each of the four individuals have separate roles at each phase of the risk initiative. Individuals are identified on the top, followed by the responsible RACI phase. Tasks are identified in the left column.

Identifying and Categorizing Risk

Risks are commonly identified by analyzing historical organizational data, trends, and lessons learned. This analysis can help identify past, current, and future risks based on actual and probability of occurrence. The next sections will provide examples of risk and emphasize the necessity of always thinking about what could go wrong. Risk falls into four general categories:

people, technology, data, and asset. Being familiar with each will make it easier to identify, categorize, and mitigate risk.

Identifying and Categorizing People-Related Risk

When contemplating risk, people are often overlooked: risk in the work environment is mostly associated with finance or operations. People, however, can cause not only financial and operational risks, but also many others. **People risk** pertains to employees, the risk in the duties they perform, and the risk a disgruntled employee could potentially cause to the organization. Another term for a disgruntled employee is an **insider threat** -- someone in a position of trust that could do harm. Privilege creep poses an even higher risk.

Privilege creep can occur when an employee maintains access or administrative rights from a previous position after moving to a new position [8]. Granting an individual additional rights without rescinding unnecessary privileges creates risk. For example, Jon is a system administrator with the ability to modify files. He advances to a managerial position and does not like Alex, who was hired into his previous position. Jon still understands the duties of his old position; because he maintains full administrative rights, Jon decides to frame Alex to make him look bad. Jon modifies a daily server and network hardware log that only Alex should have access to. The log now indicates that several systems are non-responsive, which alerts employees to initiate incident response procedures. When all systems are identified as online without issues, the blame for the event is put on Alex. Negating privilege creep and auditing employee privileges on a regular basis is just one preventative measure to reduce people-related risk to the company operations, assets, and data. Methods for lowering employee-related risk include job rotation, mandatory vacations, dual control, and separation of duties.

Job rotation [9], or rotating employees into different positions within the company, can mitigate several risk factors pertaining to employees. Job rotation is an effective way to cross train employees: if an employee were to quit without notice, having other employees who are able to perform the unexpectedly vacated job reduces the risk associated with a disruption in operations. Job rotation also lowers the possibility of fraud-related risk. For example, Mark has administrative access to an IT system that allocates payroll. Mark reconfigures the system to redistribute a dollar from each company employee's paycheck to an alternate location. Each dollar taken from the thousands of employees that work for the company globally is deposited into a personal account Mark set up for himself. A dollar may seem insignificant, but considering there are thousands of employees, Mark is receiving thousands of dollars each paycheck into his personal account. This tactic is described as a **salami technique**: shaving off small slices of money the way one would cut thin slices of deli meat [10]. In summary, job rotation provides the opportunity for the organization or other employees to identify someone performing fraudulent actions. Job rotation thus benefits cross training and will reduce the risk of people or employees committing fraud.

While dedicated employees are company assets, employees who work too much without time off can pose a risk. Employees who work constantly may have means, opportunity, or motive (**MOM**) to engage in unethical or fraudulent behavior. **Mandatory vacations** require employees to take vacation either quarterly, annually, or on another pre-specified basis [11]. Similar to job rotation, mandatory vacation is another method to help identify fraudulent activity. Time off and appropriate workloads also reduce risk and keep employees happy. When a company requires employees to take vacation, there is an opportunity to identify unethical behavior. An example would be an employee named Susan taking time off. During Susan's vacation, Mary notices some odd activity on the servers Susan administers. Mary looks closer into the activity and notices that Susan created backdoor access to the server and can then report this unauthorized access to management.

> **Looking Further**
>
> Employees who lack proper job training are more likely to make mistakes, especially in the field of information technology. Baselining and configuration management are good techniques for mitigating technology configuration errors, which will be addressed further in the technology risk related section.

Dual control is another method of controlling people-related risk. Dual control requires two individuals to authenticate a system before access is granted [12]. This control lowers the risk of a single individual exploiting a system or performing unethical actions. Remember Jon, the system administrator from the privilege creep example. If dual control had been required to modify the log, Jon would not have been able to use the administrative privileges he still maintained to modify the content that set Alex up for failure. Jon would have needed an additional employee to also enter administrative credentials, and this presumably would have lowered the probability that Jon would modify the log. Mark may also have been dissuaded from routing money to a personal account if dual control had been required to change financial routing destinations. Many banks require two people to enter codes and mandate a time delay in order to open a vault. All of these dual control processes are methods of lowering risk associated with privilege creep and fraudulent actions within an organization.

While cross training is a great technique for reducing risk of an operational failure, too many people with the ability to perform the same tasks can pose a risk as well. **Separation of duties** addresses this risk. The separation of duties ensures that only a specific team or individual can perform a given task, thereby preventing all others in the organization from engaging in unethical or fraudulent behavior pertaining to that task [13]. An Information Technology department, for example, is typically responsible for account management. The process of account vetting, creation, and management are referred to as **Account Lifecycle Management**.

When an employee requests access to a specific account, their supervisor must endorse the request. This endorsement helps to ensure that access to the account is a requirement for the employee's duties. Once the account request paperwork is submitted, another entity -- perhaps the cybersecurity team -- will validate whether the employee performs a job duty that requires access to the account. If everything checks out, the employee's account access will be created by system administrators. This account management lifecycle exemplifies the separation of duties.

People-related risk further correlates to **Human Resource Risk**. Work-related injury, lack of job training, employee lawsuits, and employee turnover are all associated with people risk [14]. Even if risk management and safe work practices are implemented, accidents will still happen. The company must decide how it will manage accidents and potential worker compensation cases. The probability of workers being injured may be a higher risk in production or commercial environments than in office or desk-based jobs. This is all part of the risk assessment process. The organization must also consider the risk of employee lawsuits. One way to mitigate this particular risk is by using a third-party insurance agency. To adequately assess people risk, all of the ways employees put the organization at risk or the organization puts the employees at risk must be addressed.

In addition to internal people risks, companies must also consider external people risks. Many nefarious actors who do not work within the organization present risk, including competitors and hackers. A competitor obtaining an advantage may serve as risk to an organization, as competitor insight would harm productivity and revenue generation. A hacker or group of hackers targeting the organization to shut down technology capabilities, interfere with business operations, or gain access to company proprietary data is a realistic threat. The success of a hacker breaching company systems or data is a scary outcome; therefore, assessing risk from both internal and external perspectives will provide a more structured threat landscape and holistic view for mitigating different people-related risks. **Threat landscapes** or threat environments describe any identified vulnerabilities or threats to a person, place, or thing.
The insurance brokerage firm Aon PLC concluded that people-related risk is one of the top 5 concerns for businesses [15]. Managing people-related risk for an organization can be more of a challenge than managing other risks. Several of the concepts discussed in this section mitigate people-related risk at a minimal expense to the organization. Fraud, espionage, and theft are among the top risks that people present to any organization. While risk-oriented culture helps alleviate people-related risk, background checks and hiring employees with the right ethics, skill sets, and expertise will enhance the overall effectiveness of people-related risk management efforts [15].

Identifying and Categorizing Technology-Related Risk

Technology risk can be costly for a modern business to mitigate depending upon the likelihood of occurrence, the impact of risk, and the establishment of compensating controls to counter the risk. A **compensating control** is an alternative action taken to help lower overall risk to an acceptable level when the risk mitigation action is too costly or simply not possible to achieve. In information technology, system vulnerabilities, environmental factors, the absence or malfunction of security mechanisms, misconfigurations, and faulty equipment are just some of many potential risk concerns that must be addressed. Technology risk can also come from outdated technology and equipment the organization still uses, or future technology and equipment the company is considering purchasing. Identifying exactly how these risks pertain to a specific organization is crucial to determining the organization's overall risk appetite and its options for reducing technology-specific risks.

System vulnerabilities, whether hardware- or software-related, can allow hackers and other nefarious actors to gain and maintain access to company-owned technology [16]. Not installing updates to software, firmware, and operating systems on enterprise technology poses a risk to organizational operations, assets, and data. System vulnerabilities can be categorized based on the impact they have on the enterprise if exploited. For example, critical and high vulnerabilities may pose the most threat to the organization, while medium and low risk vulnerabilities would be less intrusive. It is important to not take medium or low risk vulnerabilities for granted, however, as multiple small risk vulnerabilities may compile together to create a greater overall vulnerability risk for the organization. Best practice is to reduce risk by mitigating critical and high vulnerabilities first, while individually analyzing the impact of and prioritizing risk mitigation techniques for residual risk. System vulnerabilities that create risk include but are not limited to missing patches, open system ports and protocols, old firmware, unsigned or untrusted computer code, misconfiguration of systems by employees, and third party applications that may provide additional attack vectors into the system. Security controls for countering system vulnerabilities and risk will be further discussed in Chapter 7.

Environmental risk can pose a great risk to data centers and technology facilities in general. A **data center** is a term describing the facility, building, or the IT workers within the facility or a room where enterprise information technology equipment is housed. The risk of natural threats and disasters was briefly discussed earlier, in the example scenario of a flood threatening a data center. Environmental threats are not limited to mother nature, however, especially in the field of information technology. A number of other environmental risks can threaten a data center, including loss of power to hardware, electrical fires, humidity and moisture build up around electronics, temperatures that are too hot or too cold, or even particles in the air that may serve as contaminants [17].

Loss of power is a common technology risk. The loss of all power is referred to as a **blackout** [18]**.** Blackouts can cause system failure, which can in turn cause the failure of business operations. Surges or brown outs are additional risks within the scope of power. While it may provide contingency and time to recover power, an **uninterruptible power supply (UPS)** is not a fully reliable solution. A UPS must be tested consistently: battery life deteriorates over time, and a UPS will not provide any backup power if batteries have died. A **brown out**, or a reduction in power, can result in IT equipment malfunctions [18]. Typically caused by old infrastructure and wiring, the risk from brown outs can be mitigated by voltage monitoring devices. A **surge**, on the other hand, is a temporary jolt of electricity or increase in voltage that can fry or harm electronic equipment [18].

Water destroys electronic equipment. The risk of a pipe bursting or a sprinkler system leaking are realistic threats to a data center. A great way to counter the risk of a flood harming the electronics in a data center is to elevate them: keeping all server racks and IT equipment a few feet off the ground will help prevent water from flowing directly into electrical equipment. Performing quarterly or annual preventative maintenance on data center sprinkler systems is another method of reducing risk, as is selecting the most appropriate sprinkler type as well. For example, the pipes in a **pre-action sprinkler system** are filled with air while the water is held back by a pre-action valve [19]: water is not actually released until a sensor or smoke detector enacts two triggers indicating an instance of smoke or fire. Pre-action type sprinkler systems are thus ideal for data centers, as they help negate false alarms of potential fires and smoke. **Wet pipe sprinkler systems**, on the other hand, always have water in the pipes, while **dry pipe systems** are filled instead with pressurized air [19]. Wet pipe systems may thus increase risk to a data center, as water could potentially leak out. Installing the correct type of sprinkler system will assist in minimizing risk of flood, water damage, or false alarms that could cause mass amounts of water to rain down upon information technology data center hardware systems. The use of dry pipe systems reduces the possibility or risk of water leaking onto electrical equipment as pipes age.

Some data centers are housed in locations with high humidity, which means there is a lot of moisture in the air. This moisture is not good for electronics or metal in general, as it causes equipment to corrode [17]. The condition of too much or too little humidity must be addressed in contingency planning and risk assessment scenarios. Another enemy of electronic equipment is **electrostatic discharge (ESD)**: a change in electrical current between electrically charged technology components which can harm or destroy a system [17]. Risk related to humidity and moisture can be managed by installing equipment in the data center that monitors humidity levels.

Temperatures that are too hot can also pose risk to a facility. Electronics produce a lot of heat. Ensuring that air conditioning and temperature monitoring controls are installed will help alleviate the risk of equipment overheating or burning out. Risk of temperature is not limited to only the facility. Each technology component housed within the facility possesses its own manufacturer-recommended operating temperatures. While the facility temperature may contribute to risk of equipment overheating, failing components internal to each device is another potential risk pertaining to temperature damage. Monitoring internal components of equipment frequently and consistently will help manage risk of overheating and provide a signal to replace failing hardware before it is too late. Many devices have built in temperature monitoring that sends alarms when the threshold is met or exceeded. It is especially important to identify systems that do not possess built-in temperature monitoring: without having any type of temperature alert system, they would be more at risk.

Ongoing preventative maintenance and cleaning of electrical equipment will also reduce the risk of overheating and failure. Airborne particles such as dust, skin, lint, and fibers can all clog hardware cooling systems, which can result in overheating and heat-related damages [17]. Although it may seem unlikely, years of dust buildup and dirty equipment can intensify the risk of hardware failure. Routine maintenance, such as using canned air to blow dust out of electronics, will help reduce the risk of overheating and failure. The goal is to ensure that technology-related equipment can reliably support business activities and productivity. Security breaches are another common concern with technology, as technology is heavily relied upon for critical business functions. Poor security mechanisms or preventative controls raise the risk of systems being compromised, which increases overall organizational risk as well. While the bulk of cybersecurity best practices and threats will be addressed in Unit 3, it is important to note here that a lack of cybersecurity safeguards increases risk to the organization. While implementing security monitoring technology and alert systems can be expensive, the cost to install the devices is small compared to the costs of addressing breached systems and stolen data.

The misconfiguration of information technology systems can further increase risk of a breach due to human error. **Baselining**, or creating a set of standardized configurations across all similar devices, helps alleviate the risk associated with incorrectly configured systems. Baselines may include several key items such as software requirements, operating system and application configuration requirements, mandatory security settings, and version control pertaining to IT hardware. **Version control** is maintaining an inventory of previous, current, and future operating systems or applications that have been installed or managed on computer systems or technology components. Configuration management through use of baselining must align with the needs of the enterprise and be reviewed frequently as requirements and technology advance.[20]

Assessing the risk of IT hardware failure can be difficult. There are, however, several methods for calculating how to determine the current and future life expectancy of data center equipment. The **mean time between failure (MTBF)** captures the reliability of a device within a specified time frame [21] -- specifically, how long the device operates as intended without interruption or failure. MTBF can be calculated by dividing total operational time of the device by the overall total number of failures [21]. For example, if a server were operational for 100 hours but failed 2 times during the 100-hour time period, the MTBF would be 50 hours. An increasing frequency of failure means that the device may be on the brink of failing, which increases risk. MTBF can be a good indicator that it is time to respond to or investigate the behavior of a specific device: doing so will eliminate the risk of more frequent failures and complete loss of service.

Mean time to repair (MTTR) identifies how long it would take to fix a system and bring it back up to full operational standards [21]. This information can help assist in determining the level of risk an organization may face if a critical server and its services go down. MTTR includes not only the time it will take to fix the system, but also any testing that must then be performed to confirm that systems are fully operational. MTTR can be calculated by dividing the total time of maintenance by the total number repairs [21]. If a server failed 4 times in a day and required repairs that took a total of 2 hours to complete, the MTTR would be 30 minutes. In other words, it takes 30 minutes to repair the server for each failure. Knowing how long it will take to repair information technology hardware helps organizations understand the risk behind not planning for failure. It is imperative that organizations plan for information technology outages and establish effective contingency planning to counter the associated risks.

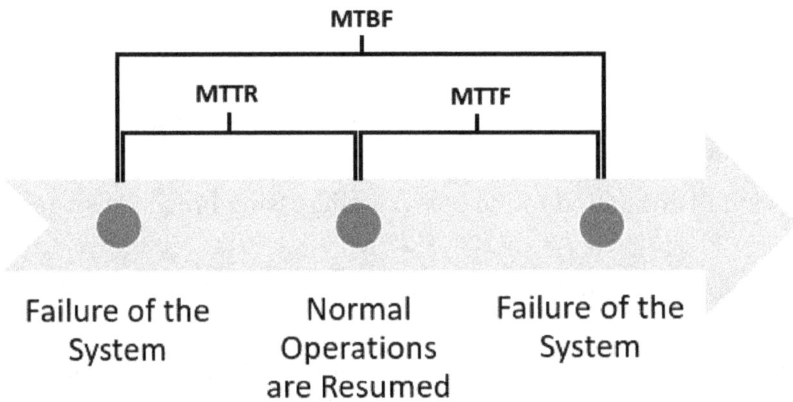

Figure 4.3. Understanding MTBF, MTTR, and MTTF

Finally, the **mean time to failure (MTTF)** estimates the entire lifecycle of a device [21]. It is imperative to not confuse MTBF and MTTF: MTTF deals primarily with a complete system failure, without the option for repair. The MTTF is calculated by dividing the complete hours of operation before failure by the sum of all units that had a failure [21]. Consider an enterprise scenario with four servers on the domain. Server 1 failed after 4,000 hours, server 2 failed after 6,000 hours, server 3 failed after 3,000 hours, and server 4 failed after 7,000 hours. The total operation hours between all servers add up to be 20,000 hours. Twenty-thousand hours, divided by the number of servers (4), provides a MTTF of 5000 hours. Five-thousand hours would be a rather bad MTTF, as this translates to approximately 208 days of operation before the system would fail completely. No organization would want to replace servers on an annual basis, as the cost to do so would be enormous. Figure 4.3 provides a visual perspective on how MTBF, MTTR, and MTTF all flow during a system lifecycle.

As technology progresses, more opportunity becomes available to support business operations. Social media, mobile devices, bring your own device to work (BYOD) solutions, and cloud computing are great additions for enhancing business capabilities. Each new opportunity, however, presents a new risk [22]. **Emerging risk** is not uncommon as enterprise architecture matures, and thus must be addressed within the risk management process. The average employee utilizes social media through a personal device during work hours, which can present a risk of protecting a company brand, exposing sensitive and confidential information, or not meeting privacy requirements. More specifically, the camera on the phone may expose critical information that could be used by a hacker if the employee is taking photos within the work environment. Exposure of a work environment layout, timelines for company activities, and company-sensitive information are countered by operational security. **Operational security (OPSEC)** develops a method to view identified risks from an attacker's perspective, while creating a solution for preventing occurrence or protecting sensitive information. The microphone on the device may capture sensitive information during a meeting that may expose certain process the organization conducts, potential vulnerabilities, or information in general that can be used against the organization. It is difficult to stop employees from randomly checking Facebook, Instagram, or social media apps during work hours without a policy dictating the use of personal devices or social media. Creating new policies that incorporate social media usage or updating existing policies to include guidance on social media can reduce the risk of employees unknowingly exposing company sensitive information, damaging a brand, or not meeting compliance requirements [22].

Mobile phones and personal electronic devices (PEDs) pose several risks to the organization that must be addressed. If personal devices are infected with malware and those devices are utilized for both personal and work-related tasks, malware could be spread on the enterprise network. The risk of business-critical information being leaked also increases if personal devices are used, and identity and access management of BYODs may serve as a challenge as well [22]. Examples of BYODs include laptops, phones, tablets or any other personal technology or equipment capable of being used for work-related duties. Baselining security requirements on BYOD technology will help reduce risk and hold employees accountable for maintaining the enterprise technology security requirements on their personal device. Cloud computing is a great solution for simplifying and centralizing technology; with this convenience, however, comes risks such as theft of data, regulatory and compliance infractions, malware, and breach [23]. Effective security policies, baselining cloud configuration security, Defense in Depth strategy, and continuous monitoring help alleviate cloud computing risk to a tolerable level. A **Defense in**

Depth strategy is a plan with many defenses in place to counter vulnerabilities, threats, risk, or security controls that do not perform as intended.

Technology is key to modern-day businesses. As there are many information technology related devices contributing to maintaining business operation capabilities, managing the risk of each device is especially imperative. Technology-related risk can be influenced by both inside and outside threats. Identifying, categorizing, and finding a solution for technology risk will help keep overall risk within the organizational threshold. Information technology risks can be categorized by specific IT assets, their services or functions, and their intended purpose to the enterprise. System vulnerabilities, environmental risks, and specific risks to data centers must be identified. Understanding MTBF, MTTR, and MTTF will contribute to managing risk associated to system lifecycles, while a Defense in Depth strategy seeks to reduce risks to all genres of possible risk.

Identifying and Categorizing Asset-Related Risk

In the context of asset-related risk, assets can include people, technology, physical devices, and even data. Assets must be identified, their values must be determined, and their levels of risk categorized. This section is going to discuss potential risk and risk responses that are specific to basic IT hardware- and software-related assets. Note that there will be different technology configurations, hardware, software, and technical implementations of IT assets based on the needs of each individual organization. A familiarity with basic information about technology-related assets will help employees understand **business impact analysis (BIA)** and how to manage the IT portion of risk within the organization. Business impact analysis is a process for determining how the loss of essential business functionality or services will affect the organization [24]. BIA is discussed in further detail in Chapter 6.

Most employees in an office-based setting use a laptop or desktop to perform their jobs. Computer system security, however, is one of the most difficult risks to regulate. Computing systems are usually all connected on the same enterprise network. If one system on the network becomes infected with malware, it is imperative to isolate the infected system, as the risk for the spreading malware is very high. Many computer risks can be mitigated by preventative maintenance and system hardening. **System hardening** is establishing security controls, reducing threat, and mitigating vulnerabilities to secure a specific system. For example, installing the latest security patches and enforcing an enterprise security control configuration across all systems will help standardize security and reduce the risk of known vulnerabilities being exploited.

Physical hardware is internal to technology-related hardware and assets. Examples include hard drives, random access memory (RAM), motherboards, central processing units (CPUs), and more. The billions of components embedded into modern day microprocessors and chips have created an increase in hardware risk and a demand for more thorough hardware preventive security measures [25]. Microprocessors and chips are utilized in nearly every type of electronic product, from vacuum cleaners to children's toys, mobile phones, tablets, automobiles, and more. When expanding computer hardware holdings, it is essential to purchase trusted hardware that has been analyzed, tested, and vetted: quality components help manage risks linked to microprocessor and internal hardware flaws. The most reliable method to identify and address risk in hardware is to include risk management best practices in the planning and development phases of the technology. Furthermore, risk identification, categorization, and monitoring must not stop. Assessing risk is a process that must occur throughout the entire lifecycle of each hardware asset.

Looking Further

According to the FBI and security subject matter expert (SME) Tom Ervin, modern day USB thumb drives, once plugged into a system, can take control of hardware assets thus allowing hackers remote access and the ability to manipulate code. The risk of webcam and microphone hardware being hijacked also increases, which raises risk to operational security by raising the likelihood of verbal or visual proprietary information being captured [28].

The risk of microprocessor vulnerabilities and exploitation was highlighted by the Meltdown and Spectre hardware flaws. The Meltdown and Spectre vulnerabilities affect several brands of processors, including the AMD and Intel processors that are in nearly every computing device [26]. Numerous hardware vulnerabilities are embedded into a single processor: this complexity makes it difficult to inventory hardware assets and associated vulnerabilities. Research must often be done to identify what type of hardware exists within company assets and whether that hardware is applicable to the Meltdown and Spectre flaws. The process of identifying these hardware vulnerabilities is also time consuming, and thus puts the organization at risk during the risk assessment process. There are many hardware flaws in addition to Meltdown and Spectre; covering specific flaws in detail, however, falls outside the scope of this book. It is important to conduct self-research on flaws applicable to systems used in the organization in order to stay aware of past and current flaws. This is a key part of risk management.

Looking Further

Hardware flaws in general sound intimidating, but the following actions will help identify and mitigate hardware risks: identifying all devices possessing a flaw, assessing technology devices for compatibility with other organizational devices, patching hardware, ensuring the correct and most current firmware or software is installed, and establishing continuous monitoring to identify any inconsistencies or abnormal behavior of hardware assets [26].

Computer peripherals include any device that connects to a computer system or technology-related hardware. Examples include keyboards, mice, chargers, headphones, devices that utilize Bluetooth technology, cameras, card readers, and more. The firmware security company Eclypsium has found that peripheral manufacturers do not verify firmware or whether code on their hardware devices comes from a trusted source. This translates to potential risk of altered firmware, capable of exploiting hardware assets. In short, unsigned firmware poses a risk [27].

> **Looking Further**
>
> Some examples of routing protocols are Routing Information Protocol (RIP), Interior Gateway Protocol (IGRP), and Open Shortest Path First (OSPF) [31]. Enterprise networks utilizing older routing protocols that are less secure, such as RIP, are exposed to higher risk.

As with internal hardware components, any technology-related additives to a system can increase risk to the hardware asset. Organizations can implement security settings that lock out or monitor Universal Serial Bus (USB) ports, unused Network Interface Cards (NICs), or even micro adapter ports on hardware. Doing so will allow the organization to ensure that only authorized peripherals are plugged into company hardware assets, and in return reduce the risk of USB attacks or other peripherals connecting with malicious intent. While peripheral specific attack vectors and USB attacks will not be covered in detail, it is wise to be familiar with each as possible risks the organization may face. Being able to identify malicious intent of unauthorized computer peripherals will reduce the probability or likeliness of the risk becoming reality. If the organization allows personal thumb drives, the risk of USB-related attacks increase.

A **switch** is a network asset that connects multiple information technology devices on a network. The repercussions of a switch being compromised are grave. Switches possess a system software known as **internetwork operating systems (IOSs).** Additionally, several services and configurations are required to reduce risk of security breach. Utilizing unmanaged switches (switches that are plug and play or that are pre-configured to work instantly upon powering on) and failing to configure security on managed switches (switches configured manually) will increase risk of nefarious actors gaining privileged access to IT hardware and applications.

In addition to security flaws, switches are also vulnerable to losing functionality during power outages and being damaged by environmental conditions such as humidity, moisture, high temperature, and corrosion. Improper configuration due to human error will also create security gaps. Switches may also experience issues with performance, capacity and storage, and network transport, all of which increase the risk to network services and business operations [29]. Like other information technology hardware, switches must remain isolated from the general population or workforce. Mounting a switch in a locked server rack in a locked data center and requiring multi-factor identification will reduce the risk of physical access and tampering. **Multi-factor authentication** uses more than one source to verify either "who you are," "what you have" or "something you know." "Who you are," for example, refers to physical characteristics such as voice, fingerprints, facial structure, or the eye retina. "Something you know" is a password or passphrase, while "something you have" may be an access card or identification badge. Using two or more of these factors is referred to as **two-factor authentication.** Again, using all 3 methods is multi-factor authentication [30].

Routers are another main component of infrastructure hardware assets. A router is much more intelligent than a switch: routers are the brains of the operation in that they receive data or packets, analyze them, and decide where they go next. Routers share many vulnerabilities with switches: power or electrical issues, misconfiguration, weak security settings, outdated software, physical access, and environmental conditions. Being more complicated than switches, routers are subject additional risks. Routers utilize routing protocol configurations geared toward the requirements of the organization. Organizations must choose the best routing protocol to suit the needs of the enterprise; to manage risk, however, security must be considered in the planning process. The risk of compromise greatly increases if a router that provides all internet functionality is using outdated or unsecure protocols. Nearly every employee in an office environment is affected by the risk associated with router hardware failure, compromise, or theft of data.

Continuously monitoring router activity, logs, and environmental controls will help reduce overall risk to routers. Incident response teams and contingency plans can alleviate the risk that the organization would face during prolonged network outages. The most difficult part of router risk mitigation is ensuring correct technical configuration, redundancy, and security. To counter the risk of a router losing its routing capabilities, the Information Technology Sector Coordinating Council & Information Technology Government Coordination Council (2011) suggested several risk mitigation actions, including the use of secure routing protocols, verification of addresses, consolidation of routes, a multi-person change commit, and signed route announcements [32]. Keeping current with vendor-tested, agency-authorized firmware and software will reduce risk exposure as well. Configurations that conform to **Security Technical Information Security Guides (STIGs)**, also known as industry recommended security configs or best security practice, will defend routers and decrease the likeliness of potential risk.
A **server** is a network asset that, as the name implies, serves other devices or assets on the network. Servers typically provide a specific service. For example, an exchange server provides email services, a database server stores logs or information, a web server stores data pertaining to a website, a print server provides network printing capabilities, and application servers provide application support. A domain controller is a server that provides authentication, account and user management, Domain Name System (DNS) capability, Dynamic Host Configuration Protocol (DHCP) services, and more. Different types of servers can be susceptible to different types of risk.

According to Stratix Systems, servers have five primary security risks. These risks can be broadly categorized into physical security, access control, application-based security and maintenance, necessary services and functionality, and software vulnerabilities [33]. Securing physical access to servers reduces the risk of unauthorized personnel either installing malicious software or physically harming servers. Administrative access must incorporate role-based access, allowing only technicians with a need to know to access and modify server settings and security. Applications must be monitored to ensure they are performing their intended purpose, while version control of updated application software is maintained, accounted for, and installed. Disabling unnecessary services can reduce risk of servers being exploited. Continuous maintenance, monitoring, updating, and appropriate change management procedures will assist in reducing organizational risk pertaining to servers and the functions they support.

Firewalls can help reduce risk of network-based attacks on the enterprise. A firewall is a network asset responsible for monitoring and filtering traffic; it blocks unrecognized connection attempts and malicious content attempting to infiltrate the network. Installing firewalls between network assets creates a barrier of protection that in return reduces risk within the **intranet**, or a company's internal private network available to employees. Although firewalls reduce risk from outside attack, the asset and hardware itself still possesses various risks. Like other network devices, the hardware requires firmware and software to function: failing to patch or update the firewall leads to exploitable vulnerabilities, rendering its original functionality useless. Protecting against outside threats is essential. The threat of an inside attack on the firewall, however, cannot be overlooked [34]. Housing firewalls in a locked data center on a locked rack helps address the risk of insider threat. Naturally, the risk of misconfiguration and human error always pose a risk as well. Dosal makes this point clearly: "having a poorly-configured firewall is kind of like filling a castle's moat with sand and putting the key to the main gate in a hide-a-key right next to the entrance—you're just making things easier for attackers while wasting time, money, and effort on your "security" measure" (2018).

Intrusion detection and intrusion prevention systems are information technology assets used to identify and halt abnormal behavior or patterns on a network. Utilizing each device can reduce the escalation of a breach by initiating incident response procedures to isolate the infected assets or system. An **intrusion detection system (IDS)** identifies abnormalities or potential breaches on the network and reports them to the appropriate person or team. Detecting a compromise quickly helps to reduce the risk of exposing multiple assets to malware that has made its way into enterprise systems. A **host intrusion detection system (HIDS)** is installed on a host or workstation, while a **network intrusion detection system (NIDS)** lies on the network to monitor traffic. While a great system to implement, an IDS does not fully mitigate risk: it cannot prevent an incident or encrypt data being sent across a network. Additionally, false positives are common, the packets containing data can be spoofed (when an untrusted source is cloaked as an accepted source), and both NIDS and HIDS can fall victim to several cyber-attacks [35]. An

intrusion prevention system (IPS), on the other hand, will not only identify potential malicious activities, but also will stop or prevent occurrences in accordance with its configured intent. Host-based intrusion systems (HIPS) are installed on computer assets, while network-based intrusion systems (NIPS) provide detection and reaction across the network itself [35]. Implementing both detection assets on an enterprise network is an effective way to manage network-related risk.

While switches are used to connect computers and IT assets to the internet, **access points** provide a means of wireless connectivity (or Wi-Fi) to the organization. Many organizations now use Wi-Fi to connect to the web. Several risks come with the convenience of wireless internet access, including unauthorized access to the wireless signal, impersonation of the access point to lure victims into connecting to them, and unauthorized use of sniffing tools to steal credentials or business sensitive information [36]. Without proper configuration and security, access points pose more risk than warranted by their convenience. Access points offer many security options, some less effective than others. Failing to choose the best security configuration for access points means higher risk and probability of unauthorized entry into the network.

When configuring a home router or access point, there are several options for encryption or security protocol selection. A **protocol** is a method of communication and security a router uses across a network. The same goes for corporate or enterprise access points. The Wired Equivalent Privacy (WEP) is the most basic and least secure. Wi-Fi Protected Access (WPA) offers more security, while the best security solution is WPA2 [37]. Configuring the most secure protocol not only negates the risk of several vulnerabilities (including the potential for "man in the middle" attacks) and of the interception of data and traffic, but it also reduces the probability of malicious intent succeeding. It is not wise to connect to non-password protected Wi-Fi, as anyone can access the same network and potentially steal data from or infect the systems connected to the access point. Part of avoiding risk is not putting oneself in a vulnerable situation in the first place. If unsecure Wi-Fi is the only option, a **virtual private network (VPN)** or encrypted tunnel for data to pass must be used to manage the risk associated with utilizing the network, thus reducing the probability of **personal identifiable information (PII)** being captured.

As discussed, a number of information technology assets exist. These assets both possess risk and help manage it. Risk management can be tricky when attempting to reduce organizational risk without understanding cumulative risk. **Cumulative risk** is defined as additional risk that is added to existing risk over time, or when changes on existing systems are made. Identifying information technology risks and their probability, impact, and severity are made easier through valuation of assets. **Asset valuation** is the process of determining fair market value of both tangible and intangible assets. **Tangible assets** are physical assets the organization possesses, while **intangible assets** are not materialistic [38]. IT hardware assets are tangible assets; the services they provide or even the reputation of the organization's ability to maintain service uptime could be considered intangible assets. Once assets are identified, their fair market value determined, and the impact of their risk assessed, the priority of addressing the risk for each asset can be decided. This priority should be assigned based on the value of the asset to the organization or the potential harm or disruption that could be caused to the organization if the asset is lost. The importance of identifying asset-related risk pertaining to common IT equipment has been discussed. Several methods for preventing and detecting cyber-attack or compromise have been reviewed to provide awareness and availability of tools to manage risk. System hardening and implementation of STIGs are ideal methods to reduce and manage asset-related risk.

Identifying and Categorizing Data-Related Risk

To protect personal and company data, check the trash. **Dumpster diving** is when a person with malicious intent searches the trash for any personally identifiable information or company-sensitive data. Not properly destroying paper records or electronic data creates risk. Different types of data must be identified and categorized by its level of sensitivity. This section will analyze various types of data from a risk viewpoint, as well as emphasize the importance of managing the risk related to handling, categorizing, storing, and destroying data in order to reduce the likelihood of sensitive or personal information being exposed.

Whether data is stored on paper or electronically, the risk of information being mistakenly or intentionally shared with the wrong party is inevitable without proper precautions. Part of managing data-related risk includes identifying what classification each piece of information requires. Employee PII, often gathered and maintained by human resource departments, must be safeguarded. The **General Data Protection Regulation (GDPR)** classifies personal data as any information related to a person that is identifiable (social security number, date of birth, address, income, etc.) [39]. GDPR will be covered in Unit 3. The risk associated with employees falling victim to identity theft because their employer failed to protect their data is a serious one. Data can generally be classified into three primary categories: public, sensitive, and confidential [40].

> **Looking Further**
>
> Data governance initiatives seek to enhance the accuracy and validity of data. More specifically, the quality of data is improved upon to ensure data management procedures are effective and successfully negating any potential risks of data exposure. Data governance will be discussed in Unit 3.

Public data is information that may be shared with the general population. Sharing public data will cause no harm to the organization or its employees. **Sensitive data**, if exposed, may cause temporary or interim harm to the organization, depending on whether consent was obtained for the release of the information. Sensitive information must be safeguarded and made available only to those with a need to know. **Confidential data**, on the other hand, poses the greatest risk of harm to the organization and its employees if it is captured or stolen.

Exposure of confidential data will harm the company over an extended period of time [40]. Handling and storing confidential data require investment and protection, as mandated by federal law or compliance regulations. Understanding the differences between various mediums of data and classifications will help safeguard company data, increase employee awareness of following proper data procedures, and reduce risk of information spillage.

Several entities within the organization must work as a team to properly manage data: the data steward, the data custodian, and the data owner. These roles help to reduce confusion as to who does what, and establishes accountability that tasks are performed accordingly. The **data steward** ensures that data is properly used in accordance with data governance initiatives. The **data custodian** maintains servers and databases and ensures that only those with a need to know have access to files or data [41]. For example, a system administrator manages who has access to specific files and directories. The company may use a file share for storing files, but the custodian ensures that the budget department and facilities maintenance department do not have access to each other's files. The **data owner** is the individual responsible for the overall risk associated with the data. The owner classifies the data, determines who can access the data, and ensures that data custodians are safeguarding the data [41]. The steward, custodian, and owner each performing their roles helps prevent the mishandling of data and reduces the risk of data falling into the wrong hands.

There are a variety of tools and methods to help protect company ideas, content, and information from theft. **Trade secrets** are any data or information a company may possess that provides a competitive advantage. Exposures of trade secrets can damage company reputation, productivity, operations, and more: this is one of the primary reasons that trade secrets must be classified as confidential and securely protected from disclosure. A **trademark** protects a brand, logo, emblem, or representation of the company [42]. Pursuing a trademark negates the risk that another company will use the same unique identifier. **Copyrights** protect "original works of authorship" and "exclusive rights" to a copyrighted expression or product [42]. Obtaining copyright reduces the risk of another company reproducing data, products, or anything else that a company originally developed. Knowing and understanding methods to protect data, information, company assets, and intellectual property is part of reducing the risk of data exposure and threat.

Paper data and electronic data are similar, despite their differing media. Records management and a data retention policy will help the organization maintain legal and regulatory data maintenance compliance, in addition to providing guidance on how to store and both when and how to destroy the data. Paper records must be identified, categorized, and marked with their classification level. Sensitive and confidential documents must always be locked in a secure location. The data retention policy indicates when specific paper data must be destroyed. Having an organized and effective records management policy reduces the risk of employees unknowingly exposing data, being uncertain as to how data should be stored, and being unaware of how to properly destroy the data. Paper files must always be shredded to prevent dumpster diving. Cross-cut shredders are the most reliable method to shred paper, as it is extremely difficult to put small pieces back together and often not worth the time. In 2011, the U.S. National Archives and Records Administration found most government agencies possessed a high-moderate risk of record integrity and authenticity compromise [43]. This survey emphasizes that records management correlates to risk management. Furthermore, in the year 2010, WikiLeaks published an immense number of diplomatic files exposing a large mass of government and organization classified data [43]. The key take-a-way from the above scenario is to always ensure data is both secure and properly destroyed. This applies both to hard copy and paper data, as well as modern data storage mediums, such as electronic data.

Electronic data is stored on various mediums, including hard drives, flash drives, SD cards, and more. **Data at rest** is data or information that is stored on one of the mediums mentioned above; **data in transit** is data being transported over a network or from one location to another. Both types of data can be safeguarded with encryption, which reduces the likelihood of information being read by those who are not meant to view it. Removing data from a hard drive can be tricky and tedious, especially if the hard drive is to be repurposed or used for other means. Not properly disposing of data on a hard drive can also leave behind traces of data known as **data remanence**, which could potentially be recovered and read. There are also different techniques for erasing data stored on the three types of hard drives: advanced technology attachment (ATA) or Serial ATA (SATA) drives, standard magnetic based hard drives, and solid-state drives (SSDs).

For standard hard drives, **clearing** is a method of removing data from risk of a keyboard attack or retrieval via file utility tools. Simply deleting files does not provide confidentiality or assurance that the data is gone. An example of clearing may involve overwriting data on the hard drive [44]. Purging reduces risk of a laboratory attack or advanced data recovery techniques within a lab. **Purging** can be accomplished in ATA hard drives through means of a firmware secure erase command [44]. **Degaussing**, another purging method, utilizes a magnetic field to sanitize the data that is stored on a magnetic based disk. It is not an effective means for destroying CD or DVD media, however, as those media must be put into a shredder. The most effective method to ensure no risk of data retrieval is destruction. Hard drives can be physically destroyed by incineration, pulverization, or shredding via a shredder made for hard drive destruction [44]. SSD drives often come with software to sanitize data. Additionally, a crypto erase method (security key deletion on the drive) can be used on an SSD drive as an alternative method of sanitizing media.

An excellent method to manage organizational risk pertaining to data is establishing **data loss prevention (DLP)** processes. Doing so provides means for managing personally identifiable information (PII), intellectual property, and visibility of data in conjunction with industry-specific regulatory compliance requirements such as GDPR, HIPAA, or PCI-DSS [45], all of which will be discussed in Unit 3. DLP consists of tools and techniques that protect data; prevent risk of exposure through means of encryption and monitoring, with additional capabilities of filtering the information; and output reports on data activity. Implementing DLP centralizes the difficult task of managing every aspect of data to reduce the probability of breach and data theft. Data-related risk is a realistic and probable modern-day threat, as proven with the Equifax data breach that exposed information of over 147.9 million Americans [46]. Data-related risk is a realistic and probable modern-day threat, as proven by the 2017 Equifax data breach discussed in the Introduction.

Chapter Summary

Identifying and categorizing risk is not a difficult process when the right tools are used. It is essential to know and understand the various risks associated with people, technology, assets, and data. Mitigating and managing these risks can be much more of a challenge when business operations, supply and demand, and regulatory requirements are constantly shifting. Risk management is a continuous process of re-evaluating an ever-evolving realm of technology capabilities and requirements. Understanding risks that apply to work-related data and personal information contribute to awareness training and data exposure prevention. Categorizing data as public, sensitive, and confidential assists in managing data by classification, and different personnel are responsible for specific tasks during data lifecycle management. Paper and electronic data must be managed and destroyed differently. Data loss prevention assists in reducing data-related risk while effectively organizing, protecting, and managing risk in a centralized approach.

Discussion Questions

1. Compare and contrast examples of people-, technology-, asset-, and data-related risks.

2. What are the differences between risk identification, categorization, and mitigation? Brainstorm activities for each.

3. Explain how risk plays a role in making a decision.

Exercises

1. Take a moment to brainstorm an activity performed within your current place of employment or at home. Construct a RACI matrix of your own indicating roles and tasks applicable to the activity.

2. Contemplate the actions taken when using social media that may expose personal information. Even if you do not use Facebook, take a moment to review actions you can take to better protect your information with Facebook's privacy settings: https://www.consumerreports.org/privacy/facebook-privacy-settings/

3. Research further into regulatory compliance requirements pertaining to your college, workplace, home internet provider, or healthcare provider. Become familiar with the context of each.

References

[1] Bryner, J. (2020, March 13). 1st Known case of coronavirus traced back to November in China. Retrieved from: https://www.livescience.com/first-case-coronavirus-found.html

[2] NIST. (2011, March). Special Publication 800-39: Managing Information Security Risk. [PDF].

[3] Jaeger, J. (2019, December 30). Top 10 Risk to Keep Executives on their Toes in 2020. *Compliance Week.* Retrieved from https://www.complianceweek.com/risk-management/top-10-risks-to-keep-executives-on-their-toes-in-2020/28239.article

[4] Usmani, F. (2020, February). Risk Appetite, Risk Tolerance, and Risk Threshold. PM Study Circle. Retrieved from https://pmstudycircle.com/2014/05/risk-appetite-risk-tolerance-and-risk-threshold/

[5] Fazlida, M. R., & Said, J. (2015, April). Information Security: Risk, Governance and Implementation Setback. Paper presented at the proceedings of the Financial Criminology, 2015 7th International Conference, Oxford, UK. doi: 10.1016/S2212-5671(15)01106-5

[6] Pearson, T. (n.d.). OODA. How to Turn Uncertainty into Opportunity. Retrieved from https://taylorpearson.me/ooda-loop/#Why_is_the_OODA_loop_so_important

[7] Fulford, M. (2018, April). How a RACI Matrix can Enhance Your Risk Management Program. *Ballast.* Retrieved from https://ballastsecure.com/resource/how-a-raci-matrix-can-enhance-your-risk-management-program/

[8] Jameel, S. (2017, September 22). Privilege Creep: Prevention & Correction. Retrieved from https://cgscomputer.com/privilege-creep-prevention-correction/

[9] Purcell, J. E. (n.d.). Secure coding. Practical Steps to Defend Your Web Apps. SANS. Retrieved from https://software-security.sans.org/resources/paper/cissp/employee-management-security-controls

[10] Mikkelson, D. (2001, February 22). The Salami Embezzlement Technique. Snopes. Retrieved from https://www.snopes.com/fact-check/the-salami-technique/

[11] Johnson, A. & Ludema, J. (2018, June 5). Three Reasons Your Company Should Make Vacation Mandatory. Forbes. Retrieved from https://www.forbes.com/sites/amberjohnson-jimludema/2018/06/05/three-reasons-your-company-should-make-vacation-mandatory/#39ea7b5238ec

[12] PCI Certificate. (2015, April 23). Dual Control or Segregation of Duties? PCI DSS. Retrieved from https://www.pcicertificate.com/dual-control-or-segregation-of-duties/

[13] Behr, A. & Coleman, K. (2017, August 3). Separation of Duties and IT Security. CSO Online. Retrieved from https://www.csoonline.com/article/2123120/separation-of-duties-and-it-security.html

[14] Struck, M. (2018, April 16). HR Risk Management – Top 8 Sources of Human Resource Risk. [Web log post]. Retrieved from http://blog.treadstonerisk.com/hr-risk-management-top-8-sources-of-human-resource-risk

[15] Donaldson, C. (2009, November 3). Human Factors: How to Manage People Risk in your Business. Finance. Retrieved from https://finance.nine.com.au/small-business/human-factors-how-to-manage-people-risk-in-your-business/65eaed43-07b4-41af-8429-374eac6d3115
[16] NIST. (n.d.). Computer Security Resource Center. Retrieved from https://csrc.nist.gov/glossary/term/vulnerability
[17] Tech Plan Inc. Environmental Threats to Your Data Center. [Web log post]. Retrieved from https://techplaninc.com/environmental-threats-to-your-data-center/
[18] Tripp Lite. (n.d.). The Five Main Power Problems. Retrieved from https://www.tripplite.com/support/common-power-problems
[19] Fire Line. (2014, December 30). 4 Types of Sprinkler Systems. [Web log post]. Retrieved from https://www.fireline.com/blog/4-types-fire-sprinkler-systems/
[20] NIST. (2013, April). Special Publication 800-53: Security and Privacy Controls for Federal Information Systems and Organizations (Rev. 4). [PDF].
[21] Christiansen, B. (2018, August 10). MTTR, MTBF, or MTTF? – A Simple Guide to Failure Metrics. Limble. Retrieved from https://limblecmms.com/blog/mttr-mtbf-mttf-guide-to-failure-metrics/
[22] Mizoguchi, T. (2012). Information Technology Risks in Today's Environment. Retrieved from https://chapters.theiia.org/san-diego/Documents/Seminars/SD_IIA___ISACA_Event_041112_Deloitte_IA_Top_Ten_Risks.pdf
[23] Akamai. (n.d.). What are the Security Risks of Cloud Computing? Retrieved from https://www.akamai.com/us/en/resources/data-security-in-cloud-computing.jsp
[24] Department of Homeland Security. (2015, December 11). Business Impact Analysis. Retrieved from https://www.ready.gov/business-impact-analysis
[25] Levine, E. V. & Pipikaite, A. (2019, December 19). Hardware is a cybersecurity risk. Here's what we need to know. Retrieved from https://www.weforum.org/agenda/2019/12/our-hardware-is-under-cyberattack-heres-how-to-make-it-safe/
[26] Kazanciyan, R. (2018, January 17). Meltdown and Spectre Microprocessor Flaws: How Tanium Can Help. [Web log post]. Retrieved from https://www.tanium.com/blog/meltdown-and-spectre-microprocessor-flaws-how-tanium-can-help/
[27] Kovacs, E. (2020, February 18). Peripherals with Unsigned Firmware Expose Windows, Linux Computers to Attacks. Retrieved from https://www.securityweek.com/peripherals-unsigned-firmware-expose-windows-linux-computers-attacks
[28] Barden, M. (2017, May 5). Hackers using devices disguised as thumb drives to steal your information. CBS. Retrieved from https://cbsaustin.com/news/local/hackers-using-devices-disguised-as-thumb-drives-to-steal-your-information
[29] Phalen, M. (2019, March 19). What is a Network Risk Assessment and Why You Need One. [Web log post]. Retrieved from https://www.ais-now.com/blog/what-is-a-network-risk-assessment-and-why-you-need-one

[30] NIST. (2019, December 9). Back to Basics: Multi-Factor Authentication (MFA). Retrieved from https://www.nist.gov/itl/applied-cybersecurity/tig/back-basics-multi-factor-authentication
[31] Keary, T. (2018, November 28). Routing Protocol Types – The Ultimate Guide. Comparitech. Retrieved from https://www.comparitech.com/net-admin/routing-protocol-types-guide/
[32] Information Technology Sector Coordinating Council & Information Technology Government Coordination Council. (2011, July). Risk Management Strategy – Internet Routing, Access and Connection Services. Retrieved from https://www.it-scc.org/uploads/4/7/2/3/47232717/itsrm_for_internet_routing_report_july20_v3.pdf
[33] Stratix Systems. (n.d.). Five Server Security Concerns You Need to Know. [Web log post]. Retrieved from https://stratixsystems.com/five-server-security-concerns-need-know-3/
[34] Dosal, E. (2018, April 12). 5 Firewall Threats and Vulnerabilities to Look Out For. [Web log post]. Retrieved from https://www.compuquip.com/blog/5-firewall-threats-and-vulnerabilities-to-look-out-for
[35] Rapid7. (2017, January 11). The Pros & Cons of Intrusion Detection Systems. [Web log post]. Retrieved from https://blog.rapid7.com/2017/01/11/the-pros-cons-of-intrusion-detection-systems/
[36] US-Cert. (2019, November 15). Security Wireless Networks. Retrieved from https://www.us-cert.gov/ncas/tips/ST05-003
[37] Scolamiero, J. (2004, April). Securing Your Wireless Access Point: What Do All Those Settings Mean Anyways? SANS. Retrieved from https://www.sans.org/reading-room/whitepapers/wireless/securing-wireless-access-point-settings-anyways-1405
[38] CFI. (n.d.). What is Asset Valuation. Retrieved from https://corporatefinanceinstitute.com/resources/knowledge/finance/asset-valuation/
[39] GDPR. (n.d.). Personal Data. Intersoft Consulting. Retrieved from https://gdpr-info.eu/issues/personal-data/
[40] Western University. (2019, April 30). What are the Data Classifications? Retrieved from https://security.uwo.ca/information_governance/standards/data_classification/data_classifications.html
[41] Reeb, B. (2019, March 21). Data Governance Roles: Steward, Owner and Custodian. [Web log post]. Retrieved from https://blog.idatainc.com/data-governance-roles
[42] Kroninger, T. K. (2019, May 1). Trademarks, Copyrights and Patents: Should Business Owners Really Care about IP? Retrieved from https://www.varnumlaw.com/newsroom-publications-trademarks-copyrights-and-patents-why-business-owners-should-care-about-ip
[43] Abraxas. (n.d.). Managing Records, Managing Risk: Assessing Records Management Risk. Retrieved from https://www.abraxasworldwide.com/managing-records-managing-risk/
[44] NIST. (2006, September). SP800-88: Guidelines for Media Sanitization. [PDF].
[45] Zhang, E. (2020, January 27). What is Data Loss Prevention (DLP)? A Definition of Data Loss Prevention. [Web log post]. Retrieved from https://digitalguardian.com/blog/what-data-loss-prevention-dlp-definition-data-loss-prevention

[46] Clements, N. (2018, March 5). Equifax's Enormous Data Breach Just Got Even Bigger. Forbes. Retrieved from https://www.forbes.com/sites/nickclements/2018/03/05/equifaxs-enormous-data-breach-just-got-even-bigger/#458d75c053bc

Chapter 5 – Risk, Vulnerability, and Threat Analysis

Overview

Vulnerability and threat analysis are important elements in calculating organizational risk and determining a risk mitigation priority. Impact, likeliness, probability, and severity of risk are all key contributors for measuring and assessing the criticality of identified vulnerabilities and threats. Risk must be assessed on a continuous basis to ensure adequate risk management. In accordance with the National Institute of Standards & Technology's (NIST's) four step risk management process (frame, assess, respond & monitor) [1], this chapter will dive into the methodology for assessing the vulnerabilities and threats that contribute to organizational risk.

Chapter Learning Objectives

1. Predict the likelihood and probability of risk occurring.
2. Develop quantitative and qualitative risk analysis methods.
3. Formulate vulnerability impact and environmental scores.
4. Compare and contrast internal and external threat analysis.
5. Determine overall risk through calculation of vulnerabilities, threats, and impact.
6. Construct a risk matrix using risk rating, likelihood, and impact.

Analyzing Risk Potential

Probability often refers to the statistical measure of the likelihood of occurrence [2]; in the context of risk, the NIST defines **probability** as the occurrence or likelihood of a vulnerability being exploited. Both the likelihood and impact of a threat occurring must be estimated in order to adequately assess the severity and total risk associated with a given risk scenario [1]. For risk assessment to serve a meaningful purpose, the method for determining probability and impact must be continually analyzed. It is not possible to identify every risk that may be applicable; however, making an honest effort to estimate the probably and impact of known risks will contribute to an effective organizational risk management strategy. Probability cannot always be measured statistically, and so must be estimated. Estimations pertaining to the likelihood of a risk event occurring can be made and are typically based on what the risk event would cost the organization if the event materialized [2]. These estimations assist in determining the likeliness that the risk will occur and what type of contingency planning and funds should be allocated towards the risk to mitigate it. Estimating uncertainty to determine probability can be complex, with a number of factors to consider throughout the process.

Those conducting risk assessments use several factors to measure uncertainty when addressing the probability of risk. These factors include proximity, manageability, familiarity, and propinquity. **Proximity** deals with time: the probability of a risk occurring may be considered higher if the potential for occurrence is sooner rather than later [2]. Risks deemed long-term probabilities may not be appropriately addressed up front, may be pushed to the side to deal with later, or can be forgotten completely if not consistently managed. **Manageability** correlates to control [2]. If the risk in question can be controlled, the probability of it being a potential threat is minimized. **Familiarity** with historical occurrences will help gauge the probability of risk, while a lack of familiarity with such occurrences will contribute to less reliable estimations of probability. **Propinquity** measures potential consequences of risk that may directly affect those involved in the risk scenario. In other words, the potential of the risk probability is analyzed for impact. The larger the impact to the organization, the higher the propinquity. Each of these factors must be considered when assessing uncertainty in the context of risk probability. One method of measuring risk probability consists of assigning risks a numerical score. A score of three may be assigned to a high risk, for example, with a score of two to a medium risk and a score of one to a low risk. Scores contribute to the quantitative risk assessment methods which will be discussed later in this chapter.

After determining risk probability, a risk **impact assessment** is done to analyze the probability and consequences of identified risk scenarios. Impacts associated with information technology and business operations include financial burdens and loss of productivity, time, operations, performance, or capabilities. Risks are then prioritized based on level of criticality correlating to the impact or harm which could be caused if the risk were to be exploited [3]. Impact of risk should be analyzed from a high, medium, and low probability of risk occurrence: doing so will ensure the organization is effectively prepared for any level of impact given each specific risk scenario. Understanding how to utilize risk probability and impact results provides measurable and realistic risk assessment results.

Risk Analysis: Qualitative and Quantitative

Qualitative risk analysis approaches assess risk using a narrative or categories that do not correlate to a measurement, system, or number. For example, risks may be identified and categorized as critical, high, medium, and low. Qualitative methods provide a straightforward method for educating management or decision makers on risks associated with the choices they make for the organization [1]. Qualitative approaches may utilize experience, expert judgement, and data analysis for identifying each risk, probability, and impact. Conducting qualitative risk analysis consists of several steps: forming a team, isolating risks, prioritizing risks, addressing risk, and monitoring and re-evaluating risk [4]. The team should consist of employees that are familiar with the area of risk being assessed. Once identified, the risks must be sorted so that the most critical risks are first and the least critical risks last. When risks are

Figure 5.1. Risk Assessment Chart

resolved, it is imperative to continually monitor and re-assess identified risks to ensure changes

Likelihood: Extremely Likely	Risk A	Risk F	Risk C
Likelihood: Very Likely	Risk H	Risk B	Risk J
Likelihood: Not Likely	Risk G	Risk I	Risk E
QUALITATIVE RISK ANALYSIS	Impact: Small	Impact: Medium	Impact: Large

Critical Risk
High Risk
Medium Risk
Low Risk

over time are not overlooked. As technology advances and changes to operations occur, risks that have been previously mitigated may become an issue yet again.

Qualitative analysis techniques have advantages and disadvantages. Advantages consist of easy to follow assessment and prioritization procedures, as well as an intuitive presentation scheme [5]. The assessment itself is rather straightforward. Describing identified risks as ranging from critical to low gives all audiences the ability to understand the impact and weight of each risk. Disadvantages of using a qualitative method include subjective evaluations or limited perceptions of risk impact and likelihood, failure to account for the impact a given risk has on other risks or entities, bias, carelessness, fatigue, and a potential inability to prioritize which risk should be mitigated first in a single category [5]. For example, if three risks are identified as high likelihood, large impact and critical risk, there is no way to decide which risk should be mitigated first.

One common method of presenting risks identified through the qualitative process is with a relatively simple chart. Figure 5.1 identifies both the impact and likelihood of various risks. Likelihood notes whether the risk is extremely likely, very likely, or not likely; impact is determined to be small, medium, or large. Risks themselves are categorized from critical to low and color coded, so it is easy to identify and prioritize the more severe risks first.

Quantitative risk assessment techniques measure risk with numerical methods, associate values to risk for use in calculations [1], and provide more validity and transparency than qualitative assessments [6]. One risk assessment method is not better than the other; choosing which method should be used depends on the need of the organization, the types of risks being assessed, and experience of those conducting the assessment. Several methods exist for performing quantitative risk analysis. Statistics can be used for characterization of parameters, interval analysis can calculate best- and worst-case scenarios, and thresholds assist the determination of when action must be taken to keep risk within the organization's level of tolerance [6]. These and other quantitative risk assessment methods will be discussed in greater detail in the next chapter.

Advantages of quantitative risk analysis vary between asset-, people-, technology-, and data-related risks. Risk associated with assets can be determined quantitatively via monetary value and through application of cost-benefit analysis.

Security levels pertaining to technology-related risk can be more accurately determined by scores based on confidentiality, integrity, and availability requirements, which will be discussed in Unit 3. Objective methods provide an additional advantage since assessment conclusions can be communicated with terminology that management comprehends. Validity is provided in the accuracy of organizational data, and management performance can be closely monitored [7]. Every category of risk can be quantified to determine likelihood, impact, and the ability to make data-backed, risk-aware decisions. Disadvantages of quantitative methods include the complexity of using calculations and information represented as monetary values: these representations may be challenging for those without experience in data analysis to interpret. Furthermore, there is no real standardized approach to performing quantitative analysis, which means that different organizations may have different methodologies and techniques for producing risk ratings. These differences could create difficulties in negotiating business or transferring risk to third parties for mitigation [7]. It is best to use a team experienced in quantitative assessment methods, in addition to having an easy-to-understand presentation for management.

> **Looking Further**
>
> *Confidentiality* represents the ability to restrict data. The opposite of confidentiality is disclosure.
>
> *Integrity* represents the accuracy of the data. Data integrity is the ability to trust the data is not altered or manipulated in a negative fashion. The opposite of integrity is destruction.
>
> *Availability* means data can be accessed, viewed, and updated when needed. The opposite of availability is denial.

Risk Management Framework and Risk Standards

Frameworks and standards provide a structured methodology for approaching an initiative. Several major globally recognized standards exist for risk assessment and risk management: The Control Objectives for Information Technologies (COBIT), the International Electrotechnical Commission (IEC), the International Organization for Standardization (ISO), and the NIST. Risk standards help an organization establish policies and procedures for effective risk management by using the most recognized risk approaches, methods, and techniques.

COBIT 5, created by the Information Systems Audit and Control Association (ISACA), provides perspectives on risk function and risk management. The framework implements governance processes to ensure information technology risk does not exceed organizational risk appetite and tolerance levels. Furthermore, managing IT-related risks are considered within the context of enterprise risk management (ERM) while costs associated with managing enterprise resource planning (ERP) are balanced. In other words, COBIT will assist in implementing risk governance for both new and mature organizations. COBIT assists in providing methods for risk identification, analysis, and response [8].

IEC 31010:2009 is a framework covering risk management and assessment techniques. A variety of risk scenarios are discussed, and guidance is provided for making risk-aware decisions and comprehending risk impact in terms of organizational objectives. The framework addresses the identification and evaluation or risk, quantifying risk rank, and selecting risk treatment methods [9].

ISO 31000:2009 *Risk Management: Principles and Guidelines* addresses top management leadership, enforcing risk management through governance and outlining risk management principles as they pertain to setting the organization up for success [10]. An open systems model is used to address risk for organizations with varying business goals, risk perspectives, and operational requirements. An **open systems model** is a way of describing an organization's internal relationship with outside relationships. In other words, being "open" would be the opposite of a closed or independent organization. An example may be an employee in an organization. The employee performs their duties internal to the organization, which allows the business to operate. The business operating affects outside customers and the services the company provides to the public. The public or customers in this case are can be referred to as outside relationships. Furthermore, ISO 31000 provides an iterative approach to risk management, encouraging organizations to learn from previous phases and actions throughout the risk management process [10].

ISO/IEC 27005:2011 *Information Technology Security Techniques: Information Security Risk Management (ISRM)* focuses on the treatment, acceptance, communication, monitoring, and review of risk. Scoping, valuation of assets, assessing impact, and vulnerability assessment techniques are reviewed [11]. **ISO/IEC 27001: 2013** *Information Technology: Security Techniques: Information Security Risk Management Systems Requirements* assists in helping organizations with reducing overall risk, optimization of business operations, and building a risk-aware culture. The intent of this standard involves reducing organizational risk by safeguarding data to lower the probability of security-related incidents [12]. Both of the ISO/IEC publications are great risk management references for building or enhancing risk management strategies.

NIST offers many publications to assist organizations with the implementation of risk management. A few of their noteworthy publications to assist with risk identification, categorization, and management are:

- **NIST SP800-30 Rev 1**: *Guide for Conducting Risk Assessments*
- **NIST SP800-37 Rev 2**: *Guide for Applying Risk Management Framework to Federal Information Systems: A Security Life Cycle Approach*

- **NIST SP800-39**: *Managing Information Security Risk*
- **NIST SP800-53 Rev 4**: *Security and Privacy Controls for Federal Information Systems and Organizations*

Each of the publications provide NIST's viewpoint or approach on managing risk. NIST SP800-53 specifically addresses the control, selection, and assessment stages, while NIST SP800-37 provides guidance on the authorize and monitor steps [13].

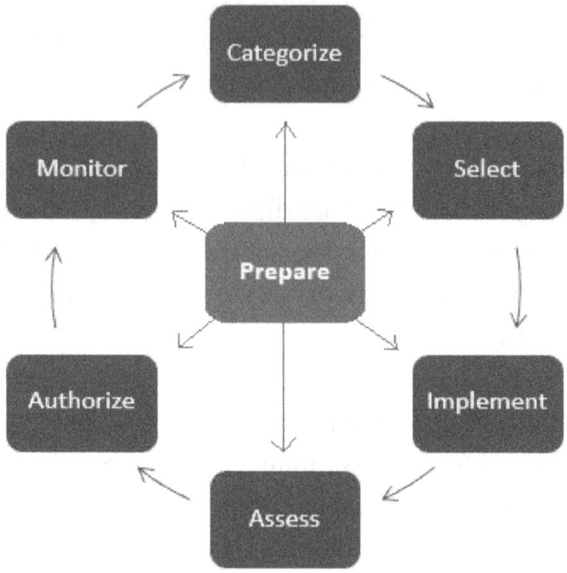

Figure 5.2. The Stages of Risk Management Framework (RMF)

The **Risk Management Framework (RMF)** is a well-recognized process for integration of both risk management procedures and organizational security in system development lifecycles. Figure 5.2 depicts the risk management framework. Preparation is where the process begins, flowing to the categorization, selection, implementation, assessing, authorizing, and monitoring controls [13]. (Controls are just another name for preventative measures the organization puts in place to manage risk associated with people, technology, assets, or data.) The **preparation** stage is where organizations plan on integrating risk management and security procedures into current policy, procedure, processes, business operations, and everyday routines. The **categorize** step involves determining how a system classifies, processes, stores, and transmits data. The **select** stage chooses a baseline control for a system that will serve as the minimum requirement for similar systems: for example, if one computer is required to have access control settings, all computers within the organization should have access control settings as well. The **implement** stage determines how controls will be implemented on the system or within the operating environment. The **assess** step investigates whether controls are effective and serving their purpose, while the **authorize** step formally recognizes controls as performing their intended function. Lastly, **monitoring** observes how controls interact, function, and change [13]. Technology and controls change over time due to new implementations or evolving requirements of the organization. Assessing and monitoring are especially important to ensure controls are still performing effectively in conjunction with new systems, requirements, or operations.

In summary, risk standards and the RMF process assist in managing information system risk through a lifecycle approach. A variety of standards are available for reference. One standard is not better than the other; they each provide guidance and insight on different perspectives for addressing organizational risk. Reviewing various perspectives on risk will help determine which approach is best for a given organization.

Vulnerability Analysis

This section will address various methods for identifying and analyzing vulnerabilities. According to NIST, a vulnerability is a weakness in computer coding, software, or hardware that, if exploited, would hinder the ability of an organization to implement confidentiality, integrity, and availability methodologies into computing systems, technology, or data [14]. **Vulnerability management** is a strategy to minimize organizational vulnerabilities by reducing the risk of exposure, attack vectors, exploitation, or malicious intent. **Attack vectors** are any method by which a system or subject may be compromised. Vulnerability management includes **patch management**, which is the process of installing the latest updates, firmware, or software on information technology hardware. As discussed in Chapter 4, failing to address technological vulnerabilities not only creates a higher risk of devices being exploited, but also puts personally identifiable information at risk of theft. Organizations rely heavily upon technology and assets to perform business operations. Nearly every employee uses computing devices for some aspect of their job. Risk management strategies, like all security systems, are only as effective as the weakest link. The exploitation of a minor vulnerability may render stronger security controls ineffective, allowing opportunity for additional exploitation and greater risk of harm to the organization.

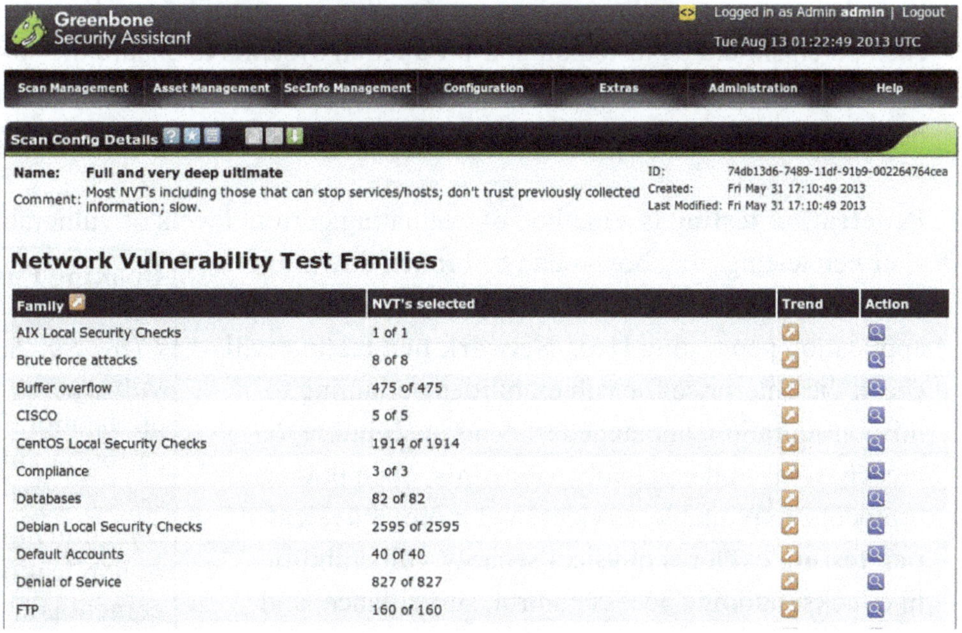

Figure 5.3. An Example of a Vulnerability Scanner

As with risk assessment, there are vulnerability assessment techniques. As shown in Figure 5.3, Greenbone Security Assistant is one of many tools available for the scanning and identification of vulnerabilities. Assessing and addressing vulnerabilities help manage and reduce risk. A **vulnerability assessment** consists of using programs or software written to scan for vulnerabilities in organizational software, hardware, and networks. The scanners should be configured to scan every IT device that has an assigned IP address on the network, including computers, printers, routers, switches, and servers. Once vulnerabilities are identified, they should be prioritized by severity and mitigated in order from most to least critical [15]. Vulnerability reports can be created to help manage vulnerability mitigation strategy and progress. Change management must be implemented to ensure patching or installing updated software does not harm the availability of services which support business operations and productivity. **Change management** is a process that vets, documents, and manages any changes to systems or an operating environment within an organization. Prior to installing new patches, each patch should be tested on non-production systems to ensure the software update will not break the system. Once the patch is verified as stable and harmless to the system, updates may be pushed out enterprise-wide on all production systems.

Penetration testing is a method of evaluating current levels of vulnerability. Penetration testing -- or pen testing, for short -- can be broken down into three general categories: network, physical, and application pen testing [16]. **Network pen testing** will check the enterprise for vulnerabilities pertaining to misconfiguration, unpatched systems susceptible to breach, weak and crackable passwords, open ports and protocols, exploitable services, and more. **Physical pen testing** explores physical security vulnerabilities like locks, building access control, surveillance, and other means of physical entry that could be breached. **Application pen testing** explores web vulnerabilities and potential attack vectors, including cross site scripting, injection flaws and cross site request forgery opportunities [16]. Conducting penetration testing helps an organization identify and fix weaknesses that increase breach risks. It is much more cost-effective to find and fix vulnerabilities than to be exploited by an attacker: costs to recover and repair damage are much greater than investing early to reduce the risk exposure and opportunity of attack.

> **Looking Further**
>
> *Cross Site Scripting (XSS)* is a vulnerability known within web applications where malicious scripts are inserted into a target.
>
> *Injection flaws* are flaws in systems or applications where malicious content is injected into the target.
>
> *Cross Site Request Forgery (CSRF)* occurs when malicious content or commands are inserted into a trusted web application. CSRF is also known as a one-click attack.

In order to accurately assess organizational risk, it is necessary to understand the impact of vulnerabilities. To quantify the impact of vulnerabilities, a scoring methodology is utilized. One such method is the **Common Vulnerability Scoring System (CVSS)**, which calculates an organization's vulnerability score in three categories: base score, temporal score, and environmental score [17]. Figure 5.4 summarizes CVSS metrics. There are manual and automated methods for calculating vulnerability scores. Automated methods can be found on the internet by searching CVSS calculators; however, it is beneficial to understand the calculation process and how scores are broken down.

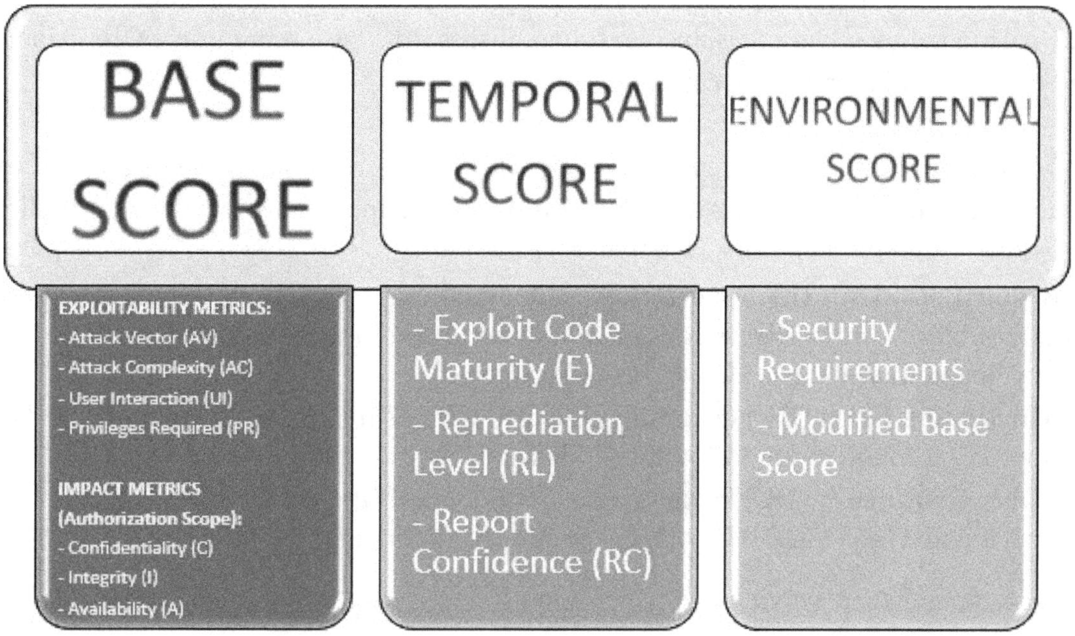

Figure 5.4. CVSS Metrics

The **base score** assesses both how easy the vulnerability is to exploit and the damage that could result from exploitation. The base score utilizes sub scores for exploitability and impact. The **exploitability sub score** considers how probable the exploit of a given vulnerability is [17]. The metrics used to calculate exploitability sub score are:

- **Attack vector (AV)** discusses how easily an attacker can access the vulnerability.
- **Attack complexity (AC)** describes the conditions which must exist for an attacker to exploit the vulnerability.
- **User interaction (UI)** determines how many users or employees in the organization are necessary for the attack to be a success.
- **Privileges required (PR)** identifies the level of access required for an attacker to exploit the vulnerability.

While the exploitability sub score measures the likeliness of an exploit, the **impact sub score** determines what impact a successful exploit will have. The **Authorization Scope** further measures the impact of the vulnerability. The authorization scope describes three impact metrics:

- **Confidentiality (C)** translates to the amount of authority an exploited vulnerability may provide.
- **Integrity (I)** refers to the amount of damage an exploited vulnerability may implement.

- **Availability (A)** is a measure of lost resources and services due to the exploitation of the vulnerability [17].

Calculating each score helps emphasize how probable and severe an exploit could be. Final scores are calculated by adding up sub scores. Establishing the base score frames the standard for assessing other potential areas of weakness.

The **temporal score** ranks the awareness level of vulnerability remediation steps and determines if threat actors are actively targeting the vulnerability. The temporal score calculation relies on three metrics:

- **Exploit Code Maturity (E)** determines the likeliness a vulnerability will be exploited successfully. This likeliness is normally based on exploit kits and coding pertaining to the vulnerability that has already been discovered.
- **Remediation Level (RL)** determines the difficulty of fixing the vulnerability and can be viewed as a counterpoint to Exploit Code Maturity.
- **Report Confidence (RC)** is the level of confidence of the vulnerability's existence, verifying that the vulnerability is real and not a rumor [17].

Calculating temporal scores, to include the previously referenced sub scores, determines how risk may be managed, mitigated, and monitored.

The **environmental score** is particular to the work environment in a specific organization. It is broken down into:

- The **security requirements sub score** is a score based on confidentiality, integrity, and availability metrics derived from the "impact sub-score." These metrics are determined based on the specific organization, environment being assessed and mandatory security requirements.
- The **modified base score** reevaluates all metrics within the "base score" to consider the specifics of the organization and environment not previously evaluated [17]. Examples of specifics may include but are not limited to: laws required from conducting business in other countries, privacy laws specific to the type of data the organization handles and specific security requirements for unique systems or applications the business may utilize to perform a service.

Environmental conditions can play a significant part in determining risk associated with vulnerability. Because environmental factors vary by organization, it is imperative to specifically assess the organizational habits, operations, and practices that may affect this area of calculation. Upon ranking the Base, Temporal, and Environmental Scores, values are assigned to reflect the potential impact and severity a vulnerability may have. Vulnerabilities are ranged on a ten-point scale: no risk (0.0), low risk (0.1-3.9), medium risk (4.0-6.9), high risk (7.0-8.9) and critical risk (9.0-10.0) [17]. Take note: values of vulnerability severity may vary depending upon the version or categorization of the CVSS used.

There are important differences between risk and vulnerability. An accumulation of unaddressed vulnerabilities increases organizational risk. Vulnerability management is required to reduce technology-related risk, which will necessarily reduce people-, asset-, and data-related risks. Assessing and mitigating vulnerabilities fall within the risk.

Threat Analysis

NIST describes a **threat** as any event or instance that may harm company operations, personnel, or assets. Furthermore, **threat sources** lead to threat events. Examples of threat sources include human error, failure of IT equipment, environmental controls, or even disaster in general [1]. Threats are generally categorized as human or not human. Examples of human threats include technicians, hackers, non-technical staff, and untrained IT personnel; they also include actions caused by humans, such as misconfigurations, theft, accidents, and more. Non-human threats could be electrical, HVAC-related, water, fire, or threats that pertain to technology, such as viruses and malware.

Threat analysis consists of four primary phases: scoping, gathering, analyzing, and acting [18]. **Scoping** involves understanding the threat and establishing priorities for addressing the threat. The **gathering** phase is where multiple sources are reviewed to harvest methodology related to the threat. The **analyze** step reviews information from the previous step to establish links between threat factors. **Threat factors** are characteristics which contribute to identifying a threat, to include but not limited to people, technology, assets, and data. The final stage is **acting** out a strategic and risk-aware decision on how to prevent or address the threat in question [18]. Using threat analysis will help lower risk to the organization, as the risk formula (discussed in the next section) includes threat in the actual calculation as well.

Threat intelligence contributes to the analysis of risk scenarios. **Threat intelligence** is defined as any information that helps the organization prevent or halt attacks. Gathering intelligence on threat specifics assists with making risk-aware decisions. Furthermore, threat intelligence helps gauge what the organization is up against, such as whether threat actors are targeting the organization, how and why they may attack, and what type of systems or hardware they commonly target [19]. Threat intelligence can generally be broken down into three distinctive categories: strategic, tactical, and operational. The **strategic category** pertains to threats commonly directed towards managerial, leadership, or executive staff. **Tactical** threat intelligence includes procedures, tactics, and techniques used by threat actors to carry out intentions. This category pertains to a technical audience. The **operational category** specifically addresses technical details about various attacks or threat-related campaigns [19]. As noted in the Introduction, hacker groups may be considered **Advanced persistent threats (APTs)**. APTs, however, may also pertain to undetected attacks that use customized malware or have exploited previous known vulnerabilities to maintain access or monitoring over a network for an extended period. APTs look to steal secrets, perform political espionage, or seek financial gain [20]. Several resources are available on the web to identify current APTs and APT groups, as well as the methods that organizations are using to counter them. The top five indicators of APTs are:

1. Random administrative login on systems during the evening or non-operation hours
2. Backdoors
3. Information flowing over the network in uncommon or different-than-established trends
4. Files appearing in locations where they previously were not
5. Spear phishing campaigns that are focused on executives or employees within the organization [20].

Spear phishing refers to attacks that target a specific person, usually management or leadership. **Backdoors** refer to any unauthorized entry a nefarious actor uses to access a system. Organizations must stay engaged on current attack trends to effectively manage threat related risks.

Threat modeling portrays the profiles, methodology, and intention of nefarious actors. A threat model also depicts potential threat scenarios and abstraction of systems. Previously, CVSS was discussed, which is one method of threat modeling. Three additional examples of threat modeling consist of STRIDE, PASTA and LINDUN [26].

STRIDE focuses on the violation of various properties by different threats. More specifically, confidentiality, integrity, availability, non-repudiation, availability, and authorization are addressed. The S in **STRIDE** addresses "spoofing identification" which violates "authentication" by a potential threat actor pretending to be someone they are not. **Spoofing** is defined as when a hacker identifies as someone or something different than they truly are. Spoofing tricks a person or system into believing the hacker is legitimate. **Authentication** is defined as a person or system proving identity or validating, they are who they say they are. The T stands for "tampering with data" which violates "integrity" by modification of data, a network or memory. The R stands for "repudiation" which violates "non-repudiation" or someone claiming they did not change or do something. The I stands for "information disclosure" which violates "confidentiality" correlating to someone accessing information they are not permitted to access. The D stands for "denial of service" and violates "availability" which pertains to resources being exhausted and services being lost. The E stands for "elevation of privilege" violating "authorization" or allow an employee to perform an action they are not authorized to conduct [26]. A system such as a server would be selected to analyze potential threats, impact and probability from each category of stride (spoofing, tampering, repudiation, information disclosure, denial of service and elevation of privilege).

PASTA stands for the Process for Attack Simulation and Threat Analysis, which uses a seven-step process for conducting risk analysis. PASTA aligns technical requirements with the business's objectives while providing an attacker's perspective on threats in conjunction with impact and risk analysis [27]. The first step in PASTA is defining objectives which include business objectives, security and compliance requirements and performing business impact analysis. The second step consists of defining the technical scope which involves capturing several factors such as the technical environment's boundary, dependences related to applications, software, and infrastructure. The third step involves application decomposition or identification of use cases, trust level, application entry points, actors, roles, services, assets, data sources and more. The fourth step covers threat analysis or attack scenarios, security event regression analysis, analytics, and threat intelligence. The fifth step is vulnerability and weaknesses analysis. This step includes issue tracking queries of vulnerability reports, threats to existent vulnerability mapping, flaw analysis of designs, scoring and enumeration. The sixth step is attack modeling which includes analysis of attack surface, attack tree structure and exploit analysis. The seventh and final step includes the risk and impact analysis. This step qualifies and quantifies the business impact, addresses countermeasures, residual risk, and mitigation strategy [26]. The process for each step goes much further in-depth but the intent is only to familiarize you with the basic methodology of the PASTA threat modeling technique.

LINDUN stands for link-ability, identifiability, non-repudiation, detectability, disclosure of information, unawareness, and non-compliance. This threat modeling technique is geared towards security of data and consists of six steps. The first three steps correlate to the "problem space" while the last three steps provide resolutions or "solution space." Defining the data flow diagram and how data moves is the first step. The second step involves mapping privacy related threats to each of the data flow diagram elements. The third step identifies threat scenarios and the fourth step prioritizes the threats. The fifth step explores mitigation possibilities while the sixth and final step selects appropriate corresponding privacy enhancing technologies (PETs) and strategic objectives [26].

Calculating Risk

RISK FORMULAS

- (Impact x Probability) / Cost
- Impact x Probability
- Threat x Vulnerability x Consequence
- Threat x Vulnerability x Asset

Now that probability, impact, vulnerabilities, and some common examples of threat have all been covered, it is time to review how each contributes to the calculation of risk. Several methods exist for calculating risk. One method involves multiplying "impact" by "probability" and dividing by "cost." Impact refers to how the risk would affect the organization if it were to occur, probability is the likelihood of the risk occurring within a specific period of time, and cost is how much it would cost in dollars to reduce or mitigate the identified risk [21]. Sometimes this formula is just calculated as "probability" times "impact." Another method of calculation involves multiplying "consequence" by "threat" by "vulnerability" to determine overall risk [22], while still another multiplies "asset" times "vulnerability" times "threat" to calculate risk [23]. Choosing the right method to calculate risk is dependent upon expert judgement, experience, and what fits the risk scenario the best. The overall goals of any method are to quantify and express the risk the organization must face, reduce, and mitigate. See Figure 5.5 for a quick reference of risk formulas.

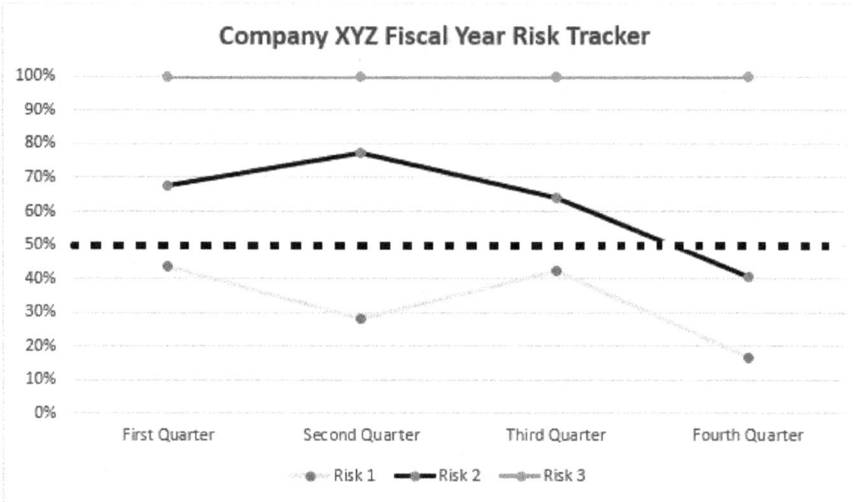

Here is one way to calculate risk. A vulnerability has been identified with a score of 8.9 (high risk). A threat has also been identified with a score of 4.2 (medium). The threat (4.2) multiplied by the vulnerability (8.9) is 37.38. That value would then be compared to a scale representing the numerical levels of risk and tolerance levels specific to the organization. Depending on where the product numerically falls on the organization's risk chart, the risk is considered to be low, medium, high, etc. Figure 5.6 shows how an organization may measure calculated risk. The example in the figure identifies three risks. In the first quarter, Risk 1 has a bit over a 40 percent chance of occurrence, Risk 2 has a bit below a 70 percent chance of occurrence, and Risk 3 has a 100 percent chance of occurrence. The organization measures the progress of risk mitigation on an annual basis. As seen in the figure, risk each quarter fluctuates dependent upon new threats, vulnerabilities, or additional risk that materializes. The dotted line at 50 percent indicates the company's risk threshold, which means that Risk 2 and 3 are way above the company threshold. This is one of many methods to map out total risk calculated throughout a standard fiscal year.

Calculating exposure of risk will help organizations estimate how much a risk or multiple risks may cost to manage. **Risk exposure** is the amount of damage or financial loss that is directly related to a risk incident occurring. Risk exposure can be calculated via three methods: single value, discrete, and continuous [24]. **Single value calculation** uses a formula very similar to one of the calculations above: probability times impact equals risk exposure. If there were a forty percent chance of critical web servers failing and that failure would cost the organization 2 million dollars in loss of productivity, the risk exposure is the probability of forty percent (.40) times the impact of two million (2,000,000) dollars, or eight-hundred thousand (800,000) dollars

Probability = P

Impact = I

Risk Exposure = RE

SCENARIO 1: COMPLETE FAILURE
.06 (P) x 3,000,000 (I) = 180,000 (RE)

SCENARIO 2: PARTIAL FAILURE
.07 (P) x 1,500,000 (I) = 105,000 (RE)

SCENARIO 3: MINIMAL FAILURE
.08 (P) x 750,000 (I) = 60,000 (RE)

TOTAL RISK EXPOSURE
180,000 + 105,000 + 60,000 = 345, 000

[24]. This calculation method is only effective for single risk scenarios and not for multiple occurrences of the same risk.

Calculating exposure of multiple risks can be done with the **discrete** method. The discrete method uses several probabilities, impacts, and exposures. While the single value calculation only addresses one risk and probability, the discrete method accounts for whether a device fails completely, partially, or minimally. As shown in Figure 5.7, if complete failure has a probability of six percent (.06) and an impact of three million (3,000,000) dollars, the risk exposure for complete failure would be one-hundred and eighty thousand (180,000) dollars. If partial failure has a probability of seven percent (.07) and an impact of 1.5 million (1,500,000) dollars, the risk exposure for partial failure would be one-hundred and five thousand (105,000) dollars. If minimal failure has a probability of eight percent (.08) and an impact of seven hundred and fifty thousand (750,000) dollars, the risk exposure of partial failure would be sixty thousand (60,000) dollars. When all three scenarios and figures are placed side by side, it is quite easy to compare risk exposure for each scenario. Revenue will still be generated but adding each risk exposure level (180,000 + 105,000 + 60,000) results in the estimated figure of 345,000 as a range for all potential levels of failure [24]. This means that in the event of all three scenarios occurring in the same fiscal year, the organization should have at least 345,000 dollars in contingency money set aside. The discrete calculation method is also a useful technique for determining the minimum and maximum damage a risk may present.

The **continuous** risk exposure calculation presents probabilities for different risk scenarios through use of a continuous curve [24]. A chart is created similar to the one in Figure 5.6, starting with maximum cost of failure and decreasing to a zero, portraying probability and impact at various levels. For example, the probabilities of failure in the example above were six percent, seven percent, and eight percent. The continuous risk exposure calculation would incorporate those probabilities along a spectrum from one percent up to one hundred percent (if it were desired to calculate that far). Realistically, a chart could be constructed to show exposure with various probabilities and impacts, and a scatter diagram would depict the actual curve. A **scatter diagram** is a chart used to analyze the relationship between two variables.

Models and Matrices

Risk is often portrayed in visual representations. Stakeholders will likely gain a better understanding of risk data and analysis results if they are displayed in a model or matrix that clearly defines the relationships between probabilities, impacts, and potential losses. **Risk models** portray a visual representation of risk-related data and results. Risk models are also used for determining what risk matrix should be used to capture the data. Examples of risk factors a model may include are impact, vulnerabilities, and threats. The risk model must be identified prior to risk assessment to determine what will be measured or estimated [1]. Understanding the differences between probability and impact matrices, threat matrices, and risk matrices will enable the results of risk assessments to be displayed more clearly.

Probability and impact matrices, often used in information technology project management scenarios, display exactly what the name implies: probability and impact. The matrix in Figure 5.8 shows the probability and cost of a network outage. There is a 70% chance that a short network outage will occur: the cost to bring the network backup would be $10,000, yielding a potential loss would be $7,000. There is a 55% chance of a mid-range outage: the recovery cost there is $50,000, with a potential loss of $27,500. A complete network outage is 10% probable: at a $500,000 cost of recovery, the potential loss would be $50,000. The chart clearly and concisely depicts the probability, impact, and cost for each risk.

PROBABILITY-IMPACT MATRIX		
PROBABILITY	IMPACT	POTENTIAL LOSS
70%	Short Network Outage Recovery Cost ($10,000.00)	$7,000.00
55%	Mid-range Network Outage Recovery Cost ($50,000.00)	$27,500.00
10%	Complete Network Outage Recovery Cost ($500,000.00)	$50,000.00

Threat matrices sort different types of threats by characteristics such as intensity, stealth, and time. **Intensity** determines the capacity of the threat and how much impact it may have. **Stealth** measures whether any information that can be confirmed regarding the threat. **Time** correlates to how much time needs to be invested in resolving the threat throughout its lifecycle [25]. The attributes of a threat matrix include threats and vulnerabilities applicable to the risk scenario, along with numerical ratings to measure or estimate the impact of each. The higher the number, the more likely the threat is to be successful; a lower number represents a lower probability of the threat occurring. An example of a threat matrix is represented in Figure 5.9. The left column contains examples of threats that may harm an information technology department, such as a virus, trojan, denial of service attack, or theft of hardware, all of which are discussed further in

Unit 3. The top row lists devices that are potentially vulnerable to each identified threat. The numbers represent how many devices or vulnerabilities exist: a virus, for example, could be installed via 4 access points and could potentially impact 8 servers, 9 computers, and 4 routers. The higher the assigned score, the more sophisticated the threat is [25]. The total score in the right column summarizes the total risk each threat serves to all identified devices on the enterprise.

THREAT MATRIX					
VULNERABILITIES ➡ **THREATS** ⬇	Servers	Computers	Routers	Access Points	Score
Virus	8	9	4	4	25
Trojan	3	8	3	3	17
Denial of Service	9	6	9	9	24
Theft	2	1	1	2	6

A **risk matrix** or risk diagram is an effective method for deciding how to prioritize risk treatment, as it allows multiple risks and their associated severities to be compared. Risk matrices identify the most troublesome risks and present overall risk scenarios in a single chart for tracking risk severity and mitigation efforts over a period. No prior information or knowledge is required to comprehend the visual depiction of risk within the matrix, and the efficiency of current risk strategies can be clearly assessed on the spot [28]. As seen in Figure 5.10, the left column lists the different severity levels or impacts of risk. The row on the bottom lists the levels of risk probability. Each risk is assigned to a specific location on the chart corresponding to its impact and probability of occurring. Seven different risks are shown in the matrix; however, there is no minimum or maximum number of risks that could potentially be shown. Color coding or shading may be used to identify risks within the company's tolerable threshold [28]. Color coding risks also simplifies the severity of each individual risk and provides a quick reference of those that need immediate attention. Looking at Figure 5.10 again, you can see the shading of color changes from the bottom left corner to the upper right corner. If using a colored graphic, red may be used to identify high risk levels, yellow to identify medium risk levels and green to identify low risk levels. Realistically, any color coding may be used as long as each color is associated to its corresponding risk level.

Chapter Summary

Vulnerabilities and threats contribute to overall risk. The ability to accurately measure and assess vulnerabilities and threats during the risk assessment process helps to determine the priority of risk mitigation. Several qualitative and quantitative techniques exist for determining risk, and a number of frameworks and standards are available for guidance on how to identify and manage organizational risk. Models and matrices are helpful tools for communicating risk to stakeholders. Now that a baseline has been established for risk, vulnerability, and threat analysis, Chapter 6 will further explore specific risk assessment methods, risk responses, various options for handling risk, and the relationship between ethics and risk.

Discussion Questions

1. Research additional matrixes not covered within the textbook. Articulate why the matrix you researched may be better than those discussed within the text, while providing justification as to why.

2. How do each of the risk formulas relate? In your opinion, which formula provides a better method to calculate max risk and why?

3. STRIDE, PASTA and LINDUN threat modeling techniques were identified. Research further another threat modeling technique and how does it compare to the others?

Exercises

1. Think of a risk scenario you have encountered in the past. Would assessing risk in the given scenario be more applicable with a quantitative or a qualitative risk assessment method?

2. Take a moment to identify potential threats or disasters that may be applicable to your home. Capture them within a matrix and determine how you can lower overall risk to your home.

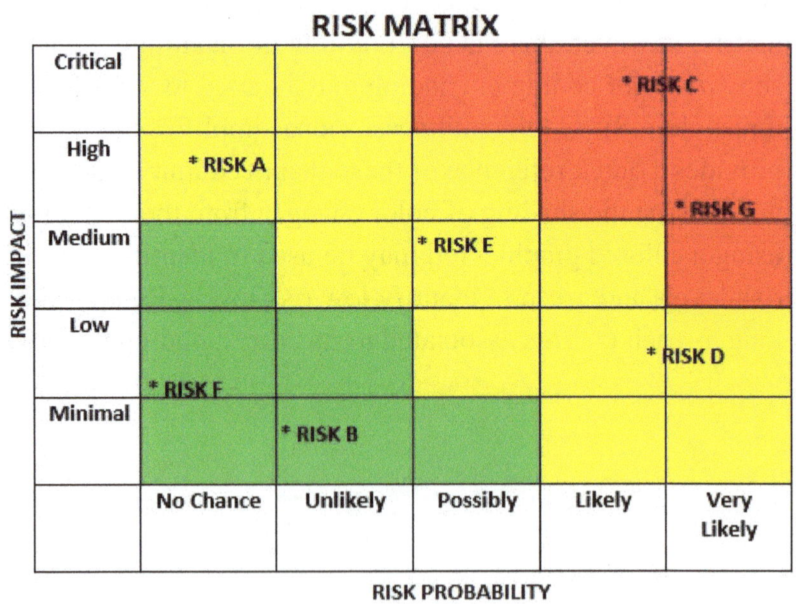

3. Research further into three of the Risk Standards you learned about in this chapter. Would any of the standards help your organization or company enhance RMF strategies?

References

[1] NIST (2012, September). SP 800-30: Guide for Conducting Risk Assessments. [PDF].
[2] Hillson, D. & Hulett, D. T. (2004, April 21). Assessing risk probability: alternative approaches. Paper presented at PMI® Global Congress 2004—EMEA, Prague, Czech Republic. Newtown Square, PA: Project Management Institute.
[3] Mitre. (n.d.). Risk Impact Assessment and Prioritization. Retrieved from https://www.mitre.org/publications/systems-engineering-guide/acquisition-systems-engineering/risk-management/risk-impact-assessment-and-prioritization
[4] Alexander, M. (2020, March 9). How to Perform a Qualitative Risk Analysis. Retrieved from https://www.techrepublic.com/article/how-to-perform-a-qualitative-risk-analysis/
[5] Safran. (n.d.). An Introduction to Qualitative Risk Analysis. Retrieved from https://www.safran.com/content/introduction-qualitative-risk-analysis
[6] U.S. Army Corps of Engineers. (n.d.). Risk Assessment – Quantitative Methods. Retrieved from https://www.iwr.usace.army.mil/Portals/70/docs/risk/Risk_Assessment_Quantitative_Methods_dft.pdf?ver=2018-07-03-134519-250
[7] Ramona, S. E. (2011, December). Advantages and Disadvantages of Quantitative and Qualitative Information risk Approaches. Retrieved from https://www.researchgate.net/profile/Ballestrazzi_Rodolfo/publication/233882852_Green_Marketing_and_Renewable_Energy_Evidence_on_Motivations_and_Behaviour_in_the_Aquacultural_Market/links/542587570cf26120b7aca1db/Green-Marketing-and-Renewable-Energy-Evidence-on-Motivations-and-Behaviour-in-the-Aquacultural-Market.pdf#page=20
[8] Ahmed, A. & Sheikh, H. (2017, July 5). COBIT 5 for Risk – A Powerful Tool for Risk Management. Retrieved from https://www.isaca.org/resources/news-and-trends/newsletters/cobit-focus/2017/cobit-5-for-riska-powerful-tool-for-risk-management
[9] Prevention Web. (n.d.). ISO/IEC 31010:2009: risk management – Risk assessment techniques. Retrieved from https://www.preventionweb.net/publications/view/12484
[10] IPMA. (2018, March 29). ISO 31000 Risk Management Second Edition Published. Retrieved from https://www.ipma.world/iso-31000-risk-management-second-edition-published/?gclid=EAIaIQobChMIrf_ZxpW56QIVxz6tBh0regipEAAYASAAEgI0_fD_BwE
[11] ISO. (2008). Introduction to ISO 27005 (ISO27005). Retrieved from https://www.27000.org/iso-27005.htm
[12] A-Lign. (n.d.). How to become ISO 27001 Certified. Retrieved from https://ip.a-lign.com/iso_27001_certification_v2/?utm_source=google&utm_medium=cpc&utm_campaign=&utm_term=what%20is%20iso%2027001&utm_content=&gclid=EAIaIQobChMIk9mA96G56QIVAz6tBh3TNAKpEAAYASAAEgIK5_D_BwE
[13] NIST. (2020, April 30). FISMA Implementation Project. Retrieved from https://csrc.nist.gov/projects/risk-management/risk-management-framework-(RMF)-Overview
[14] NIST. (n.d.). Understanding vulnerability Detail Pages. Retrieved from https://nvd.nist.gov/vuln

[15] Tobok, D. (2019, March 20). How Often Should Vulnerability Assessments be Performed? *Cytelligence.* Retrieved from https://cytelligence.com/how-often-should-vulnerability-assessments-be-performed/
[16] Talamantes, J. (n.d.). What is a Penetration Test and Why Do I Need It? [Web log post]. Retrieved from https://www.redteamsecure.com/blog/penetration-test-need/
[17] The Recorded Future Team. (2018, April 14). CVSS Scores: A Useful Guide [Web log post]. Retrieved from: https://www.recordedfuture.com/cvss-scores-guide/
[18] Bayne, J. (2019). An Overview of Threat and Risk Assessment. SANS. Retrieved from: https://www.sans.org/reading-room/whitepapers/auditing/overview-threat-risk-assessment-76
[19] Pokorny, Z. (2019, April 30). What is Threat Intelligence? Definition and Examples. *Recorded Future.* Retrieved from https://www.recordedfuture.com/threat-intelligence-definition/
[20] Grimes, R. A. (2019, February 7). 5 Signs You've Been Hit with an APT. *CSO.* Retrieved from https://www.csoonline.com/article/2615666/5-signs-youve-been-hit-with-an-apt.html
[21] Woerner, R. (2010, April 30). The Real Information Security Risk Equation. Retrieved from https://searchsecurity.techtarget.com/magazineContent/The-real-information-security-risk-equation
[22] Rolston, B. (2013, February 11). Threats Defined: Updates from INL. *SANS.* Retrieved from https://www.sans.org/cyber-security-summit/archives/file/summit-archive-1493745201.pdf
[23] Sotnikov, I. (2018, January 16). How to Perform IT Risk Assessment. [Web log post]. Retrieved from https://blog.netwrix.com/2018/01/16/how-to-perform-it-risk-assessment/
[24] Spacey, J. (2017, July 7). 3 Types of Risk Exposure. *Simplicable.* Retrieved from https://simplicable.com/new/risk-exposure
[25] Infosec Institute. (2019, February 8). Cyber Threat Analysis [Updated 2019]. Retrieved from https://resources.infosecinstitute.com/cyber-threat-analysis/#gref
[26] Shevchenko, N. (2018, December 3). Threat Modeling: 12 Available Methods. [Web log post]. Retrieved from https://insights.sei.cmu.edu/sei_blog/2018/12/threat-modeling-12-available-methods.html
[27] Threat Modeler. (2019, August 12). Stride, VAST, Trike & more: Which Threat Modeling Methodology is Right for your Organization? Retrieved from https://threatmodeler.com/threat-modeling-methodologies-overview-for-your-business/
[28] Microtool. (n.d.). Risk Matrix. Visualize Risks in a Diagram. Retrieved from https://www.microtool.de/en/knowledge-base/what-is-a-risk-matrix/
[29] Balbix. (n.d.). What are CVSS Scores? Retrieved from https://www.balbix.com/insights/understanding-cvss-scores/

Chapter 6 – Risk Assessment, Treatment and Management

Overview

Qualitative and quantitative analysis was addressed in Chapter 5. This chapter further discusses techniques for conducting both quantitative and qualitative risk analysis. Risk treatment and strategies for reducing organizational risk are explored, along with a variety of types of security controls and corresponding initiatives. The purpose of risk registers and the value of ethics in risk management provide continual emphasis on an effective, risk-aware decision-making process.

Chapter Learning Objectives

1. Determine the appropriate qualitative or quantitative risk assessment method for varying risk scenarios.
2. Determine overall risk for differing risk scenarios.
3. Compare and contrast options for risk treatment and management.
4. Assemble security controls to effectively reduce organizational risk.
5. Construct a risk register to effectively manage organizational risk.
6. Interpret the value of and correlation between ethics and risk.

Business Impact Analysis

Much of risk analysis relies on Business Impact Analysis (BIA). As previously identified, **Business impact analysis** is a process for identifying and predicting how a business would react and recover from various disaster and risk scenarios: consequences of each scenario are determined so businesses can prepare for each disruption and reduce overall organizational risk [1]. Impact can be defined as both operational and financial. Loss of business functionality can result in lost or delayed profit and sales; growing expenses associated with impact, such as paying overtime to employees or outsourcing; legal and regulatory fees; customers not being satisfied with service; hindered development or updating of current and future business plans; and contractual fees. All impacts related to finances must be quantified in order to provide a clear representation of the financial burden to the organization if the disaster or disruption were to materialize. Timelines must be developed to determine the duration of an incident and should note when the incident will have the least and greatest impact on the business [2]. Determining potential disruptions along with financial and operational impacts allows the organization to determine the level of risk it is willing to accept and must mitigate. In short, business impact analysis is a means for business continuity.

A BIA Includes:

- SCOPING
- SCHEDULING
- EXECUTING
- DOCUMENTING & APPROVAL

A business impact analysis involves several phases. As shown in Figure 6.1, these phases include scoping, scheduling, executing, documenting and approval, and completion [3]. During initial planning, the organization determines the scope of the BIA. The **scope** identifies several factors, including the who, what, when, where, why, and how pertaining to the impact analysis. More specifically: what are the intentions behind the BIA, who should be included in the BIA, when will the BIA occur, how frequently should the BIA be re-visited, why is the BIA being conducted, where will planning for the scope take place, and how much continuity planning is required? **Scheduling** includes meeting with all stakeholders. All areas of concern identified in the scope phase of the BIA must be discussed with stakeholders: each business department must clearly articulate priorities, the flow of daily operations, and any resource dependencies necessary for corresponding business operations. The **execution** stage involves collecting information and business operation dependencies by interviewing stakeholders. This stage addresses how each business activity functions from start to end: dependencies can include requirements for completing activities or how entities such as employees, applications, buildings, vendors, or additional apparatus function. Business process functionality during the execution stage expands further, determining how each dependency works, brainstorming workarounds for any issues that may arise, and identifying recovery point and time objectives in the event of a disruption [3].

The **documentation & approval** stage summarizes reports from discussing BIA efforts with each business unit. Information from the individual interviews is compiled, including newly identified issues, advice recommended by business unit leaders, and recovery time initiatives correlating to the impact of each identified risk. Following development of the documentation, the document must be reviewed by the interviewed stakeholders for accuracy and any required modifications. Upon approval from each interviewee, approved documents are compiled into a centralized report leading to the final step. The final phase, or completion stage, presents the product to management review. Primary activities, resource necessities, and risks are discussed, along with risk treatment options and recommendations [3]. Treatment and recommendations must be prioritized based on impact, from high to low. The highest impact-related risks must be addressed first to reduce organizational risk to the acceptable risk threshold. Upon completion of upper management review and approval, the document is formally accepted as a business impact analysis final product. The BIA is one of many common methods for assessing risk.

Interviews

Conducting interviews is an important part of harvesting valuable information in the business impact analysis process. Proper interview techniques must be used to gather the more detailed information contributing to risk identification and treatment. Questions must be open ended and as precise as possible, employing a Socratic methodology. The **Socratic method** involves critical thinking and debate in order to reach a decision or solution. A simple yes or no answer will not contribute any value to the risk assessment initiative. Questions should be structured around the five elements of business compliance: leadership; assessing risk; standards and controls; communication and training; and risk monitoring, responses, and conducting audits [4]. The company Lexis Nexis provides several examples of risk assessment questions pertaining to each element:

Element 1 - Leadership

- How is the organizational tone or culture perceived from business leaders/upper management?
- How are compliance initiatives and values instilled and communicated within the business?
- How are compliance requirements taken seriously within the organization?
- What types of resources are available for fulfilling and maintaining compliance requirements?

Element 2 - Assessing Risk

- Describe the established process the company uses for risk identification.
- Identify known compliance risks, the impact of each, and how the business treats each risk.
- What are the top risks the organization faces, and has management adequately dealt with each?
- What are current methods for identifying, quantifying, and mitigating organizational risk?

Element 3 - Standards & Controls

- What controls or standards are in place to ensure the organization manages risk?
- Provide a breakdown of how policy and procedure contribute to risk management activities.
- How does company policy contribute to managing organizational compliance?
- Are controls effective or have there been past scenarios that question the effectiveness of certain controls?

Element 4 - Communication & Training

- How does the organization ensure employees are trained and know how to respond to various risks?
- Is established training material accurate, updated, and relevant, or are updates required at this time?
- What methods of communication are available for communicating risk to the workforce?
- Describe how risk management is communicated within the business, from a top-down and bottom-up approach.

Element 5 - Risk Monitoring, Responses & Conducting Audits

- Does organizational culture support risk reporting, management, and mitigation?

- When, to what frequency, and how are risk audits conducted?
- Identify how the organization treats and corrects identified risks following assessments.
- How often is upper management informed of legal compliance concerns, incidents, and milestones for addressing issues [4]?

These questions are just examples and are by no means exhaustive. Questions during a real assessment should be much more in depth and focus on criteria specific to the organization being assessed. Interviews can be short or long in duration, and there is no minimum or maximum number of questions. Posing open ended questions or initiating follow-up questions during a risk assessment interview will yield a deeper analysis of current operations, trends, and processes. Many more than four questions should be asked for each element. A baseline of interview questions must be established as applicable to the organization as a whole; additional specific questions must be crafted that pertain to each business operation or function. Understanding how each business section works will make it easier to develop interview questions specific to each business function.

Event and Fault Tree Analysis

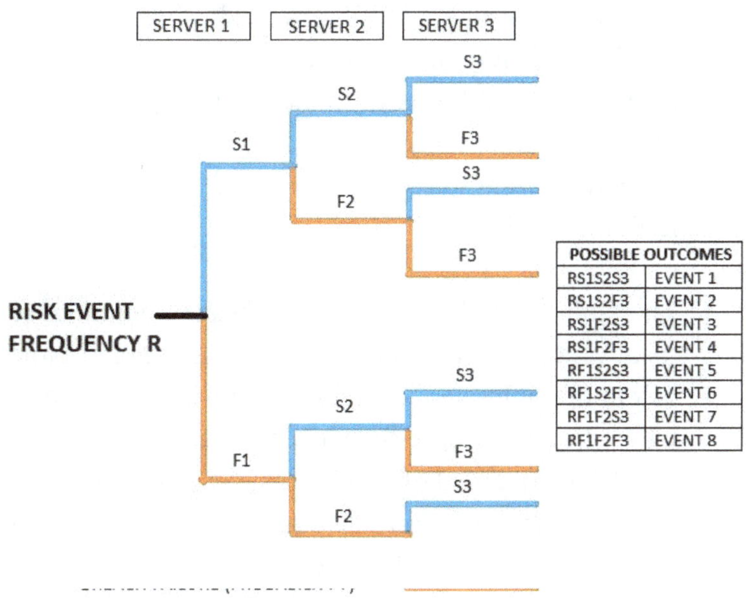

Event tree analysis (ETA) is a risk identification technique for determining potential successes and failures of an event. Scenarios are presented with corresponding impacts and outcomes [5]. The first step in conducting event tree analysis is identifying the risk scenario or anticipated event failure; once identified, potential risk preventative measures must then be established so the company can maintain control even in the event the risk scenario does occur. Figure 6.2 represents an example of an event tree. Portrayed here are risk scenarios that pertain to the probability of three servers being breached by a nefarious actor. As seen in Figure 6.2, event trees commonly utilize Boolean logic gates. A **Boolean logic gate** means that there are only two options, which in this case are success or failure of breach. To read the tree, start at the left and move right. The tree begins with the Risk Event. A **Risk Event** is defined as any incident that may result in creating new risk or enhancing previously identified risk. Each point on the branch is referred to as a node [7]. The blue line represents the breach succeeding while the orange line is failure of breach. The numbers one, two, and three represent the servers. The table to the far right in Figure 6.2 indicates the eight possible outcomes that may result from an attack on the servers. Each of the eight scenarios possesses different risk treatment options and mitigation efforts to reduce risk of the scenario leading to breach. You can trace each possible outcome on the tree to the left of the table. Frequency and probability of occurrence are analyzed to calculate potential outcomes or consequences [6]. Once all probability and frequency has been captured within the event tree, the final product may be analyzed for countering or treating associated risks.

Fault tree analysis is another method for conducting risk assessment. **Fault tree analysis (FTA)** identifies the reasons behind failures or incidents so organizations can mitigate risks prior to their occurrence. Like ETA, FTA is a top-down approach that supports problem resolution and can even provide increased efficiency of equipment or systems [8]. It is imperative to understand the differences between ETA and FTA: whereas ETA looks at measures of mitigation and the repercussions following an incident, FTA addresses what preventative measures can stop an incident from occurring in the first place [7]. Various symbols are used in FTA to differentiate events and gates. The "symbol key" to the right of the fault tree in Figure 6.3 introduces common symbols used in fault tree analysis.

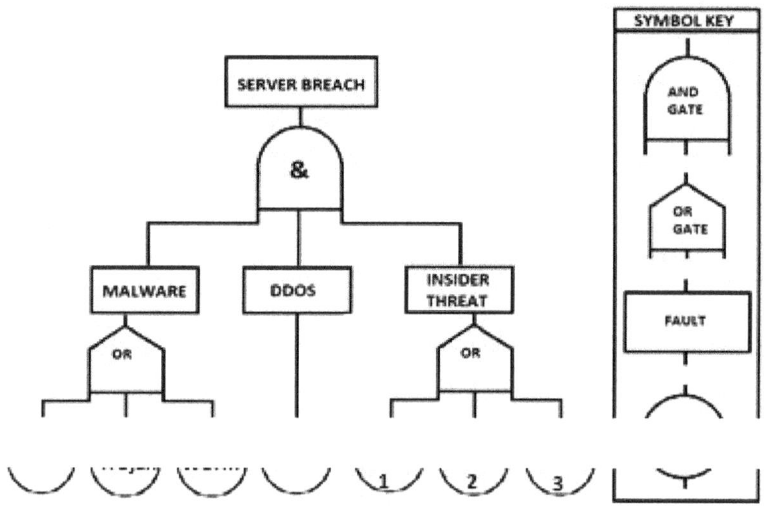

The fault tree in Figure 6.3 describes the potential scenario of a breach occurring, similar to the risk event identified in the event tree example. Note the four gates defined in the symbol key box at the right: and, or, fault, and primary failure. These symbols are used to tell the story in FTA. In this specific scenario, three potential faults for a server breach are identified: malware, a distributed denial of service attack, and an insider threat with malicious intent. The or gate specifies there are alternate attack vectors pertaining to each fault, all of which all create potential risk that could lead to a primary failure. Each fault, node, or point where the scenario can take a turn must be assessed for risk and potential methods for mitigation. (Don't get too caught up on nodes and gates, as they are just used to capture possible scenarios and outcomes.) Fault tree analysis paints a picture of potential risk scenarios, which makes it an ideal method for explaining or briefing to management or large audiences. ETA and FTA present a different perspective of utilizing the tree analysis method. As always, there is no right or wrong; the selection of which tree analysis technique is used should be dependent upon the scenario and goals, and tailored to individual risk scenario.

Cause and Effect Analysis

Cause and effect analysis identifies potential causes of an incident in order to prevent the possibility of its occurrence. A **fishbone diagram** is used to display the information. On the diagram itself, there is a main central horizontal line that presents the spine of a fish (hence the name). Branching off this main horizontal line are vertical lines that represent a possible method of how the risk scenario may occur. Additional horizontal lines branch off each risk scenario representing sub factors that may contribute to the risk scenario materializing. The factor and sub factor lines portray the thin bones that would branch off a fish's spine to form a rib cage. Some examples of factors contributing to the problem may be people, technology, equipment, external factors, or even third-party entities [9]. Several steps are involved in cause and effect analysis: identifying the problem, listing the primary causes of the problem, noting the subsidiary causes of the primary causes, and then analyzing the fishbone diagram [10].

Identifying the problem states the risk scenario in question. Figure 6.4 identifies the risk scenario being analyzed as server failure or breach. The **primary causes** of the problem include variables that either initiate or lead to the problem. In this case, there are six, listed in boxes at the top and bottom of the model: malware, electrical, theft, network, hardware, and software related risks. Each primary cause is then broken down into **plausible subsidiary causes**, which are problems or issues that could lead to the primary cause. A network outage,

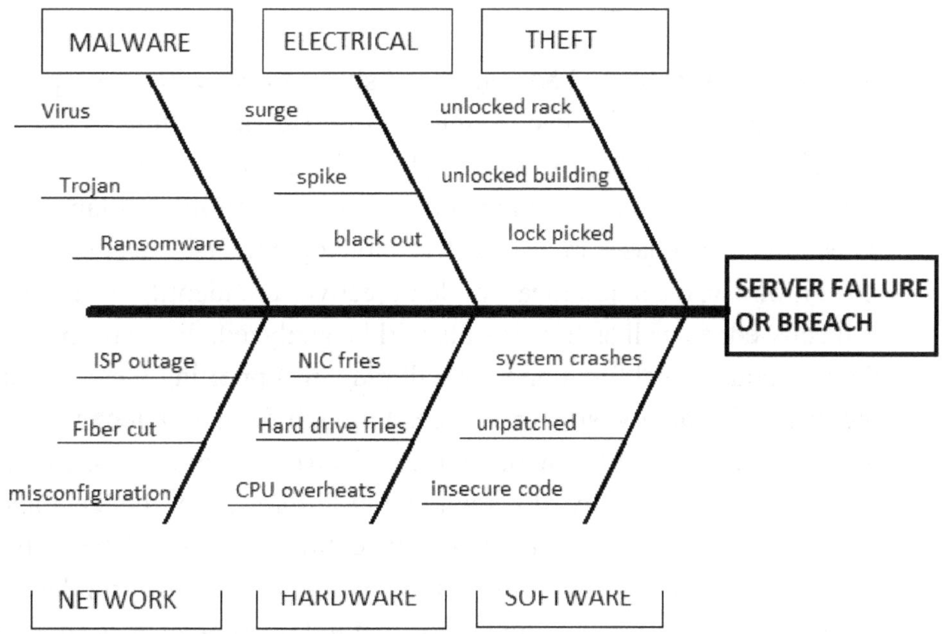

for example, will cause a server failure; an internet service provider (ISP) outage, a cut in the fiber cabling in the ground, or a misconfiguration on router or switch, however, may lead to a network failure, which would then in turn lead to server failure. Each spine of the fishbone diagram can be read in this same fashion. Hardware failure will lead to the server failure; if the network interface card (NIC), hard drive, or central processing unit (CPU) fails, the server will no longer function. Analysis of the cause and effect fishbone can help determine the risks related to an event and how to prioritize mitigation of those risks. It can even assist in uncovering uncommon or overlooked risks which may harm the organization's ability to function.

Exercises for Determining Risk

There are a number of role-playing or simulation risk-related activities, such as tabletop exercises, structured walkthroughs, functional exercises, and full-scale exercises. These activities can serve as cost-effective methods to test the organization's current risk management effectiveness. Conducting routine exercises on a quarterly or annual basis will help risk management teams analyze past problems, review lessons learned, and address risk that was previously addressed or that evolved with the recent implementation of new technologies, personnel, or services. Exercises provide a variety of other benefits as well: they evaluate the organization's level of preparedness, help identify deficiencies in a current risk management plan, validate procedural or policy modifications, clarify roles and responsibility, measure organizational improvement in conjunction with performance objectives, test the effectiveness of training, increase overall awareness of risk scenarios, help an organization to determine how to react to risk, and more [11]. The benefits of conducting routine exercises to address risk scenarios will further improve established processes and promote a well-trained and risk-aware work culture.

A **tabletop exercise (TTX)** consists of sitting down with a group of subject matter experts and discussing the roles that each employee of different sections or departments perform in the event of a disaster or risk-based scenario [11]. Tabletop exercises are often informal and include key players that would partake in incident response, continuity planning, and disaster recovery. There are three phases in an effective tabletop exercise: design, engage, and learn [12]. In the **design phase**, clear and measurable objectives are identified. The product or goal of the exercise is discussed, as well as how results will be analyzed. Exercise participants are selected based on the role and critical function they will play in supporting the end goal, which typically is recovery of a facility, site, or service. Often, information technology subject matter experts, first responders, and facilities maintenance (electricians, plumbers, etc.) are involved in the TTX to address every possibility of responding to failure. After the team and their objectives have been determined, the scenario and plan of execution is chosen. The scenario could range in the field of information technology from servers being hacked, to sprinklers leaking and damaging electrical hardware or equipment, to a natural disaster such as an earthquake or a flash flood [12]. After the design of the exercise is complete, the engagement portion of the TTX can begin.

The **engage phase** establishes relationships between participants. As professional relationships develop, comfort to participate in the exercise is raised, discussion is opened, and debate and constructive criticism are encouraged. Tabletop participants should collaborate and discuss how their individual areas of operation are linked to the operations of others. The engage stage relies upon learning from those with different perspectives than your own: this is where the actual exercise is conducted. Questions must be asked to gain insight, and utilizing a script or pre-determined topics of interest will assist in providing structure for discussions and the exercise. Questions will be based off the risk scenario being discussed and the person in charge of the exercise will manage questions, which should come from each department or section within the organization who would be affected by the risk scenario. Any identified issues or gaps must be clearly articulated in writing and contribute toward the final report and lessons learned. Examples of issues or gaps that could be uncovered during the exercise include lack of resources, personnel who do not know their role or how to perform it correctly, and external factors such as a utility company not being able to respond to an incident over the weekend. The moderator or primary person in charge of the exercise should keep it flowing and manage questions and answers. It is wise to discuss and determine resolutions pertaining to any new issues or gaps in real time while the exercise is occurring. This also simulates how leadership would react in a real risk scenario to address concerns or issues that arise.

The **learn phase** includes preparing an after-action report (AAR). The AAR can be used to develop both short- and long-term plans for mitigating any issues that arose during the TTX. For example, not having a backup point of contact for a role such as an operations manager will lead to a single point of failure. In the event the primary operations manager is not available, a secondary should be identified to ensure continuity operations are undergone. Continuous learning must be emphasized. The purpose is for all participants to enhance their individual plans and role performance, which will in turn improve the organization's response and resolution times. The AAR is a document with lessons learned, resolutions for any identified gaps, and enhancements to better overall activities and processes in the simulated event. The AAR may be referred to in future TTXs for continuous improvement and adaptation to any implemented changes since the last exercise [12].

Structured walkthroughs utilize a team of subject matter experts to conduct business continuity plan operations. Every step in the plan is conducted to assess difficulties, risk, strengths, and weaknesses [13]. Walkthroughs assist in auditing current processes, operations, and procedures: the effectiveness of established controls are weighed against new potential risks that may have been overlooked or arisen over time. Walkthroughs can further function as workshops or seminars intended to make staff more comfortable with their roles should a risk event occur. The more frequently employees practice recovery operations, the lower the risk of people making mistakes during recovery efforts. In a sense, risk within the plan itself and the risk of human error in executing that plan can both be identified and mitigated through practicing as a team. Furthermore, walkthroughs are a true realization of IT architecture and process maturity. Structured walkthroughs, repetition, and practicing continuity and disaster recovery actions create value and maturity in process.

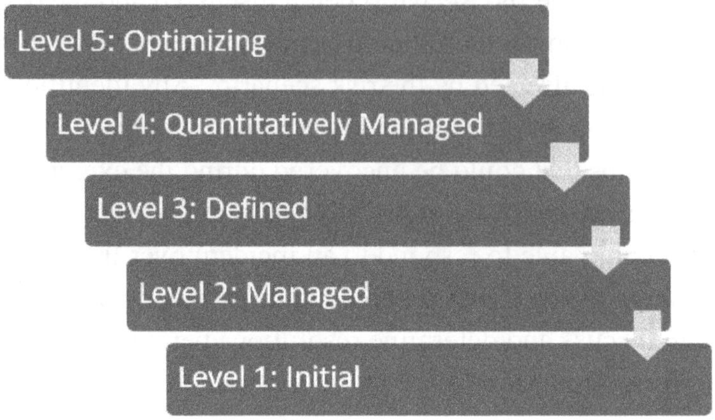

Maturity in IT can be characterized in a maturity model by five levels. As shown in Figure 6.5, the first level is defined as **initial**. This level represents ad-hoc and unpredictable processes with lack of structure. Management has very little awareness of what is processes are performed, security is ad-hoc, policy and procedure are informal, and IT processes are generally not linked to the business mission, vision, or strategy [30]. The second level is **managed**. In this level, basic processes are documented, measured, and controlled. IT vision, baselines, and business strategies are all identified. Management is in the know of architecture and process, but not fluent or well educated on processes. Security is articulated clearly, with each role and responsibility defined [30]. The next level of maturity, the **defined** level, characterizes processes while being proactive. For example, gap analyses are complete, and the IT architecture is integrated into investments and capitol planning. Governance is documented and IT security is integrated within IT architecture [30]. The **quantitatively managed** level articulates measured and controls processes. IT architecture processes are part of the organizational culture, documentation is updated frequently, and executive management are involved in reviewing architecture processes [30]. The **optimizing** or final level focuses on continuous improvements to processes. IT architecture process metrics are optimized and all operating units within the business provide valuable feedback for enhancing process improvement. Governance is emphasized in all investments and there are never any unplanned processes, purchases, or investments [30]. Practice and repetition lead to more mature processes in the organization. Structured walkthroughs are one method of evaluating process in support of evolving an organization's IT architecture process from one level to the next.

Functional exercises deal with business functions, operations, or activities; they focus on specific members of a team, the procedures they perform, and the resources they will utilize to accomplish their mission [11]. These types of exercises can assist in identifying risks to a sole functional area. For example, an organization may have an incident response team (IRT) that does not remediate a network outage quickly enough, resulting in the lack of availability of services and the loss of productivity. The functional area of incident response within the organization is failing other functional areas, such as human resources, payroll, facilities maintenance, physical security, etc. Functional exercises conducted in the cybersecurity section or with the incident response team will assist in improving this specific functional area, along with enhancing incident resolution in a more hasty and efficient manner.

Functional exercises are cost effective: they provide the opportunity to assess how resources and employees are allocated, how effective the communication and decision-making efforts are, and what risks may be present in policy, procedure, or business operations. There are several differences between a functional exercise and tabletop exercise. TTXs are not very realistic. Functional exercises, on the other hand, are as close to the real risk scenario as is possible without physically moving people and assets to a recovery location. Whereas TTXs have a laid back and relaxed atmosphere, functional exercises are much more stressful and realistic. Functional exercises are larger in scale and require much more time and planning than do tabletop exercises [14]. The needs of the organization, the scope of the risk scenario being assessed, and the available personnel and company resources will determine whether a functional exercise or a TTX is appropriate.

A **full-scale exercise** is very close to a real risk scenario, differing from a functional exercise in that resources and people are moved to the recovery location to simulate operations as realistically as possible. These exercises are lengthy, complex, and often conducted by public agencies with participation from several local businesses and third-party entities [11]. Full-scale exercises utilize an incident commander and command post team supporting the organization of functional teams to determine scope or risk scenarios and coordinate completion of assigned tasks. An **Incident Commander** is just another name for the person in charge of the exercise. The **Command post team** are the individuals under the incident commander who ensure roles and responsibilities are carried out by subordinates participating in the exercise. Critical thinking, hasty problem-solving techniques, precise response, and knowledge individuals are used to enact the exercise [15]. While it may be costly and time consuming, a full-scale exercise is a valuable technique for assessing the true effectiveness of an organization's current risk management policy, procedure, and objectives. Full scale exercises can expose risks and afford opportunities to mitigate those risks prior to the occurrence of a real risk scenario, which could easily cost the company double or triple the amount of the full-scale exercise.

TTX, structures walkthrough, functional exercises, and full-scale exercises exist for assessing the effectiveness of current risk management endeavors, policy, and procedures. Risk assessment is not a one-time event, but a process to be constantly repeated to address any new risks that arise. Performing exercises on a regular basis increases process maturity and identifies established controls that are failing to keep risk aligned with the organization's tolerance and threshold.

Selecting the appropriate exercise for the organization to assess risk depends upon the risk scenario itself, as well as the availability of business resources to contribute to the effort.

Root Cause Analysis

Root cause analysis (RCA) is a technique for assessing risk that identifies the root cause of a risk scenario materializing. Once the root cause of the risk scenario is identified, critical thinking and analysis are utilized to respond to the risk and prevent the same conflict from repeating [16]. The purpose of root cause analysis is to determine what previous decisions, risk controls, or events contributed to failure [17]. In other words, the goal is to determine what, how, and why the risk scenario occurred, as well as to identify what can prevent it from occurring again. Root cause analysis has a variety of benefits. Factors leading to a risk scenario can be resolved permanently through logic and problem-solving, and repeatable processes can be developed to address risk as it evolves in the future [16]. For example, an Internet outage is a large-scale risk that affects a whole enterprise. The root cause of the issue is linked to a router failure. With the root cause determined, redundancy can be established to address the root cause and risk of future router issues. **Redundancy** in Information Technology is defined as multiple preventative measures to prevent a single point of failure. For example, having multiple hard drives to store data will help ensure data is not completely lost in the event a single hard drive fails. The router failing is a risk on a smaller scale; however, the entire organization losing connectivity is a larger-scale risk with severe consequences. In this case, root cause analysis helps identify the primary cause of multiple risks that may all be linked.

Identifying underlying risk issues with RCA involves several steps: defining the issue, collecting data pertaining to the issue, identifying why the problem occurred, sorting the causes, identifying the solution, and monitoring continuously [18]. When defining the issue, the problem is identified, observations related to the problem are listed, and the potential impacts the issue could have on the business are determined.

Data collection involves finding data on the cause of the issue. Sometimes this data exists; other times, it may be necessary to harvest it by questioning employees who work in the risk area. When identifying why the problem occurred, the underlying cause, the factors leading to the incident, and the data from the collection phase must all be considered. A fishbone diagram can provide a visual representation of these factors. The next step involves sorting causes by priority: large-scale issues that could potentially lead to other risk scenarios must be addressed first. Finally, the solution identification phase determines how to treat the risk or scenario, with the end goal being to prevent issues from reoccurring. Roles are identified to determine who will carry out and enforce changes, as well as who will monitor and report on changes. The continuous monitoring phase then establishes a routine to track, observe, and ensure the root cause has been resolved and that no new issues arise as a result of the changes [18]. RCA utilizes a brainstorming methodology to solve large issues at their origin, rather than making multiple attempts to solve many small issues. The goal is to address the root cause in one attempt to save time and money: doing so will eliminate all correlating risk, threats, and vulnerabilities branching off the root cause.

Structured What-If Techniques / SWIFT

Everyone has experienced that one child who responds to everything with the question "what if?" Because feeding curiosity and asking questions are great methods to expand knowledge, asking "what if?" is valuable in the realm of risk assessment and risk management. **Structured What-If Techniques (SWIFT)** are an analytical method that uses questions to help identify risk, hazards, and threats within the organization. Checklists, historical occurrences, policy, and more become the basis for questions designed to thoroughly examine all aspects of a system or process [19]. While conducting structured what-if technique exercises, it is best to assign one person to create and manage a checklist of risk-based scenarios, subjects, or questions to address. As items are addressed, they may simply be checked off the list. This technique relies upon experienced individuals who have been through many conflict and resolution instances. SWIFT is a great tool to assess risk, regardless of the risk context. Some advantages of the technique include its straightforward tactics to avoid lengthy discussions, its flexibility to apply to many different risk scenarios, and its hasty methodology to avoid repetitive deviations. Because checklists summarizing in-depth and detailed questions derived from past incidents or history data are used, it is relatively convenient and easy to contact subject matter experts in the event they are not readily available for participation in brainstorming and analysis. Disadvantages include the fact that the checklist and the experience of key participants are solely relied upon. As SWIFT is qualitative in nature, it will generally cover risk scenarios and what would happen given a certain choice or action. As questions may arise both in and out of the scope, a downfall of SWIFT is its ability to determine whether potential flaws, weaknesses, or risk have been overlooked [19]. SWIFT is best used in conjunction with quantitative techniques for a more robust risk assessment and summary of risk probability and impact.

Monte Carlo Analysis

Conducting several trials or run-throughs to assess the probability and outcome of a scenario is a risk assessment technique known as **Monte Carlo Analysis**. The technique is great for not only making business- and finance-related decisions, but also for quantifying risk. The risk event is analyzed in-depth via simulations, which can number from just a few to a thousand or more, depending on how soon the result or goal is achieved [20]. The goal of Monte Carlo analysis is to quantify the overall risk that corresponds to a specific risk event on a technology system or software used by an organization. Monte Carlo helps organizations make risk-aware business decisions and implement risk management into operations and strategy. It is especially useful, due to its statistical nature and constant calculations of random what-if scenarios, for quantifying risk [21]. Using Monte Carlo Analysis in conjunction with the qualitative SWIFT method is an excellent way to simulate and categorize risk-based scenarios. Monte Carlo models are typically run using software, as software can quickly calculate and depict the frequency of risks through bell-shaped curves. As with all methods, the Monte Carlo Analysis also has drawbacks in addition to advantages. Software, unlike humans, does not possess the ability to differentiate between uncertainty or variability [21]. **Uncertainty** refers to any unknown information or outcome. Computers and software view variables as either true or false. Humans can view various perspectives to negate uncertainty. **Variability** provides alternatives or the potential to think outside the box. Machines do not possess this ability.

More specifically, computer algorithms or software may not accurately assess risk for a network when bandwidth and connection speeds vary at different times of the day or differ based on the speed the business pays the internet service provider for. Humans would have to monitor the network and manually input all the network data into Monte Carlo Analysis software in this case. Algorithms or software may not consider unknown variables, such as risk related to a specific function a server may perform or preventative technical controls configured to reduce risk. Software is not capable of thinking creatively: software only completes functions based off its pre-programmed functionality and specific purpose. Microsoft Excel is one of the easiest software tools available for constructing a Monte Carlo model. This technique can be complicated for those not familiar with Excel; there are, however, many video tutorials available on the world wide web for learning how to perform this technique. In summary, Monte Carlo analysis is one of many techniques available for conducting risk assessment. As with all risk assessment techniques, the selection of this method is dependent upon the risk scenario, available resources, and experience of the individual conducting the risk assessment.

Markov Analysis

Another technique for assessing risk is Markov Analysis. **Markov Analysis** is a method for determining a variable value based only on its current state: prior values are not considered. Markov Analysis is used to predict how certain decisions and specific actions will produce an outcome [22]. This analysis method is broad in nature, and thus not the best method for explaining a scenario or for serving as the primary model for determining why something has happened. Figure 6.6 provides an example of Markov Analysis pertaining to two critical servers within an organization. Servers are often installed in pairs to negate single point of failure in the event one fails. The theory is if both servers are installed and configured to perform the same service, one will take over if the other fails. Markov Analysis identifies four different scenarios pertaining to the servers in this situation. Each risk scenario would be further explored to consider alternatives, preventative measures, and actions to be completed in the event that a specific scenario happened.

The Markov chain further explores sequence of actions during a risk scenario, followed by determining the probability of occurrence. Within the context of information technology and servers, Markov analysis may assist in determining the time a server will remain functional in its current state, while also estimating how the server will react in different states, such as outages, failures, or breaches. The Markov chain assists in identifying states between functional and failure to include how the organization can handle the scenario. The numerical representation of probability and system state helps clarify precise dependencies between different states which are more difficult to represent with fault tree analysis techniques or similar methods [23].

Managing Risk

Methods for managing risk were introduced in Chapter Four. These methods will be further discussed and expanded upon in this section. As a review, different methods for identifying,

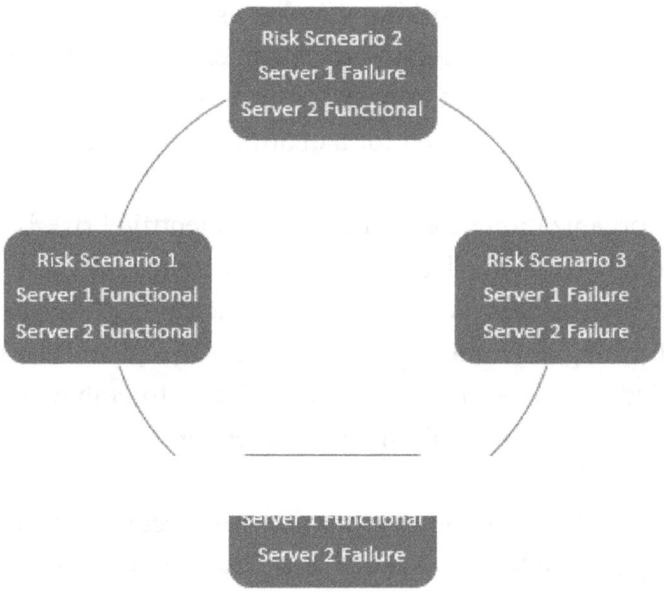

assessing, analyzing, and categorizing risk have been discussed. While one method may be more appealing than another due to the organization's financial constraints or limited resources, taking some sort of action to manage risk is the first step in developing a risk-aware climate and culture, and a risk-conscientious decision-making process. Understanding different risk treatment options will help organizations manage organizational risk effectively. Generic methods of risk treatment include risk avoidance, mitigation, transference, acceptance, sharing, contingency, enhancement, and exploitation [24].

Another way of describing risk treatment is risk response. **Risk response** is a planning process or initiative for controlling risk within the company and for supporting risk-conscientious decisions from top management down [24]. One way to treat risk is to avoid it. **Risk avoidance** is changing the process, operation, or risk scenario to eliminate the risk altogether. An example is a company using a specific port on the enterprise network that is determined to be a high risk for exploitation. Risk avoidance would occur if the company decided to completely disable the port. If, on the other hand, the company were to implement a control to counter the vulnerability, **risk mitigation** would occur [24]. Mitigating risk reduces the probability of the risk scenario materializing.

Transferring risk is commonly associated with insurance. Insurance is purchased to cover the cost a risk would inflict upon the asset, personnel, or organization. The risk is passed on to a third-party organization so the business can focus on other critical risks or additional objectives toward maintaining operations. Splitting up risk between multiple entities, business partners, or organizations is defined as **risk sharing**. An example of sharing risk is a business with multiple locations where each location possesses a security architect responsible for ensuring security controls are implemented, tested, and effective. Management decides to implement an enterprise security plan that has all security architects working together as one team, rather than specifically focusing on their individual locations. The decision results in each location sharing risk; however, if one security architect were to quit or move on to another job, that one location would not be left unattended while the company looked for a qualified security architect replacement.

Risk acceptance is when the organization determines that the identified risk is not worth the time or investment and is unlikely to occur. This decision is of course backed by qualitative and quantitative risk analysis data pertaining to what risk is being accepted. The organization accepts the risk without establishing any time, controls, or measures to address it. Often, a compensating control is applied to address and reduce the risk to a tolerable level [24]. Various types of security controls are discussed in detail in the next section.

Risk contingency is an established plan for addressing risk as it occurs. Often, it is a plan that encompasses backout procedures. **Backout procedures** are defined as actions or changes to revert from a current state to a prior state, pre-risk event occurrence. For example, a server is operational. Updates are installed that break the system. A backout procedure states to use a recovery point for reverting the server back to a point prior to the security update install. Risk is typically posed as a negative issue faced by organizations; risk, however, can also be positive in some scenarios. A project being finished early and under budget, for example, would be considered a positive risk that is beneficial in nature. **Risk enhancement** efforts are initiated to raise the likelihood of a positive risk occurring. **Risk exploitation** further attempts to reap the benefits of positive risk. Exploiting the risk could free up resources that could then in turn be reallocated elsewhere to speed up an initiative, project, or company goal [24]. It is rare to experience risk that will not deter organizational objectives or create loss; however, it is helpful to understand that some risks are good and do benefit the company if properly managed. Managing risk and choosing the best risk response and treatment method can be challenging. Addressing identified risks involves prioritizing severity and impact. Mitigating critical and high risks first is a strategy that reduces the most serious risks to the organization. Critical and high risks that cannot effectively be mitigated must be transferred to a third party, meaning that the organization must treat the risk by purchasing insurance.

Avoiding and accepting the risk are options but are often not feasible for a fully operational business to pursue. Understanding the advantages and disadvantages of each risk treatment methodology contributes to more aware risk-based decisions.

Security Controls

As noted previously, controls are implemented to help prevent an adverse risk or cybersecurity event from occurring. **Inherited risk** is defined as risk present in the organization prior to any risk management efforts, security control implementation, or contingency planning. As previously identified, **Residual risk** is the risk that remains after a security control or risk management initiative has been put in place. Both are key terms when it comes to security controls. There are three general control types: physical, technical (or logical), and administrative controls. These controls can be further broken down by the function they perform: preventative, detective, and corrective [25].

Physical controls are used for preventing access to either a system, facility, or specific location. Some common examples of physical controls are perimeter security, such as a fence or wall; surveillance technology and cameras; motion detection; or a fire suppression system. Heating, air conditioning, and humidity controls are also physical controls that reduce risk. Security identification cards used for access control are yet another example of a physical control, as they are required to gain entry into a building or restricted area. **Technical controls**, also known as logical controls, often take the form of hardware or software which protects either a system or network. Examples include firewalls, intrusion detection and prevention systems, access control lists, and data encryption. Administrative controls are any company policy or procedure that aligns performed job action with the company's enterprise security and risk management plan. **Administrative controls** are found primarily in documentation that outlines procedures and identifies requirements for task completion. More specifically, administrative controls may include processes for hiring and terminating employees, configuring company servers, classifying data, and baselining systems. These controls also often determine access control to facilities, policy for separation of duties, and security awareness training requirements for the workforce [25]. Combining and implementing these three security control types helps organizations manage inherent risk and establish an effective risk management program.

Physical, technical, and administrative controls may all serve as preventative, detective, and corrective controls in the right context.

Preventative controls are often the most expensive to implement and are focused on stopping a nefarious action from occurring: a wall prevents an intruder from entering a facility, a firewall prevents unwanted traffic from reaching its desired location, and a separation of duties policy prevents fraud. **Detective controls** are used to identify unauthorized actions on a network or within a data center [25]. Home security systems, fire alarms, and intrusion detection systems are forms of detective controls. **Corrective controls** restore systems or business operations to the state prior to the risk materializing. For example, a vulnerability may be identified during a vulnerability scan. Installing an update to mitigate the vulnerability would be considered a corrective control. Corrective controls also fix any issues that lead to risk, such as patching vulnerabilities or establishing an incident response plan for addressing risk events as they occur [25]. As emphasized multiple times in this Unit, a combination of multiple controls to establish a layered defense is the best strategy for managing people-, asset-, technology-, and data-related risks. Consistent testing and auditing of controls maintains a productive risk management strategy and a proactive defense in countering risk. Establishing and monitoring security controls in the organization relies upon adequate certification and accreditation efforts, also known as assessment and authorization.

The process previously called the **certification and accreditation** process is now called **assessment and authorization**. "Certification" or "assessment" is the process of harvesting the information technology and network artifacts (supporting documents, controls, or diagrams) that depict the layout, configuration, and accountability of equipment on the enterprise architecture. These artifacts and records of the hardware assets on the network (such as computers, printers, switches, servers, routers, etc.) are compiled into an accreditation package. The package also includes information about the organization's software, operating systems, firmware versions, and third-party software.

Security policy and procedures are also included in the package. Vulnerability scanners and port scanning are used to identify and document potential vulnerabilities, and to determine the risk tolerance of the organization. Typically, a cybersecurity subject matter expert will perform a self-assessment and include a plan of action and milestones (POA&M) for mitigating any discovered vulnerabilities. Once due care has been emphasized, the package moves on to the accreditation/authorization phase. **Due care** is defined as a reasonable and best honest effort an individual takes towards completing a task or action. For example, vulnerability scanning, identification, and remediation may be considered as emphasizing due care.

> **Looking Further**
>
> *Authorization to Operate (ATO)* means that a system has been accredited or authorized to be put into production.
>
> *Authorization to Connect (ATC)* means that a system has been accredited or authorized to fully connect to an organization s existing network infrastructure.

"Accreditation" or "authorization" is the process where upper management reviews, endorses, emphasizes accountability, and takes ownership of implemented security controls, the accreditation package, and the vulnerabilities the organization is willing to accept. Once management has made all necessary decisions regarding the package, authorization to operate and authorization to connect are granted. **Due diligence**, which is effort put into verifying the validity of all processes encompassed by due care, involves understanding the policy, procedure, and actions in place to maintain the effectiveness of an organization's cyber program. The Committee on National Security Systems (CNSS) sorts controls into specific baselines depending upon the intent of each. Controls are categorized as confidentiality, integrity, availability, or a combination of the three. Security categorization is accomplished in two steps. The first step consists of identifying the impact of data transmitted by the subject system being lost and the second step consists of categorizing the information system by impact and any additional factors. Controls vary from account management, device identification and authentication, media sanitization, vulnerability scanning, risk assessment and more [26]. The CNSS Security Categorization and Control Selection for National Security Systems (2012) is an excellent resource for determining control types to audit current control sets and manage risk related to people, assets, technology, and data.

Security control identification, selection, and implementation should be an ongoing process. Once a system or program has been accredited, the process is not over. The cycle repeats. Controls must be assessed at minimal annually to ensure effectiveness, as controls reduce and manage risk. Organizational technology constantly evolves, which results in new functionality and different services that may have not been considered when controls were first selected. Conducting audits on control functionality will ensure existing risk is continually managed and new risks are identified prior to escalating to an incident for which the organization is not prepared.

The Risk Register

Risk Index	Risk Category	Risk Title	Risk Description	Risk Effects / Impact	Probability	Risk Rank	Risk Owner	Risk Response
1	People	Insider Threat	An employee breaks into the data center.	Unauthorized access, data stolen, malicious software planted.	Likely	50 Medium Risk	Jon Doe	Implement Access Control measures.
2	Asset	Hardware Failure	A hard drive fails on a server.	Data is lost, services go down, business operations hault.	Very Likely	70 High Risk	Jane Lang	Ensure a RAID configuration is used on servers.
3	Technology	Security Breach	An unused open port/service is exploited.	A port and service is open leaving an opportunity for an attacker to compromise the host. Access to critical technology components.	Likely	62 Medium Risk	Jeff Madrid	Close the unused port/service to prevent potential breaches from occuring.

The benefits of a risk register were introduced in Chapter 4. All risk content covered in Chapters 4, 5 and 6 is stored in the risk register. The **risk register** includes identified risks, risk analysis and assessment results, and risk response initiatives. It also tracks risk treatment efforts and their effectiveness [26]. The risk register is a living document that is continuously updated. As risks evolve or are treated, the risk register must be updated. Figure 6.7 shows three lines of a risk register in Microsoft Excel.

The risk register specifies the details of each individual risk. Each component of risk is organized commonly in a Microsoft Excel spreadsheet, with components listed horizontally and risks listed vertically. The **Risk index** assigns a number to each risk component to track and quickly reference risks in the future. It is best practice to start with a four-digit system (0001, 0002, 0003, etc.) to account for the hundreds or thousands of risks that will accumulate in the register [26]. The **Risk category** organizes risk by their category to assist in identifying root cause of risk scenario or incidents. Categories may be identified as baselines by using resources such as CNSS documentation; common identifiers such as schedule, cost, scope and quality; or even industry specific categories that fall under requirements, designing, implementing, testing or deployment [26]. **Risk titles** are a short and simple description of the risk. **Risk descriptions** are more detailed summaries of the risks. The **Risk effects** section of the risk register specifically describes the potential of impact of each risk. This section is tailored towards those without a knowledge of risk management concepts. It breaks down how the risk could impact the organization in a simple narrative for quick reference [26].

The **probability** portion of the risk register captures values from quantitative risk analysis efforts and describes the likelihood of occurrence. Probability can be quantified using a numerical scale ranging from one to ten, one being the lowest and ten the highest; probability can also be identified as a high, medium, or low. **Risk rank** uses a scale from one to one hundred to sort each risk by severity. The risk rank is determined by multiplying probability by impact. The **risk owner** is listed in the register to identify who is responsible for each risk. The owner will closely monitor, manage, and report the status of the risk. Lastly, the **risk response plan** depicts specific actions taken to avoid, reduce, or mitigate each risk. If a risk is accepted and no further actions are required, that information should be noted in the register as well [26]. Risk registers may vary in content depending upon the needs of the organization and scope of the risks. There is no right or wrong method to creating a risk register if risk is effectively captured, analyzed, and frequently re-assessed. The most imperative takeaway is to remember that risk register is a living document which must be constantly updated. Without accurate data, the register is not effective and will not be of value in managing organizational risk and risk management programs.

Risk and Ethics

Ethics is essential to risk management: for risk management to be effective, ethics must be instilled within the risk culture [28]. Risk management is a process for contingency planning and decision making. Making ethical decisions that comply with rules, regulations and policy provides business value. Ethics provides guidelines on how to act and how to make decisions; risk management protects people, systems, assets, and data from harm or unethical behavior [28]. Ethics must be a way of life. Promoting and educating the workforce on the value of ethics both at work and outside of work will ultimately create a more honest, productive, and risk-aware culture.

Ethical risk, on the other hand, is risk associated with the lack of honesty, integrity, loyalty, and due care. Ethical risk can be broken down into two generic categories: corporate and personal. **Corporate risk** refers to any potential financial losses, theft, fraud, or regulatory violations the company may face due to unethical employees or actions within the organization. **Personal risk** deals with fines, prison, demotion, or termination an individual may face due to the decisions they have made [28]. Common methods for managing ethical risk include promoting values, leading by example, providing training on ethics, maintaining accountability for unethical actions, using organizational structure for deterring unethical actions, and responding fairly and firmly to instances of ethical risk [29]. In short, it is up to the individual to behave ethically. Fostering an organizational culture in which ethics and risk management are aligned will reap ongoing benefits as the company grows and matures.

Chapter Summary

Risk assessment, treatment, and management all contribute to emphasizing due care and due diligence within the organization. Risk assessment may be conducted from both a qualitative and quantitative approach; the specific method used, however, must be selected based on the individual risk scenario and scope of the assessment. It is often wise to use a combination of both methods for a more detailed conclusion on each risk the organization may face. Risk is managed through both risk actions (avoidance, transference, mitigation, acceptance, sharing, etc.) and security control implementation. Managing risk is a continuous process requiring frequent evaluation of selected controls and preventative measures.

Discussion Questions

1. Research additional qualitative and quantitative risk assessment methods not covered within the textbook. Explain how each method may be useful over those presented within the book.

2. Now that you understand what security controls are, which have you seen in action? You may have seen some implemented at work, in a business, or even at store in the mall.

3. What could happen if someone with malicious content gained access to the risk register?

Exercises

1. Identify a potential risk event you may have experienced in the past. Choose one of the risk assessment methods and conduct your own assessment of the risk event.

2. Consider each of the 5 elements discussed within the “Interviews” section of the chapter. Develop four questions for each element on your own.

3. Using the example of a risk register in Microsoft Excel, craft your own risk register with 3 risks pertaining to work, school, or your home.

References

[1] DHS. (2015, December 11). Business Impact Analysis. Retrieved from https://www.ready.gov/business-impact-analysis

[2] FEMA. (n.d.). Business Impact Analysis Worksheet. Retrieved from https://www.fema.gov/media-library-data/1388776348838-b548b013b1cfc61fa92fc4332b615e05/Business_ImpactAnalysis_Worksheet_2014.pdf

[3] Avalution Consulting. (n.d.). What is a Business Impact Analysis? Retrieved from https://avalution.com/business-impact-analysis/

[4] Martin, S. (2017, October 31). Checklist – 15 Sample Questions When Performing a Risk Assessment. *Lexis Nexis.* Retrieved from https://www.lexisnexis.com/lexis-practice-advisor/the-journal/b/lpa/posts/checklist-15-sample-questions-when-performing-a-risk-assessment

[5] Clemens, P. L., & Simmons, R. J. (1998, March). System Safety and Risk Management: NIOSH Instructional Module, A guide for Engineering Educators. Cincinnati, OH: National Institute for Occupational Safety and Health.

[6] Rausand, M. (n.d.). Event Tree Analysis. *Norwegian University of Science & Technology.* Retrieved from https://www.ntnu.edu/documents/624876/1277590549/chapt03-eta.pdf/6f3e1b19-4824-4812-adc8-9762d2201c22

[7] NEBOSH National Diploma. (2014). Fault Tree Analysis (FTA) and Event Tree Analysis (ETA). Retrieved from https://www.icao.int/SAM/Documents/2014-ADSAFASS/Fault%20Tree%20Analysis%20and%20Event%20Tree%20Analysis.pdf

[8] Ramana, P. V. (n.d.). Fault Tree Analysis. Retrieved from https://sixsigmastudyguide.com/fault-tree-analysis/

[9] Mind Tools. (n.d.). Cause and Effect Analysis Video. [Web log post]. Retrieved from https://www.mindtools.com/pages/videos/cause-effect-analysis-transcript.htm

[10] Creately. (2018, January 16). How to Use Cause and Effect Analysis to Solve Business Problems. [Web log post]. Retrieved from https://creately.com/blog/diagrams/how-to-use-cause-and-effect-analysis/

[11] DHS. (2016, January 21). Exercises. Retrieved from https://www.ready.gov/business/testing/exercises

[12] EisenHauer, J. (2014, September 30). Nine Steps to Design a Powerful Tabletop Exercise (TTX). Retrieved from https://www.nexightgroup.com/nine-steps-to-design-a-powerful-tabletop-exercise-ttx/

[13] Open Risk Manual. (n.d.). Structured Walkthrough. Retrieved from https://www.openriskmanual.org/wiki/Structured_Walkthrough

[14] Exercise Design. (n.d.). Unit 6: The Functional Exercise. Retrieved from http://www.iaem.com/documents/Exercise%20Design-IS-139-continued.pdf

[15] FEMA. (2013, July 26). Full-Scale Exercise #1. Retrieved from https://www.fema.gov/media-library-data/20130726-1917-25045-0825/cert_fullscale_1.pdf

[16] Washington State Department of Enterprise Services. (n.d.). Root Cause Analysis. Retrieved from https://des.wa.gov/services/risk-management/about-risk-management/enterprise-risk-management/root-cause-analysis

[17] Wilson, B. (2015, April 18). Root Cause Analysis. Retrieved from http://www.bill-wilson.net/root-cause-analysis
[18] Nair, R. (2018, January 16). How Do You Determine the Root Cause? [Web log post]. Retrieved from https://www.greycampus.com/blog/quality-management/how-do-you-determine-the-root-cause
[19] ASEMS. (n.d.). SWIFT. Retrieved from https://www.asems.mod.uk/printpdf/toolkit/swift
[20] Stammers, R. (2019, January 24). Using Monte Carlo Analysis to Estimate Risk. Retrieved from https://www.investopedia.com/articles/financial-theory/08/monte-carlo-multivariate-model.asp
[21] Environmental Protection Agency. (n.d.). Use of Monte Carlo Simulation in Risk Assessments. Retrieved from https://www.epa.gov/risk/use-monte-carlo-simulation-risk-assessments
[22] Kenton, W. (2019, December 6). Markov Analysis. Retrieved from https://www.investopedia.com/terms/m/markov-analysis.asp
[23] Risk Management – Markov Chain. (n.d.). Retrieved from https://project-management-basics.com/risk/risk_management_113_markov_chain
[24] Spacey, J. (2017, July 02). 8 Types of Risk Response. Retrieved from https://simplicable.com/new/risk-response
[25] Walkowski, D. (2019, August 22). What Are Security Controls? Retrieved from https://www.f5.com/labs/articles/education/what-are-security-controls
[26] Nizhebetskiy, D. (n.d.). Risk Register Example – All You Need to Know About It. Retrieved from https://pmbasics101.com/risk-register/
[27] CNSS. (2012, March 15). Security Categorization and Control Selection for National Security Systems. Retrieved from http://iassecurity.net/Resources/CNSSI_1253.SC%20Controls1.pdf
[28] Head, G. L. (2005, February). Why Link Risk Management and Ethics? Retrieved from https://www.irmi.com/articles/expert-commentary/why-link-risk-management-and-ethics
[29] Webb, R. (2017, October 31). 5 Ways to Manage Ethical Risks. Retrieved from https://www.clearrisk.com/risk-management-blog/how-to-manage-ethical-risks
[30] Visual Paradigm. (n.d.). What is Enterprise Architecture Maturity Model? Retrieved from https://www.visual-paradigm.com/guide/enterprise-architecture/what-is-enterprise-architecture-maturity-model/

Unit 2 Key Terms

account Lifecycle Management
refers to the process of account vetting, creation, and management.

acting
in the context of threat analysis, is making a strategic and risk-aware decision on how to prevent or address the threat in question.

administrative controls
are found primarily in documentation that outlines procedures and identifies requirements for task completion.

application pen testing
explores web vulnerabilities and potential attack vectors, including cross site scripting, injection flaws and cross site request forgery opportunities.

Analyzing
in the context of threat analysis, reviews information from the previous step to establish links between threat factors.

assessment
in the context of RMF, investigates whether controls are effective and serving their purpose.

asset valuation
is the process of determining fair market value of both tangible and intangible assets.

attack complexity (AC)
in the context of CVSS, describes the conditions which must exist for an attacker to exploit the vulnerability.

attack vectors
are any method by which a system or subject may be compromised, while in the context of CVSS, refer to how easily an attacker can exploit a vulnerability.

authorization
in the context of RMF, formally recognizes security controls as performing their intended function.

authorization scope
within the context of CVSS, further measures the impact of the vulnerability through means of impact on confidentiality, integrity, and availability.

backdoors
refer to any unauthorized entry a nefarious actor uses to access a system.

backout procedures
are defined as actions or changes to revert from a current state to a prior state, pre-risk event occurrence.

base score
in the context of CVSS, assesses both how easy the vulnerability is to exploit and the damage that could result from exploitation.

blackouts
are a complete loss of power.

boolean logic gates
translate to there being only two available options (failure or success).

brownouts
are a reduction in power or drop in voltage.

business continuity plans (BCP's)
are predetermined plans for returning to normal operations, in the event a disaster or disruption may occur.

business impact analysis (BIA)
is a process for determining how the loss of essential business functionality or services will affect the organization.

categorizing
in the context of RMF, involves determining how a system classifies, processes, stores, and transmits data.

cause and effect analysis
identifies potential causes of an incident in order to prevent the possibility of its occurrence.

change management
is a process that vets, documents, and manages any changes to systems or an operating environment within an organization.

clearing
is a method of sanitizing the data from risk of a keyboard attack or retrieval via file utility tools.

cold sites
are a backup location without any infrastructure stood up or available.

common vulnerability scoring system (CVSS)
calculates an organization's vulnerability score in three categories: base score, temporal score, and environmental score.

compensating controls
are an alternative action taken to help lower overall risk to an acceptable level when the risk mitigation action is too costly or not possible to achieve.

confidential data
is the most critical data or information to the organization. Exposure of confidential data will harm the company over an extended period or long range of time.

continuous risk exposure calculation
presents probabilities for different risk scenarios through use of a continuous curve.

copyrights
protect "original works of authorship" and "exclusive rights" to copyrighted expression or product.

corporate risk
refers to any potential financial losses, theft, fraud, or regulatory violations the company may face due to unethical employees or actions within the organization.

corrective controls
restore systems or business operations to the state prior to the risk materializing.

data at rest
is data stored stationary on a hard drive, SD card, flash drive or specific location.

data in transit
refers to data being transported over a network or from one location to another.

data remanence
is bits and pieces of data left behind after attempting to rewrite, overwrite or delete files.

data centers
describe the facility, building, or the IT workers within the facility or a room where enterprise information technology equipment is housed.

data custodians
maintain servers and databases and ensures that only those with a need to know have access to files or data.

data loss prevention (DLP)
describes tools and techniques that protect data, prevent risk of exposure through means of encryption and monitoring with additional capabilities of filtering the information and outputting reports on data activity.

data stewards
interpret the type of data and ensure data is properly used in accordance with data governance initiatives.

data owners
are the individuals responsible for the overall risk associated with the data. The owner classifies the data, determines who can access the data, and ensures that data custodians are safeguarding the data

defense in depth strategy
is a plan with many defenses in place to counter vulnerabilities, threats, risk, or security controls that do not perform as intended.

degaussing
utilizes a magnetic field to sanitize the data stored on magnetic based hard disks.

detective controls
are used to identify unauthorized actions on a network or within a data center.

disaster recovery plans
help identify potential disasters applicable to the organization, ranging from environmental to personnel related.

discrete risk calculation method
uses several probabilities, impacts, and exposures.

documentation & approval
within the context of BIA, summarizes reports from discussing BIA efforts with each business unit. Information from the individual interviews is compiled, including newly identified issues, advice recommended by business unit leaders, and recovery time initiatives correlating to the impact of each identified risk.

dry pipe sprinkler
systems are filled is pressurized air.

dual control
requires two individuals to authenticate a system before access is granted.

due care
is defined as a reasonable and best honest effort an individual takes towards completing a task or action.

due diligence
describes the actions the organization has taken to reduce risk.

dumpster diving
is when a person with malicious intent searches the trash for any personal identifiable or company sensitive information.

electrostatic discharge (ESD)
refers to a change in electrical current between electrically charged technology components, which can harm or destroy a system.

emerging risk
refers to any risk that materializes over the lifecycle of systems, technology, or a data center.

environmental risks
can be associated to natural disasters or in context to a data center relate to: loss of power to hardware, electrical fires, humidity or moisture build up around electronics, the temperature being either too cold or too hot and particles within the air that may serve as contaminants.

ethical risk
is risk associated with the lack of honesty, integrity, loyalty, and due care. Ethical risk can be broken down into two generic categories: corporate and personal.

event tree analysis (ETA)
is a risk identification technique for determining potential successes and failures of an event.

execution
within the context of BIA, involves collecting information and business operation dependencies by interviewing stakeholders.

exploit code maturity (E)
in the context of CVSS, determines the likeliness a vulnerability will be exploited successfully. This likeliness is normally based on exploit kits and coding pertaining to the vulnerability that has already been discovered.

exploitability sub scores
in the context of CVSS, consider how probable the exploit of a given vulnerability is. Exploitability sub-scores include attack vectors, attack complexity, user interaction and privileges required.

familiarity
in the context of risk assessment, deals with historical occurrences will help gauge the probability of risk, while a lack of familiarity with such occurrences will contribute to less reliable estimations of probability.

fault tree analysis (FTA)
is a risk assessment method that identifies the reasons behind failures or incidents so organizations can mitigate risks prior to their occurrence.

fishbone diagrams
are used to display risk information. Horizontal and vertical lines are used to capture different scenarios of a risk materializing.

functional exercises
deal with business functions, operations, or activities; they focus on specific members of a team, the procedures they perform, and the resources they will utilize to accomplish their mission.

full-scale exercises
are very close to a real risk scenario, differing from a functional exercise in that resources and people are moved to the recovery location to simulate operations as realistically as possible. These exercises are lengthy, complex, and often conducted by public agencies with participation from several local businesses and third-party entities.

gathering
in the context of threat analysis, is where multiple sources are reviewed to harvest methodology related to the threat.

general data protection regulation (GDPR)
classifies personal data as any information related to a person that is identifiable (social security number, date of birth, address, income, etc.)

hot sites
are fully prepared backup locations, offering the same information technology capabilities as the primary location.

human Resource risk
deals to risk related to people or employees. Risk can range from employee injury, lawsuits to insider threat.

identifying the problem
within context to cause and effect analysis, states the risk scenario in question.

impact assessments
identify the impact of a threat on information technology and business operations, to include financial burdens and loss of productivity, time, operations, performance, or capabilities.

impact sub score
in the context of CVSS, determines what impact a successful exploit will have.

implementation
in the context of RMF, determines how controls will be implemented on the system or within the operating environment.

inherited risk
is defined as risk present in the organization prior to any risk management efforts, security control implementation, or contingency planning.

insider threats
refer to employees in a position of trust who wish to harm the organization.

intensity
in the context of threat matrices, determine the capacity of the threat and how much impact it may have.

internetwork operating systems (IOSs)
is the primary software installed on each network switch.

intrusion detection systems (IDSs)
identify abnormalities or potential breaches on the network, reporting them to the appropriate person or team.

intrusion prevention systems (IPSs)
identify potential malicious activities and possess the capability to block or stop activities.

job rotation
refers to rotating employees into different positions within the company which can be beneficial in cross training the workforce is multiple specialties. Job rotation may assist in identifying fraudulent activity.

LINDUN
stands for link-ability, identifiability, non-repudiation, detectability, disclosure of information, unawareness, and non-compliance.

macroeconomic risk
pertains to markets and outside factors, primarily dealing with finance and currency.

mandatory vacations
require employees to take vacation either quarterly, annually, or on another pre-specified basis. Mandatory vacations may assist in identifying fraudulent activity.

manageability
in the context of risk assessment, correlates to control. If the risk in question can be controlled, the probability of it being a potential threat is minimized.

markov analysis
is a risk assessment method for determining a variable value based only on its current state without prior variables considered. It is also used to predict how certain decisions and specific actions will produce a outcome.

mean time between failure (MTBF)
captures the reliability of a device within a specified time frame. More specifically, how long the device operates as intended without interruption or failure.

mean time to failure (MTTF)
measures the estimated entire lifecycle of a device.

mean time to repair (MTTR)
captures the time it would take to fix a system, bringing it back up to full operational standards.

modified base score
in the context of CVSS, reevaluates all metrics within the "base score" to consider the specifics of the organization and environment not previously evaluated.

monitoring
in the context of RMF, observes how security controls interact, function, and change.

monte carlo analysis
is a risk assessment technique that conducts several trials or run-throughs to assess the probability and outcome of a risk scenario.

multi-factor authentication
uses more than one source to verify either "who you are," "what you have" or "something you know."

network pen testing
will check the enterprise for vulnerabilities pertaining to misconfiguration, unpatched systems susceptible to breach, weak and crackable passwords, open ports and protocols, exploitable services, and more.

OODA Loop
is a decision-making process originated by military strategist, Colonel John Boyd.

open system models
are a way of describing an organization's internal relationship with outside relationships.

operational categories
in the context of threat intelligence, specifically addresses technical details about various attacks or threat-related campaigns.

operational risk
relates to the employees, business processes, and technologies within the organization.

operational security (OPSEC)
develops a method to view identified risks from an attacker's perspective, while creating a solution for preventing occurrence or protecting sensitive information.

PASTA
stands for the Process for Attack Simulation and Threat Analysis.

patch management
is the process of installing the latest updates, firmware, or software on information technology hardware.

penetration testing
is a method of evaluating current levels of vulnerability.

personal risk
within the context of ethical risk, deals with fines, prison, demotion, or termination an individual may face due to the decisions they have made.

people risk
pertains to employees, the risk in the duties they perform, and the risk a disgruntled employee could potentially cause to the organization.

physical controls
are used for preventing access to either a system, facility, or specific location.

physical hardware
is internal to technology related hardware and assets. Examples include hard drives, random access memory (RAM), motherboards, central processing units (CPUs) and more.

physical pen testing
explores physical security vulnerabilities like locks, building access control, surveillance, and other means of physical entry that could be breached.

pre-action sprinkler systems
have pipes filled with air. Water is stopped by a pre-action valve that only opens in the event of an emergency.

preparation
in the context of RMF, is where organizations plan on integrating risk management and security procedures into current policy, procedure, processes, business operations, and everyday routines.

preventative controls
are often the most expensive to implement and are focused on stopping a nefarious action from occurring: a wall prevents an intruder from entering a facility, a firewall prevents unwanted traffic from reaching its desired location, and a separation of duties policy prevents fraud.

primary causes
of a problem, within the context of cause and effect analysis, include variables that either initiate or lead to the problem.

plausible subsidiary causes
within the context of cause and effect analysis, are problems or issues that could lead to the primary cause.

privilege creep
occurs when an employee maintains access or administrative rights from a previous position after moving to a new position.

privileges required (PR)
in the context of CVSS, identifies the level of access required for an attacker to exploit the vulnerability.

probability
in the context of risk assessment, is the occurrence or likelihood of a vulnerability being exploited.

propinquity
in the context of risk assessment, measures potential consequences of risk that may directly affect those involved in the risk scenario. In other words, the potential of the risk probability is analyzed for impact.

protocols
are referred to as a method of communication and security a router uses across a network.

proximity
in the context of risk assessment deals with time; the probability of a risk occurring may be considered higher if the potential for occurrence is sooner rather than later.

public data
is information that may be shared with the general population or public.

purging
is a data sanitization technique reducing risk of a laboratory attack or advanced data recovery techniques within a lab.

qualitative risk analysis
approaches assess risk using a narrative or categories that do not correlate to a measurement, system, or number.

quantitative risk assessment
techniques measure risk with numerical methods, associate values to risk for use in calculations and provide more validity and transparency than qualitative assessments.

redundancy
in Information Technology is defined as multiple preventative measures to prevent a single point of failure.

remediation level (RL)
in the context of CVSS, determines the difficulty of fixing the vulnerability and can be viewed as a counterpoint to Exploit Code Maturity.

report confidence (RC)
in the context of CVSS, is the level of confidence of the vulnerability's existence, verifying that the vulnerability is real and not a rumor.

residual risk
describes the amount of risk remaining or left over after implementing a control.

risk
is defined as any potential threat or vulnerability that may result in damage, loss, or disruption to company people, assets, technology, data, operations, or productivity.

risk acceptance
is when the organization determines that the identified risk is not worth the time or investment and is unlikely to occur.

risk appetite
is the amount of total risk an organization can withstand without suffering any financial or operational loss.

risk assessment
is the process of identifying and categorizing various internal and external risks.

risk avoidance
is changing the process, operation, or risk scenario to eliminate the risk altogether.

risk awareness
is the level of awareness each employee within the organization possesses regarding risk management processes.

risk categories
within context to the risk register, organize risk by their category to assist in identifying root cause of risk scenario or incidents.

risk contingency
is an established plan for addressing risk as it occurs. Often, it is a plan that encompasses backout procedures.

risk culture
summarizes the demeanor, ethics, and core values pertaining to risk within a company.

risk descriptions
within context to the risk register, are more detailed summaries of the risks.

risk effects
within context of the risk register, specifically describe the potential of impact of each risk.

risk enhancement
efforts are initiated to raise the likelihood of a positive risk occurring.

risk events
are defined as any incident that may result in creating new risk or enhancing previously identified risk.

risk exposure
is the amount of damage or financial loss that is directly related to a risk incident occurring.

risk exploitation
attempts to reap the benefits of positive risk.

risk governance
seeks to align risk management with both business and decision-making processes.

risk indexes
within context to the risk register, assign a number to each risk component to track and quickly reference risks in the future.

risk management
is a process which involves framing, assessing, responding and monitoring risks.

risk management framework (RMF)
is a well-recognized process for integration of both risk management procedures and organizational security in system development lifecycles. RMF includes preparation, categorization, selection, implementation, assessing, authorizing and monitoring of security controls.

risk matrixes
or risk diagrams are an effective method for deciding how to prioritize risk treatment, as it allows multiple risks and their associated severities to be compared.

risk models
portray a visual representation of risk-related data and results.

risk rank
in the context of the risk register, uses a scale from one to one hundred to sort each risk by severity.

risk reduction
is the process of mitigating individual risks to meet the organization's risk appetite and tolerance.

risk registers
contain necessary information for categorizing risk. This information includes identified risks, risk analysis and assessment results, risk response initiatives, the likeliness of each risk occurring, the impact each risk could have, strategies for mitigating each risk, and a method of scoring a risk's severity, etc.

risk response
is a planning process or initiative for controlling risk within the company and for supporting risk-conscientious decisions from top management down.

risk response plans
within the context of the risk register, depict specific actions taken to avoid, reduce, or mitigate each risk. If a risk is accepted and no further actions are required, that information should be noted in the register as well.

risk sharing
is splitting risk up between multiple entities, business partners, or organizations.

risk threshold
addresses the amount of risk a company will deem acceptable.

risk titles
within context to the risk register, are a short and simple description of the risk.

risk tolerance
is the agreed-upon level of risk the organization is willing to withstand.

root cause analysis (RCA)
is a technique for assessing risk that identifies the root cause of a risk scenario materializing.

salami techniques
involve shaving off small increments of money from multiple entities with the intent of financial gain.

scatter diagrams
are charts used to analyze the relationship between two variables.

scheduling
within the context of BIA, includes meeting with all stakeholders. All areas of concern identified in the scope phase of the BIA must be discussed with stakeholders: each business department must clearly articulate priorities, the flow of daily operations, and any resource dependencies necessary for corresponding business operations.

scoping
in the threat analysis, involves understanding the threat and establishing priorities for addressing the threat. Scoping in the context of BIA includes several factors, including the who, what, when, where, why and how pertaining to the impact analysis.

security requirements sub score
in the context of CVSS, is a score based on confidentiality, integrity, and availability metrics derived from the "impact sub-score." These metrics are determined based on the specific organization, environment being assessed and mandatory security requirements.

security technical information security guides (STIGs)
also known as industry recommended security configs or best security practice, will defend routers and decrease the likeliness of potential risk.

selection
in the context of RMF, chooses a baseline control for a system that will serve as the minimum requirement for similar systems: for example, if one computer is required to have access control settings, all computers within the organization should have access control settings as well.

sensitive data
is information that may not be appropriate for everyone. It must be made available to those with a need to know. Exposure of sensitive data causes temporary or interim harm to the organization, dependent upon if consent was gained for releasing the information.

separation of duties
is ensuring only a specific team or individual can perform a task or role to negate nefarious acts, fraud or the risk of employees performing unethical behavior.

single value calculation
is a risk calculation method for single risk scenarios. It will not work for multiple risk scenarios.

socratic method
involves critical thinking and debate in order to reach a decision or solution.

spear phishing
refers to attacks that target a specific person, usually management or leadership.

stealth
in the context of threat matrices, measure whether any information can be confirmed regarding a threat.

strategic categories
in the context of threat intelligence, pertains to threats commonly directed towards managerial, leadership, or executive staff.

Strategic risk
correlates to business strategy, innovation, and opportunity-related risk.

STRIDE
focuses on the violation of various properties by different threats. More specifically, confidentiality, integrity, availability, non-repudiation, availability, and authorization are addressed.

structured walkthroughs
utilize a team of subject matter experts to conduct business continuity plan operations.

structured what-if techniques (SWIFT)
are an analytical method that uses questions to help identify risk, hazards, and threats within the organization.

surges
are a temporary jolt of electricity or increase in voltage.

system hardening
is establishing security controls, reducing threat and mitigating vulnerabilities to secure a specific system.

system vulnerabilities
can be either a hardware flaw, software related flaw or weakness in a system exploited by a hacker.

tabletop exercises (TTX's)
consist of sitting down with a group of subject matter experts and discussing the roles that each employee of different sections or departments perform in the event of a disaster or risk-based scenario. TTX's include 3 phases: design, engage and learn.

tactical categories
in the context of threat intelligence, include procedures, tactics, and techniques used by threat actors to carry out intentions. This category pertains to a technical audience.

technical controls
also known as logical controls, often take the form of hardware or software which protects either a system or network.

technology risk
refers to risk pertaining to any technology related hardware or software.

temporal score
within the context of CVSS, ranks the awareness level of vulnerability remediation steps and determines if threat actors are actively targeting the vulnerability. The temporal score includes exploit code maturity, remediation level and report confidence sub-scores.

threats
are any event or instance that may harm company operations, personnel, or assets.

threat analysis
is a method of identifying threats applicable to a system or the organization. Threat analysis consists of four primary phases: scoping, gathering, analyzing, and acting.

threat intelligence
is defined as any information that helps the organization prevent or halt attacks. Threat intelligence can be broken down into three categories: strategic, tactical, and operational.

threat landscapes
or threat environments describe any identified vulnerabilities or threats to a person, place, or thing.

threat matrices
sort different types of threats by characteristics such as intensity, stealth, and time.

threat modeling
portrays the profiles, methodology, and intention of nefarious actors. A threat model also depicts potential threat scenarios and abstraction of systems.

threat sources
lead to threat events. Examples of threat sources include human error, failure of IT equipment, environmental controls, or even disaster in general.

time
in the context of threat matrices, correlates to how much time needs to be invested in resolving the threat throughout its lifecycle.

trade secrets
are any data or information a company may possess that provides a competitive advantage.

trademarks
protect a brand, logo, emblem, or representation of the company

transferring risk
is commonly associated with insurance which is purchased to cover the cost a risk would inflict upon the asset, personnel, or organization. The risk is passed on to a third-party organization so the business can focus on other critical risks or additional objectives toward maintaining operations.

two-factor authentication
uses two or more factors to authentication (something you have, something you know or something you are).

uncertainty
refers to any unknown information or outcome.

uninterruptible power supplies (UPS's)
provide backup power (batteries) to systems in the event primary power is lost.

user interaction (UI)
in the context of CVSS, determines how many users or employees in the organization are necessary for the attack to be a success.

variability
provides alternatives or the potential to think outside the box.

version control
is maintaining an inventory of previous, current, and future operating systems or applications that have been installed or managed on computer systems or technology components.

vulnerability assessment
consists of using programs or software written to scan for vulnerabilities in organizational software, hardware, and networks.

vulnerability management
is a strategy to minimize organizational vulnerabilities by reducing the risk of exposure, attack vectors, exploitation, or malicious intent.

warm sites
are partially equipped with infrastructure and IT capabilities.

wet pipe sprinkler
systems always have water within the pipes.

UNIT 3: CYBERSECURITY STRATEGY: SECURING THE ORGANIZATION'S ASSETS AND PEOPLE

Chapter 7 – Cybersecurity, Cyber Resiliency, and Convergence

Overview

Cybersecurity strategy is essential to securing the assets and people that will ensure a solvent and successful organizational future. Unfortunately, data breaches cost businesses an average of $3.62 million [1]. Sixty percent of small business close within six months of a cyber-attack [1]. Cyber-attacks are a growing concern for all organizations across our society. New digital technology continues to increase the complexity of our digital ecosystems, increasing the importance of proper cyber vision, strategy, and tactics. But even with this evolving complexity, basic approaches can eliminate most cybersecurity risk.

Chapter Learning Objectives

1. Investigate cybersecurity terms associated with attacks.
2. Compare and contrast information assurance, information security, cybersecurity, and cyber resiliency.
3. Explore convergence through the growing complexity of the digital ecosystem.

Cybersecurity comprehension is critical to organizational effectiveness and success. Cybersecurity conversations do not have to be deeply technical conversations in which the technical staff directs all decisions. Technical staff, tools, and strategies are critical for success, but everyone in leadership should comprehend core approaches to cybersecurity. Effective and impactful cybersecurity requires a simple and consistent approach.

In this Unit, we will incorporate cybersecurity strategy into the concepts of Units 1 and 2. Chapter 7 will define critical terms and present evolving concepts associated with cybersecurity, cyber resiliency, and convergence. Chapter 8 will review strategies and tactics for success. Finally, Chapter 9 will present multiple frameworks available for organizational adoption and process maturity.

Cybersecurity, Cyber Resiliency and Convergence

Cybersecurity and cyber resiliency efforts are of key importance. Every year more breaches are announced, confounding progress. Technology moves at a rapid pace, increasing in technical complexity and complicating cybersecurity. New terms and concepts such as cyber resiliency and convergence have been introduced, creating more confusion about cybersecurity. In the Introduction, key cybersecurity statistics were presented. In this Chapter, cybersecurity and its associated terms will be defined. Cyber resiliency and convergence will be discussed to provide an in-depth review of the digital ecosystem in which cybersecurity operates.

Section: Cybersecurity Terms

Unit 1 and Unit 2 provided a number of key terms and concepts surrounding information technology infrastructure and risk management. Keep in mind, infrastructure and our ability to innovate are critical items to protect. Attackers, inside and out, are focused on obtaining, altering, or manipulating our digital environments for different reasons. Every industry has jargon associated with their activities. Cybersecurity is no different. This section will provide a list of terms commonly used by cybersecurity professionals and media reporting on the cybersecurity industry. The list below may appear to be daunting, but it will increase your fluency in the terminology of cybersecurity and cyber resiliency.

Advanced Persistent Threat (APT) – Highly motivated and capable attackers, often associated with nation states or very capable cyber-criminal gangs, are known as APTs.

Attack Vector – Approach used to obtain unauthorized access on a target. Stolen credentials gained through a phishing email is an example.

Bot/Botnet – Bots are computers infected with malware, being controlled without the users' knowledge by another person or group. Botnets are groups of bots controlled by a centralized CNC server. Botnets can be leveraged for large attacks, such as DDoS attacks.

Breach – A breach is an unauthorized release of PII or obtaining unauthorized system access.

Bring Your Own Device (BYOD) – BYOD policies allow employees to use their personal devices at an organization. BYOD helps reduce direct equipment costs, but additional security implications complicate the overall cost savings.

Brute Force Attack – A brute force attack involves direct and repeated compromise attempts, often in an attempt to guess account passwords. Brute force attacks are the reason accounts are locked after multiple unsuccessful login attempts: login attempt limits directly combat brute force attacks.

Bug Bounty Program – Bug bounty programs offer rewards to researchers who identify security vulnerabilities in software and report them to the company offering the bounty. These programs are intended to encourage people to report vulnerabilities instead of selling them to threat actors for malicious use.

CAPTCHA – CAPTCHAs are designed to ensure that a human and not an automated program is attempting to login or use a digital service.

Clickjacking – Clickjacking is subverting a user's website clicks by hiding other links the user is unaware of. Clickjacking is a deceptive practice to manipulate users.

The Cloud – The cloud is the concept of services or storage on the Internet. Google Drive is an example of a cloud storage service.

Command and Control (CNC) – CNC servers provide commands to bots in a Botnet. CNC servers are also referred to as bot herders.

Controls – Controls are countermeasures intended to identify, avoid, or reduce security risks.

Cyber Criminal – A cybercriminal is a technically savvy attacker who leverages compromised remote systems for gain.

Distributed Denial of Service (DDoS) Attack - DDoS attacks are intended to overrun a website or digital asset's capability of processing. Because systems do not have limitless processing capabilities, a DDoS can stop services or websites from functioning. Botnets are often leveraged for very large DDoS attacks.

Domain – A domain is a group of computers bound together, created to identify trusted computers and enable shared services and security.

Looking Further

Bring Your Own Device (BYOD) represents different things to different groups. BYOD policies offers savings to organizations by allowing employees to use their personal devices on organizational networks. BYOD is thus often viewed as a way for an organization to save funds that would otherwise be spent on equipment.

A critical concern for BYOD, however, is cybersecurity. In most enterprise environments, policies, procedures and guidelines drive equipment usage and security measures. Typically, personal devices sit outside the realm enterprise governance. Personal devices can introduce malware, botnets, and other problematic security issues into an enterprise.

BYOD isn t necessarily all bad. Before deciding on BYOD as a strategy or tactic, security leaders should perform an objective review of goals to determine whether BYOD will have a positive or negative impact on the organization. If appropriate BYOD risk mitigations can be implemented, policies, procedures, and guidelines should be updated.

Driveby Download – Any unintended download on the Internet is a driveby download. Malware and cybercrime programs often leverage driveby downloads.

Exploit – An exploit is a software tool created to leverage conditions that create a vulnerability.

Firewall – A firewall is the portion of a computer or network intended to stop unauthorized network access or network traffic. Firewall security is accomplished through allowing outbound communications, while limiting inbound communications, based on rules.

Insider Threat – Insider threats are security risks from within an organization. Employees or contractors who steal data or commit malicious actions are insider threats.

Internet Facing – Internet facing servers and computers provide information or services over the Internet. A website server, for example, is an Internet facing machine that serves webpages to Internet users. Organizations should have all unnecessary services turned off on Internet facing machines.

Keylogger – Keyloggers are programs that capture all typed information. They are leveraged in attempts to gather PII or username and passwords.

Malware – Any software intended to negatively impact a system. Malware often disrupts, damages, or enables unauthorized access to systems.

Metadata – Metadata is digital data that describes data or files.

Open Source – Open source software is freely available and distributable.

Penetration Testing, or Pen Testing – Pen testing uses information from vulnerability scans to compromise computers. Some organizations do not consider a vulnerability to be valid if the vulnerability cannot be leveraged to gain access. More intrusive than vulnerability scans, pen tests provide clear pathways and direct evidence of exposure.

Phishing – Phishing involves sending spoofed emails intended to manipulate a person into providing passwords, credit card numbers, or some other form of gain for the attacker.

Piggyback Software – Piggyback software is a program embedded within a different program a user may download. Some utility software, for example, automatically tries to install anti-virus software along with the program you would like. The additional software is the piggyback software.

Personally Identifiable Information (PII) – PII identifies a specific person. Examples of PII include Social Security Number, Driver's License information, credit card numbers, etc.

Pretexting – Pretexting is a form of social engineering that involves an attacker attempting to create a bond their intended victim before deploying a phishing or spear phishing attempt.

Ransomware – Ransomware is malicious software that locks or encrypts data on a computer until a fee or ransom is paid.

Social Engineering – Social engineering manipulates human trust to obtain something, often privileged information.

Software – Software is programming code used for various purposes on a computer.

Spear Phishing – Spear Phishing attacks target a specific individual, often an executive or high-ranking official at an organization.

Spoofing – Spoofing is the manipulation of another with false or misleading information.

Threat – Threats are any occurrence that cause damage to a system. Threats can compromise security, access, and accuracy of data.

Threat Actors – Threat actors are any group or individual employing cyber-attacks for gain.

Trojan – A Trojan is programming code that appears to be something else. Trojans often masquerade as freeware. A mobile app may list itself as a flashlight app, but actually gather recordings, pictures, and geolocation information on a user.

Two-Factor Authentication – When you log into a system or application, you "authenticate" or prove you are the account user. Passwords are typically the first authentication factor. 2FA utilizes a second credential to verify that you are the approved account user, typically a token or special code texted to a mobile device. The additional authentication factor reduces the risk of breached or stolen accounts for nefarious purposes.

Virtual Private Network (VPN) – VPNs enable secure communications over open networks, such as the Internet. VPNs are leveraged to allow remote access into secure networks. Employees who travel and need access to organizational enterprise assets utilize VPNs for secure access.

Virus – A virus is programming code designed to have a negative impact on a computer system. A virus may open remote access to an attacker, for example, or download more malware for additional negative impacts.

Vulnerabilities – Vulnerabilities are latent conditions of weakness within hardware or software. An exploit leverages a vulnerability to gain access.

Vulnerability Scan – A vulnerability scan determines if a target contains software or hardware weaknesses that are susceptible to a threat. Keep in mind that vulnerability scans do not identify zero-days.

Web Application Framework – A web application framework is software designed for web portal creation and maintenance.

Worm – A worm is a self-replicating malware program. The worm does not need a user to interact with it to replicate and spread, especially across networks or the Internet.

Zero-Days – Zero-days are unknown vulnerabilities in software code. In particular, the vulnerabilities are unknown to the software creator, but may be known to threat actors. Without knowledge of the vulnerabilities, software creators are not able to create security patches. Zero-days represent a dangerous element to the cybersecurity environment.

Cybersecurity Concepts

Within the history of cybersecurity, a number of terms and concepts have evolved along with technology and human usage of technology. In this section, definitions of cybersecurity-related concepts will be reviewed.

Cybersecurity

Cybersecurity is associated with the protection of data assets. Information assurance is represented by practices associated with assuring information and associated risk management to employ information or data. Over time, information security has represented the practice of securing data. Traditionally, information security and information assurance represent the security and validity of data assets in a typical enterprise system environment, commonly referred to as information technology or IT. IT represents the processes and assets employed to operate, maintain, communicate, and support organization
al mission and objectives [2]. Servers and traditional digital services fall within the realm of IT. Additionally, required system patches, upgrades, and replacement components in IT and cybersecurity are implemented in a short-regimented cycle to enable frequent security modifications to support the organizational strategies.

Operational Technology (OT)

Operational technology (OT) are systems that interact, monitor, or gather data from a physical environment, as opposed to being limited to the digital realm of IT. OT operates with very different assets than IT. Building control systems (BCS), Industrial Control Systems (ICS), and Supervisory Control and Data Acquisition (SCADA) all fall into the OT domain [2].

A fundamental difference in IT and OT are the core level technologies enabling the platforms. IT leverages the microchip and standard CPU. OT leverages programmable logic controllers (PLC) and remote terminal units (RTU). Based on the difference in core components, the lifespan of equipment is also different. IT assets tend to be refreshed frequently; OT assets can be in place for decades. OT components often drive mission critical components, impacting the ability to patch and upgrade. If a laptop has an issue, it can be easily replaced. If an assembly robot has issues, the entire assembly line is impacted.

Cyber-Physical Systems

Cyber-physical systems can be defined across a wide spectrum of devices. Traditional technology (laptops, desktops and servers) generate, read, and manipulate data by interacting with users or programs. Cyber-physical systems, on the other hand, represent entirely new groups of technology operations. Computerized heating ventilation and air conditioning (HVAC) systems are a great example of operation and cyber physical systems. Cyber-physical systems can be a merge of OT and IT components to enable new functionality and innovation. Medical technology such as pacemakers, insulin pumps, and bionic eyes are examples once they are connected to wireless networks. Vehicles became cyber-physical systems with the addition of a cellular data connection. Home surveillance cameras, smart outlets, refrigerators, washers, and dryers are examples of cyber-physical IoT devices when they are connected to the Internet and controlled by an app on a smart phone.

Looking Further

Internet of Military Things (IOMT) - The Internet of Military Things (IOMT) is similar to the IoT and IIoT, but applicable to the defense industry [8]. IOMT is a great example of convergence of technologies. IOMT is expected to merge artificial intelligence, advanced analytics, sensor technologies, health systems, security, storage, and processors [8]. The combination of technologies is expected to enable an enhanced battlefield intelligence, while remaining human-centric [8].
Due to additional technologies and data points on the battlefield, machine learning and advanced analytics will be leveraged to sift and focus relevant data for war fighters [8]. Despite popular belief, artificial intelligence is still struggling with computer vision accuracy and decision explanation [8]. Reliable decision making and object identification are required for military usage, especially if drones operating in swarms are employed to replace some human fighters [8]. Overall, however, IOMT is poised to dramatically alter the battlefield of the future.

Industrial Internet of Things (IIOT)

If IoT represented a revolution of devices to the consumer market, IIoT represents a similar revolution to the manufacturing industry. Devices are being added to the assembly line and production processes to gather data and increase precision of manufacturing. These IIoT devices produce a large amount of sensor data, smart machine functionalities, and analytics for the manufacturing process through networking connectivity. Beyond sensor data acquisition, real time analytics can enable a global team to review status and real time impacts in manufacturing [11].

Cyber Resiliency

Cyber resiliency, a concept introduced by the Department of Defense (DOD) in 2018, represents an altered approach to cybersecurity. Traditionally, many groups assume and focus on cybersecurity as keeping malicious actors and attacks from breaching organizations. The best cybersecurity, however, can be circumvented through the manipulation of employees with an effective phishing email. Cyber resiliency represents planning and strategy to address ongoing functionality during an attack or compromise.

The concept hallmarked a critical shift in the approach and focus of new military assets: engineered defense posturing during compromise. DOD systems hold a different level of risk, especially in a theater of war. Threat and risk mitigation are approached and addressed more intensely in a military system than in a civilian system.

Cybersecurity is focused on identifying risks to organizational assets (data, capabilities, people, and systems), protecting prioritized organizational assets, detecting threat events as the event occurs, responding to a threat event, and recovering from the threat event. Cyber resilience, on the other hand, is focused on ensuring critical functionality during a cybersecurity threat event. Because critical IT functionality differs from critical OT functionality, we approach cyber resiliency through Convergence.

Convergence

Traditionally, IT and OT hold separate organizational responsibilities [3]. IT focuses on business applications, data assets, data protection, and data privacy, and ensuring and enabling business operations (cybersecurity) [3]. OT focuses on availability, functionality and operational capabilities, and ensuring ongoing operation of manufacturing systems (cyber resiliency) [3]. As the IIoT promises enhanced efficiency, quality and production benefits to the manufacturing process and supply chain [4], IT and OT are merging/converging disparate approaches into a unified whole. Cybersecurity within IT is converging with cyber resilience in OT to create new complex digital ecosystems (environments) [3].

Any place where technology is merging the physical worlds with the virtual worlds is a focal point for the impacts of convergence. Medical systems are now enabling network-connected lifesaving equipment. Insulin pumps, pacemakers, and other medical equipment enable the physical control of treatments or the modification of body function, simultaneously enabling data collection and transmission for physician review and updating of treatment plans. Telemedicine and robotic surgery offer updated approaches. Robotic surgery employs robots for high precision. These surgeries are often less invasive and have higher success rates and shorter healing times. Telemedicine provides remote interactions between patients and medical staff. Telemedicine removes the requirement for a patient to physically enter a health care facility unless absolutely necessary. During COVID-19, telemedicine enabled the remote assessment of non-COVID-19 medical issues.

Beyond Industry 4.0 and IIoT, convergence applies to all industries and all interface modalities. IT and OT convergence is the merger of disparate defensive approaches and strategies. In an expanded sense, convergence represents a larger and problematic impact on industries. Rather than a merger for two technology approaches to cybersecurity, convergence also represents a fundamental deepening of complexity in our technology. This deepening will continue despite our struggles to effectively address cybersecurity and cyber resiliency.

Looking Further

Industry 4.0 – The Fourth Industrial representation is sweeping the global manufacturing world. Manufacturing robots enabled Industry 3.0. Now, just as Internet enabled devices created the Internet of Things, the Industrial Internet of Things offers all new opportunities for Industry 4.0.

Embedded network devices in the manufacturing and development processes are poised to reduce engineering, development and time to market, while enabling all new capabilites.

Exploring Convergence

The Introduction presented information on the importance of understanding an organization's role in various business and social contexts. The United States' critical infrastructure is a great example of an organization's larger impact on upstream and downstream relationships. In this section, the 2015 cyber-attack on the Ukrainian power grid will illustrate the growing complexity of convergence on cybersecurity.

Ukrainian Power Grid Attacks: The Impact of Convergence in the Cybersecurity Game

On December 23rd, 2015, a worker in the Prykarpattyaoblenergo control center watched his computer's pointer move to shut down power stations and confirm through the onscreen popup box. As power stations went offline, he attempted to fight the attacker. The attacker, however, logged the worker out of his station and reset his password. Despite his best efforts, the worker watched helplessly as a remote attacker systematically set 30 substations to offline, denying power to swaths of the western Ukraine. The end result left over 230,000 Ukrainian residents in the dark two days before Christmas [3]

Similar to the Target hack, a spear phishing campaign had targeted key IT employees and system administrators working for power distribution companies in the Ukraine [4]. The email contained a Word document with macros, which installed malicious software known as BlackEnergy3 [3]. The exploit required the user to select and enable macros when opening the document. (Macros should by default be disabled to prevent malicious payloads being delivered via Word.) The initial compromise occurred in Spring 2015. Once inside the network, attackers did additional reconnaissance, mapped the network, and gained access to Windows Domain controllers. With Windows Domain access, the attackers could setup accounts and harvest the user credentials of those who had direct Virtual Private Network (VPN) access to the Supervisory Control and Data Acquisition (SCADA) network, which directly controlled and operated the electrical grid. Once they had gained access to SCADA networks, the attackers prepared for the attack.

Looking Further

Stuxnet: The First Digital Nation State Weapon - Stuxnet entered the cyber scene in 2010, although some reports indicate that it may have been in development as early as 2005. Stuxnet was a worm that spread rapidly across networks and the Internet. After infecting a machine, the worm determined if the machinewas connected to Programmable Logic Controllers (PLCs) created by Siemens [9]. The targeted PLCs were used to control industrial machines and processes -- specifically, uranium enrichment centrifuges [9]. The worm deliberately altered the spin speed of the uranium centrifuges, without reporting the change to users [9]. At the altered spin speed, uranium enrichment is impossible, and the uranium is not viable for use in weapons.

Stuxnet is assumed to have been created by the U.S. and Israeli governments to delay or prevent Iran s nuclear weapons program. Within the context of weapons development, Lt. General Michael Hayden, former director of the National Security Agency (NSA), described Stuxnet as the digital equivalent of the Hiroshima bomb. Historically, the Hiroshima bomb was the first time a nuclear weapon was deployed by a nation state against another nation state. From Hayden s perspective, the release of Stuxnet marked the first time a nation state publicly deployed a cyber weapon against another nation state.

The Ukrainian power grid was complex, as different power companies used different power distribution management systems. The attackers thus leveraged their reconnaissance to write malicious firmware, which was installed across components in the SCADA network, in essence preventing power company employees from turning the power back on remotely. Restoring power would require a manual restart by flipping a breaker at the power distribution stations. (Think *Jurassic Park*, but without the velociraptors chasing you.) At the time, this level of persistence and custom firmware had not previously been seen. To re-enable the remote control through SCADA, the infrastructure of the power companies would need to be replaced. The attackers also leveraged software titled "KillDisk," which would destroy the files on main control center workstations and thus render them unusable. In short, the APTs involved were serious, smart, and took a converged approach to take down a power grid. With their new malicious firmware installed, the attackers were prepared for their Christmas 2015 attack.

In December 2016, the attacks on the Ukrainian power grid evolved. According to *Wired*, a week before Christmas 2016 an electrical transmission station was taken down by malicious attackers. The outage impacted approximately one-fifth of the total power capacity of Kiev. With an outage duration of about an hour, the attack drew little attention. Unfortunately, analysis indicates the outage in Kiev may have been a test run for a new evolution of malware since the observation of Stuxnet [5].

Crash Override, the name of the malware used in the second attack, is capable of initiating power blackouts more quickly and with far less preparation than in the December 2015 Ukrainian attack [7]. In essence, Crash Override extends the scalability of grid attacks, reducing manual human efforts. The ultimate impact of the second attack and Crash Override malware was a worldwide wakeup call.

> **Looking Further**
>
> *Phishing Convergence* - The phone rings. You answer it. The voice sounds just like your boss and asks you do something. The voice has all of the nuances and inflections your boss uses.
>
> In the Fall of 2019, a German Chief Executive Officer was duped in a phone scam [10]. Phone scams themselves are not new; what was new is that it was an artificial intelligence-generated voice that mimicked the voice of the CEO s boss, [10]. The fake voice instructed the German CEO to transfer $243,000 to a Hungarian supplier s bank account [10]. The CEO complied. When he learned he had been duped, the CEO indicated that the fake voice exhibited all of the subtle accents and nuances of the real person [10].
>
> Convergence of the physical and the virtual worlds expand the attack surface for unprepared individuals and organizations. The next chapter will review this attack and the ways to block it.

The focus of this section is not malware, but convergence. The attacks on the Ukrainian power grid and the increasingly sophisticated malware used in them perfectly illustrate convergence. The Ukrainian power companies were heralded for having great security measures in place [3]. The attackers leveraged the corporate system to gain access and exploit the SCADA network. IT and OT networks are built in isolation, but hold clues, documentation, and tether into each other: the exploits of these separately-designed networks is a great example of how we must understand the interplay and merger of components, services, and systems that create our larger digital ecosystem.

Chapter Summary

Convergence represents a new digital ecosystem composed of components traditionally perceived as independent. As organizations approach cybersecurity and cyber resiliency, comprehension of this larger ecosystem must be explored. The Ukrainian power grid examples focused primarily on the merger of multiple systems, and the upstream and downstream impacts need to be considered. From components to configuration and change management, the Ukrainian power grid attacks illustrate that our world is evolving from manual human control to programmatic computer-controlled devices.

Convergence should be considered while studying Chapters 8 and 9. Our digital and physical worlds are converging. From electrical grids to medical facilities to artificial intelligence, the complexity of our digital ecosystems are growing. Whether an AI is generating a Deepfake or a nation state is preparing for an attack, organizations need to comprehend the complexity of in the digital ecosystem and adopt appropriate strategies and tactics to insure cybersecurity and cyber resiliency.

Discussion Questions

1. In the example of the SCADA component malicious firmware, did the manufacturers play a role in the attack?

2. Remote installation of firmware is a great feature, but how does this isolated feature play out in a larger coordinated attack, such as Crash Override?

Exercises

1. Watch the NIST video at https://www.nist.gov/video/what-internet-things-iot-and-how-can-we-secure-it and describe list two ways IoT is changing our society.

2. Research cybersecurity trends over ten years. Build a graph illustrating shifting attack patterns and industry impacts.

3. Investigate high-risk attack vectors for your industry and the top three defenses against them.

4. Identify and research a publicized breach from your industry. Review the lessons learned, evaluating the viability and potential impact of recommended actions. Evaluate whether the recommendations appear to have an impact given the breach example.

5. Research Stuxnet and Crash Override attacks. Compare and contrast the Stuxnet and Crash Override attacks. Answer the following questions:
    - Was the 2015 Ukrainian power grid attack a nation state or cyber-criminal gang orchestrated? Provide supporting points for and against each.
    - Was Crash Override created by a nation state?
    - How many zero days were leveraged in the Stuxnet attack?
    - How many zero days were leveraged in the Crash Override attack?

References

[1] R. J. II, "60 Percent Of Small Companies Close Within 6 Months Of Being Hacked," Cybercrime Magazine, 2 January 2019. [Online]. Available: https://cybersecurityventures.com/60-percent-of-small-companies-close-within-6-months-of-being-hacked/. [Accessed 16 April 2020].

[2] D. S. C. H. G. P. C. Rita Barrios, "Technology Report 2019," Automation Alley, Detroit, MI, 2019.

[3] E. F. M. S. G. P. David Schippers, "IT/OT: Convergence on the edge," Automation Alley, Detroit, MI, 2020.

[4] D. S. C. H. G. P. Rita Barrios, "Cybersecurity, Industry 4.0: From Vision to implementation," Automation Alley, Detroit, MI, 2019.

[5] K. Zetter, "Inside the Cunning, Unprecedented Hack of Ukraine's Power Grid," Wired.com, 03 March 2016. [Online]. Available: https://www.wired.com/2016/03/inside-cunning-unprecedented-hack-ukraines-power-grid/. [Accessed 11 05 2020].

[6] Wikipedia, "Screenshot of a WannaCry ransomware attack on Windows 8," Wikipedia, May 2017. [Online]. Available: https://en.wikipedia.org/wiki/WannaCry_ransomware_attack#/media/File:Wana_Decrypt0r_screenshot.png. [Accessed 30 March 2020].

[7] A. Greenburg, "'Crash Override': The Malware That Took Down a Power Grid," Wired.com, 12 June 2017. [Online]. Available: https://www.wired.com/story/crash-override-malware/. [Accessed 11 05 2020].

[8] GlobalData Thematic Research, "Internet of military things: Leading technology trends revealed," 5 November 2019. [Online]. Available: https://www.army-technology.com/comment/internet-of-military-things-leading-technology-trends-revealed/. [Accessed 2 June 2020].

[9] K. Zetter, "How Digital Detectives Deciphered Stuxnet, the Most Menacing Malware in History," 11 July 2011. [Online]. Available: https://www.wired.com/2011/07/how-digital-detectives-deciphered-stuxnet/. [Accessed 2 June 2020].

[10] J. Damiani, "A Voice Deepfake Was Used To Scam A CEO Out Of $243,000," 3 September 2019. [Online]. Available: https://www.forbes.com/sites/jessedamiani/2019/09/03/a-voice-deepfake-was-used-to-scam-a-ceo-out-of-243000/#29d935ec2241. [Accessed 2 June 2020].

[11] Rubio, J., Alcaraz, C., Roman, R., & Lopez, J. (2017). Analysis of intrusion detection systems in industrial ecosystems. 14th International Conference on Security and Cryptography.

Chapter 8 – Cyber Strategies and Tactics

Overview

Chapter 7 provided definitions and historical perspectives related to cybersecurity, cyber resiliency, and convergence, and it reviewed the complexity of the digital ecosystem. This chapter will give you a better understanding of cybersecurity strategies and tactics. Despite widespread publicity and discussion of cybersecurity, organizations ironically often miss the point.

Chapter Learning Objectives

1. Investigate confidentiality, integrity, and availability.
2. Formulating key defensive measures.
3. Critique leadership principles for cybersecurity operations.
4. Explore decision making for leadership.

All of the breaches discussed in the Introduction should drive one singular point home: there is a difference between knowledge and acting on knowledge. Comprehension and informed action can also be two very different states of mind. In short, many people think they know what cybersecurity is and how to provide it effectively. If cybersecurity is easy and everyone provides effective cybersecurity, however, why are there so many examples of breaches?

This chapter will begin with some basic statistics to illustrate how bad things really are, and will then present fundamental problems that impede successful cyber strategies and tactics. The CIA triad will be explained to address fundamental comprehension and strategy issues, and a general review of high-level strategies and tactics will be covered.

How Bad Is It?

From a cybersecurity perspective, things are bad. Really bad. Cybersecurity damages are projected to reach $6 trillion by 2021 [6]. Illegal activities involving bitcoin are estimated at $76 billion [6]. Ransomware attacks happen every 14 seconds [6]. Hacking tools are point and click, creating a low barrier of entry into the dark world of exploitation. It is estimated it only takes five minutes to hack an Internet of Things device [6]. Reports indicate that only 10% of cybercrimes are actually reported every year [6].

The Introduction reviewed some critical hacks and lessons learned. Despite ongoing review and recommendations, more hacks occur every year. As an example, the financial sector invests a significant amount of money into cybersecurity and defensive posturing. Global banks must be secure, correct? Unfortunately, a security team tested a sampling of global banks and found that 97% are vulnerable to either web or mobile attacks [6]. Organizations believe they have addressed cybersecurity effectively until they are breached. If a breached organization survives, strategies, tactics, and funding are all re-evaluated. Funding not provided before a breach is often readily available after a breach occurs. What creates the Chasm of Security?

The Chasm of Security

The defense industry has experienced significant change, particularly in the defense manufacturing industry. The DoD has created and required various standards to secure the defense supply chain. During standards rollouts, varying levels of compliance have been realized. Subsequent studies have illustrated the barriers and chasms associated with the successful adoption of and compliance with cybersecurity standards.

"The National Defense Industry Association (NDIA) completed a study on security implementations within the manufacturing supply chain in July of 2018. The NDIA study focused on the Defense Federal Acquisition Regulations Supplement (DAFRS), based on the National Institute of Standards in Technology (NIST) 800-171 publication" [4]. Despite the study's focus on DOD regulations in manufacturing, the study provides insight regarding the implementation of new requirements and technologies into the supply chain.

The NDIA report indicates that most small to medium sized (SME) suppliers do not understand the impact of cybersecurity on manufacturing capabilities – do not understand that cybersecurity enables the safe operation of manufacturing processes [4]. Survey "respondents understood the need to protect intellectual property and IT operations but saw little support in securing the operational aspects of their business" [4]. The respondents furthermore indicate they "found the NIST cybersecurity documentation for securing operations to be confusing" [4].

The NDIA (2018) provided insight on types of adopters within the supply chain. In the book *Crossing the Chasm*, Moore described four different groups of adopters: innovators, early adopters, the early majority, and the late majority and laggards [3]. Innovators embrace and adopt change first, followed by early adopters. Early adopters are focused on a competitive edge and distancing themselves from the rest of the pack: they are willing to embrace and pay for new technologies and approaches that differentiate themselves from their competition. Innovators make up approximately 2.5% of the population, while early adopters make up approximately 13% of the population. The real fulcrum point in the groups, however, is associated with the gap between early adopters and early majority [4].

The early majority accounts for about 34% of the population. The early majority group is very pragmatic in its approach [4], and leaders in the early majority and the late majority and laggards

groups are risk averse, ultimately failing on a variety of levels to understand the importance of both cybersecurity and cyber resiliency. The early majority and the late majority and laggards groups together account for approximately 84% of our population. If this study is leveraged as a blueprint for cybersecurity adoption, the size of the chasm of security is clear.
A number of approaches -- including legislation -- have been considered to address the lack of cybersecurity adoption in the manufacturing space. New legislation, research, and training will have little impact, however, until business leaders understand cybersecurity and cyber resiliency risk strategies. If traditional approaches to IT and OT are leveraged in convergence, organizations will struggle: IT and OT cultures differ significantly in their funding and expertise. Realistically, leadership needs to merge the approaches, staff, and budgets of IT and OT, integrating their risk approaches, risk strategies, management, and policies into a fundamentally new approach. Organizations looking to leverage the innovation and opportunities of technology adoption must consider a significantly different approach to find a pathway to success.

The Cost Factor

Organizations often expect to obtain cost savings when implementing cybersecurity standards and practices. Cost of quality, legal conformance, and many other factors impact the management of cybersecurity implementations. Risk-based approaches, even well intended ones, will generate wildly different costs and value if too many variables are in play. In essence, if cost projections are inaccurate in either direction, that usually means the team or organization is operating with assumed or poorly defined of terms, goals, and expected outcomes. Because the early majority is risk averse and the late majority and laggards are both risk averse and focused on tangible benefit realizations, these groups may be prone to outsourcing or abandoning cybersecurity adoptions. The late majority leadership, for example, will rarely be invested in continuing with initiatives that have growing costs and diminishing returns.

There are ways, however, to address the leadership concerns of the early majority and the late majority and laggards. Strategies that have been used to implement cybersecurity and cyber resiliency successfully include:

- Adopting a common set of definitions and terms.
- Clearly defining the organizational culture and vision for cybersecurity/cyber resiliency and cyber survivability.
- Building critical comprehension of cybersecurity and cyber resiliency for organizational growth and health.
- Aligning people to match the vision and goals for cybersecurity and cyber resiliency.
- Correlating any expenditure or action to the vision, goals, or outcomes defined by strategy or tactics.

More information on strategies and tactics will be presented in the Governance, Risk, and Compliance section. To prepare for the discussion of strategies and tactics, however, a review of the CIA triad is necessary.

The CIA Triad

The CIA triad is critical to defining and comprehending approaches in information security and cybersecurity. The CIA triad deals with the confidentiality, integrity, and availability of data. As this Unit digs into cybersecurity, differences between IT and OT approaches to the CIA triad will be discussed. These differences will be central in understanding risk mitigation and framework discussions for security implementation measures.

Confidentiality represents the ability to restrict access to data to the fewest amount of people required. For example, payroll records in a company are restricted to payroll staff. A significant amount of information about an individual employee is stored in payroll systems, so companies should not be providing full access to payroll data for everyone in the organization. People may request access to data, but their job role should clearly indicate a need to access the data. Remember: insider threats are real. Just because someone requests access to data doesn't mean that access should be granted. Unexpected or unjustified requests for access should raise red flags for leaders.

From an attack perspective, confidentiality is often the "target." If an attacker gained access to the data, confidentiality has been compromised. After access is gained, additional impacts need to be considered, such as integrity.

Integrity represents the accuracy of the data. Data integrity is the ability to trust the data has not been altered or manipulated. Part of the reason confidentiality is enforced is to ensure data integrity. Open access to data can generate integrity issues. If anybody can alter the data, data can be altered for malicious reasons, especially by insiders. A common belief is that data security is about preventing unauthorized access, which it is; data security, however, is also about ensuring data accuracy and integrity. Sometimes attackers want to alter data to impact processes: attacks are not always about stealing, especially if espionage or corporate espionage are involved.

Availability means data is available to be accessed, viewed, and updated when needed. Any attack intending to remove accessibility to a digital asset attacks availability: common attacks against availability are a denial of service (DoS) attack or a distributed denial of service attack (DDoS). The intent of a denial of service attack is to deny the service of a digital asset. Generally, these attacks generate enough requests or traffic at a digital asset to overload its capability to process the requests. With an overload of requests, the asset may lock up, become unstable, or temporarily bog down. When these requests come from multiple sources, a distributed denial of service takes place. Any of these occurrences stop the asset from being available for users. If a printer is unavailable, an alternate may be available. If an organization's webservers are unavailable, on the other hand, a significant amount of business can be lost depending on the outage duration.

In the CIA order of priority, confidentiality is first. IT groups focus on confidentiality over integrity, and integrity over availability. If one of the three slips, availability is allowed first. Of course, losing availability/access to assets is not ideal, but a loss of availability is preferred over data being altered or accessed by unauthorized individuals. In essence, the sequence of the CIA directs vision, strategy, and tactics.

Key Defensive Approaches

Ideally, organizations should be employing mature strategies and tactics, and evolving their defensive postures. Understandably, though, every organization needs to start somewhere. If an organization is not embracing an evolving and mature strategy, key defense approaches provide the minimum level of defensive posturing that every organization should be leveraging. (Note: if your organization is employing a mature and evolving defensive approach, these should be included in your approach as well.)

Key Defensive Approaches – Updates

In the introduction, the WannaCry outbreak and Equifax's breach were preventable with security updates. In July of 2017, a Ukrainian accounting software firm were breached by attackers [6]. The attackers inserted malware into the firm's accounting software, enabling the malware to be delivered with accounting software to all of the firm's clients [6]. One devastating approach to organizations is taking a perceived strength and weaponizing it against the organization. In this case, the attackers used the firm's security patch server to distribute malware [6]. Ironically, the firm's information technology staff had not installed security patches on the compromised server [6]. In addition to internal impacts for breaches, the Ukrainian firm contributed to the compromise of thousands of client computers within the digital ecosystem in which they operate. Sometimes, security is not just for one organization, but all organizations business is conducted with.

Some organizations and software vendor agreements may require the delay of security patches. In exception situations, processes and protocols need to be built to ensure patches are reviewed and implemented when applicable. Equifax thought they had installed patches and failed to detect missed patches, during their scans. Processes without validation are wish lists. Follow through.

Takeaway – Apply updates consistently and persistently.

Key Defensive Approaches – Two-Factor Authentication (2FA)

The Uber hack in the Introduction is a great illustration of the need of 2FA. If Uber had turned on 2FA for their Github account, Uber would have received validation codes when attackers attempted logins to Uber's Github account. Uber would have had forewarning that brute force attacks were in play, and the outcome of the attack would have most likely been different. 2FA can be viewed as an inconvenience, but it does add additional layers of security to increase the difficulty of exploitation.

Takeaway – Always use 2FA.

Key Defensive Approaches – Useable Backups

If an attacker gains access to your data, the data needs to be exfiltrated (removed secretly from your network). After the attacker has your data offsite, they have to decide to whom or where they will sell the stolen data. All of these additional steps increase effort and delay time to acquisition of monetary value. Ransomware, however, removes all of the steps involved with exfiltration, data movement, and monetization. Ransomware allows attackers to encrypt (lock) your data and demand a payment to obtain the key to decrypt (unlock) your data. From a monetization perspective, ransomware is the least amount of effort to payment. Attackers also know if a victim pays them once, they will most likely pay again. It is not uncommon for victims to be attacked multiple times with ransomware.

A key issue with backups is that organizations setup backup procedures and never validate the procedures are running correctly. A number of issues can complicate successful backup creation and utilization. Tape backups require tape replacements, as tapes wear out over time. Backup jobs can be misconfigured by system administrators, resulting in unusable or corrupted backups. Remember, backups are not created solely for ransomware: if a disaster such as a tornado or flood impacts a business, backups may be the only option for a business to start over. Organizations need to validate backup creations and attempt periodic recovery from backups to ensure backups are actually in a useable state.

Takeaway – Test data backups before you need them.

Key Defensive Approaches – Restrict Rogue Information Technology (IT)

Rogue IT is equipment introduced into an organization's network without knowledge of the IT staff. For example, if an employee brings a home wireless access point to the office and plugs it into the network, the wireless access point is considered rogue IT. Rogue IT can introduce unsecure equipment into a secure environment.

Takeaway – Setup network scans to identify Rogue IT occurrences.

Key Defensive Approaches – Appropriate Credential Policies

Credentials and password policies should be pretty straightforward. Password reuse is a significant issue for IT and employees in general. Password reuse is especially problematic if the password is used across work and personal accounts. If your Zoom account name and password are the same on Zoom and at work, it can be a problem if Zoom is breached. In April 2020, Zoom accounts were discovered for sale on the dark web. If buyers test those stolen credentials against other accounts, they can gain access on any platform you have registered. (Hopefully, you're using 2FA to combat this, as recommended above.)

Takeaway – Do not reuse passwords across platforms.

Key Defensive Approaches – Mature Business Processes

Leadership is targeted with attacks intended to manipulate actions or gain information. Spear phishing targets executives to obtain credentials or confidential information. An email or some type of communication is leveraged to manipulate an executive or leader to provide target information. Business process compromise involves attackers breaching an organization and exploiting the processes to obtain some type of financial gain.

The best cybersecurity in the world will not protect against the exploitation of a human being. Recall the DeepFake AI attack from the previous chapter, where technology mimicked the voice of an influential boss directing a funds transfer. The real issue here was not the failure of the technological defenses of cybersecurity: the real issue was the lack of a business process to validate funds transfer requests above a certain amount. If, for example, all funds transfers in excess of $1,000 had required double verification, the German CEO would have had to revalidate the request before initiating the transfer.

Takeaway – Build validation checks into business processes.

Key Defensive Approaches – Malicious Activity Monitoring

Knowing that your data is being stolen is critical to stopping the last stages of a successful cyberattack. In order to exfiltrate data, attackers need to move the data over your network. Monitoring for exfiltration or "data loss prevention" is the last hope of stopping a cyberattack. Quick identification of breaches through malicious activity monitoring is critical. Monitoring for malicious activity and response time are critical considerations.

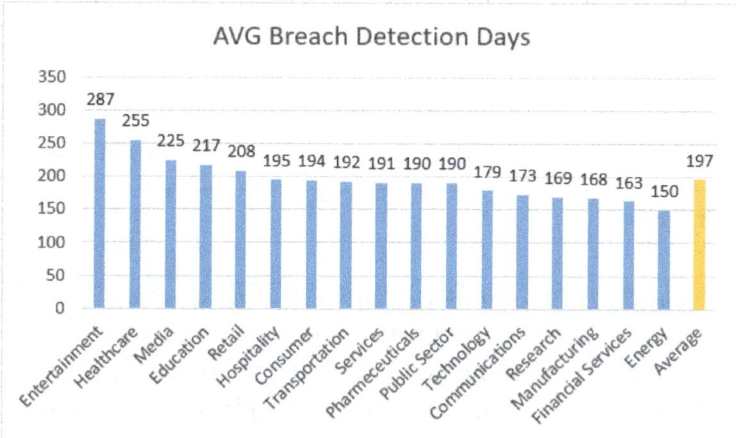

Industry response times vary for breach detection. In 2019, the energy industry had the shortest reported breach detection time at 150 days. The entertainment industry clocked in at 287 days [4]. The real question, though, is how much data can be stolen in 150 days of undetected access? Figure 1 shows the industry detection times. As discussed in the Introduction, Equifax did not detect their breach for about 30 days. Thirty days of undetected access resulted in millions of records being stolen and exfiltrated. Malicious activity monitoring/breach detection as soon as possible is critical to containment of larger losses and issues.

<u>Takeaway – Monitor traffic and systems for malicious activity.</u>

Key Defensive Approaches – Incident Response & Recovery Plan

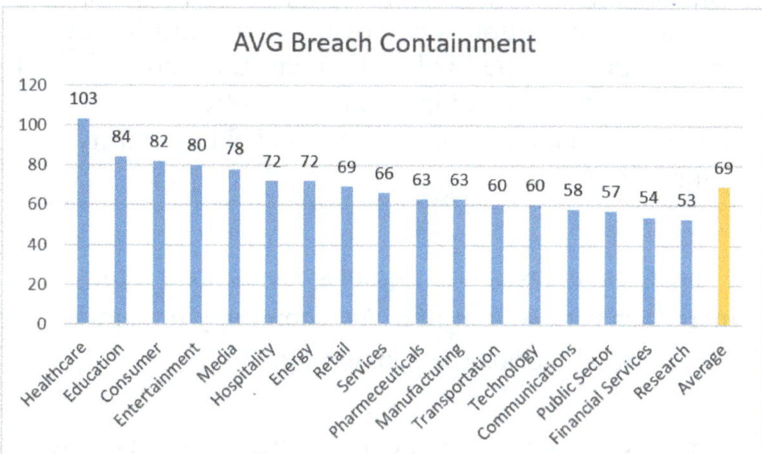

Organizations should no longer assume they cannot be breached, and the quantity and severity of data breaches should motivate organizations to plan for a breach. Incident response plans and recovery plans are critical for shortening response times. Quick response times for containment have been linked to recovery is stock values for companies after an announced data breach [4]. Longer containment response times, especially longer than 90 days, were linked with further declines in stock values [4]. Figure 2 presents average containment response times for breaches by industry. Organizations who identify roles, approaches, and priorities during incidents are better positioned to shorten response times for a cyberattack. In addition to strategy, having a knowledgeable staff with predefined roles also significantly lowers response times.

Takeaway – Create plans for incident response and recovery.

Key Defensive Approaches – Convergence

The problem with technology and security technology is complexity. As technology advances, complexity grows. Organizations are part of larger system in which their networks employ the Internet and access other organizations' networks. Organizations no longer use technology to just create, store, and leverage data. Building systems control indoor climates. Automated lock systems control access. Alexa reads our news, controls our locks, and orders our merchandise. Pacemakers, insulin pumps, and medical equipment sustain life. Our cars monitor themselves for preventative maintenance recommendations and repairs. Assembly lines gather more data than ever before, enabling virtual prototyping that reduces engineering cycles from years to months, or weeks to days. Our digital systems are a tightly integrated ecosystem that enable and maintain our very way of life. As technology integrates more fully into our lives, our real, digital, and virtual worlds are converging.

> **Terms To Know**
>
> *General Data Protection Regulation (GDPR)* is considered the strongest data protection rules in the world. Overall, GDPR operates as a framework of multiple articles [5]. It was created by the European Union and addresses personal data, or PII. PII can take many forms, including name, address, and phone number. Other data can also be combined to identify people, including network information, browser, and operating system [5].
>
> GDPR impacts individuals, organizations, and companies who either control or process the aforementioned data. Significant penalties are imposed for organizations violating GDPR requirements [5].
>
> Organizations operating outside of the EU are impacted by GDPR if the organization is processing or a controller of PII for individuals in the EU [5]. Organizations potentially impacted by GDPR should incorporate GDPR requirements into their strategic plans and cybersecurity external requirements.

Organizations must understand that cybersecurity is not just about data. Cybersecurity is about protecting our organizations and our access to partner organizations. In short, cybersecurity is about protecting an organization's ability to function and do business.

Takeaway – Ensure the entire organization comprehends the importance of cybersecurity.

Key Defensive Approaches – Leverage Frameworks

Leaders and organizations can struggle to find a reliable security posture. Different industries have different considerations for proper security postures. The complexity of technology additionally creates trepidation and uncertainty for organizations. A great starting place for cybersecurity approaches is frameworks.

Frameworks provide voluntary best practices, guidelines, and standards for considerations. In essence, frameworks are guiding documents to help organizations review internal considerations. Frameworks will not be a perfect fit for all organizations, nor are they intended to be: rather, frameworks provide a substantial road map to reliable defensive posturing. Framework investigation and adoption are intended to help organizations communicate and discuss issues that are significant to security posturing.

Chapter 9 will present and review frameworks for different industries.

Terms To Know

The *California Consumer Privacy Act* is a state statute passed in California in 2018 [6]. CCPA strives to enhance privacy rights and consumer protections for residents of California [6]. Somewhat similar to GDPR, CCPA provides residents with rights to know the data being collected, sale or disclosure of PII, the ability to say no to data sales, access to the resident s PII, the ability to request deletion of the resident s PII and avoidance of discrimination if they exercise their privacy rights [6].

CCPA impacts individuals, organizations, and companies who either control or process the aforementioned data. Penalties and sanctions can be imposed on organizations violating the CCPA for California residents [6]. Organizations meeting CCPA criteria are recommended to include CCPA requirements in strategic plans and cybersecurity process requirements.

Takeaway – Frameworks will not have all the answers, but frameworks will drive organizations to better answers.

Governance, Risk, and Compliance

All organizations have limited resources; winning organizations create a competitive edge by prioritizing and investing those limited resources to drive vision and outcomes. Leaders, often outside of the technical reporting structure, determine vision, goals, and benefits with the strategies and tactics employed. In cybersecurity and cyber resiliency, governance, risk, and compliance (GRC) approaches fundamentally dictate an organization's success for failure.

Unsuccessful GRC efforts in organizations share common themes, including:

- Ineffective oversight/strategies and tactics
- Limited/no visibility of technical assets/status
- Isolated areas within the organization
- Undefined/disjointed/erratic strategy
- Duplication of efforts (wasted labor)
- Limited/no GRC reporting
- Ineffective integration
- High costs
- Wasted efforts/resources
- Missed deadlines/goals
- Lack of integrity/ethics

When implemented correctly, GRC provides significant benefits, including:

- Reduced costs
- Effective reporting
- Enhanced information gathering
- Reduced confusion
- Consistent vision for resource allocation
- Unified efforts across organizational/functional areas
- Comprehension of cybersecurity efforts and investments

Terms To Know

Business Continuity Plans (BCP) and *Disaster Recovery Plans (DRP)* were tested by COVID-19. Leaders invest in strategic planning such as BCP and DRPs to ensure organizational continuity.

BCPs are plans designed to guide an organization through events and circumstances that impede the organization s ability to operate normally. A power outage, global pandemic, or cyber-attack qualify as events, depending on definitions. DRPs are plans to restore operations and functions to an organization after they have ceased. Ill handled BCP events can shut down organizational operations. A fire, flood, or significant loss of staffing qualify as disasters.

Strategic plans include BCPs and DRPs. Plans are designed to reduce decision making under duress. Each plan should clearly define organizational impedance (requiring BCP) or organizational disruption (requiring DRP). For example, if a server is shorted out and is a critical system, does this qualify for BCP to be invoked? If a power outage hits and backup generators fail, is this a disaster? When everything is offline, in what order do you bring systems online? (Can raptors open doors?) These are the types of questions and approaches strategic plans address.

None of the questions required for BCPs and DRPs are developed when needed. GRC and strategic plans are built in a thorough and thoughtful manner in advance. When events occur, a playbook to guide efforts is invaluable.

Strategic Plans

Strategic plans are critical to the successful adoption of cybersecurity and cyber resiliency. Successful organizations create strategic plans at the executive level, treating cyber risk and cyber requirements the same as other risks and requirements. For example, compliance with federal employer regulations are not questioned by executives. In essence, organizational compliance with federal employer requirements is considered part of doing business. Cyber risks and requirements need to be viewed in this same light.

Many people and organizations assume that definitions of basic terms and concepts are not necessary. Basic definitions and comprehensions, however, are a primary expense driver for organizations. As presented by Moore's chasm theory, comprehension and adoption of common definitions are critical factors for success. Studies indicate definition, comprehension, and consistent communication are critical barriers to success. As noted previously, wildly variable costs and delivery capabilities are prime indicators of excessive variables; a critical barrier/variable impeding cyber strategy adoption is definition and vision focus. As organizations build reliable approaches, definitions, vision, and purpose, communication is an integral component of successful strategic plans. Before any organization begins serious cyber initiatives, clear definitions, visions, and goals are required.

Security Governance: The Controls Triad

The CIA triad guiding security approaches was previously discussed. In the realm of security governance, three specific levels of controls are implemented: administrative, technical, and physical controls. All three of these are integral components of successful cyber strategy and tactics.

Administrative controls set the stage for cyber efforts and are built directly from strategies and tactics. Administrative controls leverage policies, standards, and procedures to drive organizational behavior. Policies define leadership's approaches and expectations in relation to security and achieving acceptable levels of cyber risk, and act as reference materials for unexpected events and as scope for specific tactics. For GDPR and other regulatory requirements, policies will define the organization's approach to compliance. Advisory policies provide employees with expectations of acceptable behaviors and activities and indicate punitive measures for violation of those expectations. Information policies define topics, issues, goals, and expectations in relation to cyber risks and actions.

Standards are another example of administrative controls. Standards define required activities, actions, or rules to achieve outcomes. Standards can be defined internally or externally, as by government bodies. An example of a standard is that employee

> **Looking Further**
>
> *Documentation*-Organizations sometimes view planning and strategic goal setting as red tape or unnecessary effort. Unit 1 indicated that approximately 90% of unplanned and unstructured engagements fail. Documentation in GRC formalizes approaches, identifies goals and outcomes, and is the first step in organization skill maturity and goal attainment. Some employees will cast the planning effort as futile, claiming plans rarely follow their design.
>
> Although it is true that plans do rarely follow their exact documented course, the plan creation itself builds comprehension, focus, clarity, and ultimately skill maturity for participants. In a time of crisis, the planning will pay dividends. In cyber events, the less critical thinking required in a time of crisis, the better. People handle stress differently, with some buckling and others thriving. Reducing decision making in a time of crisis and operating with predefined guidelines ultimately increases success rates.

badges/access cards must be displayed at all time. If an organization is concerned about unauthorized access to their facility, a standard is used to define this expected behavior. Standards are compulsory and only effective when enforced. Assumptions of compliance without accountability measures are ineffective; if a standard is important enough to create, the standard is important enough to enforce.

Guidelines are another administrative control. Guidelines are created as a reference for recommended actions and approaches, and they operate with some flexibility. Guidelines are most useful in hazy or gray situations. Ethical drivers and approaches appear in guidelines. Standards provide mandatory rules with expected compliance. Guidelines provide general approaches for unexpected circumstances.

Procedures are detailed tasks descriptions. As an administrative control, procedures are step-by-step actions designed to achieve a specific goal. They are the lowest level of administrative controls, defining precisely how policy, standards, and guidelines will be implemented in the organizational environment. All of the administrative controls can be rather confusing. The following example will illustrate how administrative controls operate together.

An organization decides it will adhere to and follow the confidentiality section of the CIA triad. Confidential information is a requirement of vision, strategy, and government regulation. HIPAA and FERPA are two examples of maintaining confidentiality of data. To achieve confidentiality, the organization creates the following administrative controls:

- **Policy** – The organization's leaders define policy as part of the vision and strategy. A security policy is created, indicating that information designated as confidential must be protected appropriately. The policy does not define specifically how the data will be

Looking Further

The Family Educational Rights and Privacy (FERPA) act of 1974 directly applies to educational institutions [7]. Under FERPA, the protection and dispersal of information related to education is regulated and defined.

Student performance (grade) data directly tied to a student s PII is restricted. FERPA also designates disclosure of student performance and grade information to the parents of the student if the student is a dependent.

Organizations handling education data are required by law to incorporate PII protections meeting FERPA definitions [7].

Looking Further

The Health Insurance Portability and Accountability Act (HIPAA) of 1996 addressed healthcare restrictions on PII [8]. In particular, healthcare PII impacts healthcare and healthcare insurance industries. Other provisions of the act impact other portions of the healthcare industry.

Organizations operating with healthcare data are required by law to incorporate PII protections meeting HIPAA definitions [8].

protected, but the policy does require that confidential data be protected in broad terms.

- **Standard** – Technology leadership uses the policy to create the standard/tactics to achieve the vision or strategy. A standard is created, requiring all confidential data be stored with the Advanced Encryption Standard (AES) when stored. The standard also dictates that the transmission of confidential data over the Internet requires IPSec encryption.
- **Procedure** – Technology employees use the policy and standards to create the specific actions, enabling the vision, strategy, and tactics. A procedure is created, defining step-by-step tasks to implement and maintain the AES and IPSec encryption technologies. The procedure will define operating system settings, software configurations, and specific details to enable the policy and standard.
- **Guideline** – Technology leadership and technology employees use the policy, standard, and procedure to create the guideline to be leveraged when a disaster or unexpected events occurs. Guidelines are created, defining approaches and requirements in the event encryption procedures fail. Guidelines are not necessarily as defined as procedures, but guidelines drive important principles the organization is expected to uphold while responding to deviations of procedures.

Looking Further

The Gramm-Leach-Bliley Act (GLBA), also referred to as the Financial Modernization Act of 1999, impacts financial institutions and the individuals/organizations that leverage financial institution services [9]. GLBA requires financial institutions to provide information-sharing practices to customers. Additionally, any services leveraging financial information must also ensure data protection measures are met [9].

Organizations handling PII financial data are required by law to incorporate PII protections meeting GLBA definitions [9].

Outside of administrative controls, two other controls are leveraged to govern cyber risk and derive compliance. Technical controls employ technical assets and approaches to implement and maintain administrative directives. In essence, technical controls are the actual requirements and implementations of standards and procedures from administrative controls.

Finally, physical controls are employed as the last portion of organizational controls. In addition to technical controls, physical controls are implementations of measures to achieve the vision, strategies, and tactics from administrative controls. Physical controls shift IT from traditional enterprise system to bordering or fully embracing OT. (Remember, OT prioritizes CIA as AIC, reversing the priority. Physical security must be available to be effective.) Examples of physical security include, but are not limited to:

- Security Guards
- Fencing
- Lighting
- Locks/Electronic Locks/Badging
- Fire Suppression

- Environmental (HVAC)

To recap, vision and goals build administrative controls. Strategy and tactics build technical and physical controls to implement the vision and goals. This ultimately means that cybersecurity is not a technology team issue. Cyber risks impact the entire organization: executive leadership must embed cybersecurity across the entire organization to successfully address the risks associated with cyber. Employees balk at cybersecurity training, but security training is required to properly build policies and standards. Communication is often a critical issue in compliance and comprehension across the organization.

Strategic Plan Creation

Strategic plans are critical for the allocation of limited assets and the achievement of goals. As noted above, some managers believe *ad hoc* approaches provide adaptability: if plans rarely go as designed, why create them? It is important to create plans because planning builds preparation. Project management, pre-planning, and documentation all build the probability for a better outcome.

Beyond preparation, cross-area discussions on risk mitigation and goals build organization synergies and break down silos. Cross-area discussions create a culture capable of building comprehension and support for embedding cybersecurity across the organization. Many of the frameworks discussed in Chapter 9 will offer approaches to building a strategic cyber risk plan. In this section, high level considerations will be provided.

Know What You Own

Before conversations about the allocation of assets can begin, serious discussions about current assets and systems should take place. All available digital assets and systems should be documented, and then leadership should document critical processes for business continuation and disaster recovery procedures. Think back to *Jurassic Park.* No systems or assets are functional, and they all need to be brought back online in a specific order, to ensure recovery and business continuation. What is the proper order?

Leaders from different areas of the organization will have different opinions. The key to success is developing a model to decide objectively what systems, assets, and procedures need to be restarted first. Organizations that sell commodities may say manufacturing lines need to be brought online first. But do they? What will happen if the organization can not pay their technology people for weeks?

The recommended approach here leverages the discussion of business continuity and disaster recovery to generate difficult conversations. Organizations that can't agree are unprepared. If an

organization has not conducted a prioritization exercise, the business will probably waste assets, as different areas will operate with different assumptions about priorities.
There are no absolute answers for all organizations. Each organization is different based on their assets, systems, procedures, and people. Frameworks operate as a catalyst to force organizations to align. If an organization is struggling with strategic alignment, the organization should consider hiring a consultant. Consultants can provide objective observations and feedback without the fear of long-term reprisal and political backlash. During difficult discussions, everyone needs to set egos aside and work together toward a viable solution.

Identify Regulations Impacting Your Organization

An organization next needs to understand industry regulations. Each industry faces different cyber challenges. The medical industry, for example, is highly regulated by HIPAA. Higher education is regulated by FERPA. Finance and banking industries are regulated by GLBR, and all industries are regulated by GDPR and CCPA.

Knowing industry challenges and trends for cyber risks is also critical. Frameworks tailored to specific industries will help leaders understand and develop successful cyber risk approaches. A number of these industry-specific frameworks will be discussed in Chapter 9.

Identify and Assess Organization-Specific Cyber Risks

In the context of GRC, there are associated risk activities. This section will present high level risk requirements. Risk levels help define where and how many resources are dedicated to different portions of cybersecurity and cyber resiliency.

Risk tolerance and risk appetite is established as part of overall vision and strategy. Leadership establishes the level of risk tolerance acceptable for the organization. Based on the uniqueness of each organization, each organization must determine their risk appetite and risk tolerance.

After risk tolerance and appetite are defined, the risk assessment process and procedures are built. The risk assessment process will review all of the possible threats and vulnerabilities organizations face. Risk assessment procedures and processes will enable formal procedures for identifying and mitigating risks. (Again – see Unit 2 for formal information.)

Here is an example of how risk plays into GRC. The company Alpha has pioneered a new defensive armor for tanks and is on direct contract from the DoD to produce the armor. Alpha's risk appetite is typically medium to low, depending on the system and process. The DoD, however, has established GRC, cybersecurity, and cyber resiliency requirements to maintain status as a DoD contractor; from a vision perspective, Alpha leadership sets risk tolerance and appetite low and prioritize conformance with DoD and federal standards.

Implement Impactful Decision Making

Recall from Unit 1 that human beings overestimate their decision-making abilities: we make the majority of our decisions emotionally or irrationally, and then backfill information to create the illusion of logic. Large or important decisions with multiple criteria are hotbeds for emotional decisions masked as logical outcomes. When emotional decision making is combined with poorly defined or understood visions and terms, organizational initiatives are unfulfilled and expensive. Just as project management processes help generate reliable outcomes, so too do structured decision processes.

Organizational decision making is the key to just about everything – including cybersecurity and cyber resiliency efforts. Decision making drives the creation of vision, the allocation of resources, and the implementation of processes to meet organizational goals. Reliable decision-making models and evaluation criteria are the primary key to all outcomes. Organizations that do not build valid and reliable decision processes will fail across all sectors.

Decision Interference

A number of factors can negatively impact reliable decision making, including group think, cognitive dissonance, confirmation bias, logical fallacies, and decision fatigue. Each of these factors introduces significant hurdles into the decision process.

Group think is a distinctive enemy of effective decision making. Group think occurs when multiple people are involved in making a decision and some individuals leverage their position or authority to push a perspective, effectively pressuring others to conform to their way of thinking. Group think itself is also susceptible to logical fallacies, cognitive dissonance, decision fatigue, and confirmation bias.

Confirmation bias occurs when someone looks only for information that supports their views. Confirmation bias can be readily observed on Facebook when users seek out and share memes and posts that confirm their viewpoints. These acts of finding and sharing, in the mind of the user, 'confirms' that their views are correct. As a fallacy, confirmation bias is deeply tied with cognitive dissonance.

Cognitive dissonance occurs when someone is presented with information or data that directly contradicts their perception of reality. When we are faced with contradicting data, we can either open our minds to change or simply ignore (and usually discredit) the data. Dismissing a news story on Facebook by commenting "this is a liberal news source" or "this is a conservative news

source" is a demonstration of cognitive dissonance in action. In cybersecurity, ignoring network traffic indicative of a compromise can be considered cognitive dissonance.
Logical fallacies also interfere with decision making. Logical fallacies are common errors in reasoning. Many of them exist, including:

- ***Ad hominem*** – *Ad hominem* is a personal attack [7] that denigrates the character of person to refute the validity of their argument. *Ad hominem* attacks divert the conversation from the real point to a focus on the supposed "poor" character of the person involved: for example, "President Trump is wrong to try and open the economy because he has lied on so many issues he cannot be trusted." As soon as decision conversation drops into *ad hominem*, the conversation must be shut down and refocused.
- **Alphabet Soup** – Alphabet soup leverages industry-specific terms, abbreviations, and acronyms to lull people into assuming a speaker is well versed in the subject matter and must be correct [7].
- **Appeal to Authority** – Appeal to authority is the reverse of *ad hominem* in that it works on the premise that an idea is true solely because a person in authority said so [7]. "Dr. Fauci said there is no benefit to wearing a mask during COVID-19." While there may be little to no benefit to wearing a mask, the statement is or is not true because of factual or empirical evidence – not because Dr. Fauci said it.
- **Appeal to Ignorance** – An appeal to ignorance is the view that something is obviously false if we do not have evidence to prove that it is true [7]. "Bob obviously does not have COVID-19 because he does not exhibit any symptoms associated with COVID-19" is an appeal to ignorance.
- **Bandwagon** – The bandwagon relies on group think and the actions of others to drive a decision, often citing numbers as a reason for why a decision is correct [7]: "How can 5 million people be wrong?"
- **The Circular Argument** – The circular argument is also referred to as the petitio principii, or begging the question [7]. An example of the circular argument is "Everyone watches Netflix because it's the best streaming service available." The argument provides no real factual information to confirm the points provided.
- **The Red Herring** – Red herrings are clever redirections to turn the focus away from the actual topic being assessed. Politicians reliably employ the red herring to distract the public away from critical discussion points.

Logical fallacies are barriers to decision making, and effective decision makers spot them immediately when they are not in decision fatigue.

Decision fatigue is another enemy of effective decision making and results in a drop in the quality of our decisions. As an example, an inmate's ability to gain parole is linked to the time of day the inmate appears for review [8]: inmates were granted parole 70% of the time if reviewed in the morning, but less than 10% of the time if reviewed late in the day. Because constant decisions wear down our ability to process, important decisions and decision-making sessions are conducted at times when participants will not be suffering from decision fatigue.

Decision fatigue, logical fallacies, cognitive dissonance, confirmation bias, and group think are all enemies of effective decision making. Any attempt at effective and reliable decision making holds these factors in check.

Decision Constructs

A significant approach to combating the enemies of effective decision making is to use decision constructs. Decision constructs are tools that help insure that decisions are objective, logical, and rooted in vision and values.

Humans struggle to make large decisions accurately and logically. Decision constructs break large decisions into smaller criteria that humans are capable of objectively evaluating. Decision constructs reduce decision fatigue and subjectivity, and they help organizations allocate resources to achieve their vision and objectives. A decision matrix is a construct best leveraged when choosing between multiple options. Software evaluations, for example, usually involve multiple vendors with different options and costs. To create a decision matrix, the decision options should be identified – in this case, as shown in Table 8.1, Software Vendor A and Software Vendor B. Criteria are objectively identified and defined – here, purchase price, ongoing maintenance, functionality A, functionality B, impact to business processes and procedures, and vendor reputation. Qualitative or subjective factors, such as vendor reputation, are among the criteria.

Table 8-1. Decision Matrix

Criteria	**Software Vendor A**	**Software Vendor B**
Initial Purchase Price	5	1
Yearly Maintenance Fees	1	5
Security Rating	4	5
Functionality A	4	4
Functionality B	3	4
Business Process Impact	3	4
Vendor Reputation	2	3
Total	22	26

A numeric ranking for each criteria can be employed. Typically, five is the highest score and one is the lowest. In order to avoid all of the enemies of effective decision making, decision makers should do their scoring separately and then assemble to review scores. Some organizations simply tally scores and then select the option with the highest one. Other organizations may employ a group rating. In group rating sessions, the group moderator encourages a discussion of criteria. Individuals share their scores and discuss the reasoning behind them. Each criteria and vendor score is discussed, group scores are assigned, and the highest ranked option is selected.

There are, of course, a variety of decision construct models. The primary take away here is that organizations should leverage some version of a decision construct. Decision constructs help ensure objective evaluations and build effective processes. Embracing decision constructs will also enable more efficient and effective decision making, which is another hallmark of organizational maturity.

People and Process Alignment

One critical resource alignment is people and processes. Every organization struggles with resources and work, and cybersecurity and cyber resiliency add another component to organizational workloads. GRC generates significant refocus and redirection for organizations. As organizations prepare to implement visions, strategies, and tactics for GRC, ensuring people and processes alignment generates efficient and reliable resource allocations.

As cybersecurity and cyber resiliency controls and risk mitigation factors are determined, people assets are required to install, maintain, operate, and monitor the implemented controls. As technology drives forward, some tasks and processes are candidates for automation; other positions within an organization are assigned roles, duties, and responsibilities. To meet the risk mitigations identified by the organization, controls are integrated into these duties and responsibilities. Some roles will require ongoing training and education. The vision, goals, strategies, guidelines, processes, and controls operate as a multi-layered approach to achieving cybersecurity and cyber resiliency goals.

Add KPIs

Once people and processes are aligned, key performance metrics should be identified. Also known as key performance indicators (KPI), these metrics should clearly identify the health of the organization's cyber efforts. KPIs tie metrics directly to outcomes. Some important examples of KPIs for cyber include:

- Uptime – Uptime is the amount of time resources are online and available. Uptime addresses Availability in the CIA triad.
- Resolution Time – Resolution time is the time from discovery of an incident to the resolution of an incident.
- Costs Per Incident – Time and money identifying the costs per incident. Organizations can incorporate many different factors for costs per incident, including opportunity costs.
- Incident Trends – Incident trends provide an overview of the organization's trend in relation to cybersecurity incidents. Examples include increasing time with costs per incident or reduced time with costs per incident over years.

If your metrics are consistently in a good range and your outcomes are not met, there are significant issues. KPIs consistently green with goals not met indicates the KPIs do not have a direct relationship on outcomes, the report is doctored, or a mix of both. KPIs not tied to outcomes/goals is an exercise in futility.

Enhancing Cybersecurity Process Maturity

Aligning people and process is not a one-time task. Risks, goals, and outside requirements can change over time, and organizations must establish checkpoint intervals to review people and process alignment. Incident response can also serve as a catalyst for identifying gaps in risk mitigation and cyber strategy. Questions for organizations to consider during reviews include:

- Are people and process investments resulting in desired outcomes?
- Are risks actually being mitigated as expected?
- Are processes truly effective?
- Are new risks addressed or have gaps evolved?

Incidents must not be *ad hoc* situations defined as events unfold. Successful organizations build incident response procedures, processes, and guidelines to drive success in adverse situations. All of the following are identified in incident response plans:

- Incident response team members
- Incident response roles
- Incident response triggers – conditions or events requiring incident response
- Incident response mitigation – conditions or events defining the stoppage or shut down of incident response
- Lessons Learned – a feedback loop reviewing the effectiveness of the incident response

Incident responses do not always go as planned. After each incident response, lessons learned discussions are critical to increasing organizational skill and maturity in handling cybersecurity and cyber resilience. Lessons learned are not focused on placing blame: they are a critical evaluation of the incident identification, response, and closure. From a maturity level, lessons learned are critical catalysts in pushing organizational skills, maturity, and process levels to handle growing complexity. Lessons learned questions can include, but are not limited to:

- Are existing risk strategies designed to handle the incident in the future?
- Will the existing mitigation strategies and controls be effective in detecting and responding to the incident in the future?
- Are process, procedures, and people aligned correctly to address the risk in the future? Is this an edge or rare case or viewed as an evolving threat?
- What part(s) of the incident response functioned well?
- What part(s) of the incident response functioned poorly?

Chapter Summary

After leaders identify vision and risk tolerance/appetite, industry trends are reviewed. After information and prioritization is completed, limited resources are assigned, leveraging the road maps generated.

Before any vision, strategies or tactics are implemented, decision constructs are established to ensure reliable and effective decision making is created. Difficult decisions on appropriate resource assignments is enabled with effective decision making constructs.

Discussion Questions

1. What is the anticipated impact of GDPR, globally?

2. What is the anticipated impact of CCPA?

Exercises

1. Research three data breaches for companies in your industry. Compare the defined lapse/root cause to key defensive measures listed in this chapter.

2. Go to a news site and select the first listed story. Review the story for logical fallacies and factual information. Underline factual information and box logical fallacies.

3. Research KPIs for cybersecurity for your company's industry. Identify the top three KPIs.

References

[1] R. J. II, "60 Percent Of Small Companies Close Within 6 Months Of Being Hacked," Cybercrime Magazine, 2 January 2019. [Online]. Available: https://cybersecurityventures.com/60-percent-of-small-companies-close-within-6-months-of-being-hacked/. [Accessed 16 April 2020].

[2] NDIA, (2018). "Implementing Cybersecurity in DoD Supply Chains"

[3] Moore, G. A. (1991). Crossing the chasm: Marketing and selling technology products to mainstream customers. New York, N.Y.: HarperBusiness.

[4] R. Sobers, "Data Breach Response Times: Trends and Tips," Varonis, 29 March 2020. [Online]. Available: https://www.varonis.com/blog/data-breach-response-times/. [Accessed 24 April 2020].

[5] Intersoft Consulting, "General Data Protection Regulation," [Online]. Available: https://gdpr-info.eu/. [Accessed 2 June 2020].

[6] DHCS California, "Health Insurance Portability & Accountability Act," 13 June 2019. [Online]. Available: https://www.dhcs.ca.gov/formsandpubs/laws/hipaa/Pages/1.00WhatisHIPAA.aspx. [Accessed 2 June 2020].

[7] US Department of Education, "Family Educational Rights and Privacy Act (FERPA)," 1 March 2018. [Online]. Available: https://www2.ed.gov/policy/gen/guid/fpco/ferpa/index.html. [Accessed 2 June 2020].

[8] US FTC, "Gramm-Leach-Bliley Act," [Online]. Available: https://www.ftc.gov/tips-advice/business-center/privacy-and-security/gramm-leach-bliley-act. [Accessed 2 June 2020].

[9] G. Edelman, "10 Logical Fallacies You Should Know and How to Spot Them". [Online]. Available: https://kreativcopywriting.com/10-logical-fallacies-know-spot/. [Accessed 13 May 2020].

Chapter 9 – Frameworks for Cybersecurity Success

Overview

Drawing on the definitions, concepts, strategies, and tactics previously presented, this chapter will focus on cybersecurity frameworks. Frameworks provide a skeleton approach to cybersecurity, leaving it up to each individual organization to flesh out the body of cybersecurity defense. Some frameworks, such as the NIST Cybersecurity Framework, can be used across all industries, as they are adaptable to specific industry and organizational needs. All frameworks are designed to build better organizational understanding of cybersecurity and cyber resiliency. Although many frameworks involve specific technical terms and concepts, this chapter will provide overviews and perspectives to enable non-technical business leaders to determine the best framework to adopt at their organization.

Chapter Learning Objectives

1. Investigate NIST's Cybersecurity Framework.
2. Review cybersecurity program establishment procedures.
3. Critique the Cybersecurity Maturity Model Certification.
4. Explore industry-specific frameworks.

NIST – Cybersecurity Framework

The Cybersecurity Enhancement Act (CEA) of 2014 altered the funtion of the National Institute of Standards and Technology (NIST), adding the development of cybersecurity frameworks for critical infrastructure [1]. CEA and NIST provide these frameworks to give organizations cost-effective approaches to cybersecurity and cyber risk management [1]. The NIST Cybersecurity Framework, originally released in 2014, was updated in 2018 to version 1.1 [1]. Before digging deeply into the entire framework, the next section will begin with the groups and general steps to implement the NIST-CF

Framework Implementation Groups

The NIST-CF identifies three key groups in every organization, each of which focuses on different aspects of the framework implementation. The Executive Level group defines the vision for the organization and focus on overall organizational risk, aligning with the Framework Profile. They define the Implementation Tier Level goals, as well as set the risk appetite, vision and mission priorities, and high-level budget resources to achieve defined organizational goals and objectives [1].

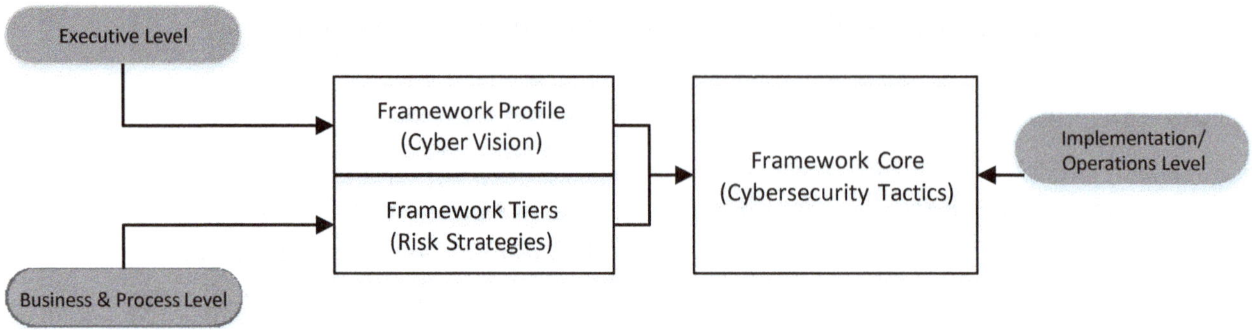

Figure 9.1. NIST-CF Groups-Framework Core Mapping

The second group is the Business and Process Level (BPL) groups, often middle management. These groups focus on translating the executive vision, budget, risk appetite, and risk tolerances into actionable profiles. Implementation Tier targets set by executive leadership are fed into process development rework and builds. Higher level budgets are broken down into people and process resource alignments. Standards and guidelines are crafted to support targeted visions from the Executive Level.

Framework Profiles and Implementation Tiers, Metrics and operational review procedures are crafted for feedback loops and continuous improvement [1]. If a large number of new objectives and actions are required to meet executive vision and risk appetite, a phased approach is the most efficient. Additionally, phased approaches are best implemented with a project management approach, as discussed in Unit 1. Project management approaches will help ensure focused and timely deliveries that meet executive expectations.

The Implementation/Operations Level (IOL) are the third group. These are the tactical IT professionals who implement resource and process alignment, and create the physical processes for reuse and efficiency. The IOL performs actions to ensure vision and process objectives are met. IOL assessments are fed back to the BPL and Executive Levels for review [1].

Establishing Cybersecurity Programs

The NIST-CF provides guidelines to establish or improve cybersecurity programs. Each organization has unique needs and challenges, in some cases restarting from scratch. Other organizations with cybersecurity tasks and tactics in place improve cyber positions through improving the organization's existing approaches and programs. Whether organizations are building new or improving, the NIST-CF provide key steps to successful cybersecurity programs [1].

The NIST-CF provides seven high level steps for executives and leaders to implement or create a cybersecurity programs. The seven steps are designed to assess, determine current status, evaluate process-resource alignment, take corrective actions, and implement [9]. The seven steps are:

- ***Prioritize and Scope*** – The organization defines vision, objectives, and organizational priorities. (No – 200 priorities is not appropriate. Leaders define manageable engagements within the context of available resources. Teams are successful with five high priorities. Other priorities can be created, but should be place on a wait list and shifted into active when one of the first five are completed.) Leadership clearly defines risk appetites and risk tolerances to guide the organization's business/process level groups and implementation level groups [1].
- ***Orient*** – With overall vision, objectives and priorities defined, current systems, assets, resources, external and internal requirements, and risk approach are identified. With a comprehensive view of current items, the business/organizational group assesses threats and vulnerabilities to the organization's vision, objectives, and priorities. (Sound like governance, risk, and compliance (GRC)? The NIST-CF implementation guides follow the general governance, risk, and compliance approach, repackaging the GRC process into a new set of terms [1].
- ***Create a Current Profile*** – After threats and vulnerabilities are assessed, the organization creates a current profile. The current profile defines current activities and processes employed to address the organization's cyber risk. During current profile inventory efforts, tasks and process inefficiencies are noted to be addressed in later phases [1]. (More information on a Current Profile will be provide in upcoming sections.)
- ***Conduct a Risk Assessment*** – In the Orient step, the overall risk approach was created. Within this step, the team leverages the overall risk management process within the organization to analyze the operational environments [1]. Analysis identifies the overall probability or likelihood a cyber risk will manifest or be leveraged against the organization. In addition to internal reviews and assessments, the organization incorporates external information and threat intelligence to assess the overall cyber risk landscape.
- ***Create a Target Profile*** – With the previous Current Profile step, the organization identifies the Target Profile for desired objectives and goals [1]. NIST-CF Profiles incorporate the categories and subcategories the organization intend to implement. In essence, Target Profiles identify the process, task, and feedback loop approaches for the organization.
- ***Analyze, Evalute and Prioritize Gaps*** – The organization examines the Current Profile and the Target Profile to determine gaps and disconnects between the two [1]. Organizational focus is targeted at the difference between the profiles. Organizational gaps and shortcomings feed into the organization's action plan to achieve the Target Profile status. Organizational action plans aligned resources to processes and objectives. Resource alignment includes efficiency discussions, metrics creation and monitoring, and phased implementation approaches. (Think Project Management approach – See Unit 1 for refreshers.)
- ***Implement Action Plan(s)*** – From the previous step, the organization implements the action plans defined from the overall implementation process [1]. Implementing the

action plan requires significant planning, execution, and troubleshooting across the organization. Project management is recommended to ensure successful implementation of the action plan. Since each organization's action plan is unique, this step is the most variable, relying on each organization's work and environment.

After an organization completes the last step, an iterative cycle begins. (Yes – another feedback loop.) Plans can miss analysis considerations and collateral impact to processes, people and resources. Missed analysis components are normal. Addressing flaws in the action plan requires a feedback loop. During the implementation processes, issues are identified. Based on the outputs from analysis and implementation, the organization starts the process, following the cycle until the target profile is achieved [1].

The overall implementation approach has been presented. The next section will dig deeply into the NIST-CF, breaking down the three core areas. To begin, we will provide an overview of the framework as a whole.

NIST Cybersecurity Framework Overview

An organization's approaches to cyber, risk, and innovation determine its Force of Technology impact. Critical infrastructure is the key target for the NIST Cybersecurity Framework (NIST-CF), which offers fundamentally sound and impactful recommendations for any organization. Cybersecurity and cyber resiliency are risks as important and as influential as financial and reputational risks [1]. Because these cyber risks must be addressed, NIST built the Cybersecurity Framework as a roadmap for organizations [1].

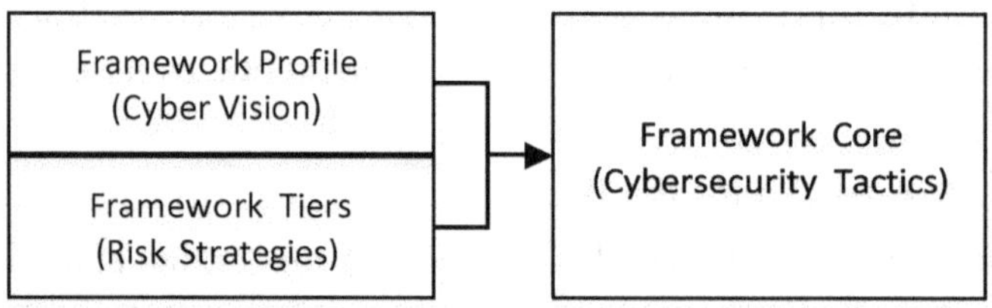

Figure 9.2. NIST CF Overview

NIST-CF has three primary pillars, organizing and driving overall vision, strategies, and tactics. As shown in Figure 2, each of the three pillars are:

- **Framework Profile** - The profile is used to drive best practices for implementation into the Framework Core. The Profile is used to define priorities and measurements while addressing organizational need. In short, the Framework Profile could be defined as the vision of how cybersecurity is implemented in the organization.
- **Framework Implementation Tier** – The Framework Implementation Tier defines the risk management strategies employed to implement the actions associated with cybersecurity efforts/Framework Core.

- **Framework Core** – The Framework Core creates a language everyone in the organization can use when discussing cybersecurity actions/tactics. The Framework Core is impacted by the Framework Profile and Framework Tiers.

NIST-CF prioritizes cybersecurity activities and embeds cybersecurity risks into the organization's overall risk approaches through the three pillars [1]. NIST-CF is designed to help organizations align, allocate, and prioritize their cybersecurity activities and resources to meet organizational strategy, requirements, and risk tolerances. (Again, think GRC from the previous chapter.) NIST clearly identifies risk tolerance and appetite (the Framework Tiers) as the gateway to appropriate and aligned cybersecurity activities. After cybersecurity activities are aligned and initiated, cybersecurity is fundamentally a risk management process, adapting and addressing to current and evolving risks in the cybersecurity landscape.

NIST-CF requires organizations to define their vision, strategy, standards, guidelines, and practices/tasks [1]. In order to assess current organizational status and developing a plan for cybersecurity excellence, NIST-CF provides approaches to:

- Defining organizational cybersecurity posture
- Defining organizational vision and goals for cybersecurity
- Identifying and prioritizing improvements for existing cybersecurity processes (Note: organizations without defined processes will need to build processes first)
- Implementing metrics to monitor and evaluate organizational progress towards defined goals
- Communicating progress and information to internal and external stakeholders

NIST-CF does not replace organizational risk management or cybersecurity programs and processes; rather, it develops organizational focus, skills, and abilities in the cybersecurity and cyber resiliency space [1]. Organizations without risk management or cybersecurity processes are encouraged to employ NIST-CF as a gateway to developing a program to work in conjunction with the NIST-CF. Let's begin with the Framework Profile.

Framework Profile

NIST-CF recognizes each organization will face a unique combination of risks, challenges, and threats. The Framework Profile sets the vision and overall approaches for cybersecurity. After an assessment of the current state of the organization, a Current Profile is identified.

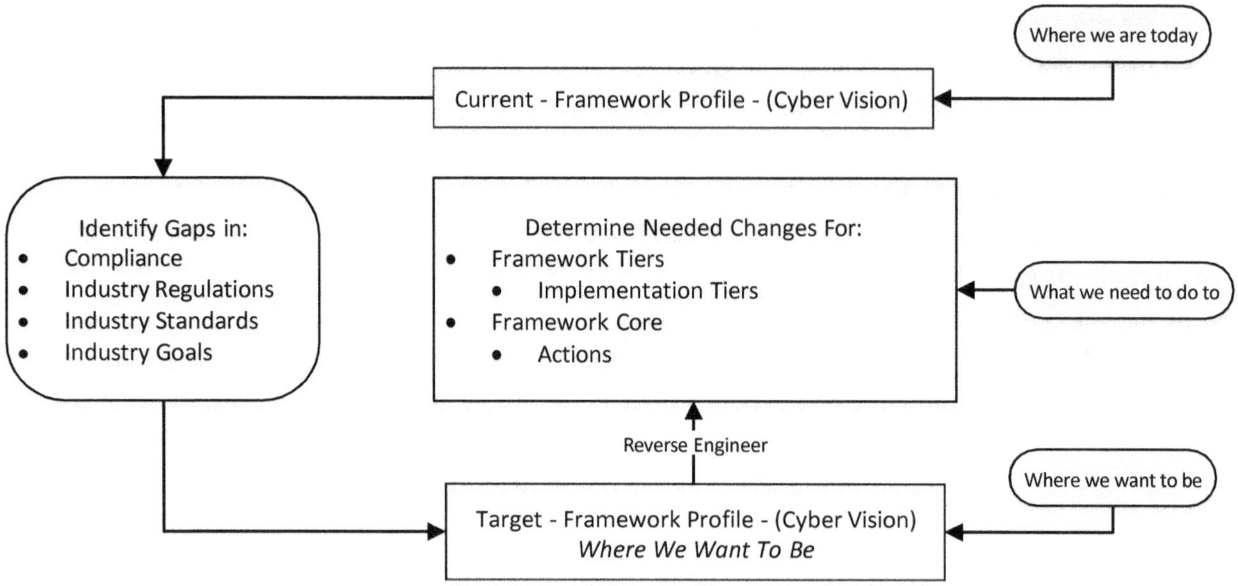

Figure 9.3. Current and Target Profiles

Current Profiles define the current state of cybersecurity efforts in the organization. As identified in Figure 3, the organization identifies gaps after a target profile is created. With the current state documented, a Target Profile is created for implementation [1]. Target Profiles, on the other hand, are typically defined to meet industry, regulatory, and organizational standards and requirements. A cross comparison of the Current and the Target profiles defines the gaps, or differences, the organization must address to meet compliance, regulations, standards, or goals [1]. The target profile is leveraged to reverse engineer what needs to change in the Framework Tier and Framework Core. Let's move into the next topic – Framework Tiers.

Framework Implementation Tiers

Framework Implementation Tiers identify the rigor and sophistication level of an organization's cybersecurity approaches. They also identify the level at which an organization's risk management is informed or driven by business need, as well as the depth that cyber risk management is integrated into the organization's overall risk management practices [1]. Three categories of implementation are defined; within each category, a tier level that matches the organization's current approaches is identified [1].

> **Looking Further**
>
> *NIST-CF* assumes organizations are actually defining, assessing, tracking, and mitigating risks based on defined risk appetites: organizations not addressing risks are recommended to create and operate a Risk Management Program.

The three Framework Implementation Tier groups are:

- ***Risk Management Process*** – Identifies the organization's process integration practices for cybersecurity and cyber resiliency risks. Organizations review whether cyber risk practices are *ad hoc*, formalized, institutionalized, or operating with an iterative cycle/feedback loop [1].
- ***Integrated Risk Management Program*** – Identifies the organization's integration of cybersecurity into the organization's overall risk management programs and processes. The Integrated Risk Management program group assesses the organization's view and handling of cyber risk compared to other risks the organization faces. Basically, this assessment focuses on whether cybersecurity and cyber resiliency risks are integrated into the overall risk management program.
- ***External Participation*** – Identifies the organization's comprehension of its role and interaction in the community or industry [9]. An organizational breach or lapse in cybersecurity, as previously noted, impacts much more than the organization itself: cyber-attacks on organizations are not always about attacking the organization breached. APTs and sophisticated attackers attack the weakly-defended organizations associated with a highly defended target. Sophisticated and mature organizations understand that cyber-attacks involve pivoting to gain access through a trusted partner who is easier to compromise.

Tier groups provide an assessment model for organizations to evaluate the efficiency and institutionalization of their implementations.

NIST-CF then uses Tier levels to describe the practices of each of the Tier groups.

- ***Partial*** – Partial level implementations are basic practices, neither defined nor efficient, often operating in an ad hoc fashion.
- ***Risk Informed*** – Risk Informed identifies defined practices, processes, or programs, but without full implementation across the entire organization (institutionalization) [1].
- ***Repeatable*** – Repeatable identifies the integration of practices, processes, and programs across the entire organization [1].
- ***Adaptive*** – Adaptive identifies efficient and adaptive practices, processes, and programs [1].

Table 9-1 integrates the NIST Cybersecurity Framework Implementation Groups and Tiers, specifying more clearly what characteristics are expected in each Tier of each Group.

Table 9-1. NIST-CF Framework Implementation Groups and Tiers

Tier Group	Tier Levels			
	Partial	**Risk Informed**	**Repeatable**	**Adaptive**
Risk Management Process	Cyber risk practices not normalized – *ad hoc*/reactive	Practices approved – not implemented organization-wide	Practices formally approved – implemented organization-wide – some updates occurring	Institutionalized practices with continuous improvement/lessons learned
Integrated Risk Management Program	Limited awareness of cybersecurity risk at organizational level	Cybersecurity risk awareness at some levels of the organization – not organization-wide	Organization-wide cybersecurity risk awareness	Organization-wide – policies, procedures, processes – executives view cyber risk on the same importance level as other risks
External Participation	Organization does not understand role in larger ecosystem or participate at a community level	Organization understands role in up or downstream ecosystem - not both	Organization understands upstream & downstream role - limited community involvement	Organization understand upstream & downstream role - community involvement

Adapted from https://nvlpubs.nist.gov/nistpubs/CSWP/NIST.CSWP.04162018.pdf

With the Framework Profile and Framework Implementation Tiers discussed, the next portion of the NIST-CS framework is where key actions happen – The Framework Core.

Framework Core

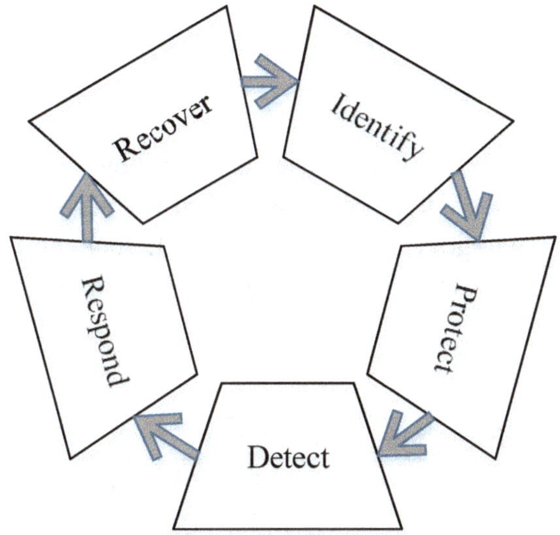

Figure 9.4 Framework Core Five Functions

The Framework Core gathers activities, processes, goals, and references for cybersecurity. It incorporates guidelines, standards, and practices enabling the communication of cyber practices across an organization at all levels. The five functions within the Framework Core, shown in Figure 4, build a high-level perception of the technical processes and tasks that organizations conduct for cybersecurity. The Framework Core defines the following five functions, processes, and tasks an organization assembles to mitigate risks [9]:

- *Identify* – Identifying builds organizational understanding of what it takes to manage the cybersecurity risks impacting people, systems, assets, data, and capabilities [1].
- *Protect* – Protecting defines approaches to engineer and implement safeguards, as well as addresses vision and strategies to deliver critical systems and services [1].
- *Detect* – Detecting is engineering and implementing processes and activities to identify cybersecurity events as the events occur [1].
- *Respond* – Responding is addressing and remediating cybersecurity events upon detection [1].
- *Recover* –Recovering refers to the activities that restore normal operations after the cybersecurity event is detected and responded to. Recovering brings the organization back into a normal/baseline state [1].

The organization's primary functions, tasks, and processes are encapsulated within the Framework Core, which is augmented by the rigor and sophistication of risk management practices – Framework Implementation Tiers.

Each of the five primary functions is a great starting point for a common vocabulary to leverage across the organization. For the cybersecurity people, more granularity and focus are needed to adequately describe, define, and categories tasks. The additional granularity is provided by the categories.

Categories

NIST-CF categories identify key cybersecurity tasks for organizations. As shown in Table 9-2, each category is associated with one of the five functions from the Framework Core. Each category also has an ID Code that can be used to associate it with the subcategories it encompasses for additional granularity.

Table 9-2. NIST Function, Category and ID Code Examples.

Function	Category	ID CODE
Identity	Asset Management	ID-AM
	Business Environment	ID-BE
	Governance	ID-GV
	Risk Assessment	ID-RA
	Risk Management Strategy	ID-RM
	Supply Chain Risk Management	ID-SC
Protect	Identity Management and Access Control	PR-AC
	Awareness and Training	PR-AT
	Data Security	PR-DS
	Information Protection, Processes and Procedures	PR-IP
	Maintenance	PR-MA
	Protective Technology	PR-PT
Detect	Anomalies and Events	DE-AE
	Security Continuous Monitoring	DE-CM
	Detection Process	DE-DP
Respond	Response Planning	RS-RP
	Communications	RS-CO
	Analysis	RS-AN
	Mitigation	RS-MI
	Improvements	RS-IM
Recover	Recovery Planning	RC-RP
	Improvements	RC-IM
	Communications	RC-CO

Adapted from https://www.nist.gov/cyberframework/online-learning/informative-references

Subcategories

NIST-CF subcategories expand the general NIST-CF categories into specific goals and objectives. (NIST-CF does not specifically list subcategories for organizations to adopt, but instead recommends that organizations review documents defined as Informative References for guidance as to which subcategories they should adopt [1].) Table 9-3 provides examples of five specific subcategories. The subcategory codes embed the Framework Core function (ID for Identify) and the Profile category (BE for Business Environment) into the code sequence. These ID codes enable the organization to combine and group tasks or subcategories into larger categories and functions.

Table 9-3. NIST-CF Subcategory Examples

Subcategory Code	Subcategory Definition
ID-BE-001	Organizational supply chain role is identified and communicated.
ID-BE-002	Organizational role and impact within its industry sector is defined and communicated.
ID-BE-003	Organizational vision, mission, objectives and activities are defined, established and communicated.
ID-BE-004	Critical services, functions, and dependencies are defined.
ID-BE-005	Business continuity and resiliency requirements are defined for all operational states, including normal operations, attacks or events, and post-attack recovery phases.

Adapted from https://www.nist.gov/cyberframework/online-learning/informative-references

NIST-CF recommends a number of sources as Informative References. These references provide critical standards and guidance to help organizations build their Framework Profile subcategories: reviewing the Informative References will help an organization determine the appropriate tasks or items that are relevant for their unique environment [1]. Some of these references are listed in Table 9-4.

Table 9-4. Informative Reference Listing

Reference	**Web Link**
NIST SP 800-53 Rev. 4	https://nvlpubs.nist.gov/nistpubs/SpecialPublications/NIST.SP.800-53r4.pdf
ISO/IEC 27001:2013	https://www.iso.org/standard/54534.html
COBIT 5	https://www.isaca.org/cobit/pages/default.aspx
CIS CSC	https://www.cisecurity.org/controls/
ISA 62443-2-1:2009	http://www.isa.org/templates/one-column.aspx?pageid=111294&productId=116731
ISA 62443-3-3:2013	https://www.isa.org/templates/one-column.aspx?pageid=111294&productId=116785

Adapted from https://www.nist.gov/cyberframework/online-learning/informative-references.

Stakeholder Communications

Communication is vital to cybersecurity and cyber resiliency operations [1]. As discussed in Unit 1, stakeholder communication is critical to success. Stakeholders are viewed as internal staff with vested interests in outcomes, and these stakeholders include external organizations. The NIST-CF, remember, includes a tier group for external participation [1]. Sharing cyber threat information creates significant threat intelligence and risk mitigation strategies, so each organization ultimately determines its success and failure with its level of internal and external communication.

The NIST-CF provides a great overall approach to cybersecurity programs and implementations. Organizations often struggle with how the NIST-CF is customized to meet the organization's specific situation. If an organization is unsure on how to create, develop, and enhance mature processes, the organization will struggle with the NIST-CF implementation. The next framework focuses on creating, building, and enhancing mature process within the DoD supply chain.

Cybersecurity Maturity Model Certification (CMMC)

On January 30, 2020, the Cybersecurity Maturity Model Certification (CMMC) was released. It represents a landmark effort by the U.S. Department of Defense (DoD) to safeguard sensitive information and fortify the cybersecurity posture of the Defense Industrial Base (DIB). This comprehensive framework was specifically designed to standardize and elevate cybersecurity practices across organizations that collaborate with the DoD, ensuring a consistent and robust approach to protecting critical data.

Figure 9.5. CMMC Certification [13].

At its core, the CMMC framework aims to shield two critical types of information: Federal Contract Information (FCI) and Controlled Unclassified Information (CUI). FCI refers to information provided from or created for the government under contract, which is not intended for public release. Meanwhile, CUI includes sensitive information that, while unclassified, requires safeguarding to prevent exploitation by adversaries. By mandating stringent security measures for handling these data types, the CMMC framework directly addresses the growing threat of cyberattacks targeting the defense supply chain.

Beyond its protective role, the CMMC also strives to enhance the security of the supply chain. The defense ecosystem relies on a complex network of contractors and subcontractors, many of whom handle sensitive information that, if compromised, could have severe implications for national security. By setting clear cybersecurity standards, the framework promotes a culture of security and resilience throughout the entire supply chain.

The applicability of the CMMC extends to all organizations seeking DoD contracts, making it a non-negotiable requirement for contractors and subcontractors alike. Whether a company provides logistical support, manufactures components, or develops software for defense applications, compliance with the CMMC is now a fundamental prerequisite for doing business with the DoD.

CMMC is impactful and impressive due to its clear delineation of the organizational skill and maturity required to address and combat top threats. CMMC defines different skills levels associated with different levels of maturity [2]; skills increase in complexity as an organization works up the levels. Although organizations typically begin in Level 1, which means they illustrate generic cyber hygiene and basic compliance approaches, CMMC defines a road map for organizations to level up their cybersecurity and cyber resilience skills [2].

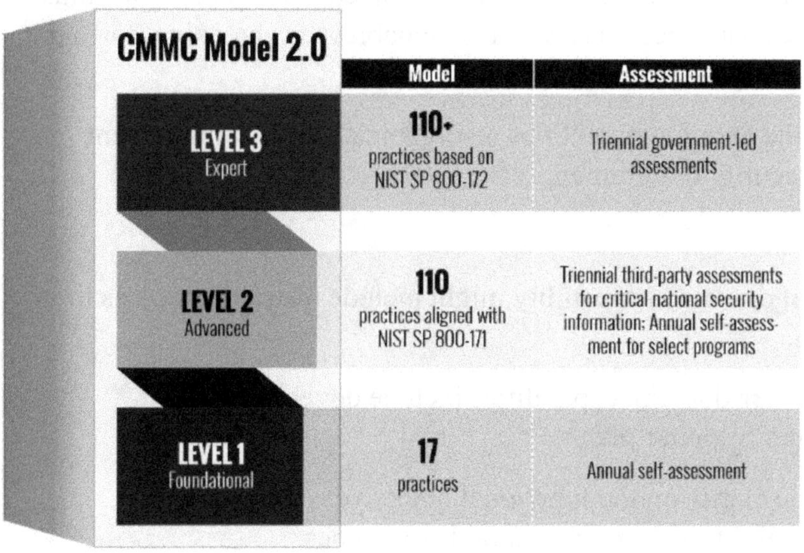

Figure 9.6. CMMC Overview [13].

CMMC Model Overview: Domains, Capabilities, Practices, and Processes

The **Cybersecurity Maturity Model Certification (CMMC)** provides a structured and systematic approach to securing sensitive information across the Defense Industrial Base (DIB). It is built upon a foundation of **domains**, **capabilities**, **practices**, and **processes** that collectively guide organizations toward achieving robust cybersecurity. This model ensures all key aspects of cybersecurity are addressed holistically, integrating both technical requirements and organizational behaviors [13]. Below is a detailed exploration of each component.

Domains: Key Areas of Cybersecurity Focus

The **domains** of the CMMC framework represent the broad categories of cybersecurity an organization must address to achieve compliance. Each domain focuses on a specific aspect of security, encompassing critical functions necessary to safeguard systems, data, and networks [13].

- **Definition:** Domains are high-level groupings of related cybersecurity practices which collectively address major areas of risk.
- **Examples:**
  - **Access Control (AC):** Focuses on managing who can access systems, networks, and data based on roles and permissions.
  - **Incident Response (IR):** Prepares organizations to detect, respond to, and recover from security incidents.
  - **System and Information Integrity (SI):** Ensures systems are secure, uncorrupted, and protected from malware or other threats.
- **Purpose:** Domains provide a framework for comprehensively addressing cybersecurity challenges, ensuring no critical aspect is overlooked.

Capabilities: Functions Within Each Domain

Within each domain, **capabilities** define the specific functions or objectives organizations must achieve to meet their security goals. Capabilities serve as the actionable steps breaking down the domain's broad focus into manageable, goal-oriented tasks [13].

- **Definition:** Capabilities are the core functionalities an organization must implement within a domain to address security requirements effectively.
- **Examples:**
  - In the **Access Control** domain, a capability might include restricting access to only authorized users.
  - In the **Incident Response** domain, capabilities include developing and maintaining an incident response plan.
- **Purpose:** Capabilities provide clarity on the functional objectives of each domain, helping organizations align their efforts with measurable outcomes.

Practices: Specific Technical and Procedural Requirements

The **practices** of the CMMC framework detail the exact technical and procedural actions organizations must take to achieve compliance. These practices are mapped to specific maturity levels and become progressively more rigorous as an organization advances through the framework [13].

- **Definition:** Practices are the explicit tasks, controls, and requirements organizations must implement to meet the cybersecurity objectives defined by the capabilities.
- **Examples:**
    - At **Level 1**, practices include basic measures such as requiring passwords and antivirus software.
    - At **Level 3**, practices include advanced requirements such as multifactor authentication, encryption, and vulnerability scanning.
- **Purpose:** Practices ensure organizations have the necessary technical and procedural safeguards to mitigate risks and protect sensitive data effectively.

Processes: Management and Institutionalization of Cybersecurity Practices

While practices focus on specific tasks, **processes** emphasize the management and institutionalization of those practices. Processes ensure cybersecurity measures are not only implemented but also consistently applied, monitored, and improved over time [13].

- **Definition:** Processes are the activities and management strategies which embed cybersecurity practices into the organization's culture and workflows.
- **Examples:**
    - At **Level 2**, processes include documenting policies and procedures to guide cybersecurity actions.
    - At **Level 5**, processes include continuous monitoring, improvement, and adaptation to emerging threats.
- **Purpose:** Processes promote consistency, accountability, and long-term sustainability of cybersecurity efforts. They ensure security practices evolve alongside an organization's maturity.

Integration of Components

The integration of **domains**, **capabilities**, **practices**, and **processes** is what makes the CMMC framework comprehensive and effective. Domains define the focus areas, capabilities outline functional goals, practices specify actionable requirements, and processes ensure those actions are institutionalized and scalable. Together, these components enable organizations to build a resilient cybersecurity posture protecting both their operations and the broader defense supply chain [13].

By addressing all four components, organizations can systematically assess, enhance, and maintain their cybersecurity measures, ensuring compliance with the CMMC framework and safeguarding critical data [13].

Understanding CMMC Domains

Having explored the overarching structure and purpose of the Cybersecurity Maturity Model Certification (CMMC) framework, it is crucial to delve deeper into its foundational elements: the domains. These domains represent the key areas of cybersecurity focus, encompassing the broad and interconnected aspects of protecting sensitive information such as Federal Contract Information (FCI) and Controlled Unclassified Information (CUI) [13].

The domains form the framework's backbone, serving as high-level categories that organize and define the capabilities and practices required to achieve robust cybersecurity. Each domain addresses a specific dimension of cybersecurity, ensuring all critical facets, from access control to incident response, are systematically covered. By breaking down cybersecurity into these distinct focus areas, the CMMC provides a roadmap for organizations to identify, prioritize, and implement security measures that align with their operational needs and the sensitivity of the data they handle [13].

In this section, we will explore the individual CMMC domains, examining their purpose, the capabilities they encompass, and their role in creating a comprehensive and resilient cybersecurity posture. Deep diving into the domains will reveal how they collectively guide organizations through the complexities of safeguarding sensitive information and achieving compliance within the broader defense supply chain [13].

The **Cybersecurity Maturity Model Certification (CMMC)** framework is organized into **14 domains**, each representing a critical area of cybersecurity focus. These domains encompass the foundational practices, processes, and capabilities required to secure systems, networks, and sensitive data, such as **Federal Contract Information (FCI)** and **Controlled Unclassified Information (CUI)**. By addressing cybersecurity comprehensively across these domains, the CMMC ensures organizations implement targeted measures to protect themselves and the broader defense supply chain [13].

Each domain serves a distinct purpose, and together they provide a holistic approach to cybersecurity. Below is a detailed explanation of the **14 CMMC domains**:

1. Access Control (AC)

- **Purpose:** Ensure that only authorized users and systems can access sensitive information.
- **Key Capabilities:**
    - Manage user accounts and permissions.
    - Limit access to information systems based on roles and responsibilities.
- **Examples of Practices:**

- Implement role-based access controls.
- Use multifactor authentication for enhanced security.

2. Asset Management (AM)

- **Purpose:** Identify and manage both physical and digital assets within the organization.
- **Key Capabilities:**
  - Maintain an inventory of devices, systems, and software.
  - Track ownership and usage of information assets.
- **Examples of Practices:**
  - Regularly update asset inventories.
  - Monitor endpoints for unauthorized access.

3. Audit and Accountability (AU)

- **Purpose:** Monitor and log system activities to detect anomalies and ensure compliance.
- **Key Capabilities:**
  - Record and review audit logs.
  - Maintain accountability for actions performed on systems.
- **Examples of Practices:**
  - Enable log collection for critical systems.
  - Conduct regular audits to identify unauthorized activities.

4. Awareness and Training (AT)

- **Purpose:** Ensure personnel are educated about cybersecurity policies, risks, and best practices.
- **Key Capabilities:**
  - Provide role-based training on security protocols.
  - Foster a security-first culture within the organization.
- **Examples of Practices:**
  - Conduct regular phishing simulations.
  - Train employees on recognizing and reporting threats.

5. Configuration Management (CM)

- **Purpose:** Establish and maintain secure system configurations to minimize vulnerabilities.
- **Key Capabilities:**
    - Define and enforce secure baseline configurations.
    - Track and control changes to system settings.
- **Examples of Practices:**
    - Use automated tools to manage system configurations.
    - Regularly review and update security settings.

6. Identification and Authentication (IA)

- **Purpose:** Verify the identities of users and devices accessing systems.
- **Key Capabilities:**
    - Authenticate users and devices before granting access.
    - Prevent unauthorized system access.
- **Examples of Practices:**
    - Require strong passwords and password rotation.
    - Implement identity verification tools like biometrics.

7. Incident Response (IR)

- **Purpose:** Prepare for, detect, and respond to cybersecurity incidents to minimize damage.
- **Key Capabilities:**
    - Develop and test incident response plans.
    - Conduct post-incident analyses to improve response strategies.
- **Examples of Practices:**
    - Create an incident response team and procedures.
    - Perform tabletop exercises to simulate incident scenarios.

8. Maintenance (MA)

- **Purpose:** Ensure systems are maintained securely and functionality is preserved.
- **Key Capabilities:**
    - Perform routine maintenance and updates.

    - Monitor systems for signs of wear or compromise.
- **Examples of Practices:**
    - Patch operating systems and software regularly.
    - Secure remote maintenance activities with encryption.

9. Media Protection (MP)

- **Purpose:** Safeguard sensitive data stored on physical and digital media.
- **Key Capabilities:**
    - Control access to media containing sensitive information.
    - Dispose of media securely to prevent unauthorized data recovery.
- **Examples of Practices:**
    - Encrypt USB drives and portable storage devices.
    - Shred or degauss retired hard drives.

10. Personnel Security (PS)

- **Purpose:** Manage risks related to personnel handling sensitive information.
- **Key Capabilities:**
    - Conduct background checks for employees and contractors.
    - Monitor personnel for insider threats.
- **Examples of Practices:**
    - Enforce policies for access revocation when employees leave the organization.
    - Train employees in the ethical handling of sensitive information.

11. Physical Protection (PE)

- **Purpose:** Secure physical access to facilities, systems, and data.
- **Key Capabilities:**
    - Control access to secure areas.
    - Protect systems from physical tampering or theft.
- **Examples of Practices:**
    - Use security cameras and badge-based entry systems.
    - Implement policies for visitor access.

12. Risk Management (RM)

- **Purpose:** Identify, assess, and mitigate cybersecurity risks to the organization.
- **Key Capabilities:**
    - Perform regular risk assessments.
    - Develop mitigation strategies for identified risks.
- **Examples of Practices:**
    - Maintain a risk register to document vulnerabilities and remediation steps.
    - Conduct threat modeling to anticipate potential attacks.

13. Security Assessment (CA)

- **Purpose:** Evaluate the effectiveness of security controls and practices.
- **Key Capabilities:**
    - Perform self-assessments and third-party audits.
    - Identify gaps and areas for improvement.
- **Examples of Practices:**
    - Use automated tools to scan for vulnerabilities.
    - Engage certified assessors for compliance evaluations.

14. System and Communications Protection (SC)

- **Purpose:** Ensure the confidentiality, integrity, and availability of data in transit and at rest.
- **Key Capabilities:**
    - Protect communication channels from interception.
    - Safeguard data from unauthorized access.
- **Examples of Practices:**
    - Encrypt sensitive data in transit using TLS.
    - Secure network perimeters with firewalls and intrusion detection systems.

Integrating the Domains for Comprehensive Security

The 14 domains of the CMMC framework provide a roadmap for achieving a comprehensive cybersecurity posture. Each domain addresses a specific aspect of security, but they work together to form an integrated and cohesive defense strategy. By implementing these domains systematically, organizations can ensure their systems and processes are resilient against evolving threats, aligning with the requirements of the Department of Defense and the broader objectives of protecting national security [13].

Understanding CMMC Capabilities
The **Cybersecurity Maturity Model Certification (CMMC)** organizes its framework around **capabilities**, which are the functional objectives organizations must achieve to implement effective cybersecurity measures. These capabilities are embedded within the framework's 14 domains, providing a structured approach to safeguarding sensitive information like **Federal Contract Information (FCI)** and **Controlled Unclassified Information (CUI)** [13].

Capabilities bridge the gap between high-level security goals and specific practices, ensuring that each domain's focus is actionable and results oriented. By defining these functional building blocks, the CMMC allows organizations to systematically implement, assess, and refine their cybersecurity measures [13].

What Are Capabilities?

In the context of CMMC, **capabilities** are actionable goals or functions that organizations must fulfill to meet the security objectives of each domain. These capabilities guide the design and implementation of practices and processes, ensuring organizations align with the framework's maturity levels [13].

- **Definition:** Functional objectives which outline what an organization must achieve within a domain to establish a strong cybersecurity posture.
- **Purpose:** Ensure organizations address key aspects of cybersecurity systematically, progressing toward a resilient and proactive defense strategy.

CMMC Capabilities Across Key Domains

Below are examples of capabilities aligned with some of the CMMC domains to illustrate their purpose and importance:

1. Access Control (AC): Managing Permissions and Access

- **Capabilities:**
    - Restrict system access to authorized users, devices, and processes.
    - Enforce policies to prevent unauthorized access.
- **Examples:**
    - Implement role-based access control (RBAC).
    - Limit access based on the principle of least privilege.
- **Objective:** Ensure sensitive systems and data are accessible only to those with legitimate needs, reducing the risk of unauthorized exposure.

2. Incident Response (IR): Detecting and Mitigating Threats

- **Capabilities:**
  - Develop an incident response plan.
  - Detect, identify, report, and respond to cybersecurity incidents promptly.
- **Examples:**
  - Establish procedures for incident containment and recovery.
  - Conduct post-incident reviews to improve response capabilities.
- **Objective:** Minimize the impact of incidents through rapid detection and effective response strategies.

3. Risk Management (RM): Identifying and Mitigating Risks

- **Capabilities:**
  - Identify risks to systems and operations.
  - Develop risk mitigation strategies.
- **Examples:**
  - Perform regular risk assessments.
  - Maintain a risk register documenting vulnerabilities and action plans.
- **Objective:** Proactively identify and address potential threats to reduce vulnerabilities.

4. System and Communications Protection (SC): Safeguarding Data and Systems

- **Capabilities:**
  - Protect the confidentiality, integrity, and availability of information in transit and at rest.
  - Implement secure communication protocols.
- **Examples:**
  - Use encryption for sensitive data.
  - Monitor and control data flows between systems.
- **Objective:** Secure data from interception, tampering, or unauthorized access during transmission or storage.

5. Audit and Accountability (AU): Ensuring Traceability

- **Capabilities:**
  - Log system activities for monitoring and accountability.

    - Detect and analyze unauthorized activity through audit logs.
- **Examples:**
    - Implement centralized logging for critical systems.
    - Use automated tools to monitor log data for anomalies.
- **Objective:** Maintain visibility into system activities to detect and respond to threats.

6. Awareness and Training (AT): Empowering Personnel

- **Capabilities:**
    - Provide training on cybersecurity policies and practices.
    - Enhance user awareness of threats and vulnerabilities.
- **Examples:**
    - Conduct security awareness workshops.
    - Simulate phishing attacks to test and educate employees.
- **Objective:** Build a security-conscious culture within the organization.

Capabilities Across Maturity Levels

Capabilities are scaled across the **five maturity levels** of the CMMC framework, becoming more advanced and sophisticated as organizations progress [13].

Level 1: Basic Cyber Hygiene

- Focus: Foundational capabilities like managing user access and ensuring basic endpoint security.
- Example: Restricting system access to authorized users.

Level 2: Intermediate Cyber Hygiene

- Focus: Formalizing capabilities with documentation and repeatable processes.
- Example: Developing and documenting an incident response plan.

Level 3: Good Cyber Hygiene

- Focus: Achieving full compliance with **NIST SP 800-171** to protect CUI.
- Example: Implementing multifactor authentication and advanced risk management.

Level 4: Proactive

- Focus: Anticipating and mitigating Advanced Persistent Threats (APTs).
- Example: Integrating threat intelligence into monitoring processes.

Level 5: Advanced/Progressive

- Focus: Optimizing capabilities with continuous improvement and automation.
- Example: Deploying machine learning tools for threat detection and response.

The Importance of CMMC Capabilities

The focus on **capabilities** ensures the CMMC framework is practical and results driven. By emphasizing what organizations must achieve rather than prescribing how to achieve it, capabilities allow flexibility and scalability, enabling organizations to adapt their cybersecurity measures to their unique needs [13].

Benefits of CMMC Capabilities:

1. **Clarity:** Provide actionable objectives aligning with organizational goals.
2. **Scalability:** Allow organizations to progress through maturity levels at their own pace.
3. **Adaptability:** Encourage tailored solutions aligning with unique operational contexts.
4. **Resilience:** Promote proactive and evolving cybersecurity measures to counter emerging threats.

Conclusion

CMMC capabilities are the foundation of the framework's structured approach to cybersecurity. They provide organizations with clear, actionable goals within each domain, ensuring a comprehensive defense strategy. By focusing on capabilities, the CMMC enables organizations to build a resilient cybersecurity posture, meet compliance requirements, and safeguard the broader defense supply chain against ever-evolving threats.

Understanding CMMC Practices

The **Cybersecurity Maturity Model Certification (CMMC)** framework is underpinned by **practices**, which represent the specific actions, technical controls, and procedural measures that organizations must implement to meet their security objectives. These practices are the actionable elements of the framework, directly tied to the capabilities and domains which structure the CMMC. As the backbone of the framework, practices ensure organizations implement a comprehensive and effective approach to safeguarding sensitive information, including **Federal Contract Information (FCI)** and **Controlled Unclassified Information (CUI)** [13].

What Are CMMC Practices?

CMMC practices are defined actions and requirements that organizations must follow to achieve and maintain compliance with the framework. These practices are tailored to progressively strengthen cybersecurity measures as organizations advance through the five **maturity levels** of the CMMC [13].

- **Definition:** Practices are specific technical and procedural requirements addressing the functional objectives (capabilities) of each CMMC domain.
- **Purpose:** Ensure organizations implement tangible security controls and processes to protect against evolving cyber threats.

Each practice is mapped to a specific **domain** and maturity level, creating a clear and actionable path for organizations to achieve their cybersecurity goals.

The Role of Practices in the CMMC Framework

Practices provide the "how-to" for achieving the broader security objectives defined by the domains and capabilities. They translate high-level cybersecurity goals into concrete, actionable steps organizations can implement, measure, and refine. By detailing specific controls and actions, practices help standardize cybersecurity measures across organizations, ensuring consistency and reliability in protecting sensitive data [13].

Examples of CMMC Practices Across Domains

Below are examples of CMMC practices, categorized by domain, to illustrate their scope and implementation:

1. Access Control (AC): Controlling System Access

- **Example Practices:**
  - Limit access to information systems based on user roles and responsibilities.
  - Implement multifactor authentication for all users accessing sensitive data.
  - Enforce the principle of least privilege by restricting access to only what is necessary.
- **Purpose:** Ensure only authorized personnel can access sensitive systems and data, minimizing the risk of unauthorized access or data breaches.

2. Incident Response (IR): Preparing for and Managing Cyber Incidents

- **Example Practices:**
  - Develop, test, and maintain an incident response plan.
  - Train organizational personnel on individual roles and responsibilities during a cybersecurity incident.
  - Document and analyze security incidents to improve future response efforts.
- **Purpose:** Help organizations detect and respond to incidents quickly and effectively, reducing their impact.

3. Risk Management (RM): Identifying and Addressing Cyber Risks

- **Example Practices:**
  - Perform regular risk assessments to identify vulnerabilities.
  - Maintain a risk register documenting identified risks and mitigation strategies.
  - Monitor the evolving threat landscape to adapt risk management efforts.
- **Purpose:** Proactively identify and mitigate cybersecurity risks, enhancing organizational resilience.

4. Audit and Accountability (AU): Ensuring Transparency and Oversight

- **Example Practices:**
  - Enable logging of critical system activities, such as user logins and file accesses.
  - Regularly review audit logs for suspicious or unauthorized activities.
  - Use automated tools to analyze and alert on unusual system behaviors.
- **Purpose:** Ensure traceability and accountability for system actions, facilitating compliance and threat detection.

5. System and Communications Protection (SC): Securing Data and Communication Channels

- **Example Practices:**
  - Encrypt sensitive data at rest and in transit using secure protocols (e.g., AES-256, TLS).
  - Implement firewalls to monitor and control network traffic.
  - Use intrusion detection and prevention systems to identify and block malicious activities.
- **Purpose:** Safeguard data and communication channels against unauthorized access, interception, and manipulation.

6. Awareness and Training (AT): Building a Security-Conscious Workforce

- **Example Practices:**
  - Conduct regular training sessions on recognizing phishing attempts.
  - Simulate real-world cybersecurity threats to test and educate employees.
  - Provide specialized training for employees with access to sensitive systems or data.

- **Purpose:** Empower personnel to recognize and respond to cybersecurity threats effectively, reducing human vulnerabilities.

Practices Across CMMC Maturity Levels

The CMMC framework scales its practices across **five maturity levels**, with each level adding complexity and rigor:

Level 1: Basic Cyber Hygiene

- Focus: Basic security practices to protect FCI.
- Example Practices: Require passwords, update software regularly, and restrict access to sensitive systems.

Level 2: Intermediate Cyber Hygiene

- Focus: Establishing formalized practices to protect both FCI and CUI.
- Example Practices: Document policies for managing system configurations and handling security incidents.

Level 3: Good Cyber Hygiene

- Focus: Implementing the full set of **NIST SP 800-171** practices to protect CUI.
- Example Practices: Use multifactor authentication, encrypt sensitive data, and conduct regular vulnerability scans.

Level 4: Proactive

- Focus: Advanced practices to counteract Advanced Persistent Threats (APTs).
- Example Practices: Integrate threat intelligence, conduct real-time monitoring, and use behavioral analytics.

Level 5: Advanced/Progressive

- Focus: Optimizing and automating cybersecurity practices for continuous improvement.
- Example Practices: Deploy machine learning-based tools for threat detection and automate incident response workflows.

The Importance of Practices

CMMC practices are critical because they:

1. **Standardize Cybersecurity:** Ensure consistent security measures across the defense supply chain.

2. **Promote Accountability:** Define clear, actionable steps that organizations must implement and monitor.
3. **Scale with Maturity:** Allow organizations to build upon basic measures, progressing toward advanced cybersecurity capabilities.
4. **Bridge Strategy and Action:** Translate high-level goals into tangible actions directly protecting systems and data.

Conclusion

CMMC practices are the actionable elements bringing the framework to life. By detailing specific technical and procedural requirements, they provide organizations with a roadmap for implementing effective cybersecurity measures. These practices ensure every organization, regardless of size or resources, can systematically improve its security posture, protect sensitive information, and contribute to the resilience of the defense supply chain [13].

Understanding CMMC Processes

In the **Cybersecurity Maturity Model Certification (CMMC)** framework, **processes** are as vital as technical practices. While practices outline the specific actions organizations must take to protect their systems and data, **processes** focus on how those actions are institutionalized, managed, and sustained. Processes ensure cybersecurity measures are not only implemented but are also consistently maintained, improved, and embedded into the organization's culture [13].

CMMC processes define the organizational maturity required at each level, emphasizing the need for robust management practices which evolve as cybersecurity demands increase. These processes create the foundation for operational resilience and continuous improvement, ensuring security efforts remain effective over time [13].

What Are CMMC Processes?

Processes in the CMMC framework refer to the management activities, policies, and procedures that guide the implementation, oversight, and institutionalization of cybersecurity practices. They ensure cybersecurity is integrated into the organization's operations and is not treated as a one-time initiative [13].

- **Definition:** Processes are structured activities that formalize and sustain the implementation of cybersecurity practices across the organization.
- **Purpose:** Establish a culture of accountability and consistency, enabling organizations to manage cybersecurity as a continuous process rather than a static goal.

The Role of Processes in the CMMC Framework

Processes are critical for scaling cybersecurity maturity across the **five CMMC levels**. They provide the structure and governance necessary to manage the complexity of increasing cybersecurity requirements as organizations advance through the maturity levels [13].

- **Institutionalization:** Processes ensure cybersecurity practices are repeatable, documented, and consistently applied.
- **Adaptability:** Processes facilitate continuous improvement, allowing organizations to respond to evolving threats and regulatory changes.
- **Accountability:** Well-defined processes ensure roles and responsibilities are clear, and outcomes can be tracked and measured.

Processes Across CMMC Maturity Levels

The CMMC framework defines different levels of process maturity, which correspond to the five **maturity levels**. Each level reflects an increasing degree of formality and rigor in how cybersecurity practices are managed and institutionalized [13].

Level 1: Performed

- **Description:** At this entry level, processes are performed informally and may vary across the organization.
- **Characteristics:**
    - Practices are implemented as needed, but there is no formal documentation or consistency.
    - Cybersecurity efforts are largely reactive and reliant on individual initiative.
- **Example:** Employees may implement password protection or antivirus software without a formal policy guiding these actions.

Level 2: Documented

- **Description:** Organizations begin to formalize processes by documenting policies and procedures.
- **Characteristics:**
    - Policies are developed to guide the consistent implementation of cybersecurity practices.
    - Documentation ensures practices can be repeated and are not dependent on individual employees.
- **Example:** A documented incident response plan outlines steps for identifying and mitigating security breaches.

Level 3: Managed

- **Description:** Processes are actively managed and regularly reviewed for effectiveness.

- **Characteristics:**
  - Cybersecurity activities are planned, monitored, and controlled to ensure alignment with organizational goals.
  - Management oversight ensures accountability for cybersecurity performance.
- **Example:** Regular reviews of system logs and periodic risk assessments are conducted to identify and address vulnerabilities.

Level 4: Reviewed

- **Description:** Processes are proactively reviewed and refined based on performance metrics and lessons learned.
- **Characteristics:**
  - Organizations use feedback loops to improve processes, integrating advanced risk management and threat intelligence.
  - Processes are evaluated for their effectiveness in mitigating Advanced Persistent Threats (APTs).
- **Example:** Continuous monitoring tools generate reports which inform updates to incident response plans.

Level 5: Optimized

- **Description:** Processes are fully optimized and continuously improved through automation and innovation.
- **Characteristics:**
  - Organizations adopt advanced tools and techniques to enhance process efficiency and effectiveness.
  - A culture of continuous improvement ensures processes evolve alongside emerging threats and technologies.
- **Example:** Automated systems use machine learning to detect and respond to threats in real time, reducing response times and improving accuracy.

Key Components of CMMC Processes

To achieve institutionalization of cybersecurity practices, CMMC processes emphasize several key components [13]:

1. **Documentation:**
   - Policies, procedures, and guidelines are created to ensure clarity and consistency in cybersecurity activities.

   - Example: A formalized risk management policy outlines how risks are identified, assessed, and mitigated.

2. **Planning:**
   - Cybersecurity efforts are integrated into broader organizational planning to ensure alignment with business goals.
   - Example: Cybersecurity requirements are incorporated into project planning for new IT systems.
3. **Monitoring and Measurement:**
   - Regular monitoring and measurement of cybersecurity activities ensure processes are effective and aligned with objectives.
   - Example: Metrics such as the number of detected vulnerabilities or incident response times are tracked and analyzed.
4. **Feedback and Improvement:**
   - Processes are continually improved based on feedback from audits, assessments, and incident reviews.
   - Example: Lessons learned from a phishing attack are used to update employee training programs.
5. **Accountability and Ownership:**
   - Clear roles and responsibilities ensure processes are implemented and maintained consistently.
   - Example: A dedicated cybersecurity manager oversees the implementation of security practices across departments.

The Importance of Processes in CMMC

Processes are a critical component of the CMMC framework because they:

1. **Ensure Consistency:** Formalized processes provide a repeatable and predictable approach to cybersecurity, reducing variability and human error.
2. **Promote Sustainability:** Institutionalized processes ensure cybersecurity efforts are maintained over time, even as personnel or organizational priorities change.
3. **Enable Scalability:** Processes provide the structure needed to scale cybersecurity practices across larger and more complex organizations.
4. **Facilitate Compliance:** Documented and managed processes demonstrate an organization's commitment to meeting CMMC requirements and protecting sensitive data.

Conclusion

CMMC processes are essential for embedding cybersecurity into the fabric of an organization. By focusing on institutionalization, accountability, and continuous improvement, processes ensure cybersecurity practices are consistently applied, monitored, and refined. As organizations progress through the CMMC maturity levels, the increasing rigor of processes allows them to adapt to evolving threats and regulatory demands, ultimately achieving a resilient and proactive cybersecurity posture [13].

CMMC Levels

The **Cybersecurity Maturity Model Certification (CMMC)** is structured around five maturity levels, each integrating a combination of **processes** and **practices** to enhance an organization's cybersecurity capabilities. These levels provide a roadmap for achieving robust cybersecurity by progressively advancing from basic protections to highly sophisticated measures. The framework ensures organizations implement appropriate safeguards based on the sensitivity of the data they handle, such as **Federal Contract Information (FCI)** and **Controlled Unclassified Information (CUI)** [13].

Understanding CMMC Maturity Levels: A Progressive Path to Cybersecurity Excellence

The **Cybersecurity Maturity Model Certification (CMMC)** framework defines **five maturity levels** to help organizations improve their cybersecurity practices progressively. Each level builds upon the previous one, creating a structured path toward more advanced and comprehensive cybersecurity capabilities. This tiered approach ensures organizations of varying sizes and resources can implement security measures aligning with their unique needs, the sensitivity of the data they handle, and their role within the Defense Industrial Base (DIB) [13].

The CMMC maturity levels range from **basic cybersecurity hygiene** to **optimized, proactive defenses** against advanced threats. These levels guide organizations from addressing fundamental security measures to achieving a state of continuous improvement and innovation [13].

Overview of the Five Maturity Levels

Level 1: Basic Cyber Hygiene

- **Focus:** Protecting Federal Contract Information (FCI) through essential security measures.
- **Key Features:**
    - Practices at this level are straightforward and focus on protecting FCI with minimal resources.
    - No formal processes are required; practices are performed as needed.
- **Examples of Practices:**
    - Implementing basic access controls (e.g., password protection).

    - Ensuring antivirus software is installed and updated.
- **Purpose:** Provides a foundational level of protection suitable for smaller organizations or those new to cybersecurity.

Level 2: Intermediate Cyber Hygiene

- **Focus:** Establishing a bridge between Level 1 and the more stringent requirements for protecting Controlled Unclassified Information (CUI).
- **Key Features:**
    - Practices include a mix of basic and advanced controls.
    - Processes begin to be documented and repeatable, ensuring consistency.
- **Examples of Practices:**
    - Developing a written incident response plan.
    - Conducting user awareness training to mitigate phishing risks.
- **Purpose:** Prepares organizations to handle CUI by formalizing cybersecurity practices and introducing process management.

Level 3: Good Cyber Hygiene

- **Focus:** Fully implementing **NIST SP 800-171** standards to protect CUI comprehensively.
- **Key Features:**
    - Practices expand to include 130 controls, covering all NIST SP 800-171 requirements and additional CMMC-specific measures.
    - Processes are institutionalized, actively managed, and regularly reviewed.
- **Examples of Practices:**
    - Employing multifactor authentication (MFA) for secure access.
    - Encrypting sensitive data both at rest and in transit.
    - Conducting vulnerability scans to identify and remediate risks.
- **Purpose:** Ensures organizations can effectively safeguard CUI and handle a broader range of cybersecurity threats.

Level 4: Proactive

- **Focus:** Defending against **Advanced Persistent Threats (APTs)** through proactive measures and advanced capabilities.

- **Key Features:**
    - Practices emphasize advanced threat detection, response, and mitigation.
    - Processes are continuously reviewed and improved, leveraging data-driven insights.
- **Examples of Practices:**
    - Integrating threat intelligence to identify and respond to emerging threats.
    - Using behavioral analytics to detect unusual user activity.
- **Purpose:** Equips organizations to anticipate and respond to sophisticated cyberattacks, protecting critical assets and data.

Level 5: Advanced/Progressive

- **Focus:** Achieving a state of continuous improvement and optimization for maximum cybersecurity resilience.
- **Key Features:**
    - Practices focus on automation, innovation, and advanced threat hunting techniques.
    - Processes are fully optimized, embedding cybersecurity into the organization's culture.
- **Examples of Practices:**
    - Deploying artificial intelligence (AI) to automate threat detection and response.
    - Conducting red team/blue team exercises to test and improve defenses.
- **Purpose:** Positions organizations as leaders in cybersecurity, capable of adapting to the most advanced and evolving threats.

Maturity Level	Processes	Practices	Focus
Level 1	Performed informally, ad hoc	17 basic practices	Protecting FCI with minimal formalization.
Level 2	Documented and repeatable	72 practices (subset of NIST SP 800-171)	Bridging basic hygiene to full CUI protection.
Level 3	Fully institutionalized and managed	130 practices (full NIST SP 800-171 compliance)	Comprehensive CUI protection and risk management.
Level 4	Proactively reviewed and improved	156 practices	Countering APTs with advanced defenses.
Level 5	Optimized for continuous improvement	171 practices	Maximizing resilience through innovation.

Benefits of the CMMC Maturity Levels

1. **Scalability:** The maturity levels allow organizations to start with basic cybersecurity measures and progress to advanced capabilities as resources and needs grow.
2. **Customization:** Each level aligns with the sensitivity of the data handled by the organization, ensuring appropriate security without overburdening smaller entities.
3. **Structure:** The progression provides a clear, step-by-step path to improving cybersecurity, making it manageable and achievable.
4. **Resilience:** Higher maturity levels focus on proactive and optimized measures, enabling organizations to adapt to and counter emerging threats.

Why the CMMC Maturity Levels Matter

The maturity levels of the CMMC framework are more than a compliance checklist; they represent a strategic approach to building a strong cybersecurity posture. By starting with basic protections and scaling to sophisticated, automated defenses, organizations can ensure their systems are secure, adaptable, and capable of withstanding even the most advanced threats. This progressive model not only protects sensitive information but also fortifies the integrity of the defense supply chain as a whole.

Conclusion

The CMMC maturity levels provide a roadmap for organizations to improve their cybersecurity practices incrementally and effectively. Each level reflects a deeper integration of cybersecurity into an organization's operations, moving from basic measures to advanced, proactive, and optimized defenses. By following this structured approach, organizations can achieve a robust and resilient cybersecurity posture, meeting the demands of the Department of Defense and safeguarding sensitive information from evolving threats.

Key Components of the Cybersecurity Maturity Model Certification (CMMC)

The **Cybersecurity Maturity Model Certification (CMMC)** is built on key components which ensure a standardized and comprehensive approach to safeguarding sensitive information. These components provide a foundational understanding of the data types being protected, the scope of assessments, and the implications for organizations within the Defense Industrial Base (DIB). Below, we explore the key components: **Controlled Unclassified Information (CUI), Federal Contract Information (FCI)**, and the **Assessment Scope** [13].

Controlled Unclassified Information (CUI): Definition and Importance

Controlled Unclassified Information (CUI) refers to information which is not classified but requires safeguarding due to its sensitivity. This category includes data that could have national security or operational implications if improperly accessed or disclosed. Examples of CUI include technical drawings, procurement data, or research and development materials shared under government contracts [13].

- **Definition:** According to the National Archives and Records Administration (NARA), CUI is defined as "information the government creates or possesses, or that an entity creates or possesses for or on behalf of the government, which requires safeguarding or dissemination controls consistent with applicable laws, regulations, and government-wide policies."
- **Importance:**
    - Protecting CUI ensures sensitive but unclassified information does not fall into the hands of adversaries or unauthorized entities.
    - Loss of CUI can compromise national security, disrupt defense supply chains, and damage the reputations of organizations entrusted with handling this data.
    - CMMC compliance ensures organizations handling CUI implement robust controls to protect it, aligning with standards such as **NIST SP 800-171**.

By defining and prioritizing the protection of CUI, the CMMC framework addresses a critical gap in national cybersecurity defenses, ensuring consistent safeguards across the entire DIB.

Federal Contract Information (FCI): Overview and Handling

Federal Contract Information (FCI) refers to information provided by or generated for the government under a contract, which is not intended for public release. Unlike CUI, FCI does not require the same stringent level of protection but still demands baseline cybersecurity measures to prevent unauthorized access [13].

- **Definition:** As described in the Federal Acquisition Regulation (FAR) Clause 52.204-21, FCI includes any information that is "not intended for public release" and is "provided or generated for the Government under a contract to develop or deliver a product or service to the Government."

- **Handling Requirements:**
    - Organizations handling FCI must meet basic cybersecurity practices outlined in **Level 1 of the CMMC framework**, including measures like password protection, antivirus usage, and restricting system access to authorized personnel.
    - While not as sensitive as CUI, safeguarding FCI is critical to maintaining trust within government-contractor relationships and preventing unauthorized disclosures that could lead to reputational harm.

Incorporating FCI into the CMMC framework ensures even the most fundamental information shared under contracts is adequately protected, creating a baseline of security for all participants in the defense supply chain [13].

Assessment Scope: Identifying Systems and Networks within Certification Boundaries

One of the most critical steps in achieving CMMC compliance is defining the **assessment scope**, which identifies the systems, networks, and processes which fall within the certification's boundaries. This component ensures all aspects of an organization's infrastructure involved in handling FCI or CUI are appropriately evaluated and secured [13].

- **Scope Definition:**
    - The scope includes any **information systems, devices, and networks** used to process, store, or transmit FCI or CUI.
    - It also encompasses connected systems which may indirectly impact the security of FCI or CUI, such as cloud services or third-party vendor solutions.
- **Importance:**
    - Establishing clear boundaries helps organizations focus their resources on securing the most critical assets and processes.
    - A well-defined scope reduces the risk of overlooking vulnerabilities in systems that could be exploited to access sensitive information.
- **Process:**
    - Organizations perform a **system inventory** to identify all devices, applications, and data flows.
    - They document system interdependencies and ensure all components within the scope meet the required CMMC practices for their desired certification level.

Proper scoping is essential for achieving certification efficiently and effectively, ensuring every element of the organization's cybersecurity program aligns with the CMMC framework's requirements.

Bringing the Components Together

Together, these key components—**CUI, FCI, and Assessment Scope**—form the backbone of the CMMC framework. They define what needs protection, establish baseline requirements, and ensure a focused and thorough approach to cybersecurity. By addressing these components, organizations can better safeguard sensitive data, comply with DoD requirements, and contribute to the overall security and resilience of the defense supply chain [13].

The CMMC Certification Process

The **Cybersecurity Maturity Model Certification (CMMC)** introduces a structured certification process to ensure organizations within the Defense Industrial Base (DIB) implement effective cybersecurity measures. This process is critical for verifying that organizations can safeguard sensitive information, such as **Federal Contract Information (FCI)** and **Controlled Unclassified Information (CUI)** and comply with Department of Defense (DoD) requirements [13].

The certification process involves several phases, from preparation to final certification, with the goal of creating a verified and robust cybersecurity posture. Below is a detailed explanation of the **CMMC certification process** [13].

1. Preparation Phase

The preparation phase is the foundation of the certification process. During this phase, organizations assess their current cybersecurity practices, identify gaps, and take corrective actions to align with the desired CMMC maturity level [13].

- **Key Steps:**
    1. **Self-Assessment:**
        - Conduct an internal review of existing cybersecurity practices and compare them to CMMC requirements.
        - Use tools such as the **DoD's Assessment Guide** or third-party readiness tools to evaluate compliance.
    2. **Gap Analysis:**
        - Identify deficiencies in both practices and processes relative to the targeted maturity level.
        - Document areas requiring improvement, such as missing controls or unformalized policies.
    3. **Remediation:**
        - Address identified gaps by implementing necessary technical controls, updating policies, and formalizing processes.
        - Examples include upgrading system configurations, training employees, and establishing incident response plans.

- **Outcome:** The organization is prepared to undergo formal assessment with a strong understanding of its cybersecurity posture.

2. Assessment Phase

In this phase, the organization undergoes a formal assessment by a Certified Third-Party Assessment Organization (**C3PAO**). The assessment determines whether the organization meets the requirements of the targeted CMMC maturity level [13].

- **Key Steps:**
    1. **Engage a C3PAO:**
        - Select a DoD-approved C3PAO to conduct the assessment. These organizations are accredited by the **CMMC Accreditation Body (CMMC-AB)** to perform evaluations.
    2. **Assessment Scope:**
        - Define the systems, networks, and processes within the certification boundary. The scope should include all assets handling FCI or CUI.
    3. **Assessment Execution:**
        - The C3PAO evaluates the organization's compliance with the required practices and processes.
        - Assessors review documentation, interview personnel, and test technical controls to verify implementation.
    4. **Preliminary Results:**
        - The assessors provide preliminary feedback on areas of compliance and potential gaps that need attention.
- **Outcome:** The C3PAO determines if the organization meets the requirements of the desired maturity level.

3. Certification Phase

If the organization successfully meets the requirements during the assessment, it receives formal certification for the targeted CMMC maturity level.

- **Key Steps:**
    1. **Certification Issuance:**

    - The C3PAO submits the results to the **CMMC-AB**, which validates the findings and issues the certification.
    - The certification specifies the maturity level achieved and is valid for **three years**.
  2. **Compliance Reporting:**
    - The organization's certification status is recorded in the DoD Supplier Performance Risk System (SPRS).
    - Contractors and subcontractors may be required to provide proof of certification when bidding on DoD contracts.
- **Outcome:** Certification demonstrates the organization meets the required cybersecurity standards and is eligible to participate in DoD contracts at the specified maturity level.

4. Maintenance Phase

Certification is not a one-time activity; organizations must continuously maintain and improve their cybersecurity practices to retain their certification and adapt to evolving threats.

- **Key Steps:**
  1. **Continuous Monitoring:**
    - Monitor systems and networks for vulnerabilities, threats, and compliance lapses.
    - Conduct regular internal audits to ensure ongoing adherence to CMMC requirements.
  2. **Incident Response:**
    - Respond promptly to cybersecurity incidents and document lessons learned to improve practices.
  3. **Renewal:**
    - Certifications must be renewed every three years through a reassessment by a C3PAO.
- **Outcome:** By maintaining compliance, organizations ensure sustained eligibility for DoD contracts and ongoing protection of sensitive information.

Key Considerations in the Certification Process

1. **Target Maturity Level:**

- Organizations must determine the appropriate CMMC maturity level based on their role in handling FCI or CUI and the contract requirements.

2. **Cost Implications:**
   - Certification costs vary based on the targeted maturity level, the size and complexity of the organization, and the C3PAO selected.
3. **Resource Allocation:**
   - Smaller organizations may need to allocate additional resources or seek external expertise to prepare for certification.
4. **Timelines:**
   - The certification process can take several months, depending on the organization's readiness and the availability of C3PAOs.

Benefits of the CMMC Certification Process

1. **Enhanced Cybersecurity Posture:**
   - The process ensures organizations implement robust cybersecurity measures, reducing vulnerabilities and strengthening defenses.
2. **Contract Eligibility:**
   - Certification is a prerequisite for bidding on DoD contracts, providing a competitive advantage.
3. **Supply Chain Security:**
   - By requiring certification across the DIB, the DoD ensures the entire supply chain is resilient against cyber threats.
4. **Reputation and Trust:**
   - Certification demonstrates an organization's commitment to cybersecurity, fostering trust with partners and clients.

Conclusion

The **CMMC certification process** is a comprehensive pathway to achieving and demonstrating cybersecurity compliance. By progressing through the preparation, assessment, certification, and maintenance phases, organizations can align with DoD requirements, secure sensitive information, and contribute to the resilience of the defense supply chain. This structured approach ensures cybersecurity measures are not only implemented but also sustained, enabling organizations to stay ahead of evolving threats while maintaining eligibility for critical government contracts [13].

Key Stakeholders in the CMMC Ecosystem

The **Cybersecurity Maturity Model Certification (CMMC)** framework involves a collaborative network of key stakeholders who play critical roles in its implementation, enforcement, and compliance. These stakeholders ensure the success of the framework by aligning its objectives with the cybersecurity needs of the Defense Industrial Base (DIB) and the U.S. Department of Defense (DoD). Below is a detailed explanation of the primary stakeholders and their respective roles [13].

1. Department of Defense (DoD): Regulator and Enforcer

The **Department of Defense (DoD)** is the driving force behind the CMMC framework. As the regulator and enforcer, the DoD is responsible for mandating cybersecurity standards across its supply chain to protect sensitive information from cyber threats [13].

- **Role and Responsibilities:**
  - **Mandating Requirements:** The DoD requires all contractors and subcontractors within the DIB to achieve CMMC certification at the appropriate maturity level based on the sensitivity of the data they handle.
  - **Protecting National Security:** By enforcing CMMC compliance, the DoD ensures the protection of **Federal Contract Information (FCI)** and **Controlled Unclassified Information (CUI)**, thereby safeguarding the integrity of defense operations.
  - **Oversight and Policy Development:** The DoD collaborates with the **CMMC Accreditation Body (CMMC-AB)** to develop policies and oversee the framework's implementation.
- **Significance:** The DoD's leadership ensures the consistency and credibility of the CMMC framework, making cybersecurity a priority across the defense supply chain.

2. Defense Industrial Base (DIB) Contractors: Organizations Seeking Certification

The **Defense Industrial Base (DIB)** comprises contractors and subcontractors who provide products, services, and support to the DoD. These organizations are required to achieve CMMC certification to remain eligible for DoD contracts [13].

- **Role and Responsibilities:**
  - **Achieving Certification:** DIB contractors must undergo CMMC assessments and obtain certification at the level specified in their contracts.
  - **Implementing Cybersecurity Practices:** Contractors are responsible for aligning their cybersecurity practices with CMMC requirements, ranging from **basic hygiene** to **advanced proactive defenses**.
  - **Maintaining Compliance:** Contractors must sustain their certification through continuous monitoring, regular audits, and periodic recertification.

- **Challenges and Opportunities:**
    - **Challenges:** Small and medium-sized businesses (SMBs) may face resource constraints in meeting CMMC requirements, necessitating investment in cybersecurity tools and expertise.
    - **Opportunities:** Certification provides a competitive advantage by demonstrating a commitment to robust cybersecurity measures, fostering trust with the DoD and other clients.
- **Significance:** As the backbone of the defense supply chain, DIB contractors play a critical role in ensuring the overall resilience and security of the DoD's operations.

3. Certified Third-Party Assessment Organizations (C3PAOs): Conductors of Official CMMC Assessments

Certified Third-Party Assessment Organizations (C3PAOs) are independent entities accredited by the **CMMC Accreditation Body (CMMC-AB)** to conduct official assessments. These organizations evaluate whether DIB contractors meet the CMMC requirements for the targeted maturity level [13].

- **Role and Responsibilities:**
    - **Conducting Assessments:** C3PAOs perform detailed evaluations of contractors' cybersecurity practices and processes, verifying compliance with CMMC standards.
    - **Providing Feedback:** Assessors review documentation, interview personnel, and test technical controls, offering preliminary feedback and identifying areas for improvement.
    - **Certifying Compliance:** Upon successful assessment, C3PAOs recommend certification to the CMMC-AB, specifying the maturity level achieved.
- **Significance:** C3PAOs act as impartial evaluators, ensuring organizations meet the rigorous standards required to protect sensitive DoD information.

4. CMMC Accreditation Body (CMMC-AB): Oversees Implementation and Compliance

The **CMMC Accreditation Body (CMMC-AB)** is a non-profit organization tasked with overseeing the implementation, governance, and enforcement of the CMMC framework. It serves as the central authority for maintaining the integrity of the certification process [13].

- **Role and Responsibilities:**
    - **Accrediting Assessors and C3PAOs:** The CMMC-AB ensures C3PAOs and assessors meet stringent qualifications and adhere to ethical standards.
    - **Managing Certification Processes:** The Accreditation Body reviews assessment reports submitted by C3PAOs and issues official certifications to contractors.

  - **Providing Guidance and Training:** The CMMC-AB develops training programs for assessors, consultants, and contractors to ensure consistent understanding and application of the framework.
  - **Evolving the Framework:** The Accreditation Body collaborates with the DoD and industry experts to refine the CMMC model, addressing emerging threats and technological advancements.
- **Significance:** The CMMC-AB ensures the credibility, consistency, and fairness of the certification process, establishing trust across the DIB and the DoD.

Collaboration Among Stakeholders

The success of the CMMC framework relies on the effective collaboration among these stakeholders:

1. **The DoD** sets the strategic objectives and enforces compliance requirements.
2. **DIB contractors** implement cybersecurity practices and seek certification to maintain eligibility for contracts.
3. **C3PAOs** conduct impartial assessments to verify compliance with CMMC standards.
4. **The CMMC-AB** governs the entire certification ecosystem, ensuring integrity and consistency across the process.

Together, these stakeholders create a robust system that strengthens the cybersecurity posture of the defense supply chain, reduces vulnerabilities, and enhances national security.

Conclusion

The **CMMC certification process** involves the coordinated efforts of key stakeholders, each fulfilling a critical role in the framework's success. The Department of Defense enforces the framework, contractors adopt and implement required practices, C3PAOs ensure compliance through assessments, and the CMMC Accreditation Body oversees the entire process. This ecosystem ensures that cybersecurity measures are consistently applied, effectively evaluated, and continually improved, safeguarding the integrity of the nation's defense operations.

Understanding the Relationship Between CMMC and NIST SP 800-171

The **Cybersecurity Maturity Model Certification (CMMC)** and **NIST Special Publication 800-171** (NIST SP 800-171) are closely interconnected frameworks designed to enhance cybersecurity within organizations handling sensitive government information. While CMMC builds on the foundational principles of NIST SP 800-171, it introduces additional requirements, scalability, and a structured certification process. Understanding the relationship between these frameworks is critical for organizations aiming to achieve compliance with CMMC requirements while aligning with established cybersecurity standards [13].

1. Relationship Between CMMC Practices and NIST Standards

NIST SP 800-171 provides a set of standardized security controls for protecting **Controlled Unclassified Information (CUI)** in non-federal systems and organizations. The CMMC framework incorporates these controls and expands on them to create a comprehensive, scalable model for improving cybersecurity maturity across the Defense Industrial Base (DIB) [13].

Key Aspects of the Relationship:

1. **Foundation:**
    - NIST SP 800-171 serves as the baseline for CMMC's cybersecurity requirements, particularly at **CMMC Level 3** and above. The 110 controls in NIST SP 800-171 are fully included in CMMC, ensuring organizations implement industry-accepted best practices for CUI protection.
2. **Enhanced Scope:**
    - While NIST SP 800-171 focuses on protecting CUI, the CMMC framework also includes requirements for safeguarding **Federal Contract Information (FCI)**, addressed primarily in **CMMC Level 1**. This broader scope ensures the protection of less sensitive information while building a foundation for more advanced cybersecurity practices.
3. **Additional Requirements:**
    - CMMC adds new practices and processes to go beyond the technical controls outlined in NIST SP 800-171. For example:
        - CMMC includes **process maturity requirements**, such as documenting and managing cybersecurity efforts.
        - It introduces additional practices, such as advanced threat detection and response capabilities at higher maturity levels.
4. **Certification:**
    - Unlike NIST SP 800-171, which relies on self-assessments, CMMC requires third-party assessments to verify compliance. This certification process adds an external layer of accountability.

2. Mapping Practices to NIST SP 800-171 Requirements

To ensure alignment and clarity, CMMC maps many of its practices directly to the controls in NIST SP 800-171. This mapping helps organizations already compliant with NIST SP 800-171 transition to CMMC more efficiently. Below is a breakdown of how practices are mapped across the frameworks [13]:

CMMC Levels and NIST SP 800-171 Controls:

1. **CMMC Level 1: Basic Cyber Hygiene**
    - **Focus:** Protecting FCI through basic security measures.
    - **Relationship to NIST SP 800-171:**
        - Practices at Level 1 align with basic safeguarding requirements outlined in FAR 52.204-21, which form a subset of NIST SP 800-171 controls.
        - Example Practices:
            - Limit information access to authorized users (NIST 3.1.1).
            - Use antivirus software to protect against malicious code (NIST 3.14.1).
2. **CMMC Level 2: Intermediate Cyber Hygiene**
    - **Focus:** Bridging basic practices and the full implementation of NIST SP 800-171.
    - **Relationship to NIST SP 800-171:**
        - Includes a subset of NIST SP 800-171 controls and additional practices to prepare for full CUI protection.
        - Example Practices:
            - Establish and enforce security configuration settings (NIST 3.4.1).
            - Monitor and control remote access (NIST 3.1.12).
3. **CMMC Level 3: Good Cyber Hygiene**
    - **Focus:** Fully implementing all 110 controls from NIST SP 800-171 to protect CUI.
    - **Relationship to NIST SP 800-171:**
        - Achieves full compliance with NIST SP 800-171 and adds additional CMMC-specific practices.
        - Example Practices:
            - Encrypt data in transit and at rest (NIST 3.13.8 and 3.13.11).
            - Implement multifactor authentication (NIST 3.5.3).
4. **CMMC Levels 4 and 5: Proactive and Optimized**
    - **Focus:** Defending against Advanced Persistent Threats (APTs) and optimizing cybersecurity practices.
    - **Relationship to NIST SP 800-171:**

    - Builds on NIST SP 800-171 controls with additional advanced practices for real-time threat detection, response, and continuous improvement.
    - Example Practices:
        - Utilize threat intelligence to improve defenses.
        - Automate security processes for rapid response to incidents.

Key Benefits of Mapping CMMC to NIST SP 800-171

1. **Streamlined Transition:**
    - Organizations already compliant with NIST SP 800-171 have a head start in achieving CMMC certification, particularly at Level 3 and higher.
2. **Clarity and Continuity:**
    - The mapping provides clear guidance on how existing NIST SP 800-171 controls align with CMMC practices, reducing ambiguity in implementation.
3. **Enhanced Security:**
    - By adding advanced practices and process maturity requirements, CMMC builds on the strong foundation of NIST SP 800-171 to address evolving cybersecurity threats.

Challenges in Transitioning from NIST SP 800-171 to CMMC

1. **Process Maturity Requirements:**
    - CMMC introduces process-focused requirements, such as documenting and institutionalizing cybersecurity practices, which go beyond the technical controls of NIST SP 800-171.
2. **Certification Requirements:**
    - Unlike NIST SP 800-171's self-assessment approach, CMMC requires independent third-party assessments, adding complexity and cost.
3. **Additional Practices:**
    - Higher CMMC levels include practices not found in NIST SP 800-171, such as advanced analytics and threat intelligence, which may require additional investment in tools and expertise.

Conclusion

The relationship between **CMMC** and **NIST SP 800-171** highlights a natural progression from compliance to certification, enabling organizations to scale their cybersecurity efforts effectively. While CMMC incorporates all NIST SP 800-171 controls, it enhances them with additional practices and process maturity requirements to address evolving threats and ensure accountability. Mapping practices between the two frameworks provides clarity and continuity, helping organizations protect sensitive information while meeting the stringent demands of the Department of Defense. Through this alignment, CMMC ensures a higher standard of cybersecurity across the Defense Industrial Base, contributing to national security and supply chain resilience [13].

Implementation Challenges of the CMMC Framework

The **Cybersecurity Maturity Model Certification (CMMC)** framework aims to standardize and improve cybersecurity across the Defense Industrial Base (DIB). While its goals are critical for safeguarding sensitive information, implementing the framework poses significant challenges for organizations, particularly for smaller businesses. These challenges arise from **cost implications**, **resource constraints**, and the need to adapt to **evolving requirements**. Below is a detailed examination of these challenges and their impact on organizations [13].

1. Cost Implications

Implementing the CMMC framework involves both direct and indirect costs, which can vary widely depending on the organization's current cybersecurity maturity, size, and targeted CMMC level.

Direct Costs

- **Assessments:**
  - Organizations must engage a Certified Third-Party Assessment Organization (**C3PAO**) to conduct formal CMMC assessments. The cost of these assessments depends on the organization's size, scope, and complexity.
  - For small businesses, these costs can represent a significant portion of their operating budgets.
- **Technology Upgrades:**
  - Many organizations, particularly those at lower cybersecurity maturity levels, must invest in new technologies to meet CMMC requirements. These may include:
    - **Endpoint protection tools** (e.g., antivirus and anti-malware software).
    - **Multifactor authentication (MFA)** solutions.
    - **Encryption tools** for data at rest and in transit.
    - **Logging and monitoring systems** for audit and accountability.

    - Upgrading outdated infrastructure to modern, secure systems can also result in substantial expenses.

Indirect Costs

- **Training:**
    - Employees need training to understand and adhere to new cybersecurity policies and practices. This includes awareness training, role-specific technical training, and simulated phishing exercises.
    - Developing and delivering such training requires time, effort, and financial resources.
- **Staffing:**
    - Organizations may need to hire dedicated cybersecurity personnel or engage external consultants to implement, manage, and maintain CMMC compliance.
    - The cost of recruiting, onboarding, and retaining qualified cybersecurity professionals can strain budgets, especially in a competitive labor market.

Impact of Costs:

For smaller organizations, these direct and indirect costs can be prohibitive, potentially deterring them from pursuing DoD contracts altogether. Larger organizations, while more financially capable, may also face challenges in scaling these costs across their operations.

2. Resource Constraints

Resource limitations, particularly for small and medium-sized businesses (SMBs), are a major barrier to implementing CMMC.

Challenges for Smaller Businesses:

- **Limited Budget Allocation:**
    - Many smaller contractors operate on tight budgets, leaving little room for substantial cybersecurity investments.
    - Competing priorities, such as operational expenses, can make it difficult to allocate resources toward CMMC compliance.
- **In-house Expertise:**
    - SMBs often lack dedicated cybersecurity staff or expertise, making it challenging to understand and implement the technical and procedural requirements of CMMC.
    - This reliance on external consultants or managed service providers (MSPs) adds further costs and complexities.

- **Scalability:**
    - Smaller organizations may struggle to scale their operations to align with the documentation, monitoring, and reporting requirements of CMMC.

Impact of Resource Constraints:

Resource constraints disproportionately affect smaller businesses, increasing the risk of losing their eligibility for DoD contracts. This could lead to a reduction in the diversity and competitiveness of the defense supply chain.

3. Evolving Requirements

The dynamic nature of the CMMC framework and cybersecurity threats presents a continual challenge for organizations.

Regulatory Updates:

- The **CMMC framework itself is evolving**, with changes such as the transition from CMMC 1.0 to **CMMC 2.0**, which introduced simplified levels and reduced practices in some areas. While these changes aim to streamline the framework, they require organizations to stay informed and adapt their strategies.
- The DoD regularly updates its requirements to address emerging threats and align with broader cybersecurity standards, such as NIST SP 800-171 updates.

Adapting to Emerging Threats:

- Cybersecurity threats evolve rapidly, requiring organizations to continuously enhance their defenses to stay compliant. This may involve:
    - Updating systems and controls to counter new vulnerabilities.
    - Incorporating advanced tools like threat intelligence platforms and automated response systems.
- For smaller organizations, these adjustments can feel like moving targets, adding complexity to compliance efforts.

Compliance Fatigue:

- The effort required to track, interpret, and implement regulatory updates can lead to compliance fatigue, particularly for organizations already stretched thin on resources.
- Organizations must also ensure alignment with overlapping regulatory frameworks (e.g., NIST, GDPR, or CISA guidelines), adding another layer of complexity.

Impact of Evolving Requirements:

Organizations that fail to keep pace with regulatory updates risk non-compliance, certification delays, or lose eligibility for DoD contracts. The uncertainty and complexity of these evolving requirements can also discourage smaller businesses from pursuing certification.

Addressing the Challenges

Organizations can mitigate these challenges through proactive planning and strategic investments:

1. **Cost Mitigation:**
    - Leverage government programs and grants designed to support SMBs in improving their cybersecurity posture.
    - Partner with managed service providers (MSPs) or consultants to access expertise without hiring full-time staff.
2. **Efficient Resource Allocation:**
    - Prioritize cybersecurity investments based on risk assessments and the organization's role within the DIB.
    - Utilize automation tools to reduce the burden of monitoring and reporting.
3. **Staying Informed:**
    - Engage with the **CMMC Accreditation Body (CMMC-AB)** for updates and resources.
    - Join industry groups or forums to share best practices and stay ahead of regulatory changes.
4. **Incremental Implementation:**
    - Start with the foundational requirements of CMMC Level 1 and build capabilities over time, especially for smaller organizations aiming to achieve higher levels.

Conclusion

The implementation of the CMMC framework presents significant challenges, particularly in terms of **cost implications**, **resource constraints**, and adapting to **evolving requirements**. While these challenges can be daunting, they are not insurmountable. By understanding the costs, prioritizing resources effectively, and staying proactive in response to regulatory updates, organizations can navigate these hurdles. Achieving CMMC compliance not only ensures eligibility for DoD contracts but also strengthens an organization's cybersecurity posture, ultimately contributing to the resilience and security of the entire defense supply chain [13].

Benefits of CMMC Certification: Strengthening Cybersecurity and Competitiveness

The **Cybersecurity Maturity Model Certification (CMMC)** offers significant benefits to organizations, both in terms of enhancing their cybersecurity defenses and providing strategic business advantages. By achieving CMMC certification, organizations demonstrate their commitment to safeguarding sensitive information, strengthening the security of the defense supply chain, and positioning themselves for long-term success. Below is a detailed exploration of the key benefits of CMMC certification [13].

1. Enhanced Cybersecurity Posture

One of the most critical benefits of CMMC certification is the substantial improvement in an organization's cybersecurity defenses.

Protection Against Cyber Threats

- **Addressing Modern Threats:**
    - The CMMC framework provides a structured approach to implementing robust cybersecurity practices, enabling organizations to defend against a wide range of cyber threats, including phishing, ransomware, and Advanced Persistent Threats (APTs).
    - By adhering to practices such as access control, encryption, and incident response, organizations can reduce vulnerabilities and limit the potential impact of breaches.
- **Comprehensive Safeguards:**
    - The framework encompasses technical controls (e.g., multifactor authentication, endpoint protection) and process-oriented measures (e.g., risk assessments, incident response planning) to ensure a well-rounded security posture.
- **Proactive and Evolving Defenses:**
    - Higher maturity levels of CMMC emphasize continuous improvement, enabling organizations to stay ahead of emerging threats through proactive monitoring, automation, and threat intelligence.

Organizational Impact:

- Enhanced cybersecurity reduces the risk of financial loss, reputational damage, and operational disruptions caused by cyberattacks.
- Protecting sensitive data, such as **Federal Contract Information (FCI)** and **Controlled Unclassified Information (CUI)**, fosters trust with the Department of Defense (DoD) and other stakeholders.

2. Competitive Advantage

CMMC certification positions organizations to gain a significant edge in the highly competitive defense contracting landscape.

Eligibility for DoD Contracts

- **Meeting Contractual Requirements:**
  - CMMC certification is a mandatory prerequisite for bidding on most DoD contracts. Without certification, organizations risk being excluded from these opportunities, regardless of their expertise or capabilities.
- **Expanding Market Access:**
  - Certified organizations gain access to a wider range of contracts, including those requiring higher maturity levels for handling CUI. This expands business opportunities and revenue potential.
- **Differentiation from Competitors:**
  - Certification demonstrates a commitment to cybersecurity, distinguishing certified contractors from non-certified competitors. This can enhance an organization's reputation and credibility in the eyes of both the DoD and other clients.

Long-Term Business Growth:

- Beyond immediate eligibility for contracts, CMMC certification signals an organization's commitment to excellence and compliance, fostering stronger relationships with partners and stakeholders in the defense industry.

3. Supply Chain Security

CMMC certification contributes to the broader goal of strengthening the resilience and security of the entire defense supply chain.

Strengthening the Overall Ecosystem

- **Mitigating Weak Links:**
  - Cybersecurity vulnerabilities in any part of the supply chain can have cascading effects on the entire ecosystem. CMMC ensures that all participants, from prime contractors to small subcontractors, adhere to a consistent set of cybersecurity standards.
- **Reducing Risks to National Security:**
  - By safeguarding FCI and CUI, CMMC certification protects critical information from adversaries, enhancing the security of DoD operations and national defense initiatives.
- **Fostering Collaboration:**
  - A certified supply chain builds trust and facilitates smoother collaboration among contractors, subcontractors, and government entities. This reduces friction and ensures that all parties operate with aligned cybersecurity expectations.

Resilience Against Systemic Threats:

- **Cybersecurity Awareness and Accountability:**
    - CMMC certification promotes a culture of cybersecurity awareness and accountability, making the entire supply chain more resilient to systemic threats like ransomware attacks and supply chain intrusions.

Additional Benefits of CMMC Certification

1. **Compliance with Industry Standards:**
    - CMMC aligns with established frameworks such as **NIST SP 800-171**, enabling organizations to meet broader compliance requirements.
2. **Improved Organizational Efficiency:**
    - The structured processes required for certification, such as risk management and continuous monitoring, often lead to improved operational efficiency and better resource utilization.
3. **Enhanced Stakeholder Confidence:**
    - Certification reassures stakeholders, including customers, partners, and investors, that the organization prioritizes cybersecurity and adheres to industry best practices.

Conclusion

CMMC certification offers a wide range of benefits, from enhancing an organization's cybersecurity posture to unlocking new business opportunities and strengthening the defense supply chain. By protecting against cyber threats, gaining a competitive advantage in the defense contracting space, and contributing to the overall security of the ecosystem, certified organizations position themselves as leaders in both cybersecurity and operational excellence. Achieving CMMC certification is not just a compliance requirement—it is a strategic investment in the resilience, reputation, and long-term success of the organization [13].

Tools and Resources for Achieving CMMC Compliance

The journey to **Cybersecurity Maturity Model Certification (CMMC)** compliance can be complex, but organizations have access to various tools and resources which can simplify the process and ensure successful implementation. These tools and resources fall into three primary categories: **pre-assessment tools**, **technical solutions**, and **training resources**. Each category plays a vital role in preparing organizations to meet CMMC requirements, from initial readiness evaluation to implementing robust technical controls and educating personnel [13].

1. Pre-assessment Tools

Before undergoing a formal CMMC assessment, organizations need to evaluate their current cybersecurity posture, identify gaps, and address deficiencies. Pre-assessment tools provide a structured way to perform this self-evaluation and prepare for certification.

a. Readiness Checklists

- **Purpose:**
  - Readiness checklists help organizations systematically evaluate their compliance with CMMC practices and processes. These checklists are particularly useful for understanding which requirements have been met and which need attention.
- **Key Features:**
  - Break down CMMC requirements into manageable tasks, categorized by maturity level and domain.
  - Provide a clear roadmap for addressing gaps in compliance.
- **Examples:**
  - **DoD Readiness Checklists:** Official tools aligned with CMMC requirements.
  - Vendor-provided checklists tailored to specific industries or organization sizes.

b. CMMC Model Documentation

- **Purpose:**
  - Official CMMC documentation outlines the framework's domains, capabilities, practices, and processes, serving as the definitive guide for organizations pursuing compliance.
- **Key Features:**
  - Detailed explanations of CMMC requirements for each maturity level.
  - Guidance on how practices and processes should be implemented.
- **Examples:**
  - CMMC 2.0 model overview documents and assessment guides available from the **CMMC Accreditation Body (CMMC-AB)**.

2. Technical Solutions

To meet CMMC requirements, organizations must implement a range of technical controls to protect sensitive information like **Federal Contract Information (FCI)** and **Controlled Unclassified Information (CUI)**. Technical solutions such as **Security Information and Event Management (SIEM)** systems and **Endpoint Detection and Response (EDR)** tools are essential for ensuring compliance.

a. Security Information and Event Management (SIEM)

- **Purpose:**
  - SIEM systems collect, analyze, and correlate security event data from across an organization's network to detect and respond to potential threats.

- **Key Features:**
  - Real-time monitoring of network activity for suspicious events.
  - Log management and reporting capabilities to satisfy CMMC audit and accountability requirements.
  - Automated alerts for unusual or unauthorized activities.
- **Examples:**
  - Tools like Splunk, IBM QRadar, or Azure Sentinel that integrate with existing IT systems.
- **Alignment with CMMC:**
  - SIEM solutions help meet requirements in domains like **Audit and Accountability (AU)** and **System and Communications Protection (SC)**.

b. Endpoint Detection and Response (EDR)

- **Purpose:**
  - EDR solutions provide advanced protection for endpoint devices (e.g., laptops, desktops, and servers), identifying and mitigating threats at the device level.
- **Key Features:**
  - Continuous monitoring and analysis of endpoint activity.
  - Rapid detection and containment of malware, ransomware, and other endpoint-specific threats.
  - Incident response capabilities, including root cause analysis.
- **Examples:**
  - Solutions like CrowdStrike Falcon, Carbon Black, or Microsoft Defender for Endpoint.
- **Alignment with CMMC:**
  - EDR tools align with practices in domains such as **System and Information Integrity (SI)** and **Incident Response (IR)**.

3. Training Resources

Successful implementation of CMMC requirements depends on a well-trained workforce. Training resources equip employees with the knowledge and skills to understand, implement, and sustain cybersecurity practices across the organization.

a. Workshops

- **Purpose:**
    - Interactive sessions designed to provide hands-on guidance for implementing CMMC requirements.
- **Key Features:**
    - In-person or virtual workshops led by cybersecurity experts.
    - Focused on specific aspects of CMMC, such as risk assessments, incident response planning, or documentation processes.
- **Examples:**
    - Workshops organized by the **CMMC Accreditation Body (CMMC-AB)** or industry associations.

b. Online Courses

- **Purpose:**
    - Flexible, self-paced learning options for employees at all levels of the organization.
- **Key Features:**
    - Comprehensive coverage of CMMC requirements, domains, and certification processes.
    - Modules tailored to specific roles, such as IT administrators, compliance officers, or executives.
- **Examples:**
    - Online platforms like Coursera, Udemy, or vendor-specific training from companies like Microsoft or Splunk.

c. Guides

- **Purpose:**
    - Written resources that provide in-depth explanations and step-by-step instructions for achieving CMMC compliance.
- **Key Features:**
    - Practical advice for addressing common challenges and pitfalls.
    - Checklists, templates, and case studies to facilitate implementation.
- **Examples:**

- Guides from the **CMMC Accreditation Body** or third-party consultants specializing in cybersecurity compliance.

Integration of Tools and Resources

The tools and resources for achieving CMMC compliance work together to create a comprehensive support system:

1. **Pre-assessment tools** help organizations evaluate their current state and plan for improvements.
2. **Technical solutions** enable the implementation of required security controls.
3. **Training resources** ensure employees have the knowledge and skills to maintain compliance over time.

By leveraging these resources effectively, organizations can streamline the compliance process, reduce costs, and build a sustainable cybersecurity posture.

Conclusion

Achieving CMMC compliance requires more than technical implementation; it demands a strategic approach supported by the right tools and resources. **Pre-assessment tools** provide clarity and direction, **technical solutions** implement essential controls, and **training resources** empower personnel to maintain and sustain compliance. Together, these resources enable organizations to navigate the complexities of CMMC certification, protect sensitive information, and contribute to the overall security of the defense supply chain [13].

The Future of CMMC: Navigating Change and Cybersecurity Challenges

The **Cybersecurity Maturity Model Certification (CMMC)** is evolving to address the changing needs of the defense supply chain and the growing sophistication of cyber threats. The future of CMMC, marked by the introduction of **CMMC 2.0**, signals a shift toward simplification, broader adoption, and enhanced adaptability. These changes aim to make the framework more accessible to contractors while maintaining robust security standards to protect **Federal Contract Information (FCI)** and **Controlled Unclassified Information (CUI)**. Below is a detailed exploration of the future direction of CMMC and its implications for contractors [13].

1. CMMC 2.0: A Streamlined Framework

Simplified Levels

- Under CMMC 2.0, the maturity levels have been reduced from five to **three levels** to simplify compliance and align requirements more closely with contractor capabilities and DoD needs:
    - **Level 1 (Foundational):** Focused on protecting FCI with basic security practices, similar to the original Level 1.

- **Level 2 (Advanced):** Based on the 110 controls in **NIST SP 800-171**, this level addresses CUI protection and aligns with the original Level 3. It includes a bifurcated approach:
  - **Self-assessments** for non-critical programs.
  - **Third-party assessments** for critical programs.
- **Level 3 (Expert):** Designed for organizations handling the most sensitive DoD information, incorporating controls from **NIST SP 800-172** to address Advanced Persistent Threats (APTs).

Enhanced Alignment with NIST SP 800-171

- CMMC 2.0 reinforces its reliance on **NIST SP 800-171** as the foundational standard for protecting CUI:
  - By directly aligning with NIST SP 800-171, CMMC eliminates additional practices and simplifies implementation for contractors already familiar with NIST requirements.
  - Organizations at Level 2 must fully implement all NIST SP 800-171 controls, making the framework more predictable and easier to navigate.
- **Streamlined Processes:**
  - CMMC 2.0 eliminates process maturity requirements (e.g., documenting and managing practices), focusing solely on technical controls.
  - This shift reduces administrative burdens and simplifies the path to certification for smaller organizations.

2. Impact on Contractors

Broader Adoption Requirements

- **Expansion Across the Defense Industrial Base (DIB):**
  - CMMC certification will become mandatory for a broader range of contractors, including small businesses, subcontractors, and non-traditional defense suppliers.
  - Organizations previously relying on self-assessments for compliance with **NIST SP 800-171** must now achieve certification for contracts requiring CUI protection.
- **Tiered Approach:**
  - The bifurcated approach at Level 2 (self-assessment versus third-party assessment) makes compliance more flexible while ensuring critical programs meet stringent security standards.

- Contractors handling less sensitive information may find the self-assessment pathway less resource intensive.

- **Increased Accountability:**
  - The requirement for third-party assessments for critical programs ensures contractors demonstrate accountability and adhere to security standards under independent scrutiny.

Challenges and Opportunities for Contractors

- **Challenges:**
  - Smaller businesses may face difficulties allocating resources for assessments, technology upgrades, and ongoing compliance.
  - Third-party assessments introduce additional costs and complexity for organizations pursuing higher levels of certification.
- **Opportunities:**
  - Certification differentiates contractors by demonstrating a commitment to cybersecurity, offering a competitive edge in securing DoD contracts.
  - The streamlined framework under CMMC 2.0 reduces redundancies and lowers administrative barriers, making compliance more achievable.

3. Evolving Threat Landscape

The future of CMMC is shaped by the need to address the rapidly changing cybersecurity threat landscape. As adversaries employ increasingly sophisticated methods to exploit vulnerabilities, CMMC must evolve to protect the defense supply chain effectively.

Addressing New Cybersecurity Challenges

- **Advanced Persistent Threats (APTs):**
  - CMMC 2.0 emphasizes proactive measures at Level 3 to counter APTs, leveraging advanced controls from **NIST SP 800-172**.
  - Contractors handling sensitive DoD information must implement threat intelligence, advanced monitoring, and automated response capabilities to detect and neutralize APTs.
- **Emerging Technologies:**
  - As technologies such as **artificial intelligence (AI)**, **machine learning (ML)**, and **quantum computing** become more prevalent, CMMC must adapt to address new vulnerabilities introduced by these advancements.
- **Supply Chain Risks:**

- Threat actors increasingly target weak links in the supply chain to compromise entire ecosystems. CMMC's focus on consistent security standards across all tiers of contractors mitigates these risks.

Future Enhancements:

- CMMC will likely incorporate additional guidance and tools to address new cybersecurity challenges, such as:
  - **Zero Trust Architectures:** Implementing "trust but verify" principles to secure access to systems and data.
  - **Continuous Monitoring:** Encouraging real-time threat detection and response to ensure ongoing compliance and security.

Benefits of the Future Direction

1. **Simplified Compliance:**
   - The streamlined levels and enhanced alignment with NIST SP 800-171 make CMMC more accessible, especially for smaller organizations.
2. **Enhanced Security:**
   - By adapting to the evolving threat landscape, CMMC ensures that the defense supply chain remains resilient against emerging cyber threats.
3. **Flexibility for Contractors:**
   - The bifurcated approach at Level 2 balances the need for rigorous oversight with flexibility for less critical programs.
4. **Sustainability:**
   - CMMC 2.0 reduces administrative burdens, making it easier for contractors to maintain long-term compliance.

Conclusion

The future of CMMC, embodied by the transition to **CMMC 2.0**, reflects a thoughtful response to the needs of contractors and the evolving cybersecurity landscape. By simplifying maturity levels, aligning more closely with NIST SP 800-171, and addressing emerging threats, CMMC 2.0 aims to strengthen the defense supply chain while reducing barriers to compliance. For contractors, these changes present both challenges and opportunities, emphasizing the need for proactive planning, resource allocation, and a commitment to continuous improvement. As the framework evolves, CMMC remains a cornerstone of cybersecurity for national defense, protecting sensitive information and ensuring the resilience of critical operations [13].

Conclusion: The Critical Role of CMMC in Cybersecurity and Competitive Advantage
The **Cybersecurity Maturity Model Certification (CMMC)** is more than a regulatory framework; it is a strategic initiative designed to safeguard national security and ensure the resilience of the Defense Industrial Base (DIB). By establishing robust cybersecurity standards, the CMMC framework addresses the growing threat of cyberattacks, particularly from nation-state actors, while also offering significant strategic advantages to contractors who achieve compliance [13].

Importance of CMMC in Safeguarding National Security

Protecting Sensitive Information

- The modern threat landscape is increasingly complex, with adversaries targeting sensitive government data such as **Federal Contract Information (FCI)** and **Controlled Unclassified Information (CUI)**. Breaches of this data can compromise national security, disrupt defense operations, and weaken the integrity of the defense supply chain.
- CMMC plays a critical role in mitigating these risks by:
    - Ensuring consistent cybersecurity standards across all tiers of the DIB.
    - Protecting critical data from unauthorized access and cyberattacks.
    - Fortifying the defense supply chain against systemic vulnerabilities.

Strengthening the Defense Supply Chain

- National security depends on a resilient supply chain, with contributions from both large defense contractors and small businesses. A single weak link in this chain can lead to cascading vulnerabilities.
- By requiring all participants to meet specific cybersecurity standards, CMMC ensures every organization, regardless of size, contributes to the overall security of the supply chain.

Adapting to Emerging Threats

- As cyber threats evolve, particularly from **Advanced Persistent Threats (APTs)** and other sophisticated attackers, CMMC provides a proactive framework to address these challenges.
- The framework's alignment with evolving standards, such as **NIST SP 800-171** and **NIST SP 800-172**, ensures organizations remain equipped to handle both current and future threats.

In essence, CMMC is a vital tool in the DoD's strategy to protect critical information and maintain the integrity of national defense efforts [13].

Strategic Advantage of Compliance for Contractors

Eligibility for DoD Contracts

- CMMC certification is increasingly a requirement for organizations seeking to bid on Department of Defense contracts. Without certification, contractors risk losing access to lucrative opportunities within the defense sector.
- By achieving compliance, contractors demonstrate their commitment to meeting the DoD's stringent cybersecurity requirements, positioning themselves as trusted partners.

Competitive Differentiation

- Certification provides a tangible proof point of an organization's cybersecurity maturity, setting it apart from competitors who may lack the same level of diligence.
- Organizations who achieve higher levels of CMMC certification gain a distinct advantage in securing contracts involving sensitive or classified information.

Long-Term Business Growth

- Beyond immediate contract eligibility, CMMC compliance signals a contractor's commitment to excellence, reliability, and security. This reputation can open doors to new partnerships, strengthen existing relationships, and foster trust with both government and private sector clients.
- Compliance also prepares organizations to navigate other regulatory frameworks, creating a foundation for broader market access.

Strengthened Internal Operations

- The structured approach to cybersecurity required by CMMC enhances internal efficiency and resilience:
    - Improved risk management practices.
    - Enhanced employee awareness and training.
    - Better integration of cybersecurity into overall business operations.

Conclusion

The **CMMC framework** represents a critical intersection of cybersecurity, national security, and strategic business opportunity. Its role in safeguarding sensitive information and fortifying the defense supply chain cannot be overstated, particularly in the face of an evolving threat landscape. For contractors, compliance with CMMC offers more than just eligibility for DoD contracts—it provides a strategic advantage, fostering trust, enhancing competitiveness, and positioning organizations for sustained growth [13].

As cyber threats continue to grow in scope and sophistication, the importance of CMMC in protecting national security will only increase. By embracing CMMC compliance, contractors not only contribute to a secure and resilient defense ecosystem but also secure their place as key players in the defense industry. CMMC is not just a requirement—it is a strategic investment in the future of both national security and organizational success.

Additional Frameworks and Considerations

The previous sections in this Chapter presented information on the NIST-CF and the CMMC. NIST-CF is adaptable to most industries and approaches; CMMC, on the other hand, is specific to the DoD supply chain for DoD contracts. This section will present a high-level overview of other frameworks used in specific industries.

Cybersecurity: Risk Management Oversight - Accounting and Auditing

Certified Public Accounts (CPAs) have a special relationship with the cybersecurity industry, as CPA firms conduct audits for many industries. The accounting industry views cybersecurity from a risk perspective: audits, tools, recommendations, and approaches are all sources for comprehension of cybersecurity organizational risk [3].

The American Institute of Certified Public Accountants (AICPA) provides a number of resources for the accounting profession, including the "Cybersecurity: Risk Management Oversight" publication. AICPA provides questions and approaches CPAs use when auditing publicly traded companies. (Note: the SEC has designated requirements for cybersecurity.)
The AICPA document focuses on the following areas:

- Financial statement auditors' cyber risk considerations
- The role of management and management's responsibilities in cybersecurity disclosures
- Management's approach to cybersecurity risk management
- Board oversight and cybersecurity risk management assistance [4]

AICPA also recommends topics and questions for boards to ask organizational leadership [4]. Examples of categories and questions include:

Situational Awareness

- How many cyberattacks has the organization suffered?
- Was the board notified of the attacks as they occurred?
- How does the organization identify breaches as they occur?
- What systems are the most critical for the organization? [4]

Strategy and Operations

- How do the organization's cybersecurity practices mirror or differ from defined best practices?
- Do approaches differ for critical and non-critical organizational assets?

- What cybersecurity framework has been adopted? [4]

Insider Threats

- How do organizational policies address insider threats?
- What are the supply chain and other third-party risks?
- How are the supply chain and third-party risks flexibility addressed?
- How are cybersecurity requirements incorporated into supply chain and third-party contracts? [4]

Incident Response

- What is the defined incident response approach?
- Are there incident response procedures defined for the incident response team? [4]

Every organization employing third-party auditors is impacted by audit recommendations. Again, the accounting industry is a significant driver of approaches, especially when the approaches are impacted by risk. Business leaders must be fully aware of the auditing industry questions and approaches to investigating cybersecurity measures.

FFIEC Frameworks for Banking

Cybersecurity plays a critical role in banking and finance industries. The Federal Financial Institutions Examination Council (FFIEC) operates as a cross-agency body that defines uniform principles, standards, and recommendations. FFIEC has created multiple documents for banking institutions. These documents include:

User's Guide – An overview and explanation of how to use the FFIEC documents [6].

Overview for Chief Executive Officers and Boards of Directors – This document provides benefits to the institution, identifies roles, approaches and explanations of the FFIEC cybersecurity documents [5].

Inherent Risk Profile – Technical identifiers are listed with an equivalent risk level. Each category is rated from least to most risk based on objective criteria. Criteria is very granular and pointed for specific categorization of risk level [7]. Banking and finance industries are deeply intertwined with technology, enabling a focused assessment tool for risk assessments. Categories include:

- **Technologies and Connection Types**: Internet Service Providers, unsecured external connections, wireless access, personal device access (BYOD), third parties/contractors with system access, wholesale customers with dedicated access, internally hosted third-party services, end of life systems, open-source software, network devices, third-party storage or processing of critical operations, and externally hosted cloud services [7].

- **Delivery Channels**: Online presence for customers, mobile, and automated teller machines [15].
- **Online/Mobile Products and Technologies**: Issuance of debit or credit cards, prepaid cards, emerging payment technologies, person-to-person (P2P) payments, originating ACH payments, originating wholesale payments, wire transfers, merchant remote deposit capture, global remittances, treasury services and clients, trust services, interbank transfers, merchant acquirer, and IT service reseller [7].
- **Organizational Characteristics**: Mergers and acquisitions, direct employees, IT and cybersecurity staffing changes, privileged access, IT system changes, branch/business locations, and operations/data centers [7].
- **External Threats**: Attempted cyber-attacks [7].

Cybersecurity Assessment Tool for Cybersecurity Maturity-

The assessment tool is broken down into five domains, with multiple assessment factors for each domain 10]. Maturity levels are rated with the following designations:

- Baseline – Meets basic expectations of the assessment factor.
- Evolving – Processes exist and are leveraged for the assessment factor.
- Intermediate – Processes are embedded across the organization.
- Advanced - Processes are adaptive and evolve with performance at a high level for the assessment factor.
- Innovative – Processes are highly engineered, adaptive, and respond quickly for the assessment factor. [7]

The five domains and assessment factors include:

- Cyber Risk Management and Oversight
- Threat Intelligence and Collaboration
- Cybersecurity Controls
- External Dependency Management

FFIEC follows the same path as many other frameworks: governance, risk, and compliance lead first to risk management and mitigation, and then technical operations are assessed. The banking industry is deeply embedded with the Force of Technology.

With the embedded approach to technology, banking incorporates a number of technical assessments. Not surprisingly, some documents list specific technical measurements to identify levels of risk. With many designed and deployed electronically, banking industry executives must have a deeper level of technical concept comprehension.

Fintech represents evolving consumerism erupting from technology combined with financial services. Fintech represents the evolving needs of consumers for personal banking, while also enabling business transactions. Fintech is poised to face the same challenges every industry has faced when heavily pairing technology with their core offerings: fast development with low focus on security. Following governance, risk, and compliance approaches from previous sections, comparisons of Fintech solutions to organizational requirements enables organizations to design or purchase effective solutions. Of course, Fintech organizations are required to define vision, objectives, goals, and standards before any design or solution purchase is engaged. Failure to define overall vision, objectives, requirements, and standards will place Fintech organizations at a disadvantage. Individuals involved with creating/deploying Fintech functionality should:

- Require security in all selected solutions
- Validate sales information through testing software functionality
- Investigate Impacts on Organizational Operations
- Review solution offerings

Fintech professionals and organizations are cautioned to learn the lessons of preceding industries. Unfortunately, history repeats itself. The computer industry suffered significant security issues. So has the smartphone industry. So has the automotive industry. Fintech needs to leverage the lessons learned in order to avoid the same issues.

ISO 2700 Family – Manufacturing and International Organizations

The International Organization for Standardization (ISO) provides a number of standards for manufacturing and international organizations, including the ISO 2700 Cybersecurity Framework Series [8]. Similar to the NIST cybersecurity documentation, ISO 2700 is designed to enable certification of external standards [8]. Although the NIST-CF and ISO 2700 frameworks enable similar approaches, ISO 2700 does have unique features.

The ISO 2700 family focuses on the implementation of information security within an organization [8]. Executive and leadership considerations are defined. Objectives, policies, roles, responsibilities, and competencies are defined. Risk management plays a heavy role in the 2700 family [8]. ISO places a heavy focus on performance efficiencies and KPIs. ISO documentation provides the following critical considerations for security metrics:

- Metrics must be measurable, duplicable, and comparable across temporal and organizational areas.
- Metrics must be based on sound statistical and mathematical foundations for reliable measurements.
- Metrics must be relevant (up-to-date and applicable) with an acceptable frequency of data collections for reporting.

- Metrics must measure performance in relationship to objectives. Metrics not tied to performance indicating objective and goal progress are not measured.
- Metrics should provide an assessment of the overall cyber risk approach and systematic controls evaluating cyber risk.
- Metrics should generate a cohesive whole measurement, avoiding disparate unrelated measurements [8].

Organizations with ISO certification find ISO 2700 a welcome approach for cybersecurity. Manufacturing and international organizations align with the ISO standards. Organizations adopting the ISO 2700 family are recommended to compare overall ISO standards to overall organizational goals. Organizations with federal contracts are recommended to employ both the NIST and the ISO frameworks, mapping each to the organization's cybersecurity approaches.

Healthcare Sector Cybersecurity Framework Implementation Guide

Under Presidential Policy directive, the National Infrastructure Protection Plan required public and private sector collaboration to improve cybersecurity and cyber resiliency in 2016 [9]. The U.S. Department of Health and Human Services (HHS) coordinates cybersecurity and cyber resiliency for the public health sector [9]. A number of agencies combined together to create the Healthcare and Public Health (HPH) Sector Critical Infrastructure Partnership [9]. A Joint HPH Cybersecurity Working Group was created to develop and recommend a framework for the healthcare industry [9].

The HPH group leveraged the NIST-CF. The Healthcare Sector Cybersecurity Framework follows the same implementation sequence as the NIST-CF [9]. Overall, the sequence and approach match other industries, as outlined by NIST in the NIST-CF.

COBIT Cybersecurity Framework - Leadership and Management

The Information Systems Audit and Control Association (ISACA) created the Control Objectives for Information Related Technology (COBIT) framework to ensure operational integrity of enterprise infrastructure [11]. In Unit 1, enterprise technology and innovation were presented. Remember, cybersecurity exists to protect the enterprise digital ecosystem. Frameworks often focus on enterprise governance or security. Successful organizations design and engineer intertwined processes across innovation, operations, risk management, and security. The key benefit of COBIT 5 is the perspective of enablers.

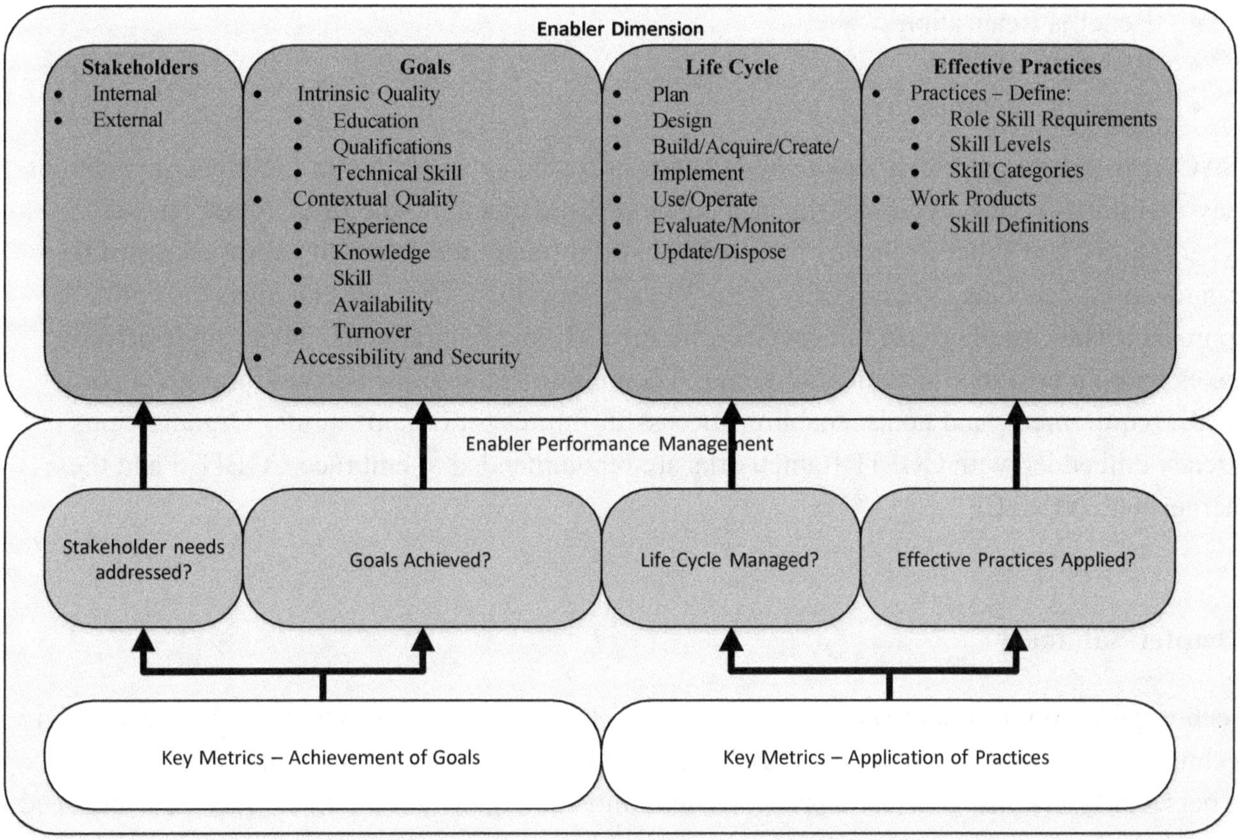

Figure 4. COBIT 5 Enabler Perspective. Adapted from COBIT 5 [11].

Enablers drive the vision and strategy for success in COBIT 5. The primary component from COBIT 5 is the clear connection between leadership vision, goals, life cycles, and practices. ISACA delineates specific criteria for quality or effective and impactful processes [12]. ISACA also identifies how metrics are leveraged to evaluate the ongoing ability to maintain effective processes, operate within the life cycle, meet goals, and address stakeholder and leadership needs and expectations [11]. Similar to CMMC, COBIT 5 defines the enabler's impact on mature and monitored processes.

ISACA also provides a mapping of COBIT 5 to implementing the NIST-CF [12]. ISACA views COBIT 5 and the NIST-CF as mutually enhancing [12], providing important synergies between overall governance and process optimizations with cybersecurity and cyber resiliency operations. ISACA views cybersecurity success as dependent on four key principles:

- Meeting stakeholder needs and requirements
- Approaching vision, strategy, and tactics holistically
- Addressing the enterprise from end-to-end
- Employing a single framework

ISACA views the combination of COBIT 5 with NIST-CF as a catalyst to drive value across the enterprise [12]. ISACA defines value as:

- Benefits Realization
- Risk Optimization
- Resource Optimization

ISACA provides a great perspective on cybersecurity and cyber resiliency. While organizations may traditionally view cybersecurity as a cost to the organization, the ISACA emphasizes cybersecurity and cyber resiliency is actually an investment in the stability and success of the organization. Viewing cybersecurity as an investment rather than a cost changes the entire approach. The cost approach to cybersecurity meets basic requirements, ticks simple activity boxes without creating impactful solutions. The investment approach drives through vision, needs, requirements and goals, enabling successful futures for organizations. Organizations already embedded with COBIT frameworks are recommended to embrace COBIT 5 and the merger with NIST-CF.

Chapter Summary

Technology is not just hardware and software. Technology is a force. Organizations decide how technology is harnessed. Innovation; risk management; enterprise architecture; and cybersecurity visions, goals, and priorities determine an organization's fate. Success is destined for those who prepare, plan, work plans, update plans, and mature processes.

Technology is not free. Technology is not easy. Security technology requires skill and process maturity. Each organization chooses between success and failure based on how IT harnesses innovation, mitigates risk, and secures assets.

Cybersecurity and cyber resiliency have different meanings and approaches. Many approaches are common, whether the AIC or CIA triad are embraced. Organizations are faced with a mix of data and asset security. Organizations must choose a framework, approach, metrics, or solution provider, but one framework is not guaranteed to provide an organization with everything it needs. Ultimately, the mindset and approach to enterprise technology, innovation, risk management, cybersecurity, and cyber resiliency will determine the success or failure of an organization. Viewing cybersecurity and cyber resilience as an investment versus a cost defines an organization's core belief in terms of the role technology and all of its components will play. In addition to a return on investment view, process and skill maturity of the organization determines the long-term success or failure of an organization. Ticking boxes for short term gain is not addressing cybersecurity. Multiple examples were presented on organizations without robust and mature processes who failed. Organizations define their future success or failure with their commitment and dedication to the many choices outlined through this book. Choose wisely.

Discussion Questions

1. From the frameworks and standards provided in this chapter, do any of them apply to your organization? Cite why or why not with detailed explanations

2. Does your organization have a written and defined cybersecurity vision, strategy and tactics? If so, is it appropriate? If not, what do you think the vision and strategy should be?

Exercises

1. Review your organization's cybersecurity posture. From the NIST-CF, assess your organization's current Framework Implementation Tier, providing supporting examples and data.

2. Assess your organization's status from an adoption status and discuss how NIST-CF or CMMC can alter your organization's status.
    a. *Crossing the Chasm's* adopter's categories:
        i. Innovators
        ii. Early adopters
        iii. Early majority
        iv. Late majority and laggards

3. CMMC was created for the DoD supply chain. Based on your organization, does it have a place in your industry?

References

[1] NIST, "Framework for improving critical infrastructure cybersecurity," 2018.

[2] Carnegie Mellon University and The John Hopkins University Applied Physics Laboratory, LLC, "Cybersecurity maturity model certification (CMMC)," 2020.

[3] AICPA, "SOC for cybersecurity," [Online]. Available: https://www.aicpa.org/interestareas/frc/assuranceadvisoryservices/aicpacybersecurityinitiative.html. [Accessed 02 June 2020].

[4] AICPA, "Cybersecurity: Risk management oversight," 2018.

[5] FFIEC`, "Cybersecurity assessment tool:User's guide," 2017.

[6] FFIEC, "Cybersecurity Assessment Tool: Overview for Chief Executive Officers and Boards of Directors," 2017.

[7] FFIEC, "Cybersecurity assessment tool: Inherent risk profile," 2017.

[8] International Standards Organization, "ISO/IEC 27002 Information technology — Security techniques — Code of practice for information security controls," 2013.

[9] HITRUST Alliance Inc., "Healthcare Sector Cybersecurity Implementation Guide v1.1," 2016.

[10] ISACA, "COBIT 6: A business framework for the governance and management of enterprise IT," 2012.

[11] ISACA, "COBIT 5: An ISACA Framework," 2012.

[12] ISACA, "Governance playbook: Integrating frameworks to tackle cybersecurity".

[13] Carnegie Mellon University and The John Hopkins University Applied Physics Laboratory, LLC, "Cybersecurity maturity model certification (CMMC): Version 2.0," 2021.

Dr. David A. Schippers is a recognized authority in cybersecurity, risk management, technology leadership and innovation. With over two decades of experience spanning academic and private sector leadership, Dr. Schippers currently serves as the Vice President and Chief Academic Officer at Walsh College, an upper division and graduate business and technology college.

Dr. Schippers has revolutionized academic programs by aligning them with industry needs, increasing doctoral program enrollment and retention by over 50%, and redesigning key business and technology curricula most recently leveraging advances in artificial intelligence and machine learning.

Dr. Schippers holds a Doctor of Science (Sc.D.) in Cybersecurity, with groundbreaking dissertation on Digital Image Source Authentication, and multiple advanced degrees in information systems and digital forensics. His career blends academic excellence with real-world impact, including his role as a licensed Professional Investigator specializing in digital forensics and cyber intelligence.

A Certified Information Systems Security Professional (CISSP), Dr. Schippers has earned numerous accolades for his contributions to technology and education. He has co-authored influential publications, including *The Force of Technology: Understanding Innovation, Risk Management, and Cybersecurity,* and has spoken at global conferences on topics like IT/OT convergence, digital forensics, and agile cybersecurity education.

As a consultant and thought leader, Dr. Schippers continues to shape the future of cybersecurity and risk management through innovative research and practical solutions. His dedication to advancing knowledge and practice makes him a trusted voice in navigating the complexities of today's connected world.

Dr. Schippers resides in Michigan, where he combines his passion for teaching, research, and innovation to empower the next generation of business and technology leaders.

Dr. Michael J. Simko brings over 20 years of diverse experience in information technology, cybersecurity, and leadership to the forefront of his work. A veteran of the United States Marine Corps and a lifelong learner, Dr. Simko's academic and professional accomplishments reflect his unwavering commitment to excellence and innovation in the field of cybersecurity.

Dr. Simko holds a Doctor of Science in Cybersecurity from Capitol Technology University, as well as master's degrees in Cybersecurity and Business Administration. His dedication to professional growth is further evidenced by earning 20 industry-recognized certifications across IT, cybersecurity, and project management. His leadership journey includes accolades such as the Eagle Scout Award and participation in elite executive leadership programs in Washington, D.C.

Currently serving as a director at a Department of Defense military installation, Dr. Simko has held roles ranging from cybersecurity architect to IT operations officer. His Marine Corps tenure included deployments in support of Operation Enduring Freedom in Afghanistan and Operation Tomodachi in Japan, earning him the rank of Staff Sergeant.

Dr. Simko is also an adjunct professor at Walsh College, where he has inspired graduate and doctoral students for over six years. His contributions to academia include co-authoring *The Force of Technology: Understanding Innovation, Risk Management, and Cybersecurity,* as well as publishing groundbreaking research on IT and OT convergence.

Outside of his professional endeavors, Dr. Simko is a martial artist, California state champion in Taekwondo, and dedicated family man. He resides in California, with his wife and three children, where he continues to balance his passions for technology, teaching, and mentoring the next generation of leaders.

www.ingramcontent.com/pod-product-compliance
Lightning Source LLC
LaVergne TN
LVHW060046210926
848481LV00013B/3967